THE CULTURAL REVOLUTION

THE CULTURAL REVOLUTION

A PEOPLE'S HISTORY, 1962–1976

FRANK DIKÖTTER

BLOOMSBURY PRESS

NEW YORK · LONDON · OXFORD · NEW DELHI · SYDNEY

Bloomsbury Press
An imprint of Bloomsbury Publishing Plc

1385 Broadway	50 Bedford Square
New York	London
NY 10018	WC1B 3DP
USA	UK

www.bloomsbury.com

BLOOMSBURY and the Diana logo are trademarks of Bloomsbury Publishing Plc

First published in Great Britain 2016
First U.S. edition 2016

© Frank Dikötter, 2016
Map by John Gilkes

ISBN: HB: 978-1-63286-421-5
ePub: 978-1-63286-422-2

Library of Congress Cataloging-in-Publication Data has been applied for.

2 4 6 8 10 9 7 5 3 1

Typeset by Newgen Knowledge Works (P) Ltd., Chennai, India
Printed and bound in USA by Berryville Graphics Inc., Berryville, Virginia

To find out more about our authors and books visit www.bloomsbury.
com. Here you will find extracts, author interviews, details of forthcoming
events, and the option to sign up for our newsletters.

Bloomsbury books may be purchased for business or promotional use.
For information on bulk purchases please contact Macmillan Corporate and
Premium Sales Department at specialmarkets@macmillan.com.

Who are our friends? Who are our enemies?
This is the main question of the revolution.

Mao Zedong

CONTENTS

Preface   ix

Chronology   xix

Map   xxvi

PART ONE: THE EARLY YEARS (1962–1966)

 1. Two Dictators   3

 2. Never Forget Class Struggle   15

 3. War on the Cultural Front   27

 4. Clique of Four   42

PART TWO: THE RED YEARS (1966–1968)

 5. Poster Wars   53

 6. Red August   66

 7. Destroying the Old World   80

 8. Mao Cult   94

 9. Linking Up   101

10. Rebels and Royalists   115

11. Enter the Army   128

12. The Arms Race   147

13. Quenching the Fires   163

PART THREE: THE BLACK YEARS (1968–1971)

14. Cleansing the Ranks   183

15. Up the Mountains, Down to the Villages   192

16. Preparing for War   206

17. Learning from Dazhai   219

18. More Purges   232

19. Fall of an Heir   242

PART FOUR: THE GREY YEARS (1971–1976)

20. Recovery   255
21. The Silent Revolution   270
22. The Second Society   285
23. Reversals   301
24. Aftermath   312

Notes   323
Select Bibliography   361
Acknowledgements   381
Index   383

Preface

In August 1963, Chairman Mao received a group of African guerrilla fighters in the State Council meeting hall, an elegant wood-panelled pavilion in the heart of the leadership compound in Beijing. One of the young visitors, a big, square-shouldered man from Southern Rhodesia, had a question. He believed that the red star shining over the Kremlin had slipped away. The Soviets, who used to help the revolutionaries, now sold weapons to their enemies. 'What I worry about is this,' he said. 'Will the red star over Tiananmen Square in China go out? Will you abandon us and sell arms to our oppressors as well?' Mao became pensive, puffing on his cigarette. 'I understand your question,' he observed. 'It is that the USSR has turned revisionist and has betrayed the revolution. Can I guarantee to you that China won't betray the revolution? Right now I can't give you that guarantee. We are searching very hard to find the way to keep China from becoming corrupt, bureaucratic and revisionist.'[1]

Three years later, on 1 June 1966, an incendiary editorial in the *People's Daily* exhorted readers to 'Sweep Away All Monsters and Demons!' It was the opening shot of the Cultural Revolution, urging people to denounce representatives of the bourgeoisie who were out to 'deceive, fool and benumb the working people in order to consolidate their reactionary state power'. As if this were not enough, it soon came to light that four of the top leaders in the party had been placed under arrest, accused of plotting against the Chairman. The mayor of Beijing was among them. He had tried, under the very nose of the people, to turn the capital into a citadel of revisionism. Counter-revolutionaries had sneaked into the party, the government and the army, trying to lead the country down the road to capitalism. Now was the beginning of a new revolution in China, as the people were encouraged to stand up and flush out all those trying to transform the dictatorship of the proletariat into a dictatorship of the bourgeoisie.

Who, precisely, these counter-revolutionaries were, and how they had managed to worm their way into the party, was unclear, but the number-one representative of modern revisionism was the Soviet leader and party secretary Nikita Khrushchev. In a secret speech in 1956 that shook the socialist camp to the core, Khrushchev had demolished the reputation of his predecessor Joseph Stalin, detailing the horrors of his rule and attacking the cult of personality. Two years later, Khrushchev proposed 'peaceful coexistence' with the West, a concept that true believers around the world, including the young guerrilla fighter from Southern Rhodesia, viewed as a betrayal of the principles of revolutionary communism.

Mao, who had modelled himself on Stalin, felt personally threatened by deStalinisation. He must have wondered how Khrushchev could have single-handedly engineered such a complete reversal of policy in the mighty Soviet Union, the first socialist country in the world. Its founder Vladimir Lenin had, after all, successfully overcome concerted attacks from foreign powers after the Bolsheviks seized power in 1917, and Stalin had survived the assault of Nazi Germany a quarter of a century later. The answer was that too little had been done to remould the way people thought. The bourgeoisie was gone, but bourgeois ideology still held sway, making it possible for a few people at the top to erode and finally subvert the entire system.

In communist parlance, after the socialist transformation of the ownership of the means of production had been completed, a new revolution was required to stamp out once and for all the remnants of bourgeois culture, from private thoughts to private markets. Just as the transition from capitalism to socialism required a revolution, the transition from socialism to communism demanded a revolution too: Mao called it the Cultural Revolution.

It was a bold project, one that aimed to eradicate all traces of the past. But behind all the theoretical justifications lay an ageing dictator's determination to shore up his own standing in world history. Mao was sure of his own greatness, of which he spoke constantly, and saw himself as the leading light of communism. It was not all hubris. The Chairman had led a quarter of humanity to liberation, and had then succeeded in fighting the imperialist camp to a standstill during the Korean War.

The Chairman's first attempt to steal the Soviet Union's thunder was the Great Leap Forward in 1958, when people in the countryside were herded into giant collectives called people's communes. By substituting labour for capital and harnessing the vast potential of the masses, he thought that he could catapult his country past its competitors. Mao was convinced that he had found the golden bridge to communism, making him the messiah leading humanity to a world of plenty for all. But the Great Leap Forward was a disastrous experiment which cost the lives of tens of millions of people.

The Cultural Revolution was Mao's second attempt to become the historical pivot around which the socialist universe revolved. Lenin had carried out the Great October Socialist Revolution, setting a precedent for the proletariat of the whole world. But modern revisionists like Khrushchev had usurped the leadership of the party, leading the Soviet Union back on the road of capitalist restoration. The Great Proletarian Cultural Revolution was the second stage in the history of the international communist movement, safeguarding the dictatorship of the proletariat against revisionism. The foundation piles of the communist future were being driven in China, as the Chairman guided the oppressed and downtrodden people of the world towards freedom. Mao was the one who inherited, defended and developed Marxism-Leninism into a new stage, that of Marxism-Leninism-Mao Zedong Thought.

Like many dictators, Mao combined grandiose ideas about his own historical destiny with an extraordinary capacity for malice. He was easily offended and resentful, with a long memory for grievances. Insensitive to human loss, he nonchalantly handed down killing quotas in the many campaigns that were designed to cow the population. As he became older, he increasingly turned on his colleagues and subordinates, some of them longstanding comrades-in-arms, subjecting them to public humiliation, imprisonment and torture. The Cultural Revolution, then, was also about an old man settling personal scores at the end of his life. These two aspects of the Cultural Revolution – the vision of a socialist world free of revisionism, the sordid, vengeful plotting against real and imaginary enemies – were not mutually exclusive. Mao saw no distinction between himself and the revolution. He was the revolution. An inkling of dissatisfaction with his authority was a direct threat to the dictatorship of the proletariat.

And there were many challenges to his position. In 1956, some of the Chairman's closest allies had used Khrushchev's secret speech to delete all references to Mao Zedong Thought from the constitution and criticise the cult of personality. Mao was seething, yet had little choice but to acquiesce. The biggest setback, however, came in the wake of the Great Leap Forward, a catastrophe on an unprecedented scale directly caused by his own obstinate policies. Mao was hardly paranoid in believing that many of his colleagues wanted him to step down, holding him responsible for the mass starvation of ordinary people. Plenty of rumours were circulating, accusing him of being deluded, innumerate and dangerous. His entire legacy was in jeopardy. The Chairman feared that he would meet the same fate as Stalin, denounced after his death. Who would become China's Khrushchev?

There were quite a few candidates, starting with Peng Dehuai, a marshal who had written a letter in the summer of 1959, criticising the Great Leap Forward. But Liu Shaoqi, the number two in the party, was a still more plausible contender for the title, having described the famine as a man-made disaster before thousands of assembled party leaders in January 1962. The moment the conference was over, Mao started clearing the ground for a purge. As he put it in December 1964, 'We must punish this party of ours.'[2]

But Mao carefully concealed his strategy. The rhetoric of the Cultural Revolution was deliberately vague, as 'class enemies', 'capitalist roaders' and 'revisionists' were denounced in general terms. Few leading party officials would have felt threatened, since by 1965 there were no real 'capitalist roaders' inside the upper ranks of the party, least of all Liu Shaoqi and Deng Xiaoping, the party's general secretary. Although they were the main targets of the Chairman's wrath, they had no inkling of what was coming. Liu, between 1962 and 1965, presided over one of the most vicious purges of the communist party in modern history, punishing 5 million party members. He was desperate to prove himself a worthy successor to the Chairman. Deng, on the other hand, was one of the most vociferous critics of Soviet revisionism. Leonid Brezhnev, who assumed power in

1964, called him an 'anti-Soviet dwarf'. Both men were vocal supporters of the Chairman, assisting him in purging the early victims of the Cultural Revolution, including the unwitting mayor of Beijing.

Mao set about ensnaring his enemies with the precision of a trapper. But once the stage was set and the Cultural Revolution erupted in the summer of 1966, it took on a life of its own, with unintended consequences that even the most consummate strategist could not have anticipated. Mao wished to purge the higher echelons of power, so he could hardly rely on the party machine to get the job done. He turned to young, radical students instead, some of them no older than fourteen, giving them licence to denounce all authority and 'bombard the headquarters'. But party officials had honed their survival skills during decades of political infighting, and few were about to be outflanked by a group of screaming, self-righteous Red Guards. Many deflected the violence away from themselves by encouraging the youngsters to raid the homes of class enemies, stigmatised as social outcasts. Some cadres even managed to organise their own Red Guards, all in the name of Mao Zedong Thought and the Cultural Revolution. In the parlance of the time, they 'raised the red flag in order to fight the red flag'. The Red Guards started fighting each other, divided over who the true 'capitalist roaders' inside the party were. In some places, party activists and factory workers rallied in support of their besieged leaders.

In response, the Chairman urged the population at large to join the revolution, calling on all to 'seize power' and overthrow the 'bourgeois power holders'. The result was a social explosion on an unprecedented scale, as every pent-up frustration caused by years of communist rule was released. There was no lack of people who harboured grievances against party officials. But the 'revolutionary masses', instead of neatly sweeping away all followers of the 'bourgeois reactionary line', also became divided, as different factions jostled for power and started fighting each other. Mao used the people during the Cultural Revolution; but, equally, many people manipulated the campaign to pursue their own goals.

By January 1967 the chaos was such that the army intervened, seeking to push through the revolution and bring the situation under control by supporting the 'true proletarian left'. As different military leaders supported different factions, all of them equally certain they represented the true voice of Mao Zedong, the country slid into civil war.

Still, the Chairman prevailed. He was cold and calculating, but also erratic, whimsical and fitful, thriving in willed chaos. He improvised, bending and breaking millions along the way. He may not have been in control, but he was always in charge, relishing a game in which he could constantly rewrite the rules. Periodically he stepped in to rescue a loyal follower or, contrariwise, to throw a close colleague to the wolves. A mere utterance of his decided the fates of countless people, as he declared one or another faction to be 'counter-revolutionary'. His verdict could change overnight, feeding a seemingly endless cycle of violence in which people scrambled to prove their loyalty to the Chairman.

The first phase of the Cultural Revolution came to an end in the summer of 1968 as new, so-called 'revolutionary party committees' took over the party and the state. They were heavily dominated by military officers, concentrating real power in the hands of the army. They represented a simplified chain of command that the Chairman relished, one in which his orders could be carried out instantly and without question. Over the next three years, they turned the country into a garrison state, with soldiers overseeing schools, factories and government units. At first, millions of undesirable elements, including students and others who had taken the Chairman at his word, were banished to the countryside to be 're-educated by the peasants'. Then followed a series of brutal purges, used by the revolutionary party committees to eradicate all those who had spoken out at the height of the Cultural Revolution. The talk was no longer of 'capitalist roaders', but of 'traitors', 'renegades' and 'spies', as special committees were set up to examine alleged enemy links among ordinary people and erstwhile leaders alike. After a nationwide witch-hunt came a sweeping campaign against corruption, further cowing the population into submission, as almost every act and every utterance became potentially criminal. In some provinces over one in fifty people were implicated in one purge or another.

But Mao was wary of the military, in particular Lin Biao, who took over the Ministry of Defence from Peng Dehuai in the summer of 1959 and pioneered the study of Mao Zedong Thought in the army. Mao had used

Lin Biao to launch and sustain the Cultural Revolution, but the marshal in turn exploited the turmoil to expand his own power base, placing his followers in key positions throughout the army. He died in a mysterious plane crash in September 1971, bringing to an end the grip of the military on civilian life.

By now, the revolutionary frenzy had exhausted almost everyone. Even at the height of the Cultural Revolution, many ordinary people, wary of the one-party state, had offered no more than outward compliance, keeping their innermost thoughts and personal feelings to themselves. Now many of them realised that the party had been badly damaged by the Cultural Revolution. They used the opportunity quietly to pursue their lives, even as the Chairman continued to play one faction against the other during his final years in power. In the countryside in particular, if the Great Leap Forward had destroyed the credibility of the party, the Cultural Revolution undermined its organisation. In a silent revolution, millions upon millions of villagers surreptitiously reconnected with traditional practices, as they opened black markets, shared out collective assets, divided the land and operated underground factories. Even before Mao died in September 1976, large parts of the countryside had abandoned the planned economy.

It was to be one of the most enduring legacies of a decade of chaos and entrenched fear. No communist party would have tolerated organised confrontation, but cadres in the countryside were defenceless against myriad daily acts of quiet defiance and endless subterfuge, as people tried to sap the economic dominance of the state and replace it with their own initiative and ingenuity. Deng Xiaoping, assuming the reins of power a few years after the death of Mao, briefly tried to resurrect the planned economy, but soon realised that he had little choice but to go with the flow. The people's communes, backbone of the collectivised economy, were dissolved in 1982.[3]

The gradual undermining of the planned economy was one unintended outcome of the Cultural Revolution. Another was the destruction of the remnants of Marxism-Leninism and Mao Zedong Thought. By the time Mao died, not only were people in the countryside pushing for much greater economic opportunities, but many had also broken free of the ideological shackles imposed by decades of Maoism. Endless campaigns

of thought reform produced widespread scepticism even among the party
members themselves.

But there was also a much darker heritage. Even if, in terms of human
loss, the Cultural Revolution was far less murderous than many earlier
campaigns, in particular the catastrophe unleashed during Mao's Great
Famine, it left a trail of broken lives and cultural devastation. By all
accounts, during the ten years spanning the Cultural Revolution, between
1.5 and 2 million people were killed, but many more lives were ruined
through endless denunciations, false confessions, struggle meetings and
persecution campaigns. Anne Thurston has written eloquently that the
Cultural Revolution was neither a sudden disaster nor a holocaust, but an
extreme situation characterised by loss at many levels, 'loss of culture and
of spiritual values, loss of status and honour, loss of career, loss of dignity',
and, of course, loss of trust and predictability in human relations, as people
turned against each other.[4]

The extent of loss varied enormously from one person to the next. Some
lives were crushed, while others managed to get through the daily grind
relatively unscathed. A few even managed to flourish, especially during the
last years of the Cultural Revolution. The sheer variety of human experience during the final decade of the Maoist era, one which resists sweeping
theoretical explanations, becomes all the more evident as we abandon the
corridors of power to focus on people from all walks of life. As the subtitle
of the book indicates, the people take centre stage.

A people's history of the Cultural Revolution would have been unimaginable even a few years ago, when most evidence still came from official party
documents and Red Guard publications. But over the past few years increasingly large amounts of primary material from the party archives in China
have become available to historians. This book is part of a trilogy, and like its
two predecessors, it draws on hundreds of archival documents, the majority
of them used here for the first time. There are details of the victims of Red
Guards, statistics on political purges, inquiries into conditions in the countryside, surveys of factories and workshops, police reports on black markets,
even letters of complaint written by villagers, and much more besides.

There are, of course, many published memoirs on the Cultural
Revolution, and they too have found their way into this book. In order to

complement some of the more popular ones, for instance Nien Cheng's *Life and Death in Shanghai* or Jung Chang's *Wild Swans*, I have read through dozens of self-published autobiographies, a relatively recent publishing phenomenon. They are called *ziyinshu* in Chinese, a literal translation of samizdat, although they are a far cry from the censored documents that were passed around by dissidents in the Soviet Union. Many are written by the rank and file of the party or even by ordinary people, and they offer insights that cannot be gleaned from official accounts. An equally important source are interviews, some openly available, others gathered specifically for this book.

A wealth of secondary material is also available to readers interested in the Cultural Revolution. From the moment that the Red Guards appeared on the stage, they captured the imagination of both professional sinologists and the wider public. Standard bibliographies on the Cultural Revolution now list thousands of articles and books in English alone, and this body of work has immeasurably advanced our understanding of the Maoist era.[5] But ordinary people are often missing from these studies. This book brings together the broader historical sweep with the stories of the men and women at the centre of this human drama. From the leaders at the top of the regime down to impoverished villagers, people faced extraordinarily difficult circumstances, and the sheer complexity of the decisions they took undermines the picture of complete conformity that is often supposed to have characterised the last decade of the Mao era. The combined total of their choices ultimately pushed the country in a direction very much at odds with the one envisaged by the Chairman: instead of fighting the remnants of bourgeois culture, they subverted the planned economy and hollowed out the party's ideology. In short, they buried Maoism.

Chronology

25 February 1956:

At the Twentieth Congress of the Soviet Communist Party, Nikita Khrushchev denounces the brutal purges, mass deportations and executions without trial under Stalin.

Autumn 1956:

At the Eighth Chinese Communist Party Congress, a reference to 'Mao Zedong Thought' is removed from the party constitution and the cult of personality denounced.

Winter 1956–spring 1957:

Mao, overriding most of his colleagues, encourages a more open political climate with the Hundred Flowers campaign. People demonstrate, protest and strike across the country.

Summer 1957:

The campaign backfires as a mounting barrage of criticism questions the very right of the party to rule. Mao changes tack and accuses these critical voices of being 'bad elements' bent on destroying the party. He puts Deng Xiaoping in charge of an anti-rightist campaign, which persecutes half a million people. The party unites behind its Chairman, who unleashes the Great Leap Forward a few months later.

1958–1961:

During the Great Leap Forward, villagers everywhere are herded into giant collectives called people's communes. In the following years, tens of millions of people die of torture, exhaustion, disease and hunger.

January 1962:

At an enlarged party gathering of thousands of cadres in Beijing, Liu Shaoqi describes the famine as a man-made disaster. Support for Mao is at an all-time low.

Summer 1962:

Mao condemns the breaking up of collective land and promotes the slogan 'Never Forget Class Struggle'.

Autumn 1962:

A Socialist Education Campaign is launched to educate people on the benefits of socialism and to clamp down on economic activities that take place outside the planned economy.

1963–4:

Liu Shaoqi throws his weight behind the Socialist Education Campaign and sends his wife Wang Guangmei to the countryside to head a work team. Entire provinces are accused of taking the 'capitalist road'. Over 5 million party members are punished.

16 October 1964:

China explodes its first atom bomb.

October–November 1964:

Khrushchev is deposed in a bloodless coup in Moscow. At a Kremlin reception a few weeks later, an inebriated Soviet minister advises a delegation headed by Zhou Enlai to get rid of Mao.

January 1965:

Mao has the guidelines of the Socialist Education Campaign rewritten, aiming at 'people in positions of authority within the party who take the capitalist road'.

10 November 1965:

Yao Wenyuan publishes an essay alleging that a play entitled *The Dismissal of Hai Rui*, written by Wu Han, a prominent historian and vice-mayor of Beijing, obliquely criticises the Great Leap Forward.

8–15 December 1965:

Mao, on the advice of Lin Biao, removes Luo Ruiqing as chief of staff of the army.

7 May 1966:

Mao writes a letter to Lin Biao projecting a utopian vision of military organisation and political indoctrination in which the army and the people fuse to become indistinct. This letter will later be known as the 7 May Directive.

4–27 May 1966:

Peng Zhen, the mayor of Beijing and Wu Han's superior, as well as Luo Ruiqing, Lu Dingyi and Yang Shangkun are accused of anti-party crimes. An inner-party document entitled the 16 May Circular accuses 'representatives of the bourgeoisie' of having penetrated the ranks of the party and the state.

25 May 1966:

Nie Yuanzi puts up a big-character poster in Peking University accusing its leadership of being 'a bunch of Khrushchev-type revisionist elements'.

28 May 1966:

A Cultural Revolution Group is established, headed by Chen Boda and including Madame Mao (Jiang Qing), Kang Sheng, Yao Wenyuan and Zhang Chunqiao.

1 June 1966:

The *People's Daily* exhorts the nation to 'Sweep Away All Monsters and Demons!' School classes are suspended across the country.

June–July 1966:

Liu Shaoqi and Deng Xiaoping dispatch work teams to middle schools and colleges to lead the Cultural Revolution. They soon clash with some of the more outspoken students, denouncing them as 'rightists'.

16 July 1966:

Mao swims in the Yangtze, signalling his determination to carry through the Cultural Revolution.

1 August 1966:

Mao writes a letter in support of a group of students who, inspired by the 7 May Directive, call themselves Red Guards and vow to fight against those who conspire to lead the country back to capitalism. Students throughout China form Red Guard units, attacking people from a bad class background.

5 August 1966:

The *People's Daily* publishes Mao's own big-character poster, entitled 'Bombard the Headquarters'. Mao accuses 'leading comrades' who have dispatched work teams of having adopted the 'reactionary stand of the bourgeoisie' and organised a reign of 'white terror'. Students labelled as 'rightists' are rehabilitated.

12 August 1966:

At a plenum of the Central Committee, Lin Biao replaces Liu Shaoqi as second-in-command.

18 August 1966:

Mao, wearing a military uniform and a Red Guard armband, welcomes a million students in Tiananmen Square. Over the following months, he reviews a total of 12 million Red Guards in Beijing.

23 August 1966:

The *People's Daily* applauds Red Guard violence and their campaign to destroy all remnants of the old society.

5 September 1966:

Red Guards are given free transportation and accommodation. Many come to Beijing to be reviewed by the Chairman, while others travel the country to establish revolutionary networks, attacking local party authorities as 'capitalist roaders'.

3 October 1966:

Party organisations beleaguered by Red Guards ask for help, but instead of supporting them, the party journal *Red Flag*, edited by Chen Boda, publishes an editorial denouncing 'counter-revolutionary revisionists' inside the ranks of the party who follow a 'bourgeois reactionary line'.

1 November 1966:

A further *Red Flag* editorial accuses leading party members of 'treating the masses as if they were ignorant and incapable', unleashing ordinary people against their party leaders and encouraging them to set up rebel organisations.

26 December 1966:

Madame Mao meets representatives of a newly forged nationwide alliance of temporary workers and demands that all those who have been dismissed since the start of the Cultural Revolution for criticising party leaders be reinstated. That evening, as he turns seventy-three, the Chairman gives a toast to welcome 'the unfolding of a nationwide civil war'.

6 January 1967:

In what will become known as the 'January Storm', a million rebel workers seize power from the municipal party committee in Shanghai. The Chairman encourages rebels elsewhere to 'seize power'.

23 January 1967:

The army is ordered to support the 'revolutionary masses'.

11 and 16 February 1967:

At a meeting of the central leadership chaired by Zhou Enlai, several veteran marshals take members of the Cultural Revolution Group to task. Mao soon denounces them, prompting an even greater shift of power towards Lin Biao and the Cultural Revolution Group.

6 April 1967:

In some parts of the country, the army, ordered to assist the 'proletarian left', sides instead with party leaders. On 6 April new directives prohibit the army from firing on rebels, disbanding mass organisations or retaliating against those who raid military commands.

May 1967:

Factional violence, in which the military is often involved, spreads across the country.

20 July 1967:

In Wuhan local soldiers abduct two envoys of the Cultural Revolution Group who are seen as favouring a rebel faction in their mediation between two opposing forces there. Lin Biao portrays the incident as a mutiny by the regional military commander and urges the Chairman, on a secret visit to the city, to leave immediately for Shanghai.

25 July 1967:

The Cultural Revolution Group members arrested in Wuhan are welcomed back to Beijing, where the incident is denounced as a 'counter-revolutionary riot'. Lin Biao uses the occasion further to tighten his grip on the army.

1 August 1967:

A *Red Flag* editorial hails Lin Biao as the most faithful follower of the Chairman and demands that 'capitalist roaders' be removed from the army. Throughout the summer, armed conflicts between different factions spread across the country.

22 August 1967:

A rebel faction at the Ministry of Foreign Affairs critical of Zhou Enlai sets the British mission in Beijing on fire.

30 August 1967:

The Chairman reins in the violence and has several members of the Cultural Revolution Group arrested. A few days later, mass organisations are once again forbidden from seizing weapons from the military.

September 1967:

Mao tours the country, calling for a great alliance of all revolutionary forces.

22 March 1968:

Lin Biao further consolidates his hold on the army by having several military leaders arrested.

27 July 1968:

A Mao Zedong Thought propaganda team is sent to Tsinghua University, marking the end of the Red Guards, who are brought to heel and disciplined.

7 September 1968:

With revolutionary committees established in all provinces and major cities, Zhou Enlai announces an all-round victory.

Summer 1968–autumn 1969:

The new revolutionary committees use a campaign to 'cleanse the party ranks' to denounce their enemies as 'spies' and 'traitors'.

22 December 1968:

The *People's Daily* publishes a directive from the Chairman ordering that students in the cities be re-educated in the countryside. Between 1968 and 1980, some 17 million students in all will be banished from the cities.

March 1969:

Weeks before the Ninth Party Congress, Chinese and Soviet troops clash along the Ussuri River. Lin Biao uses the incident to militarise the country even further.

April 1969:

At the Ninth Party Congress, Lin Biao is designated as Mao's successor.

February–November 1970:

Two overlapping campaigns, referred to as the 'One Strike and Three Antis', target 'counter-revolutionary activities' and 'economic crimes', implicating up to one in every fifty people and cowing the population.

Summer 1970:

Mao uses the issue of the post of president of state to question Lin Biao's loyalty.

April 1971:

The Chairman invites the United States table-tennis team to visit China.

Summer 1971:

The Chairman tours the south of the country, undermining Lin Biao without ever mentioning him by name.

12 September 1971:

Mao returns to Beijing. Just after midnight, Lin Biao, his wife and son hurriedly board a plane outside the summer resort of Beidaihe. The plane crashes in Mongolia, killing all aboard.

21–28 February 1972:

President Richard Nixon visits China.

August 1972:

The military return to their barracks. Over the following months many government administrators and party cadres are rehabilitated.

November 1973–January 1974:

Madame Mao, Zhang Chunqiao, Wang Hongwen and Yao Wenyuan band together against Zhou Enlai and are soon referred to as the 'Gang of Four'. A nationwide campaign aimed at Zhou is launched.

April 1974:

The Chairman promotes Deng Xiaoping, who heads the Chinese delegation at the United Nations.

January 1975:

With the approval of the Chairman, Zhou Enlai launches the 'Four Modernisations' programme to upgrade China's agriculture, industry, national defence and science and technology.

November 1975–January 1976:

Mao fears that Deng Xiaoping will undermine his legacy. Deng is taken to task at several party meetings and removed from most of his official positions.

8 January 1976:

Premier Zhou Enlai dies.

4–5 April 1976:

An outpouring of popular support for Zhou Enlai culminates in a massive demonstration on Tiananmen Square, brutally repressed by the police and the army.

9 September 1976:

Mao Zedong dies.

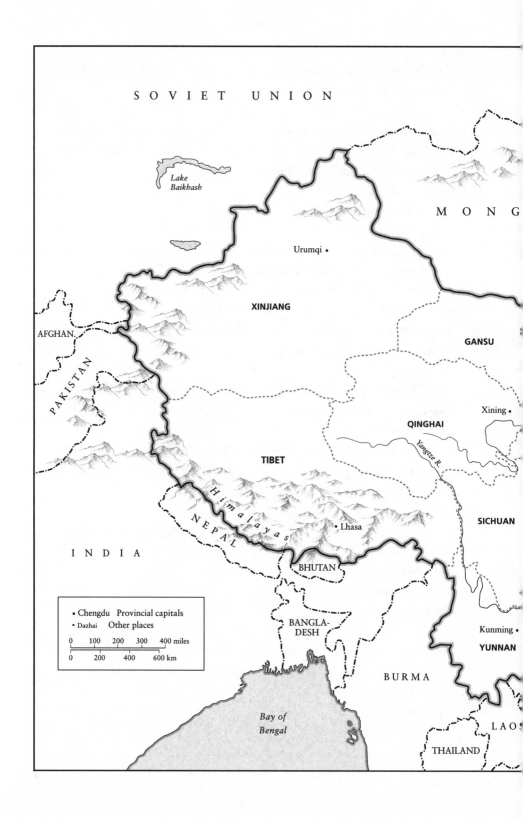

PART ONE

THE EARLY YEARS (1962–1966)

I

Two Dictators

At the heart of Beijing, a vast, monolithic building with marble columns and pillars casts a shadow over Tiananmen Square, much as the Communist Party of China dominates the political life of the country. The Great Hall of the People was built in record time to be ready for the tenth anniversary of the Chinese Revolution, celebrated with much fanfare in October 1959. It is a grand, intimidating structure, heavily inspired by Soviet architecture, with a large auditorium that can seat over 10,000 delegates. A giant red star surrounded by hundreds of lights shines down from the ceiling. Everything is drenched in red, from the banners and curtains on the podium to the thick carpet on the gallery and balconies. There are also dozens of cavernous rooms named after the provinces of the country, giving the building more floor space than the Forbidden City, the sprawling ancient quarter of pavilions, courtyards and palaces that had served the emperors of the Ming and Qing dynasties, facing Tiananmen Square.

In January 1962, some 7,000 cadres arrived from all parts of the country to attend the largest conference ever held in the Great Hall of the People. They had been called to Beijing because the leadership needed their support. For several years they had worked under relentless pressure, as Chairman Mao had set ever higher targets, from steel output to grain production. Those who failed to meet the quotas were labelled rightists and purged from the party. They were replaced by hard, unscrupulous men who trimmed their sails to benefit from the radical winds blowing from Beijing. Many lied about their achievements, inventing the production figures reported to their masters higher up the echelons of power. Others imposed a reign of terror during which the villagers under their supervision were worked to death. Now they were being blamed for the catastrophe unleashed by Mao with the Great Leap Forward.

Four years earlier, in 1958, Mao had thrown his country into a frenzy, as villagers were herded into giant people's communes that heralded a great leap from socialism into communism. People were conscripted to fight in a continuous revolution and forced to tackle one task after another, from giant water-conservancy projects during the slack winter months to steel production in backyard furnaces over the summer. 'Battle Hard for Three Years to Change the Face of China' was one slogan of the Great Leap Forward, as a world of plenty beckoned ahead. 'Catch up with Britain and Overtake the United States' was another. But despite the propaganda about outstripping capitalist economies, Mao's real aim was to propel China past the Soviet Union. Ever since the death of Stalin in 1953, Mao had wished to claim leadership of the socialist camp.

Even during Stalin's lifetime, Mao had considered himself a more accomplished revolutionary. It was he who had brought a quarter of humanity into the socialist camp in 1949, not Stalin. And it was he who had fought the Americans to a standstill in Korea a year later, not Stalin. But Mao was also a faithful follower of his master in Moscow, and for good reason. From the start, the Chinese Communist Party had been dependent on financial help and political guidance from the Soviet Union. Stalin personally assisted Mao's rise to power. The relationship between the two men was often tumultuous, but once the red flag flew over Beijing in 1949, Mao wasted no time in imposing a harsh communist regime modelled on the Soviet Union. Mao was a Stalinist attracted to the collectivisation of agriculture, an unlimited cult of the leader, the elimination of private property, all-pervasive control of the lives of ordinary people and huge expenditure on national defence.[1]

Ironically, it was Stalin, fearing the emergence of a powerful neighbour that might threaten his dominance, who constrained the Stalinisation of China. In 1929–30, Stalin had launched a ruthless campaign of dekulakisation, resulting in the execution of thousands of people classified as 'rich peasants' and the deportation of close to 2 million to labour camps in Siberia and Soviet Central Asia. But in 1950 Stalin advised Mao to leave the economy of the rich peasants intact so as to speed up China's recovery after years of civil war. Mao ignored his advice, forcing rural populations to participate in the denunciation, and sometimes murder, of traditional village leaders. All the assets of the victims were handed over to the crowd. The land was measured and distributed to the poor. By implicating a majority in the murder of a carefully designated minority, Mao managed permanently to link the people to the party. No reliable figure exists for the number of victims killed during land redistribution, but between 1947 and 1952 it is unlikely to have been less than 1.5 to 2 million people. Many other millions were stigmatised as exploiters and class enemies.

Once land reform had been completed in 1952, Mao approached Stalin with a request for a large loan to help China's industrialisation. Stalin, ever the contrarian, rebuffed his plea by judging that the growth rate that China sought to pursue was 'rash'. He imposed deep cuts, vetoed several projects related to military defence and reduced the number of industrial complexes to be built with Soviet assistance. Yet Stalin himself had presided over the collectivisation of agriculture in the Soviet Union between 1929 and 1933, using the grain he extracted from collective farms in the countryside to feed a growing industrial workforce and pay for imports of machinery from the West. The experience led to mass starvation in the Ukraine and other parts of the Soviet Union. The death toll has been estimated at 5 to 10 million people.

Stalin was the only person capable of restraining Mao. After the death of his master in Moscow in March 1953, Mao cranked up the pace of collectivisation. A monopoly on grain was introduced by the end of the year, forcing farmers to sell their crops at prices fixed by the state. In 1955–6, collectives resembling state farms in the Soviet Union were introduced. They took back the land from the farmers, transforming the villagers into bonded servants at the beck and call of the state. In the cities all commerce and industry also became functions of the state, as the government expropriated private enterprises, small shops and large industries alike. Mao termed this the Socialist High Tide.

But in 1956 Mao's programme of crash collectivisation encountered a huge setback. On 25 February, the final day of the Twentieth Congress of the Soviet Communist Party, Nikita Khrushchev denounced the brutal purges, mass deportations and executions without trial under Stalin.

Speaking for several hours without interruption in the Great Kremlin Palace, the former Moscow residence of the Russian tsars, Khrushchev criticised Stalin's cult of personality and accused his erstwhile master of ruining agriculture in the early 1930s. Stalin, he said, 'never went anywhere, never met with workers and collective farmers' and knew the country only from 'films that dressed up and prettified the situation in the countryside'. Mao interpreted this as a personal attack on his own authority. He was, after all, China's Stalin, and Khrushchev's speech was bound to raise questions about his own leadership, in particular the personality cult surrounding him. Within months, premier Zhou Enlai and others used Khrushchev's critique of state farms to check the pace of collectivisation. It looked as if Mao was being sidelined.

Mao's response to deStalinisation came on 25 April 1956. When addressing a meeting of the Politburo, he championed the ordinary man. He posed as a protector of democratic values in order to regain moral leadership over the party. Mao outdid Khrushchev. Two months earlier he had been forced on the defensive, seemingly an ageing dictator out of touch with reality clinging to a model that had failed in the past. Now he reclaimed the initiative, striking a far more liberal and conciliatory tone than his counterpart in Moscow. A week later, on 2 May, he encouraged freedom of expression among intellectuals, asking the party to 'let a hundred flowers bloom, let a hundred schools contend'.

Still, Mao was forced to make major concessions to his colleagues. At the Eighth Party Congress, convened in September to elect the first new Central Committee since 1945, the Socialist High Tide was quietly dropped, all references to Mao Zedong Thought deleted from the constitution and the cult of personality denounced. Collective leadership was praised. Hemmed in by Khrushchev's secret speech, Mao had little choice but to acquiesce in these measures. While he retained the chairmanship of the party, he indicated that he wanted to relinquish the chairmanship of the state, a largely ceremonial position he disliked. Seeking to test his colleagues' loyalty, he hinted that he might want to step back for health reasons. But, instead of begging him to remain, Liu Shaoqi and Deng Xiaoping created a new position of honorary chairman, for Mao to take up as soon as he resigned the chairmanship of the party. In private, the infuriated Mao did not hide his anger.[2]

The Hungarian revolt gave Mao an opportunity to regain the upper hand. As Soviet troops crushed the rebels in Budapest in early November, the Chairman blamed the Hungarian Communist Party for having brought misfortune on itself by failing to listen to popular grievances and allowing them to fester and spiral out of control. The danger in China, he opined, was not so much popular unrest as rigid adherence to party policy. 'The party needs to be given some lessons. It is a good thing that students demonstrate against us.' He wanted the communist party to welcome critical views from outsiders in a great reckoning: 'Those who insult the masses should be liquidated by the masses.'[3]

Encouraged by Mao's call for more open debate in May, discontented people from all walks of life had begun to speak out. The Hungarian revolt further fuelled popular unrest, as students and workers started invoking Budapest in acts of defiance against the state. Hundreds of students gathered in front of the mayor's office in Nanjing to chant slogans in favour of democracy and human rights. In cities across the country, workers went on strike, complaining of decreasing real income, poor housing and dwindling welfare benefits. In Shanghai some demonstrations attracted thousands of supporters.

The unrest was not confined to the cities. By the winter of 1956–7, farmers started withdrawing from the collectives, raising a clamour against the party and beating up local cadres who stood in their way. In parts of Guangdong province, across the border from Hong Kong, up to a third of the villagers forcibly took back the land and started planting their own crops. In other parts of the country, too, villagers left the collectives in droves, claiming their cattle, seed and tools, determined to make it on their own.[4]

Since the Chairman himself had posed as a champion of the people and defended their democratic rights to express themselves, the party was in no position to clamp down on popular opposition. In February 1957, Mao went further by encouraging intellectuals who had remained on the sidelines to speak out. His voice rang with sincerity as he enumerated examples of serious errors made by the communist party, accusing it in harsh terms of 'dogmatism', 'bureaucratism' and 'subjectivism'. Mao appealed to the public at large to help party officials improve their work by airing their grievances so that social injustices could be redressed. In a portent of what was to come during the Cultural Revolution, Mao was using students and workers as a way of putting his comrades on notice.

Soon a torrent of criticism burst out, but Mao had badly miscalculated. He had hoped for an outpouring of adulation in which activists would follow his cues and punish a party that had sidestepped him and written his Mao Zedong Thought out of the constitution. Instead, people wrote pithy slogans in favour of democracy and human rights, some even demanding that the communist party relinquish power. Students had been striking and demonstrating sporadically since the summer of 1956, but now tens of thousands took to the streets. On 4 May 1957, some 8,000 of them converged on Beijing, marking the anniversary of the May Fourth Movement, an abortive student uprising dating back to 1919. They created a 'Democracy Wall' covered with posters and slogans charging the communist party with 'suppression of freedom and democracy in all the country's educational institutions'. In Shanghai, local cadres were reviled, insulted and jeered at by angry mobs. Major labour disturbances involving over 30,000 workers erupted in hundreds of enterprises, dwarfing anything the country had seen, even during the heyday of the nationalist regime in the 1930s.[5]

Mao was stung by the extent of popular discontent. He put Deng Xiaoping in charge of a campaign that denounced half a million students and intellectuals as 'rightists' bent on destroying the party. Many were deported to remote areas in Manchuria and Xinjiang to do hard labour.

Mao's gamble had backfired, but at least he and his comrades-in-arms were united again, determined to suppress the people. Back at the helm of the party, Mao was keen to push through the radical collectivisation of the countryside. In Moscow, where he and other communist party leaders from all over the world had been invited to celebrate the fortieth anniversary of the October Revolution in November 1957, he gave his showpiece pledge of allegiance to Khrushchev by recognising him as the leader of the socialist camp. But he also challenged his opposite number in Moscow. When Khrushchev announced that the Soviet Union would catch up with the United States in per-capita production of meat, milk and butter, Mao boldly proclaimed that China would outstrip Britain – then still considered a major industrial power – in the production of steel within fifteen years. The Great Leap Forward had just begun.

Back home, leaders like Zhou Enlai who had shown insufficient enthusiasm for the Socialist High Tide a few years earlier were taken to task, humiliated by Mao in private meetings and party conferences. Under the drumbeat of propaganda, several provincial party leaders and many of their underlings were purged and replaced by close followers of Mao, who herded the villagers into giant people's communes that heralded the leap from socialism into communism. In the countryside, people lost their homes, land, belongings and livelihoods. In collective canteens, food, distributed by the spoonful according to merit, became a weapon used to force people to follow the party's every dictate. Combined with the elimination of private property and the profit motive, these experiments resulted in a steep decline in grain output. But instead of sounding the alarm, local cadres were pressured by their superiors to report falsely ever greater yields. To protect their jobs, they handed over a correspondingly bigger share of the crop to the state, putting villagers on a starvation diet.

In the summer of 1959, as the party leaders convened in the mountain resort of Lushan for a conference, Marshal Peng Dehuai and others cautiously criticised the Great Leap Forward. At the same time, while visiting the Polish town of Poznań, Khrushchev publicly condemned the communes under Stalin. It looked like a carefully planned attack on Mao. The Chairman, suspecting a plot to overthrow him, denounced Peng and his supporters as an anti-party clique guilty of conspiring against the state and the people.

A witch-hunt against 'rightist' elements ensued, as over 3 million cadres were replaced by willing executioners, prepared to do everything it took to achieve the goals set by their Chairman. Faced with constant pressure to meet and exceed the plan, many resorted to ever greater means of coercion, resulting in an orgy of violence that became all the more extreme as the incentives to work were removed. In some places both villagers and cadres became so brutalised that the scope of intimidation had to be constantly expanded, creating an escalating spiral of violence. People who did not work hard enough were hung up and beaten; some were drowned in ponds. Others were doused in urine or forced to eat excrement. People were mutilated. A report circulated to the top leadership, including Chairman Mao, describes how a man called Wang Ziyou had one of his ears chopped off, his legs bound with wire and a 10-kilo stone dropped on his back before he was branded – as punishment for digging up a potato.[6] There were even cases of people being buried alive. When a boy stole a handful of grain in a Hunan village, local boss Xiong Dechang forced his father to bury his son alive. The man died of grief a few days later.[7]

But the most common weapon was food, as starvation became the punishment of first resort. Throughout the country those who were too ill to work were routinely deprived of food. The sick, the vulnerable and the elderly were banned from the canteen and starved to death, as cadres recited Lenin's dictum: 'he who does not work shall not eat'. Countless people were killed indirectly through neglect, as local cadres were compelled to focus on figures rather than on people, making sure they fulfilled the targets prescribed by the planners in Beijing. The experiment ended in one of the greatest mass killings in history, with at least 45 million people worked, starved or beaten to death.[8]

By the end of 1960, the sheer scale of the catastrophe forced Mao to allow Zhou Enlai and others to introduce measures designed to weaken the power of the communes over villagers. Local markets were restored, private plots allowed once more. Grain was imported from abroad. It was the beginning of the end of mass starvation. But as the pressure to deliver grain, coal and other commodities to the state abated, some of the large cities started facing massive shortfalls. In the summer of 1961, Minister of Finance Li Xiannian announced that empty state granaries were the most pressing issue confronting the party.[9] The countryside was effectively cutting off Beijing, Tianjin and Shanghai, forcing the centre to listen.

———

Mao's star was at its lowest in January 1962 during the Seven Thousand Cadres Conference – so named because of the number of attendees. If ever there had been a time to depose him, it would have been during this massive gathering, as cadres from all corners of the country finally assembled to compare notes and rail against the disaster brought by the Great Leap Forward. There were even rumours that a couple of months before the meeting, Peng Zhen, a tall, thin man with a limp hand who was mayor of Beijing, had asked one of his underlings, a party intellectual called Deng Tuo, to compile a dossier of documents critical of the famine and Mao's role in it. The investigation was carried out with the knowledge of Liu Shaoqi and Deng Xiaoping, and several meetings were held away from the public view in a baroque-style palace built for the empress dowager in the Beijing Zoo. Peng Zhen, it was alleged, intended to confront the Chairman.[10]

Decades earlier, Stalin had faced a similar challenge. During the Congress of Victors, held in the Great Hall of the Kremlin in 1934, some 2,000 delegates had assembled to celebrate the success of agricultural collectivisation and rapid industrialisation. They welcomed Stalin with rapturous applause; behind the scenes, they grumbled about his methods and feared his ambition. Critical of the extent of the cult of personality surrounding him, several leading party members met privately to discuss his replacement. Rumour had it that he received so many negative votes that some of the paper ballots had to be destroyed. Much of the dissent in the ranks was caused by the famine, for which Stalin was held responsible. However, nobody criticised the leader directly.[11]

In Beijing, too, Mao was applauded. Many delegates relished the opportunity to have their picture taken with the Chairman.[12] Not even the top leaders confronted Mao directly. But in his official report, delivered to a packed audience, Liu Shaoqi spoke at length about the famine. Liu was a dour, puritanical man with a lined and flabby face, who often worked through the night. Most leaders went bare-headed, but Liu always wore a proletarian cloth cap. A year earlier, in April 1961, he and other leaders had been sent to the countryside by Mao to investigate the famine. Liu had been genuinely shocked by the disastrous state in which he found his home village. Now he reported that the farmers in Hunan believed that the disaster was 70 per cent man-made with 30 per cent attributed to natural causes. The very use of the term 'man-made disaster' (*renhuo*) was a bombshell, drawing gasps from the audience. Liu also dismissed the expression 'nine fingers to one', Mao's favourite phrase to emphasise achievements over setbacks. The tension was palpable. 'I wonder if we can say that, generally speaking, the ratio of achievements to setbacks is seven to three, although each region is different. One finger versus nine fingers does not apply to every place. There are only a small number of regions where mistakes are equal to one finger and successes equal to nine fingers.' Mao interrupted Liu, visibly annoyed: 'It's not a small number of regions at all, for instance in Hebei only 20 per cent of regions decreased production and in Jiangsu 30 per cent of all regions increased production year after year!' Liu, refusing to be intimidated, carried on: 'In general, we cannot say it is merely one finger, but rather three, and in some places it is even more.'[13]

But Liu did try to defend the Great Leap Forward. As in Moscow more than thirty years before, every delegate hastened to proclaim that the 'general line' was correct. It was its implementation that was at fault.

One man in particular threw his full weight behind the Chairman. Lin Biao was widely considered one of the most brilliant strategists of the civil war. A gaunt man with a chalky-white complexion, he suffered from a wide array of phobias about water, wind and cold. The mere sound of running water gave him diarrhoea. He did not drink liquids at all, and relied on his wife feeding him steamed buns dipped in water to stay hydrated. Most of the time he wore his military cap to hide a scraggy bald head. He often called in sick, but in the summer of 1959 he had left his mole-like existence to rally to the defence of the Chairman at the Lushan plenum. In reward, his performance won him Peng Dehuai's job as head of the army. Now he eulogised the Chairman again, hailing the Great Leap Forward as an unprecedented accomplishment in Chinese history: 'The thoughts of Chairman Mao are always correct . . . He is never out of touch with reality . . . I feel very deeply that when in the past our work was done well, it was precisely when we thoroughly implemented and did not interfere with Chairman Mao's thought. Every time Chairman Mao's ideas were not sufficiently respected or suffered interference, there have been problems. That is essentially what the history of our party over the last few decades shows.'[14]

Mao was pleased with Lin, but suspicious of everyone else. He put on his best face, acting the fatherly, benevolent elder, 'a gentle giant spouting Chinese history, citing classical fiction, an Olympian deity ready to admit that he, too, could err'.[15] He tried to disarm the delegates and put them at their ease. He encouraged an open and democratic climate in which all could speak without fear of retribution. He was trying to find out where everybody stood. In the smaller discussion groups which gathered separately from the main party speeches, some delegates aired dangerously critical views. A few provincial leaders believed that the entire famine was a man-made catastrophe. Others wondered how many millions had perished, comparing notes from their respective provinces. Some even thought that the Chairman could hardly escape blame: 'Such a huge problem, Chairman Mao should assume responsibility.'[16] One delegate pointed out that the people's communes had been the Chairman's idea. Mao read the transcripts of these debates with great contempt: 'They complain all day long and get to watch plays at night. They eat three full meals a day – and fart. That's what Marxism-Leninism means to them.'[17]

But Mao did offer a token apology, admitting that as Chairman of the party he was at least in part accountable. It was an astute move, one which obliged other leaders to follow suit and acknowledge their own mistakes. A chorus of confessions followed. Zhou Enlai, for instance, took personal responsibility for excessive grain procurements, inflated production figures, the draining of grain away from the provinces and growing exports of food. A faithful and adroit assistant, with strongly marked features, large eyes under bushy eyebrows and slightly effeminate manners, he had made himself indispensable as a first-rate administrator. Early in his career as a revolutionary, Zhou had resolved never to challenge Mao, although his master still periodically abased him in front of other leaders, as in the early months of 1958, when Mao had censured Zhou for lacking sufficient enthusiasm for agricultural collectivisation. Zhou worked tirelessly at the Great Leap Forward to prove himself. Now he declared that 'shortcomings and errors of the last few years have occurred precisely when we contravened the general line and Chairman Mao's precious instructions'.[18] Wang Renzhong, a sycophantic follower of Mao and party secretary of Hubei, confessed that his province had misled Beijing by inflating production figures. Liu Zihou accepted that Hebei, the province under his purview, had invented the bumper harvest in several counties that Beijing had heralded as models. Zhou Lin, the boss of Guizhou, went further, acknowledging that under his leadership the villagers had been wrongly persecuted for allegedly hiding grain.[19]

These admissions of culpability deflected attention away from Mao. More importantly, they undercut Peng Zhen's attempt to discredit the Chairman. The lengthy report the mayor of Beijing had allegedly prepared months earlier never saw the light of day. In effect, instead of making sure that their leader would never again be able to perpetrate a disaster, the party allowed him to save face.

Mao survived the Seven Thousand Cadres Conference. But more than ever he feared losing control of the party. In the Soviet Union, back in 1934, the Congress of Victors would turn out to be a congress of victims. Over the next four years, more than half of the 2,000 delegates were either executed or sent to the gulag. Stalin excelled at hunting down his enemies during the Great Terror. As the historian Robert Service has noted, 'his brutality was as mechanical as a badger trap'.[20] Mao would be much more whimsical, deliberately turning society upside down and stoking the violence of millions to retain his position at the centre.

2

Never Forget Class Struggle

One of the first steps Mao took when he could no longer deny the extent of the famine was to blame it on class enemies. 'Bad people have seized power, causing beatings, deaths, grain shortages and hunger,' he wrote in November 1960. 'The democratic revolution has not been completed, as feudal forces, full of hatred towards socialism, are stirring up trouble, sabotaging socialist productive forces.'[1] A few months later, he expressed his surprise at the extent of the counter-revolution: 'Who would have thought that the countryside harboured so many counter-revolutionaries? We did not expect the counter-revolution to usurp power at the village level and carry out cruel acts of class revenge.'[2]

It was a predictable move. Decades earlier, Stalin, too, had declared that the success of collectivisation had 'infuriated the lickspittles of the defeated classes'. As his *History of the All-Union Communist Party: A Short Course* put it, 'they began to revenge themselves on the Party and the people for their own failure, for their own bankruptcy; they began to resort to foul play and sabotage against the cause of the workers and collective farmers, to blow up pits, set fire to factories, and commit acts of wrecking in collective and state farms, with the object of undoing the achievements of the workers and collective farmers'.[3]

More than 42 million copies of the *Short Course* were published in Russian alone, and it was translated into sixty-seven languages.[4] Chinese was one of them. The red book, as the *Short Course* was known at the time, was studied like the holy Bible in the years after 1949, when 'The Soviet Union's Today is Our Tomorrow' became the motto. According to one of Mao's secretaries, 'Stalin's ideas provided Mao with handy shortcuts.' The core message of the *Short Course* was that every significant development was the result of political struggles between the correct line, represented by Lenin and Stalin, and incorrect positions, adopted by a string of anti-party groups that had been successfully eliminated on the path to socialism. The book's prominence came to an end after Khrushchev denounced Stalin, although it was never officially repudiated.[5]

Mao revered the text even after 1956. Of particular importance was Stalin's notion that 'as the socialist revolution deepens, class struggle intensifies'. In the *Short Course*'s words, it was 'opportunist complacency' to assume that 'as we grow stronger the enemy will become tamer and more inoffensive'. In reality, the exact opposite was happening, and this called for vigilance, 'real Bolshevik revolutionary vigilance'. The enemy was no longer out there, but hiding in plain sight, inside the very ranks of the party.

At the Seven Thousand Cadres Conference in January 1962, Mao had merely hinted at the issue of class struggle. 'There are some people who adopt the guise of communist party members, but they in no way represent the working class; instead they represent the bourgeoisie. All is not pure within the party. We must see this point, otherwise we shall suffer.'[6] He was in retreat, unable to press the point any further.

A year earlier, as the leadership desperately tried to find an escape route from the famine that was claiming millions of lives, several provincial leaders had favoured returning small plots of communal land to the farmers. Anhui had been one of the first provinces to sink into famine, but was also one of the first to emerge from it as Zeng Xisheng began to allow farmers to rent the land. Tao Zhu, a powerful Politburo member, supported the move. 'This way people won't starve to death,' he said, adding that 'if this is capitalism, then I prefer capitalism. Do we really want everyone to be poor under socialism?'[7] But others, like Zhou Enlai, kept their counsel, having attracted the wrath of the Chairman in the past for trying to slow down the pace of collectivisation.

After the Seven Thousand Cadres Conference, Liu Shaoqi, Deng Xiaoping and a small group of advisers continued to discuss ways of recalibrating the economy. Mao was away from the capital, touring the south and observing his colleagues from afar. Much of what had been left unsaid at the party gathering in January 1962 was now voiced more openly, sometimes in harsh terms. 'Lack of modesty and lack of experience are the main reasons why we made such a big mess of it,' Liu allegedly said. 'We should place the market on top of everything else.' He and others proposed delegating responsibility for working the fields directly to the farming households rather than the collective. It was private farming in all but name.[8] A few months later, in May, Liu pressed for the right of some villagers to leave the collectives altogether: 'if we don't allow 20 per cent of the peasants to go it alone, I don't think we can keep the collective economy'.[9]

But the defining moment probably came one hot afternoon in July, when Mao was resting by the side of his swimming pool in Beijing in a bad mood. Liu Shaoqi had asked him to return to the capital for important business. The Chairman demanded an explanation. Liu opened by reporting that Chen Yun and Tian Jiaying, two of the most outspoken critics of the Great Leap Forward, wished to present their views on returning the land to the farmers. Mao became angry. Hastily, Liu said: 'So many people have died of hunger!' Then he blurted out, 'History will judge you and me, even cannibalism will go into the books!' Mao now fell into a rage. 'The Three Red Banners [meaning the main components of the Great Leap Forward, including the people's communes] have been shot down, now the land is being divided up again,' he shouted. 'What have you done to resist this? What's going to happen after I'm dead?' The two men soon calmed down, but the episode must have left Mao wondering whether Liu Shaoqi was his nemesis, the Chinese Khrushchev who would denounce him after his death and launch a campaign of deMaoification.[10]

More irritation followed on 1 August, as a revised version of Liu Shaoqi's 1939 essay *How to be a Good Communist* was published after having been serialised in the *People's Daily*, the mouthpiece of the party.[11] Liu had been chairman of the state since 1959, and Mao's heir apparent was clearly trying to build an image for himself as an independent and creative thinker.

Five days later the Chairman decided that it was time to counter-attack. He delivered a major speech on class struggle at the leadership's annual retreat by the beach resort of Beidaihe. 'Never Forget Class Struggle' became the slogan of the day a month later, as the powerful Central Committee elected in 1956 convened in the capital. Mao's first target was the breaking up of collective land. He homed in on Deng Zihui, one of Liu Shaoqi's underlings. Years earlier, the Chairman had already harshly condemned Deng for 'tottering along like a woman with bound feet' on the road to collectivisation. Deng was the most vocal advocate of contracting production out to individual households. Mao condemned the practice as 'capitalist' and Deng as a 'rightist'. He also rounded on several provincial leaders who had defended the system. Zeng Xisheng, the leader of Anhui province who had pioneered a return of the land to the farmers, was now attacked as a 'capitalist roader'.

For good measure, Peng Dehuai, already purged at the Lushan plenum in the summer of 1959, was condemned once again. After the Seven Thousand Cadres Conference, Deng Xiaoping had begun rehabilitating cadres who had fallen victim to the purges carried out in the wake of the Lushan plenum. Even Peng had submitted an appeal for his political rehabilitation, but instead Mao escalated the charges, accusing him of having colluded with reactionary forces the world over.[12]

Mao was back in charge, for all to see. A few leaders waited to see which way the wind would blow. Most of them, sensing a change of direction, rallied behind him. Liu Shaoqi, silent at first, acquiesced.[13] Once again, it had become dangerous to disagree with the Chairman. The days of the Seven Thousand Cadres Conference were over.

By the time the plenum reached its conclusion a few weeks later, Mao enjoyed the full backing of his colleagues. He announced that 'We must acknowledge that classes will continue to exist for a long time. We must also acknowledge the existence of a struggle of class against class and admit the possibility of the restoration of reactionary classes. We must raise our vigilance and properly educate our youth as well as the cadres, the masses and the middle- and basic-level cadres. Otherwise a country like ours can still move towards its opposite.'[14]

To raise revolutionary vigilance and educate the masses on the benefits of socialism, a Socialist Education Campaign was launched a few months later, with the motto 'Never Forget Class Struggle'. Among its instruments were committees of poor and middle peasants. In the Xingtai region of Hebei, many thousands were established and then unleashed on 'capitalists' and 'go-it-aloners'. They clamoured for the return of all holdings larger than the small private plots allowed since 1960. In Anhui province, the countryside was recollectivised within half a year, as countless production teams were forced to surrender their land to the people's communes. Villagers who worked on their own on the margins of the communes were accused of undermining the collective economy. In Guizhou, where Zhou Lin had followed a path similar to that adopted by Zeng Xisheng, land was also claimed back from individual households.[15]

Any type of activity that took place outside the collectives was viewed with suspicion, even raising chickens or weaving baskets in the evening to earn some extra income. Speculators seemed to be everywhere. In Xi'an over 2,000 merchants were going it alone, some of them starting to charge higher interest than their counterparts in the state sector. Shenyang, all the way up in Manchuria, had an astounding 20,000 private entrepreneurs, while in Wuhan, the commercial and industrial centre on the middle Yangtze, 3,000 profiteers made a living by exploiting loopholes in the planned economy, colluding with cadres to buy rationed commodities at state-controlled prices and selling them back for a profit on the black market. Many carried out their trade across several provinces. Private networks were constructed far and wide, involving not only agricultural products but also gold and silver. From Guangdong in the subtropical south, some communes sent their own agents with rare produce around the country by plane. A shadow economy flourished in the interstices of the collectives. There were underground factories, underground construction teams, underground transportation corps.[16] Even opium, the very symbol of imperialist oppression, was being resurrected, its silky flowers, held high on elegant stems, turning entire fields white, pink, red and purple, from Heilongjiang to Shanxi. In Zunyi, a town in Guizhou where the communists had stopped during the Long March in 1935 to elect Mao Zedong as their leader, dozens of opium dens operated with impunity.[17]

To the leadership, it appeared that a whole new bourgeois class was emerging from the ruins of Mao's Great Famine. Much of this underground activity had indeed sprung to life since the dead hand of the state had been relaxed in the last year or so. But in an odd twist of fate, the attempt to replace individual rewards with moral incentives during the Great Leap Forward had already produced a nation of entrepreneurs.

People had not simply waited to starve to death. In a society in disintegration, they had resorted to every means available to survive. So destructive was radical collectivisation that at every level the population tried to circumvent, undermine or exploit the master plan, covertly giving full scope to the profit motive that the party was trying to eliminate. As the catastrophe unfolded, claiming tens of millions of victims, the very survival of an ordinary person came to depend on the ability to lie, charm, hide, steal, cheat, pilfer, forage, smuggle, trick, manipulate or otherwise outwit the state.

Theft became routine. One survivor of the famine summed it up: 'Those who could not steal died. Those who managed to steal some food did not die.'[18] Sometimes entire villages banded together, hiding the grain and keeping two sets of books, one with the real figures and another with fake numbers for the grain inspectors. People learned to trade. One of the many paradoxes of the Great Leap Forward was that everything was for sale, as bricks, clothes and fuel were bartered for food. Millions also left the countryside to work in underground factories, despite formal restrictions on the freedom of movement. They sent remittances back home to keep their families alive.

Higher up the social hierarchy, local cadres showed extraordinary entrepreneurial guile in devising novel ways to defraud the state. State enterprises sent purchasing agents to bypass the rigid supply system. In Nanjing alone, hundreds of units had been involved in the direct trading of scarce commodities between themselves, outside the state plan. Some counterfeited shipping permits, used false names, forged certificates and even shipped in the name of the army in order to secure a profit.[19]

Everywhere – or so it seemed, as the campaign unfolded, going through many political twists and turns – there existed government organs, state enterprises and people's communes where cadres took the lead in undermining the socialist economy. They became the focus of the Socialist Education Campaign. Teams were organised to scrutinise the records of party members, in rural areas in particular. In the people's communes, they scrutinised corruption in accounting, food distribution, the division of the land and ways in which work points, given to commune members instead of a salary, were distributed.

Liu Shaoqi threw his full weight behind the campaign. In February 1963, he had interrupted a report by Peng Zhen on corruption in the cities to warn gravely that the Socialist Education Campaign was 'a very acute class struggle', one that would determine 'the life or death of our party'.[20] Trying to prove that he was a determined revolutionary and worthy heir to the Chairman, Liu was veering even further to the left than Mao himself. By the end of 1963, he had sent his own wife to the countryside to head a work team. Wang Guangmei departed from Beijing with much fanfare. In Funing county, just outside the beach resort of Beidaihe, she set up her headquarters in a small village called Peach Garden, determined to 'take power back from class enemies'. She showed herself to be a fierce class warrior, inciting ever greater punitive violence against alleged enemies of the party. Suspects were beaten, forced to stand naked in the cold and threatened with execution. It was rumoured that she introduced a new torture method, known as the jet plane, as victims were made to stand for hours with bent knees and arms pulled straight back to increase the strain. The jet plane would become very popular with Red Guards a few years later. The conclusion of her inquiry was that all the cadres, 'big or small', had problems, and that none could be trusted.[21]

Across the country work teams exposed corruption on a staggering scale. In Hunan province, up to 80 per cent of all cadres in the countryside were found to be corrupt, working hand in hand with people from bad class backgrounds – those who had been condemned in earlier campaigns as landlords, rich peasants, counter-revolutionaries and bad elements. The slogan of the day was 'class struggle is a struggle to the death'. The work teams carried out violent purges, as corrupt cadres and bad elements were denounced in public rallies, paraded through the streets and forced to confess to their wrongdoings. In every people's commune, several victims were beaten to death.[22]

The enemy was ubiquitous, bribing local cadres to be reclassified as poor or middle peasants rather than the landlords and counter-revolutionaries they really were. Entire counter-revolutionary organisations had managed to infiltrate the ranks of the party. In Daoxian, a county of great natural beauty, with orange groves and hot springs, one in ten cadres had gone the capitalist way: 'many people have no understanding of the meaning of class or class struggle, and no class awareness of the distinction between those who exploit and those who are exploited'. The whole region, it seemed, was still mired in feudal relations, as clan and lineage held sway over a superstitious population.[23]

So rotten were parts of the country that power was no longer in the hands of the communist party. This became particularly clear in the case of Baiyin, an arid county located on a loess plateau in Gansu province. In March 1962, in the wake of the Seven Thousand Cadres Conference, the local party committee had not only criticised Zhang Zhongliang, the provincial boss who had caused millions to die during the famine, but also pointed the finger at Liu Shaoqi, Zhou Enlai and the Chairman himself. 'If Chairman Mao is not examined and corrected, he will commit the same errors as the later Stalin.' Somebody denounced the party committee as a revisionist clique. Beijing dispatched a team 1,500 strong in March 1963. They scrutinised the Baiyin Silver and Non-Ferrous Metals Company and interrogated, denounced in public meetings and tortured around 2,000 of its employees. Hundreds were accused of one crime or another, from 'speculation' to 'moral decadence'. Fourteen committed suicide. 'Power', it was announced, 'had been seized by counter-revolutionaries.' Mao liked the report, and the investigation was broadened to include the entire municipality. From the mayor and the party secretary to the head of the police, hardly anyone in a position of authority came out clean.[24]

Baiyin was proof that entire counties could fall into the hands of the enemy. On 8 July 1964, even Liu Shaoqi wondered: 'We should think it over, could revisionism appear in China in the future? If we don't pay attention it could.'

Mao retorted: 'It has already appeared!' He invoked the example of Baiyin. 'The way I look at it, a third of the power in this country is no longer in our hands, it is in the hands of our enemies.'

Liu Shaoqi agreed: 'Right now, problems appear at the lower level because we don't go after the top; it's precisely at the top that problems appear. In Funing county the peasants say that it's easy to be an official if you have friends at court [to protect you when you are in trouble].'

'What shall we do if a Khrushchev appears in China?' Mao reflected. 'If a revisionist centre appears, we will have to stop it.'[25]

Khrushchev, by now, had become a byword for revisionism. After the Soviet leader had visited Camp David in November 1959 and agreed to a reduction of 1 million Soviet troops, seeking a rapprochement with the United States, Beijing had begun to challenge Moscow openly for the leadership of the socialist camp, denouncing Khrushchev in increasingly vituperative terms for pursuing 'appeasement with imperialists'.²⁶ In July 1960 an angry Khrushchev retaliated by ordering thousands of Soviet advisers and their dependants to pack up and leave China. Economic relations between the two countries collapsed, scores of large-scale projects were cancelled and transfers of high-end military technology were frozen. After the world had come to the brink of atomic war during the 1962 Cuban missile crisis, the Soviet Union, Britain and the United States tried to restrict the production of nuclear weapons by other nations. Mao, who years earlier had been promised help by Khrushchev developing an atomic bomb, viewed this as an attempt to isolate China. From September 1963 to July 1964, Beijing published a series of commentaries in the *People's Daily* portraying the Soviet Union as a country on the road towards capitalism and Khrushchev as the staunchest enemy of revolution.²⁷ Mao was making his claim for leadership in the communist world, causing ripples across communist parties from Albania to Cuba. But he also used the conflict to undermine his real and imagined enemies inside China.

In the summer of 1964, Liu Shaoqi formally assumed command of the Socialist Education Campaign. He was now determined to show his mettle. He toured the country, explaining to provincial leaders how the international fight against revisionist forces had to be linked to the suppression of revisionism at home. He even wondered whether Mao had been too conservative in venturing that a third of all power was in the hands of the enemy: 'It may well be more than a third.' Jiang Weiqing, the leader of Jiangsu province, dared to express doubts about the extent of the counter-revolution, but Liu forced him to make an abject self-criticism. Wang Renzhong, the sycophantic follower of Mao who had volunteered a confession at the Seven Thousand Cadres Conference, now shifted his loyalty and proclaimed that he, too, deserved to be thoroughly criticised by Liu Shaoqi.²⁸ By asserting his personal authority over the party elders, Liu was stealing Mao's thunder.

On 1 August 1964, Liu reported back to a packed meeting in Beijing, with the top brass in attendance. The audience was eerily quiet as Zhou Enlai led the chairman of the state to the podium. Instead of speaking from the lectern, Liu paced the podium, his hands clasped behind his back. He asked that everyone emulate his wife, and take part in the campaign by joining work teams in the countryside: 'Hurry and go!' Those who declined, he insinuated, were not fit to serve on the Politburo. The whole performance took less than an hour. On their way out, many leading officials wondered what had just happened. 'What the hell was that? Were we being lectured?', some of them muttered. Several army officials cursed Liu under their breath. They did not like taking orders from anyone but the Chairman, and they certainly did not appreciate how Liu publicly promoted his own wife.[29]

By now, the campaign was escalating beyond isolated towns and counties. Whole provinces were being accused of taking the capitalist road. One such was Guizhou province, where the entire leadership was denounced as 'rightist', with the capital, Guiyang, branded a 'nest of counter-revolutionaries', a 'small Taiwan' teeming with agents of imperialism. The work team in charge of Guizhou hunted them down, investigating the dossiers and background histories of all party members, searching their households for incriminating evidence, encouraging people to denounce each other, dragging prominent victims in front of assembled crowds for public trials. Zhou Lin, party secretary of Guizhou, was purged, his underlings hounded across the province. The head of the work team, a close associate of Liu Shaoqi, took over the province in September 1964. Over the following two months, up to a quarter of party members in some counties vanished from public view. Some were issued a formal warning, others put under arrest or sent away to the gulag.[30]

Guizhou was an extreme example, but the situation elsewhere was not all that different. Exact figures are hard to come by, but one historian has estimated that during the Socialist Education Campaign conducted by Liu Shaoqi, over 5 million party members were punished, with more than 77,000 people hounded to their death. The vast majority were innocent, and many of these verdicts were overturned in the 1980s. Liu pushed through one of the longest and most vicious purges of party members in the history of the People's Republic.[31]

As whole provinces were being toppled by Liu Shaoqi, a dramatic turn of events took place in Moscow in October 1964. In a surgical, bloodless coup, led by one of his own protégés, Leonid Brezhnev, Khrushchev's colleagues deposed him, ending his ten-year reign. A delegation headed by Zhou Enlai was sent to Moscow. Hopes for a better relationship were quickly dashed. At a Kremlin reception on 7 November, the highly inebriated Soviet defence minister staggered towards Marshal He Long and said in the hearing of everyone present: 'We've already got rid of Khrushchev; you ought to follow our example and get rid of Mao Zedong. That way we'll get on better.'[32]

At Beijing airport one week later, in a show of defiance against the Soviet Union, a grim Chairman flanked by his colleagues welcomed the delegation back. The *People's Daily* denounced Moscow for practising 'Khrushchevism without Khrushchev'. Mao could not help but wonder whether his colleagues might contemplate Maoism without Mao.

The Chairman now started distancing himself from his heir apparent. He was deeply suspicious of Liu's increasing assertion of authority over the party. By the end of November, Mao goaded his ambitious next in line. 'Let's change over now. You be Chairman; you be the Qin Emperor [the ruthless emperor to whom Mao was often compared]. I have my weak points. When I tell people off it has no effect. You're vigorous. You should take over the role of telling people off.'[33] A few weeks later, he began mentioning 'leaders taking the capitalist road', hinting darkly at a bureaucratic class that was drinking the blood of the workers. Then, on 26 December, to celebrate his seventy-first birthday, Mao summoned a group of party leaders to the Great Hall of the People for a banquet, where he harped on revisionism and attacked 'independent kingdoms' at the centre. The atmosphere was glacial.[34]

The following day, Mao referred enigmatically to the existence of two factions within the party, a socialist one and a capitalist one. 'In Beijing, and I don't mean the Beijing party committee, there are two independent kingdoms. I will let you guess, I have said enough.'[35] On 28 December, as Deng Xiaoping suggested that the Chairman need not attend a meeting on the Socialist Education Campaign, Mao brandished copies of the party and state constitutions, reading out a passage asserting his right to speak as a citizen and party member. 'One person told me not to attend the meeting [alluding to Deng Xiaoping], and another didn't want me to speak [meaning Liu Shaoqi].' Outside the meeting room, Mao complained: 'Somebody is shitting on my head.'[36]

Over the following weeks, Mao continued carping over how the Socialist Education Campaign was being implemented, constantly interfering with the work of his colleagues. In January 1965, he put his foot down, demanding the retraction of accusations against Zhou Lin, the head of Guizhou. What rattled the Chairman was that Liu Shaoqi was placing his own men in positions of power in Guizhou, including several who had been trained in Moscow and had worked as secret agents in the pre-1949 communist underground. Like Stalin in the Great Terror, Liu sought to use the public security and party organs to push through his purge.[37]

But, most of all, the Socialist Education Campaign focused on the rank and file in the countryside. If revisionism was to be prevented from taking over the country, power holders ensconced in high office should come under fire. Liu had sent his own wife to investigate the grassroots, demanding that others follow her lead by joining large work teams across the country. Mao did not appreciate this top-down approach, preferring a bottom-up campaign in which ordinary people would shine the spotlight on the very leaders who were heading those work teams. In January 1965, he had the guidelines for the campaign rewritten. One key point was 'to rectify those people in positions of authority within the party who take the capitalist road'.[38] Red Guards would turn to this passage just over a year later during the Cultural Revolution, which would subsume the Socialist Education Campaign.

3

War on the Cultural Front

At the Congress of Victors, Stalin had declared that fierce battles lay ahead. As the *Short Course* explained:

> He warned the party that although its enemies, the opportunists and nationalist deviators of all shades and complexions, had been defeated, remnants of their ideology still lingered in the minds of some party members and often asserted themselves. The survivals of capitalism in economic life and particularly in the minds of men provided a favourable soil for the revival of the ideology of the defeated anti-Leninist groups. The development of people's mentality does not keep pace with their economic position. As a consequence, survivals of bourgeois ideas still remained in men's minds and would continue to do so even though capitalism had been abolished in economic life.[1]

Stalin believed that socialism demanded nothing less than a complete rupture with the attitudes and ideas of the past. In the years following the Congress of Victors, war was declared on traditional culture. Private printing houses were closed down. Religion was stamped out, and intellectuals 'battered into submission or else discarded'. Those who joined the war on the cultural front were called 'engineers of human souls'. Stalin became the arbiter of high culture, lauding a few novelists as great proletarian intellectuals, sending countless others to their deaths. Stalin wanted culture for the masses.[2]

As early as 1942, Mao had brushed aside the idea that art could exist simply for art's sake. After tens of thousands of students, teachers, artists, writers and journalists had poured into Yan'an, a remote and isolated mountain area in Shaanxi where the communist party had established its headquarters, the Chairman launched a campaign to eradicate any lingering influence of free thinking among the young volunteers. They were interrogated in front of crowds, made to confess in indoctrination meetings and forced to denounce each other in a bid to save themselves. Some were incarcerated in caves, others put through mock executions. Mao demanded absolute loyalty from intellectuals. 'All literature and art belong to definite classes and are geared towards definite political lines,' he declared.

After 1949, the party spared no effort to crush independent thought. Private newspapers were closed within months of liberation, while thousands of titles were withdrawn from circulation. Entire libraries were burned. The beat of drums and the chant of revolutionary song displaced classical music, decried as bourgeois. Jazz was banned. New plays celebrating class struggle were brought to the villagers by travelling drama troupes. Most foreign films were deemed reactionary and replaced by Russian ones, for instance *Lenin in October*, one of Stalin's favourites. Religion, too, came under attack, as monasteries, temples, churches and mosques were converted into barracks or prisons. Religious leaders were persecuted, their congregations forced to renounce their faith at public meetings – after much pressure, not to mention outright threats to themselves and their families. Sacred objects were melted down for their metal.[3]

Millions of teachers, scientists and writers – termed 'intellectuals' in communist jargon – found themselves forced to prove their allegiance to the new regime. Like everyone else, they attended indoctrination classes to learn Marxist-Leninist orthodoxy, studying official pamphlets, newspapers and textbooks. The party line was periodically enforced through a witch-hunt, as thousands were denounced for 'bourgeois idealism' and packed off to labour camps. This happened in 1955, when under cover of an attack on Hu Feng – a famous writer who had compared the stultifying literary theories of the party to knives thrust into the brains of writers – over a million individuals, from primary school teachers up to leading party theoreticians, were forced to defend themselves against accusations of treason. Many committed suicide; even more ended up in an ever expanding gulag. Two years later, a further 500,000 were labelled 'rightists' by Deng Xiaoping, as the Hundred Flowers campaign reached its tragic conclusion.

Although Mao disparaged intellectuals, like Stalin he tried to keep a few of them as occasional companions. Like Stalin, he would break them at the merest hint of disagreement. One example is Liang Shuming, a remarkable thinker hired in 1918 at the age of twenty-four by the philosophy department in Peking University, when Mao was still an obscure school teacher. On a brief visit to Yan'an in 1938, Liang presented the Chairman with copies of his work. Mao was flattered, and after 1949 cultivated the professor, on occasion sending his own car to ferry him to Zhongnanhai, the headquarters of the party. The relationship cooled after Liang wrote a letter in 1952 to defend private entrepreneurs. A year later, at a meeting of the Political Consultative Conference, an advisory body designed to create the appearance of democracy, Liang insisted that, in the wake of land reform, villagers lived 'in the ninth ring of hell'. The delegates shouted him down and a stern Mao remonstrated with him, publishing a lengthy 'Criticism of Liang Shuming's Reactionary Ideas', in which he came down hard on the philosopher: 'There are two ways of killing people: one is to kill with the gun and the other with the pen. The way which is most artfully disguised and draws no blood is to kill with the pen. That is the kind of murderer you are.' Liang was neither the first nor the last intellectual whom Mao courted and then discarded as unworthy of his trust.[4]

At the Seven Thousand Cadres Conference in January 1962, when Mao was forced to be on his best behaviour, he had magnanimously accepted at least partial responsibility for the Great Leap Forward, drawing on historical examples of emperors who had strayed by failing to listen to their advisers. He told the story of Xiang Yu, an emperor who 'hated listening to opinions which differed from his', and was ultimately defeated by his rival Liu Bang, an 'open-minded man who took advice and was as relaxed as a flowing river'.[5]

But eight months later, as Mao spearheaded the Socialist Education Campaign, he quashed an appeal for rehabilitation from his greatest critic at the 1959 Lushan plenum, Marshal Peng Dehuai. Almost simultaneously, Kang Sheng, head of the party's Ideology Steering Committee, concocted the idea of a high-level plot against the party. A tall, slightly bowed man with a sparse moustache and a sinister look, Kang had been trained in Moscow by Nikolai Yezhov, the head of the secret police. During the great purges Stalin launched in 1934, he worked closely with the Soviet secret police in eliminating hundreds of Chinese students in the Soviet Union. A few years later Stalin sent him to Yan'an on a special plane. He quickly sided with Mao, using the expertise he had acquired in the Soviet Union to oversee security and intelligence. He was the hand behind the persecution of intellectuals in Yan'an, and so brutal were his methods that in 1945 he was forced to step down. He adopted a low profile throughout the 1950s, suffering from bouts of psychosis and epilepsy, and was further demoted at the Eighth Party Congress in 1956 at which Mao Zedong Thought was written out of the constitution.[6]

But Mao protected this master of intrigue, and was now using him to regain control over the party. Kang alleged that a historical novel about a fallen party leader named Liu Zhidan was in fact an attempt to exonerate Peng Dehuai. Kang slipped a note to Mao: 'Using novels to carry out anti-party activities is a great invention.' Mao read out the note, which Kang interpreted as licence to accuse several leaders of being part of a plot. Its mastermind, he contended, was Xi Zhongxun, a party elder who sometimes acted as premier in the absence of Zhou Enlai and had sided with Peng Dehuai at the Lushan plenum. Under Mao's watchful eye, Xi was purged.[7]

Mao now talked about the importance of class struggle in the realm of ideology. 'Writing novels is popular these days, isn't it? The use of novels for anti-party activity is a great invention. Anyone wanting to overthrow a political regime must create public opinion and do some preparatory ideological work. This applies to counter-revolutionary as well as to revolutionary classes.'[8]

The sheer scale of the ideological rot was highlighted during the Socialist Education Campaign. In June 1963, the leadership warned that 'right now there is a serious, acute class struggle taking place inside the country relating to ideology, education, theory, science, arts, newspapers, periodicals, broadcasting, publishing, health, physical education and other fields, and all of these merit close attention.' In Xi Zhongxun's home province, plays inspired by the West were performed in the cities, while feudal opera was enjoying a revival in the countryside. In some of the villages scattered along the fertile valley of the Wei River, often seen as the cradle of civilisation, tutors in private schools were returning to the classics of Confucianism. In the ancient city of Xi'an, which had once housed hundreds of Buddhist shrines, pagodas and monasteries inside its walls, counter-revolutionary organisations spewed their venom in publications openly on sale at bookstalls clustered around the main thoroughfares. Some followed Hu Feng, others praised Chiang Kai-shek, head of the Nationalist Party that had been defeated by the communists and forced to flee to Taiwan in 1949. Several government units even ordered reading material from abroad. The Xi'an Foreign Language Institute, which had churned out Russian graduates in the 1950s, subscribed to scores of foreign magazines and newspapers. In Hanzhong University, the first lesson in English was 'The United States' Today is Our Tomorrow', an ironic inversion of the official slogan that had spread after 1949, namely 'The Soviet Union's Today is Our Tomorrow'.[9]

Xi'an was not unique. In Wuhan, the commercial powerhouse on the shores of the Yangtze, hundreds of unlicensed pedlars had since 1961 been doing thriving business lending and selling books. Many of these publications were reactionary, for instance the *Guidelines for Members of the Nationalist Party*. Copies of popular folk ballads were also on sale, and not just a few dozen rescued from the recycling plant. The contents of the majority of some 15,000 libretti were condemned as 'feudal, superstitious, Confucian, preposterous and pornographic'. At the railway station and on the wharfs, travellers could purchase photos of 'politically incorrect leaders', not to mention foreign actresses. The rot reached far beyond Hubei's busy port, as feudal literature was common in the countryside. In Gong'an county hundreds of primary schools relied on the Three Character Classic, a simple text used before liberation to teach children Confucian values.[10]

A cloud of superstition seemed to hang over the countryside. In the Xingtai region of Hebei, where poor peasants were being unleashed on 'capitalists' and 'go-it-aloners' in the Socialist Education Campaign, cadres had colluded with reactionary elements to build temples, stage plays, burn incense and invoke the spirits. In Jiangxi province too, class struggle against farmers who cultivated their own plots proceeded apace, but failed to tackle the much deeper-rooted phenomenon of religious revival. In the

Qujiang region, more than a hundred Buddhist temples had been rebuilt. Idols appeared across the country. And much more sinister habits were making a comeback, as parts of the countryside seemed to be slipping back into a feudal past from which communism was supposed to have rescued the villagers. Hundreds of women were sold into wedlock. Xu Rongda spent 2,200 yuan to purchase his bride. The party secretary of his commune, for his part, bought a fifteen-year-old girl. Across the country, villagers returned to their old habits, disenchanted with communism: 'Year in, year out there is a catastrophe, day in, day out the talk is about difficulties, when will it be over?' In Shunde, not far from Hong Kong, the outlook was bleak: 'Did we really walk down the right road to socialism?'[11]

Even Christianity seemed impervious to fifteen years of harsh persecution. Over Easter, hundreds of Christians celebrated the resurrection of Jesus Christ in Yidu, Shandong province, while the church in Changwei claimed thousands of followers, most of them converted in the wake of the Great Leap Forward. In Qingdao, the port of Shandong, churches were packed over Christmas.[12]

Many of the converts were children and adolescents, as the young appeared to be particularly vulnerable to counter-revolutionary poison. In Qingdao, a third of all children took part in religious activities. Reactionary songs were common. Many mocked the party by twisting the lyrics of well-known propaganda songs. 'Without the Communist Party, There Would be No New China', an obligatory song belted out in schools, factories and offices, became 'Without the Communist Party, There Would be No Dried Yam', as the sweet potato, cut and dried in the sunshine, stood as a symbol for famine. Another subversive take was 'The Sky Above the Liberated Areas is Bright and the People are Happy', which perhaps predictably became 'The Sky in the Liberated Areas is Dark and the People are Unhappy'. More than a hundred similar songs existed.[13]

In Beijing, right under the noses of the party elders, some students took their defiance much further, proudly calling themselves 'Tito' or 'Khrushchev'. A few spoke openly of the overthrow of the communist party. Wang Cuiwen, aged twenty-seven, was a graduate student in biology at Peking University who talked ceaselessly about the famine and referred to the party as the worst of all possible dictatorships. He and his friends had tried to flee to Hong Kong in the spring of 1962. He failed, but many others succeeded. In May, the exodus reached 5,000 a day.[14]

The Socialist Education Campaign was meant to teach people to appreciate the benefits of socialism. It was also used to stamp out corruption in the party ranks and ferret out counter-revolutionary plots, real or imagined. As we have seen, more than 5 million party members were punished in one way or another. But repression alone would not suffice to counteract the pervasive effects of a counter-revolutionary ideology that had taken hold in the wake of the Great Leap Forward. The Chairman was particularly concerned with educating the young, who were the heirs to the revolution. Lei Feng was part of the answer.

On 5 March 1963, Mao exhorted the nation to learn from Lei Feng, a young soldier who had dedicated his life to serving the people. Lei Feng had died the previous year at the age of twenty-one, struck by a falling telephone pole. His posthumous diary, a record of his ideological progress, was published and studied across the country. There had been other models for emulation in the past, but most had been war heroes and heroines who had died before 1949 fighting the Japanese or the nationalists. Lei Feng was different: he had joined the army after liberation, and he was designed to appeal to a generation of young readers raised in an era of peace. Lei Feng turned Mao into an everyman's philosopher, as his diary showed how the Chairman's political aphorisms could be used to solve everyday problems. Lei Feng was an invention of the propaganda department.

In his diary, Lei Feng explained how 'the blood given by the party and Chairman Mao has penetrated every single cell of my body'. Mao even appeared in a vision: 'Yesterday I had a dream. I dreamt of seeing Chairman Mao. Like a compassionate father, he stroked my head. With a smile, he spoke to me: "Do a good job in study; be forever loyal to the party, loyal to the people!" My joy was overwhelming; I tried to speak but could not.'[15]

Glowing testimonials from factory workers and farm labourers were published in letters to newspapers all over China. For the benefit of the younger generation, tens of thousands of meetings extolling Lei Feng as the ideal communist were held. Plays and movies were produced. Songs were composed, some of them running into dozens of verses. Storytellers roamed the villages to enthral illiterate villagers with his exploits and his love of the Chairman. A Lei Feng exhibition opened at the Beijing Army Museum, where a huge screen at the entrance inscribed with Mao Zedong's calligraphy exhorted visitors to 'Learn from Comrade Lei Feng!' On display under glass was Lei Feng's only uniform, his hat, bag and handkerchief. Slogans culled from his diary adorned the walls. Everywhere were huge, life-size photographs of Lei Feng, a chubby, eternally smiling young soldier among groups of smiling workers, peasants and children. As one shrewd observer noted, Lei Feng was the poor man's Mao, a simplified Mao for the masses. Most of all, he was the young man's Mao, 'a rejuvenated Mao, speaking the language of enthusiastic adolescents'. He was meant to rouse people from the apathy caused by Mao's Great Famine and heighten their hatred for class enemies.[16]

Other heroes were promoted for emulation. Ouyang Hai appeared in 1963. He, too, had been an army hero who had left a diary revealing his devotion to the Chairman. Yet another incarnation of Lei Feng turned up in November 1965, this one called Wang Jie. Wang, who also kept a diary, had thrown himself on a land mine that had been accidentally triggered by local militia, saving twelve bystanders. In 1963 the slogan was 'Learn from Lei Feng', now it became 'Learn from Wang Jie'. Identical posters were produced, identical articles were published. Other young role models succeeded one another rapidly, including Mai Xiande, a sailor critically wounded in 1965; Wang Jinsi, a pioneer worker at the Daqing oilfields, nicknamed 'Man of Iron'; and Liu Yingjun, a soldier who died aged twenty-one by saving children from runaway horses. All of them were resurrected briefly from death to flit across the stage and help the younger generation feel closer to the Chairman. But only Mao was to be remembered eternally.[17]

Zhai Zhenhua, the daughter of dedicated communists, was twelve when she and her classmates were asked to emulate Lei Feng: 'All students had a copy of *Excerpts from Lei Feng's Diary* . . . The "Learn from Lei Feng" movement began when I was in grade five and lasted until the Cultural Revolution. People were encouraged to be like him: to obey orders, to work hard, to do good deeds, to be selfless, and to study the writings of Chairman

Mao.'[18] Xu Xiaodi, aged ten, identified so closely with Lei Feng that she cried for him.[19] In Sichuan, Jung Chang left school with her classmates each afternoon to 'do good deeds like Lei Feng'. As the campaign started taking hold, some students became ready to submit themselves 'unquestioningly to the control of the Great Leader'.[20]

Helping old ladies at the railway station, as Lei Feng had done, was all well and good, but students were warned not to assist class enemies. The motto of the Socialist Education Campaign, after all, was 'Never Forget Class Struggle'. To instil class hatred in them, regular sessions of 'Recalling Bitterness' were organised, where elderly workers and peasants came to tell of the harsh and miserable days before liberation. 'We heard of childhoods dominated by starvation, freezing winters with no shoes, and premature, painful deaths. They told us how boundlessly grateful they were to Chairman Mao for saving their lives and giving them food and clothing.' Jung Chang came out of those sessions feeling devastated by the atrocities committed by the nationalist regime and passionately devoted to Mao.[21] In cities like Nanjing, some retired workers evoked their personal memories of torture and rape by evil capitalists to tens of thousands of people. The packed theatres were so shaken by sobs that the workers' accounts were barely audible.[22]

Students were also taken to 'museums of class education' where capitalist exploitation was on full display, showing how class enemies had wallowed in luxury while the masses lived in poverty. There were sculptures of starving peasants forced to pay exorbitant rents. There were torture chambers and dungeons with iron cages, all recreated to convey the dread of the feudal past. Now, the students were told, class enemies threatened to undermine the dictatorship of the proletariat and return the country to the old days of feudal exploitation, snatching their winter shoes, stealing their food, turning them into slaves.[23]

The army was behind Lei Feng, and the army was behind the drive to spread Mao Zedong Thought. At the Lushan plenum in the summer of 1959, Lin Biao had rallied to the defence of the Chairman, accusing Peng Dehuai in his frail, squeaky voice of being 'ambitious, conspiratorial and hypocritical'. Then he crowed that 'Only Mao is a great hero, a role to which no one else should dare to aspire. We are all very far behind him, so don't even go there!'[24] In private, Lin was in fact decidedly more critical than Peng, confiding in his private diary that the Great Leap Forward was 'based on fantasy and a total mess'.[25] But he knew that the best way to maintain power was to shower the Chairman with flattery. Lin had realised long before how crucial it was to promote Mao's cult of personality: 'He worships himself, he has blind faith in himself, adores himself, he will take credit for every achievement but blame others for his failures.'[26]

Immediately after taking over the Ministry of Defence from Peng Dehuai, Lin Biao begun promoting the study of Mao Zedong Thought as a shortcut to mastering Marxism-Leninism. Soldiers were asked to commit short passages from Mao's collected writings to memory. From April 1961, the *Liberation Army Daily* started carrying a quotation from the Chairman prominently displayed on the front page. Readers cut out the epigraphs and started compiling their own collections. Then, in January 1964, a mimeographed compendium of these quotations was published, with a fuller version distributed to the People's Liberation Army in May. It came covered in gaudy red plastic, and was no bigger than the palm of a hand, easily fitting inside the pocket of a standard military uniform. Lin Biao provided an inscription, taken from Lei Feng's diary: 'Read Chairman Mao's book, listen to Chairman Mao's words, act according to Chairman Mao's instructions and be a good fighter for Chairman Mao.' By the time a new edition appeared in August 1965, millions of copies of the *Quotations of Chairman Mao Zedong*, also known as the Little Red Book, were being distributed far beyond the ranks of the army.[27]

Mao basked in the adulation, and ordered the country to emulate Lin Biao and the People's Liberation Army. 'The merit of the Liberation Army', he said, 'is that its political ideology is correct.'[28] In response, the army started to assume a more prominent role in civil life, setting up political departments in government work units to promote Mao Zedong Thought. The army also fostered a more martial atmosphere, in tune with the Socialist Education Campaign. Military 'summer camps' for students and workers were organised in the countryside. In primary schools, children were taught how to use airguns by shooting at portraits of Chiang Kai-shek and American imperialists. At the Shanghai Children's Palace, originally built by Sun Yat-sen's wife with marble imported from Europe, special advisers organised military games for the Young Pioneers, easily identifiable by the red scarves they wore. Military training camps were set up for older students from reliable backgrounds, where they learned how to throw grenades and shoot with live bullets. In the summer of 1965, more than 10,000 university and 50,000 middle-school students in Shanghai spent a week in camp. Athletic clubs for 'national defence' were also founded by the army, offering classes in primary and secondary schools. 'The most important instruction was in shooting and communications.' There were rifle clubs, radio clubs, navigation clubs, electrical engineering clubs, flag signal clubs and parachuting clubs. Young people of dubious class background were excluded.[29]

On 1 October 1964, to celebrate National Day, the army organised a monumental show on Tiananmen with several choirs and ballet dancers in military uniform. A colossal figure of Chairman Mao opened the procession, which edged forward to the tune of 'Chairman Mao, the Sun in our Hearts'. Peng Zhen, the mayor of Beijing, proclaimed that the Chinese people, 'armed with Mao Zedong Thought', could overcome 'capitalist and feudal attempts at restoration as well as attacks by our enemies at home and abroad'.[30]

A passion for the military model went hand in hand with contempt for formal learning. 'Politics in Command' was Lin Biao's slogan. Mao had always been scathing of intellectuals, but he now began to express doubts about the entire education system. On 13 February 1963, on the occasion of the Spring Festival, when the country welcomed the Chinese New Year, he compared tests in high schools and universities to the old eight-legged essay, a written form of argumentation that candidates for the imperial examinations had been required to master under the Qing dynasty. 'I do not approve of this. It should be changed completely. I am in favour of publishing the questions in advance and letting the students study them and answer them with the aid of books.' He struck an even more rebellious note when he suggested that there were benefits to cheating. 'If your answer is good and I copy it, then mine too should be counted as good.' He praised students who dozed off when teachers rambled on with their tedious lectures. 'You don't have to listen to nonsense, you can rest your brain instead.'[31]

Mao went further, accusing the education system of favouring students from bad class backgrounds – capitalists, landlords – as they were better equipped to succeed in education than the proletariat and the peasants. Worst of all, schools were run by bourgeois intellectuals who were failing in their mission of training 'revolutionary successors'.[32]

Some students were quick to pick up the message. Hua Linshan, still a young boy in Guilin, a scenic town in Guangxi where karst hills rise sharply from the green plains, embraced Mao's Spring Festival report: 'Each word was like a precious stone.' Like many other students, he felt crushed by an oppressive system based on blind obedience to teachers, mindless theory and rote learning. Mao was taking their side. As another future Red Guard put it, 'Classes are wasting my time and teachers are wasting my time.'[33] Many were awaiting the Chairman's call.

———

Mao also took aim at literature and the arts. In November 1963, he attacked the Ministry of Culture for failing to curb the spread of feudal, superstitious and revisionist ideas. He suggested that it should change its name to the 'Ministry of Gifted Scholars and Beautiful Ladies'. An even more appropriate name was the 'Ministry of Foreign Dead People'. A month later he complained again that 'dead people are still in control'. He also accused the All-China Federation of Literature and Art of tottering on the edge of revisionism: 'For the last fifteen years, they have not been carrying out the party's policy.'[34]

Spurred on by the Chairman, a national campaign was launched in the summer of 1964, aimed initially at traditional opera, one of the most popular art forms in the countryside. Five thousand leading cadres and artists were invited to attend the Peking Opera Festival under the auspices of Zhou Enlai. Peng Zhen, mayor of Beijing, condemned revisionism in ringing tones and exhorted his audience to ask whether opera served socialism or capitalism. 'Does it take the road of Marxism-Leninism or the road of revisionism?' Mao was pleased, but the real star of the festival was his wife.

Jiang Qing had been an up-and-coming actress in Shanghai in her early years, but after Japan had attacked the city in 1937 she headed for Yan'an, joining tens of thousands of other volunteers eager to dedicate their lives to the revolution. She was an attractive young woman, with fair skin and large eyes. She was also ambitious, ready to use sex to win power. Soon she attracted the attention of the Chairman. Mao was twenty years older and estranged from his third wife. The affair caused a stir among his comrades-in-arms, who disapproved of their leader abandoning a wife of long standing to marry an actress from Shanghai. Rumours circulated about her past, and an investigation even produced a report suspecting her of being an agent for Chiang Kai-shek. Kang Sheng, in charge of security, stepped in and vouched that she was a party member in good standing. He encouraged her liaison with the Chairman. Kang Sheng and Jiang Qing were old friends from Shandong, and they used each other to cement their relationship with Mao. A divorce was pronounced, as the Chairman's wife was shipped off to the Soviet Union for medical treatment. Mao married his fourth wife in 1938, but the new Madame Mao had to agree to refrain from political activities, leaving her seething with resentment for years to come.[35]

The initial passion soon faded. Mao had an enormous appetite for sex, and after liberation a string of young women were recruited to service his needs. 'Women were served to order like food.' As Mao's infidelities became more blatant, Jiang Qing became increasingly ill and lonely, suffering from a string of real and imaginary diseases. She was heavily medicated, suspected plots around her and complained all day long about noise, wind and glaring light. Pink and brown colours hurt her eyes, and she insisted that everything in her residence be painted light green – including the furniture. She demanded constant attention, but quarrelled incessantly with those around her. She had huge political ambitions, craving an active political role, but had become a helpless appendage to Mao.[36]

In 1961, Mao became smitten by one of the stewardesses on the special train that he used to travel through China. Zhang Yufeng was eighteen, with strikingly beautiful looks and a sharp tongue. She would soon become his closest female companion. Whether Jiang Qing agreed not to interfere in her husband's numerous affairs in return for a public role is not known, but Mao introduced his wife to the political stage the following year. On 29 September 1962, a few days after the party conference at which Mao had launched the slogan 'Never Forget Class Struggle', Jiang Qing made her first public appearance. The occasion was a visit by President Sukarno, and a photo in the *People's Daily* showed Jiang Qing standing next to Hartini, the Indonesian president's wife. Liu Shaoqi and his wife Wang Guangmei also posed for the camera. The photos aroused widespread attention, in China and abroad, as even *Time* magazine noted how 'the Peking matrons plainly competed for attention' with Hartini. Jiang Qing appeared in a neat Western-style suit, but was outclassed by Wang Guangmei, dressed in a gown of opulent velvet.[37]

The occasion signalled the entrance of Madame Mao into the party politics from which she had been banned more than twenty years earlier. Mao allowed Jiang Qing to try her hand at culture and the arts. As Mao's doctor noticed, 'the more involved in politics she became, the more her hypochondria and neurasthenia eased'.[38]

In 1963 Jiang Qing homed in on a historical play about a concubine executed by a cruel and jealous despot. The turning point in the play came after the concubine blurted out her admiration for a handsome young scholar within earshot of her ageing master, sealing her death sentence. The play was staged at Zhongnanhai, with all the top leaders in attendance, but Mao looked glum. At the end of the performance, he slowly clapped his hands three or four times and then walked away in silence. The play had cut too close to the bone, as the Chairman took it as a dig at his own philandering.[39]

Jiang Qing, now spurred into action, started investigating the extent of feudal and foreign plays staged by drama troupes across the country. Before long, as self-appointed overseer of culture, she started issuing instructions on the production of drama, music and film.[40]

But she was not acting on her own. Liu Shaoqi, who had rallied behind Mao's battle cry of 'Never Forget Class Struggle', also threw his weight behind the war on culture. In January 1964, he condemned Tian Han, author of the play that had offended Mao, saying that his work was 'aimed at the communist party'. He, too, wanted a cleansing fire to burn through the very foundations of culture. Just as Liu claimed that over a third of all power in the countryside was in the hands of the enemy, he suggested that over a third of all art and culture, from universities down to village schools, was revisionist and ought to be overthrown in a revolution.[41]

Peng Zhen, too, had never believed in freedom for intellectuals, and he headed a small Group of Five charged by the party with revolutionising culture. It was in his capacity as head of the Group of Five that Peng Zhen gave the key speech on the danger of revisionism at the Peking Opera Festival. Kang Sheng was another member of the group.

Jiang Qing sided with her former mentor, Kang Sheng, who two years earlier had presided over the purge of Xi Zhongxun. At the Peking Opera Festival, they took Tian Han to task. In a thick Shandong accent, before a radiant Madame Mao, Kang denounced his work as 'poisonous weeds that are anti-party and anti-socialist'. The playwright, pale as a sheet, stared at his shoes. He was one of Jiang Qing's many foes, having offended her during her acting days in Shanghai.[42]

In the second half of 1964, the purge was expanded far beyond theatre. War was waged across the entire spectrum of intellectual activity, from fine arts to history, economics and philosophy. Endless 'tools of Peng Dehuai' and 'mini-Khrushchevs' were uncovered. By the time the campaign came to a formal end in April 1965, even the head of the Ministry of Culture had fallen from grace.[43]

But Mao had not brought his wife into the political arena to attack a few playwrights. He needed somebody he could trust for a much more important mission, one that aimed far above the Ministry of Culture. In February 1965 he sent Jiang Qing on a secret assignment to Shanghai, as culture would become the stage from which the next revolution was launched.

4

Clique of Four

In January 1965, Edgar Snow was invited to share a meal with Mao Zedong in one of the spacious rooms of the Great Hall of the People. The two went back to 1936, when Snow, a young, idealistic reporter from Missouri, had been one of the first foreigners to reach Yan'an. Mao told him his story, and Snow accepted it eagerly. *Red Star over China*, published a year later, was the scoop of the century, introducing the Chairman to the rest of the world and swaying opinion in favour of the communists, portrayed as agrarian reformers who lived cheek by jowl with the peasants in a great, unfolding democracy.

Now the Chairman was using Snow to convey another message to the outside world, this time on Vietnam: no troops would cross the border as long as the United States did not attack China. The interview was never published in China but read avidly by those with access to it.[1]

A few months earlier, on 16 October 1964, a mushroom cloud had soared into the atmosphere above Lop Nor, a salt lake in Xinjiang, China's westernmost province. The explosion had been powerful enough to set off Geiger counters on rooftops in Japan, where radiation watching had become something of a national hobby since the bombing of Hiroshima. China had just exploded its first atom bomb, becoming the fifth member of an exclusive club, joining the United States, the Soviet Union, Britain and France. The test came just two months after a congressional resolution gave President Lyndon B. Johnson the power to respond to communist aggression in Vietnam. Would an atomic China allow its armies to overrun South-east Asia in a major clash with the United States?

Korea had set a dire precedent. Thirteen years earlier, on 18 October 1950, more than 180,000 Chinese troops had crossed into Korea under cover of night. In what one historian has called 'the largest ambush in the era of modern warfare', they took the United Nations forces completely by surprise, forcing them to retreat.[2]

Mao used the Korean War to build up a first-class arms industry, all with Soviet help. Stalin, on the other hand, was keen to see more American troops destroyed in Korea, and probably not unhappy to have a potential rival locked into a costly conflict. The war dragged on for three years, as neither Mao nor Stalin was willing to bring it to an end. The human cost of the conflict was enormous. China sent some 3 million men to the front, of whom an estimated 400,000 died, in addition to the hundreds of thousands of Korean casualties. The United States suffered more than 30,000 deaths on the battlefield. Mao indicated that Vietnam would not be a repeat of Korea.

A month after Snow's visit, another guest was welcomed in Beijing. After the disaster of the Cuban missile crisis in 1962, Khrushchev had worked hard to improve relations with the United States. He did not want to get involved in Vietnam. But Brezhnev was eager for a harder line. In February 1965, as the United States dramatically escalated its involvement in Vietnam, he sent his premier Kosygin to Hanoi, where a defence treaty was agreed that provided the revolutionary leader Ho Chi Minh with a flood of financial aid, military equipment and technical advisers. En route back to Moscow, Kosygin stopped in Beijing to press for a joint effort in the Vietnam War. Young Pioneers with flowers welcomed him at the airport. But Mao, in the presence of the entire leadership, lectured Kosygin for several hours and rejected his pleas for unity.[3]

Mao wished to focus on the revolution at home. But not all his colleagues agreed that internal class struggle should have priority over world revolution. As US troop numbers began to rise in South Vietnam, Luo Ruiqing, chief of staff of the People's Liberation Army, compared the United States to Nazi Germany and warned of a new East Asian Munich. On 5 May 1965, he used the notion of 'active defence', reminiscent of the Korean War, to warn that escalation was leading towards a 'local war of the Korean type'. The communist party, he asserted, was prepared 'to send our men to fight together with the people of Vietnam when they need us'.[4]

Lin Biao, minister of defence, came to the rescue, providing the Chairman with a rationale by proposing the notion of a 'people's war'. In June he abolished formal saluting, epaulettes, hard-peak caps, medals, insignia of rank, tailored uniforms for officers and other privileges in the People's Liberation Army. From a general all the way down to a soldier, every fighter was now to wear a single red star on an identical cap. Several months later, on 3 September, Lin expounded a strategy that avoided confrontation with the United States on the one hand and collaboration with the Soviet Union on the other. His vision hinged on a single term, one that would run throughout the Cultural Revolution: self-reliance. Revolutionary forces around the world, from Asia to Africa, would rely on their own military forces to destroy American imperialism: 'In order to fight a revolution and to fight a people's war and be victorious, it is imperative to adhere to the policy of self-reliance, rely on the strength of the masses in one's own country and prepare to carry on the fight independently even when all material aid from outside is cut off.'[5]

Luo Ruiqing had picked the anniversary of the Soviet defeat of Nazi Germany to make his speech. Lin Biao published his statement on the twentieth anniversary of China's victory over Japan. The very same day that Lin's piece appeared in the *People's Daily*, Luo, flanked by Liu Shaoqi and Deng Xiaoping at a political rally in the Great Hall of the People, repeated the key elements of his spring talk.[6]

The rivalry between Lin Biao and Luo Ruiqing dated back to the Lushan plenum in 1959, when both had been promoted to important military positions. Lin was formally Luo's superior, but his chief of staff often went straight to Mao instead. There were deeper disagreements. Russian help with military technology – from jet fuel and spare parts for aircraft to ballistic missiles – came to an abrupt end with the withdrawal of Soviet experts from China in the summer of 1960. Lin Biao's answer was to advocate the primacy of man over weapon. Luo was disdainful. Ideology was paramount for Lin, who distributed the Little Red Book to the army in 1964 and promoted the slogan 'Politics in Command'. Luo was appalled.

Ye Qun, the tight-lipped, middle-aged wife of Lin Biao, went to see Mao in November 1965. She accused the chief of staff of undermining her husband and plotting for control over the army. Mao was easily swayed, relying on Lin Biao far more than on Luo Ruiqing. Relentless pressure was applied for months on end, as Luo was investigated, questioned, harangued and finally subjected to struggle sessions by groups of up to ninety-five participants, included Liu Shaoqi and Deng Xiaoping, his erstwhile supporters. Luo was a party stalwart and tough as nails. Before becoming chief of staff in 1959, he had built up the labour-camp system as minister of public security, presiding over the deaths of millions of ordinary people. But even he broke down under the strain, jumping from a window. He managed only to break his legs, but his suicide bid was interpreted as conclusive evidence of his guilt. Liu Shaoqi was disparaging: 'He should have jumped head first, he dropped down with his feet in front of him.' Deng Xiaoping also shrugged off the episode: 'He dived like an ice lolly.'[7]

Even before Luo Ruiqing sealed his own fate, another obstacle on the road to revolution was removed. Around the time that Khrushchev had denounced Stalin in 1956, clerks had started using tape recorders to ensure that their transcripts of major party conferences were accurate. Mao grumbled when two years later even his meetings with local leaders started being recorded. But he exploded when in 1961 his flirtations with Zhang Yufeng, the female attendant on his air-conditioned East German train, were caught on tape. Yang Shangkun, head of the General Office in charge of technical and logistical affairs, was spared, as several of his underlings took the fall. But Mao wondered whether his colleagues were collecting material to tarnish his reputation, possibly even preparing a report similar to the one Khrushchev had delivered on his former boss.[8]

The Chairman's paranoia increased after the coup against Khrushchev in October 1964. But, most of all, Mao was preparing the terrain for revolution. He wanted somebody he could trust with the paper flow through the party machine. In November 1965, Yang Shangkun was removed from his post and replaced by Wang Dongxing, one of the Chairman's most trusted bodyguards.

In early 1957, when the Chairman had appealed to intellectuals to air their grievances and help party members improve their work, Peng Zhen had used his clout as the mayor of Beijing to hold the campaign back. The *People's Daily*, based in the capital, took several weeks to publicise Mao Zedong's most important speeches on the Hundred Flowers. Deng Tuo, chief editor of the party's official organ, was following cues from the mayor. Many of Mao's colleagues were dismayed by the Hundred Flowers, especially Liu Shaoqi, who feared that the situation might spiral out of control if people were encouraged to vent their grievances. But none pushed defiance as far as Peng Zhen. A burly, hardened revolutionary who had little time for books and newspapers, he had played a key role in the persecution of intellectuals in Yan'an in the early 1940s. After liberation he transformed Beijing from a sleepy backwater into a communist capital of 6 million people, and little happened in the city without his consent.[9]

Peng Zhen eventually fell into line, but years later the Chairman complained that his control of the capital was so tight that 'you can't poke a hole in it with a needle or force a single drop of water through'.[10]

Peng and Liu, of course, were proven right: in the spring of 1957 people took to the streets in an outpouring of discontent with communist rule, forcing the party to backtrack. A ruthless campaign of repression started, and Peng Zhen made sure that no stone was left unturned in the capital. Soon throngs of students, teachers, artists and writers could be seen at the railway station, wearing heavy cotton-padded clothes and clunky winter shoes, some with coarse sheepskin overcoats under their arms, waiting to depart for labour camps in the Great Northern Wilderness.[11]

Peng Zhen was also in charge of the Group of Five, charged by the party with purifying literature and the arts in July 1964. It was an appropriate choice, given the relish with which Peng had persecuted intellectuals in 1942 and again in 1957. But his role as chief prosecutor in the field of culture, combined with his grip on the capital, were obstacles the Chairman sought to remove.

Mao first tried to undermine him through Kang Sheng, who was one of the Group of Five. As work teams were sent around the country during the Socialist Education Campaign, Kang decided to focus on Peking University. His hope was that, by scrutinising one institution, he could undermine the entire city, as had happened in Baiyin. A work group was dispatched in July 1964, finding a willing collaborator in Nie Yuanzi, party secretary of the philosophy department. The group secretly examined the files of every cadre and declared that the party committee of the university was 'rotten to the core'. Peng Zhen was enraged. A new inquiry was held, hundreds of investigators now poring over every aspect of the university's activities, including its relationship with the Beijing Municipal Party Committee. They concluded that the university and the municipality had colluded in taking a 'bourgeois line'. Peng Zhen, with the help of several members of the capital's party committee, denounced the 'wild criticisms' of the work team in January 1965. Two months later, Deng Xiaoping rallied to the mayor's defence, condemning the work team for having gone too far. Kang Sheng was criticised in all but name. More than sixty cadres who had been accused of 'anti-party' activities were rehabilitated.[12]

As Kang Sheng's strategy started to backfire, Mao opted for a more elaborate approach, sending his wife on a secret mission to Shanghai in February 1965. Jiang Qing had already cut her teeth in the field of theatre. Now the plan was to denounce another historical play, one in which an upright mandarin named Hai Rui confronted a tyrannical emperor and was dismissed for his honesty. Its author was Wu Han, a prominent historian and vice-mayor under Peng Zhen.

The use of historical allusion as a means of political attack had a long tradition in China, but in this case the Chairman himself had urged party leaders to study the character of Hai Rui in the first half of 1959. Mao was fascinated by the Ming-era official, who was both courageous in speaking out to the emperor and genuinely loyal to him. Most of all, Hai Rui accused not the emperor himself, but rather his misguided ministers. Mao used this historical figure to blame the party leadership for the mounting disaster caused by the Great Leap Forward. He had been told lies by his underlings and fed inflated statistics on the grain output. To promote the Hai Rui spirit, plays were staged, articles published, biographies written.[13]

But after the purge of Peng Dehuai in the summer of 1959, the political climate changed completely. It now seemed that the marshal who had spoken out at the Lushan plenum was Hai Rui. Wu Han's play, entitled *The Dismissal of Hai Rui*, could be read in a very different light: 'In your early years you may have done a few good deeds. But now? The country has been dissatisfied with you for a long time, a fact known by all officials of the inner and outer courts. So set on cultivating the Tao, you have become bewitched; so bent upon dictatorial ways, you have become dogmatic and biased.'[14]

A revised play written by Wu Han was performed in Beijing in February 1961, and its allegorical significance must have been clear to some leading party officials. During the fateful Seven Thousand Cadres Conference in January 1962, behind the scenes a few of them had started to compare Peng Dehuai to Hai Rui. The play was not staged again, but remained popular in print. In the immediate aftermath of the famine, there was little the Chairman could do about it.[15]

Jiang Qing knew Shanghai well from her actress days. The port city was a bastion of communism with a long history of labour unrest, run by a powerful mayor named Ke Qingshi who had the Chairman's trust. Two of the mayor's henchmen came forward to help Madame Mao. Both would become part of what was later called the 'Gang of Four'. One was Zhang Chunqiao, a taciturn, brooding man who was director of propaganda in the Shanghai party machine. The other was Yao Wenyuan, a stout young man with a round face who, in 1955, had enthusiastically joined a campaign against Hu Feng, the famous writer who had excoriated official dogma. When a string of intellectuals were condemned as members of the 'Hu Feng clique' and sentenced to do hard labour, Yao rejoiced, ready to use his pen again to help the Chairman.

Yao became a hatchet man. On Jiang Qing's advice, he retired to a sanatorium for the summer, pretending to be ill, and wrote a lengthy diatribe against the play, accusing Wu Han of supporting private farming and obliquely criticising the Great Leap Forward. It took nine drafts, three of which Mao personally edited. Even then, it was a turgid piece of prose running to 10,000 words.

Mao was in Shanghai to oversee the opening volley of the Cultural Revolution, published in two local newspapers on 10 November 1965, the very same day that Yang Shangkun was dismissed.

Peng Zhen had a choice. If he shielded Wu Han – a friend, colleague and respected intellectual – he could be accused of allowing the capital to harbour revisionist elements at the highest level. If he turned against him, he would be exposed for failing to spot the danger in the first place.

The mayor tried to sidestep the issue by forbidding the *People's Daily* and other newspapers in Beijing to reprint the article. After Zhou Enlai had telephoned Peng Zhen to tell him that the Chairman himself was behind the polemic, he relented, but tried to argue that the debate about the allegorical connection between Hai Rui and Peng Dehuai was a purely academic one. In February 1966, with his Group of Five, Peng went to seek guidance from the Chairman, now hunkering down in a secluded villa on the shore of East Lake in Wuhan. During the meeting Kang Sheng, one of the five members, denounced the play as a 'poisonous weed', but Peng Zhen insisted on portraying the whole affair as a scholarly controversy. Mao feigned ignorance and brushed off the conflict, adding: 'You people work it out.'[16]

Mao had lulled Peng into a false sense of security. The trap was sprung a month later, as Mao denounced the mayor for 'running an independent kingdom'. The Beijing Municipal Party Committee, the Chairman told Kang Sheng, should be dissolved for having shielded bad people and opposed the revolution. Kang travelled to Beijing to convey the message to Zhou Enlai, who followed his political instinct and threw in his lot with the Chairman. At a top meeting of party elders, Zhou Enlai and Deng Xiaoping gave Peng the coup de grâce, accusing their erstwhile colleague of 'contravening Mao Zedong Thought' and 'opposing Chairman Mao'.[17]

The fourth and final obstacle was Lu Dingyi, the man in charge of propaganda. He was one of the members of the Group of Five, and his fall followed hard upon that of his boss Peng Zhen, with whom he had sided in the controversy over the historical play *The Dismissal of Hai Rui*. Like Peng, Lu had been keen to regiment literature and the arts, declaring in December 1964 that the Ministry of Culture was 'entirely rotten' and run by the joint forces of capitalism and feudalism.[18] He purged the ministry from top to bottom, but this was not enough. Jiang Qing and Lin Biao, now increasingly working together, convened a meeting in Shanghai in February 1966 to discuss literature and the arts in the army. Their report concluded that since the founding of the People's Republic, 'the literary field and most professors have stood as a black force trying to dominate our politics'. Now it was Lu Dingyi's turn to be purged. He fell from power in March for having 'vilified' Mao Zedong Thought.[19]

Mao insisted that all four men – Peng Zhen, Luo Ruiqing, Lu Dingyi and Yang Shangkun – were part of an 'anti-party clique' that had been plotting a coup d'état. In front of the party elders, Lin Biao read out the accusation, prepared for him by Kang Sheng on orders from the Chairman. 'There is a bunch of bastards who want to take a chance and are biding their time. They want to kill us, so we have to crush them! They are fake revolutionaries, they are fake Marxists, they are fake followers of Mao Zedong Thought, they are traitors, they want to betray Chairman Mao as he is still in good health, they overtly agree with him but covertly oppose him, they are careerists, they play tricks, right now they want to kill people, they are using all sorts of tricks to kill people!'

Lin Biao denounced the four conspirators as the leaders of a revisionist, counter-revolutionary clique. He also heaped praise on the Chairman: 'Isn't Chairman Mao a genius? Don't we say that without Chairman Mao there would be no new China? Why is it that others won't do, and only Chairman Mao will do? Isn't Mao Zedong Thought creative? If it is not creative, then why would we hold high the banner of Mao Zedong Thought?' Zhou Enlai threw in his lot with Lin Biao: 'I entirely agree with comrade Lin's words, he has spoken very well.'

On 23 May 1966 the four leaders were dismissed. Their fall was a 'victory for Mao Zedong Thought', Zhou Enlai gushed, adding that 'Chairman Mao is a genius leader just like Lenin, he is the leader of all the people of the world!'[20]

PART TWO

THE RED YEARS (1966–1968)

5

Poster Wars

In May 1966, at the end of a rainy spring, a twenty-three-year-old worker employed at a scissor factory in Yangzhou trekked 50 kilometres inland to Purple Mountain, a historic location said to be haunted by spirits. Its peak, now in every shade of green, often vanished in mysterious clouds of gold and purple at sunset. The mountain dominated Nanjing, which had once been the capital of the Ming dynasty. It was the final resting place of several emperors and high-ranking mandarins. Amid the bamboo groves and ancient oak trees growing in the shade of a mausoleum where the Hongwu emperor, founder of the Ming, had been entombed, Chen Zhigao swallowed a vial of cyanide. After a child had glued a poster on his front door with brisk characters reading 'Embrace Deng Tuo!', he had been unable to bear the pressure. He became one of the first ordinary people to fall victim to the Cultural Revolution.[1]

Yao Wenyuan's essay had unleashed a whirlwind against Wu Han in November 1965. Peng Zhen asked Deng Tuo, the man who years earlier had delayed the publication of the Chairman's main speeches on the Hundred Flowers, to write in defence of Wu Han. After both Peng and Wu had fallen from power, Deng was next in the line of fire. On 6 May 1966, the *People's Daily* – now firmly in the hands of Mao – denounced him and several of his acolytes. In the wake of the Great Leap Forward, they had written hundreds of essays that had appeared in magazines controlled by the Beijing Municipal Party Committee, and their writings were now alleged to have attacked the Chairman through historical allegory and satire. Ten days later, on 16 May, the *People's Daily* demanded blood: 'What kind of person is Deng Tuo? Investigations now reveal that he is a traitor.'[2] Two days later, Deng took a large dose of sleeping pills and died at home, surrounded by a sprawling collection of rare calligraphy and ancient paintings that he had been able to amass as a leading hack under Peng Zhen.

The *People's Daily* was the party's mouthpiece, with its editorials carefully studied across the nation, read out at meetings, broadcast over the radio and posted in display cases at busy street intersections. In middle schools, party secretaries denounced Wu Han, Deng Tuo and their followers before assembled student bodies. For several years, students had been brought up in the militant doctrine of 'class struggle', and the Socialist Education Campaign had warned them of class enemies lurking in every corner, plotting to overthrow the party. Like the model soldier Lei Feng, many were eager to become loyal fighters for Chairman Mao.

Now they were given a task. They set to work, having been asked to write big-character posters. Bundles of brush pens, bottles of ink and stacks of old newspapers were provided. Cauldrons were set up to make glue from sweet-potato starch. Big, bold characters were painted on the newspapers, sometimes one to a sheet, and then they were pasted on walls with a broom. Soon the headlines were plastered across the country: 'Smash the Black Gang!', 'Down with the Anti-Socialist Cabal!', 'Carry the Revolution Through to the End!'[3]

Some of the more politically astute students also spent time in the library, studying commentaries and editorials from the *People's Daily* and other newspapers to understand what was wrong with Wu Han and his followers. They were on the alert for incriminating evidence, and every day fresh posters reported the latest findings. In Zhengding, a city where several schools of Buddhism had been founded, a group of students claimed to have identified a sword hanging over Chairman Mao's head in a photograph that showed him standing on the rostrum in Tiananmen Square. The search spread, and soon problems were discovered with short stories, novels, movies and plays. Many of the young activists tried to imitate the prose style of Yao Wenyuan, the man who had brought down Wu Han with his pen. Gao Yuan, one of the students in Zhengding, explained: 'The method was, first, to declare yourself a defender of Marxism-Leninism and Mao Zedong Thought; second, to pose a series of accusatory questions about your target; and third, to expose it as yet another example of counter-revolutionary infiltration of the Party.'[4]

Still, while some of the students were thirsty for action, many of their teachers were confused. Some actually defended Wu Han. In a middle school in Jinan, an entire article was penned to refute Yao Wenyuan's allegations. But most were cautious, and for good reason. Unlike the students, they remembered the Hundred Flowers. One teacher who had been labelled a rightist in 1957 had an inkling that the Cultural Revolution would be worse: 'This time around, with the Cultural Revolution, we teachers are in the dock. It will be even worse than the Anti-Rightist Campaign of 1957.' Many waited to see in which direction the wind would blow: 'It's best not to say too much, if you say something wrong you will be in trouble.' A few were so worried that they sought out the school's party secretary to volunteer a full confession of their ideological mistakes, hoping for leniency. Posters appeared questioning the background of some teachers.[5]

Even more excitement followed as the entire Beijing Municipal Party Committee was reorganised. While the clique of four was still being denounced behind closed doors, a notice was circulated within the party ranks on 16 May to announce that Peng Zhen had turned the capital into a citadel of revisionism. Mao called on the whole party to 'repudiate those representatives of the bourgeoisie who have sneaked into the party, the government, the army and various cultural circles'. They were a 'bunch of counter-revolutionary revisionists'. They wanted to seize political power and turn the dictatorship of the proletariat into a dictatorship of the bourgeoisie as soon as conditions were ripe. Mao issued a dire warning: 'Some of them we have already seen through, others we have not. Some are still trusted by us and are being trained as our successors, persons like Khrushchev, for example, who are still nestling beside us.'[6]

The message sent a chill through the party ranks. If the powerful head of the capital could fall, others might soon follow. Party members started eyeing each other across the table at meetings where the Chairman's words were studied. A few began to believe that the only safe option was to trust nobody but the Chairman himself: 'Right now I feel that Chairman Mao is the only one we can trust . . . we must doubt all others, we must denounce anyone who does not follow the Chairman's instructions.'[7]

Ordinary people who read the *People's Daily* had an inkling that something was happening in the corridors of power. Wild rumours started circulating. Some alleged that Peng Zhen was bringing troops to the capital. Others whispered that criminals were being recruited from the prisons in Beijing in a final showdown. The fact that Mao had not been seen in public for many months only deepened the mystery.[8]

Mao, meanwhile, moved to dissolve the small Group of Five headed by Peng Zhen. A Cultural Revolution Group appeared instead, stacked with the Chairman's cronies. The group would soon direct the entire course of the Cultural Revolution, becoming the most important political organ by which all the top decisions were made. Like the inner courts created by emperors to bypass the opposition of their cabinets, the group would rule over party, state and army.

The group's head was Chen Boda, a mean, petty and ambitious man with a heavy Fujianese accent who had been trained in Moscow in the 1930s. Chen became the Chairman's ghostwriter in Yan'an, and served as one of his political secretaries after liberation. In 1958 he welcomed the Great Leap Forward as the dawn of communism. Two years later, he absolved his master of all responsibility for the catastrophe, claiming that the millions of deaths were 'an unavoidable phenomenon in our forward march'.[9]

The Cultural Revolution Group included Jiang Qing, Kang Sheng, Yao Wenyuan and Zhang Chunqiao, as well as several other close followers of the Chairman. Its composition would change with every shift in the balance of power, but it would remain in the eye of the storm throughout much of the Cultural Revolution. The group moved into two buildings at the Diaoyutai State Guesthouse, a complex located a few kilometres to the west of the Forbidden City. Surrounded by lakes and gardens, the site had been a favourite fishing spot of the Zhangzong emperor in the twelfth century, although the buildings themselves, like the Great Hall of the People, had been erected in 1959. The group soon took over another four buildings, with a crew of telephonists, typists, recorders and other assistants who helped to deal with the several bags of telegrams and letters that arrived from every corner of the country each day. Madame Mao took up permanent residence in its quarters, safely ensconced as chaos raged outside.[10]

On 1 June, celebrated as International Children's Day, the Cultural Revolution Group dropped its first bombshell. Written by Chen Boda, an inflammatory editorial in the *People's Daily* urged the population to 'Sweep Away All Monsters and Demons!' It was the public inauguration of the Cultural Revolution, as people were urged to sweep away the representatives of the bourgeoisie who were trying to 'deceive, fool and benumb the working people in order to consolidate their reactionary state power'. The editorial singled out the 'bourgeois specialists', 'scholarly authorities' and 'venerable masters' who were entrenched in 'ideological and cultural positions'.[11]

As if the editorial was not yet drama enough, that very same evening the Central People's Radio broadcast the text of a big-character poster written by Nie Yuanzi a week earlier. Nie was the party secretary of the philosophy department who had helped Kang Sheng and his work team expose the leadership of Peking University for 'taking the capitalist road' more than a year before. Kang's strategy had backfired, as Peng Zhen had used his political clout to have the work team dismissed in March 1965. Nie was severely criticised and about to lose her job, but in early May 1966 she realised that with the fall of Wu Han and Deng Tuo, the very people who were persecuting her would soon be in trouble. She received a nudge from Kang Sheng, who sent his wife to foment a revolution on campus. On 25 May, Nie put up a big-character poster which claimed that the university was under the control of the bourgeoisie. Its leaders were 'a bunch of Khrushchev-type revisionist elements'. News of the poster spread within minutes. Thousands of similar ones appeared the following day. Kang sent a copy to the Chairman, who opined that the document was 'even more significant than the manifesto of the Paris commune'. He gave it his stamp of approval.[12]

On 2 June, one day after radio stations all over the country had broadcast the full text of the poster, it was printed in the *People's Daily*. Classes in the capital were suspended. The following day the fall of Peng Zhen finally became public knowledge, as a new Beijing Municipal Party Committee was inaugurated. Portraits of Mao flanked by red flags with hammer and sickle were hoisted above the main entrance of the party headquarters. Arc lamps flooded the building with light, as lorries conveyed one delegation after another to express their support for the new leadership. Schoolchildren cheered, their cheeks painted red. Firecrackers were lit, drums rolled, cymbals clashed. The demonstration finally tapered off at 8.00 the following morning.[13]

To heighten the tension, a mass trial took place on 13 June in the Workers' Stadium, a huge concrete structure built in 1959 to mark the tenth anniversary of the Chinese Revolution, like the Great Hall of the People and the Diaoyutai State Guesthouse. Yang Guoqing, a nineteen-year-old from Beijing, was accused of having stabbed two foreigners a month earlier. In front of television cameras, Yang was led on to a raised platform by three policemen. He bowed his head, submitting to the fury of a crowd of 13,000 people who raised their fists at every slogan, chanting in chorus: 'Never Forget Class Struggle', 'Down with the Counter-Revolutionaries'.[14]

China was now in the grip of a militant campaign against counter-revolutionary plots, seen to be everywhere. In every town and city, large placards went up bearing full-length portraits of the Chairman. His sayings proliferated on the walls of factories, offices and schools. In the streets, according to one observer, the number of slogans alerting readers to the dangers of a revisionist coup 'seemed to have multiplied by ten'. Across the country, the militia were put on alert. They practised Morse code, prepared for air raids and trained in bayonet fighting. Girls as young as six took part, shouting 'kill' in shrill voices as they lunged forward. In some factories in Jinan, the capital of Shandong, model aeroplanes were stretched on wires between buildings for anti-aircraft practice. In Qingdao, the province's main port, squads of militia crowded the streets, armed with rifles and light machine guns. Foreign powers, it was feared, could use Shandong as a beachhead for the invasion of China.[15]

Further inland the situation was similar. Travelling along the Yangtze River, Alan Donald, with years of experience at the British mission in Beijing, wrote: 'I had never seen, at any time during my stay in China, such a visual and aural attack on the propaganda plane.' Exhortations to revolutionary vigilance against anti-party groups were common, with slogans daubed on walls, printed in newspapers, broadcast over loudspeakers and, in the countryside, even placed on moveable boards.[16]

But the clearest indication of what the Chairman had in mind was evident in Yan'an, the crucible of revolution where the communists had holed up decades earlier during the Second World War. Cut off from the rest of the country, isolated from Moscow except for intermittent radio contact, they had turned austerity into a virtue with the principle of self-reliance. Throughout the base areas under their control, grassroots units assumed responsibility for the livelihood of all of their members. Specialisation was banned, as the ideal communist man was simultaneously soldier, worker and student, fusing with the collective in war and work alike. Students were required to contribute to the revolution through manual labour, while soldiers were asked to immerse themselves in political study.

Yan'an became the capital of red tourism in the summer of 1966, as throngs of visitors were shown documentaries about reclamation projects, with long lines of soldiers hacking away at the rough mountainside, convinced that selfless perseverance and collective action could change the face of nature. In communes and factories in Yan'an, the most popular text was 'The Foolish Old Man who Moved the Mountain', a traditional tale given a new twist by Mao in 1945.[17] A ninety-year-old man, so the story went, had tried to remove a mountain that obstructed his view with a hoe and a basket. When asked how he would ever complete the task, he had answered that the mountain would eventually be carted off if his children, and their children and other generations after them, would persevere. Mao reinterpreted the tale by saying that imperialism and feudalism were two mountains oppressing the people, but through sheer willpower and hard work they would be cleared away. It would become one of the three most frequently read stories from the Little Red Book during the Cultural Revolution.

Mao himself had praised the Yan'an spirit a month earlier, writing to Lin Biao on 7 May to state that the army should carry out 'military–educational, military–agricultural, military–industrial and military–civilian work', aiming 'to unite the army and people as one'. Workers, likewise, should 'learn military affairs, politics and culture', while students 'ought to learn industrial, agricultural and military work in addition to class work'. Mao's letter was widely distributed in the following weeks. What the Chairman projected was a fanatical vision of military organisation and political indoctrination in which every man and every woman became a soldier. China was moving forward to the past.[18]

———

The moment Nie Yuanzi's accusation against Peking University was broadcast on 1 June 1966, posters went up in offices, factories and schools across the nation. Some were as big as a door, written in black ink with the main accusations underlined in red. Others were lengthy diatribes denouncing local leaders for betraying the party, corrupting the people, undermining the revolution or even working for a capitalist restoration. But Nie had put up her text at exactly the spot where posters had appeared ten years earlier during the Hundred Flowers. As readers pressed around these hoardings, they wondered what to make of it all. In 1956 the party had called on everybody to speak out, only to denounce the critics a year later. Were the authors of these posters disciplined party members dedicated to the revolution? 'Or are they self-seekers, troublemakers, anti-party and anti-socialist elements, themselves counter-revolutionaries?' as one participant in the Foreign Language Bureau in Beijing put it. Some cynics suggested that they were mere agents of the party, inciting people to stick out their necks until the axe fell.[19]

The leadership was just as confounded. Having stirred up the party with his message on 16 May, Mao went into retreat, staying away from the capital: 'Let others stay busy with politics.' Liu Shaoqi and Deng Xiaoping, left to their own devices, decided to do what the party always did. They agreed on a well-established routine, namely sending in work teams to lead the Cultural Revolution. Still, they flew to Hangzhou to solicit the Chairman's consent. He remained evasive, refusing to be pinned down. 'Let them handle the problems of the movement by themselves,' he told his doctor after the two leaders had left. Then the Chairman sat back and watched the country descend into chaos.[20]

Tens of thousands of cadres were sent to join work teams in educational units across the capital, from middle schools to publishing companies. The largest one, entering Tsinghua University on 9 June, had more than 500 members, including Liu Shaoqi's wife Wang Guangmei. The rest of the country took its lead from the capital and also hastily dispatched work teams. Wherever they went, they found the schools and colleges under their care plastered with big-character posters.

The work teams encouraged the students to denounce the 'monsters and demons' who, according to the earlier editorial in the *People's Daily*, had monopolised culture to oppress the working people. The students needed little encouragement. For weeks they had been tracking the followers of Wu Han and Deng Tuo, and the more radical ones among them had already started scrutinising the backgrounds of some of their own professors. Class enemies were no longer abstract shadows of the past, but real people threatening to drag the country back to the days of feudal exploitation. Soon the posters about Wu Han were buried by layers of denunciations against teachers.

Spurred on by the work teams, at first the students lashed out at faculty members who had humiliated them in the past. Rae Yang, a fifteen-year-old student at one of the most prestigious middle schools of Beijing, took to task a teacher who had reprimanded her in front of all the other students, accusing her in a shrill voice of lacking proletarian feelings when she had grumbled about physical labour. The teacher was exactly the kind of person who, in the Chairman's words, 'treated the students as their enemies'. Dipping her brush pen in black ink, Rae wrote a poster that used the very rhetorical devices that the teacher had used against her: the teacher, she wrote, had lacked proletarian feelings towards her students and suppressed differing opinions. One of her classmates castigated a tutor whom he had caught rifling through the students' desks and reading their diaries during class breaks. As the students began to scrutinise textbooks, teaching methods and even the faculty themselves, more dirty secrets were exposed as other posters went up.[21]

Some students were more circumspect, or reluctant to join the campaign against teachers with whom they had established a good relationship. In Chengdu, Jung Chang was instinctively averse to all militant activities and frightened of the violence that screamed from the wall posters. Aged fourteen, she began to play truant. But there was no standing on the sidelines. At interminable meetings she was criticised for 'putting family first'.[22]

Some 1,500 kilometres away from Chengdu, in the coastal city of Xiamen overlooking the small archipelago of Quemoy, still administered by Taiwan, the work team produced a blacklist of suspect teachers. One was accused of having been a member of Chiang Kai-shek's party, another was linked to the nationalist Youth Corps during the Second World War. 'Now it is in front of you,' the work team told Ken Ling, one of the school's students. 'Let's see what stand you take.'[23]

Soon teachers started hurling accusations against each other in order to save themselves, leading to furious poster wars. They knew far more about each other than students could possibly discover, and some had access to confidential records or boasted powerful contacts further up the echelons of power. As they blackened each other's reputations, they dug further and further into the past, accusing one another of having colluded with counter-revolutionary elements, secretly joined underground organisations or sexually abused members of the proletariat. A few wrote self-criticisms or produced false confessions in the hope of gaining clemency. The list of accusations grew longer. In Zhengding there were 'hooligans and bad eggs, filthy rich peasants and son-of-a-bitch landlords, bloodsucking capitalists and neo-bourgeoisie, historical counter-revolutionaries and active counter-revolutionaries, rightists and ultra-rightists, alien class elements and degenerate elements, reactionaries and opportunists, counter-revolutionary revisionists, imperialist running dogs and spies'.[24]

As an atmosphere of hatred was whipped up, the war of words started to escalate into physical attacks on the targets singled out by the work teams. Some victims were made to carry dunces' caps, and others had placards hung around their necks, identifying them as 'Running Dogs of Capitalism', 'Black Gang Elements', 'Imperialist Spies' or other incriminating categories. Many were paraded around the campus, pushed and shoved, sometimes splashed with ink. As the days went by, the dunces' caps became longer and heavier, the wooden placards larger and weightier. Sometimes they were replaced by buckets filled with rocks. This happened to the principal of Ken Ling's school, who carried a load so heavy that the wire cut deep into his neck. He and others were forced to march around the campus barefoot, hitting broken gongs or pots, declaiming their crimes: 'I am a Black Gang Element!'[25]

Beatings came soon enough. After all, this was class struggle, a fight to the death against an implacable enemy. As students egged each other on, trying to outdo each other in their demonstrations of revolutionary fervour, the abuse intensified. Some of the accused had their heads shaved, others were given so-called yin and yang haircuts, where only one half of the head was shorn. Some were exposed to the summer heat for hours on end. In Xiamen a few were forced to kneel on broken glass. The majority of these torture methods had been commonly used on class enemies since liberation, most recently during the Socialist Education Campaign. But one was new, namely the jet-plane position, perfected by Wang Guangmei two years earlier. On campuses across Fujian province, dozens died or committed suicide after being tormented by students in June and early July.[26]

Counter-revolutionary monsters and demons had to be segregated from the community, and many of the suspects were locked up at night in makeshift prisons, disparagingly called 'cow sheds': these included storehouses, classrooms and dormitories. The most reliable students were assigned to sentry duty by the work teams. Some armed themselves with improvised weapons, others rummaged through the sports equipment room and used fencing foils, wooden swords and metal javelins. 'I felt the same kind of excitement I had felt playing spy games in primary school,' Gao Yuan remembered.[27]

————

At this early stage of the Cultural Revolution, the violence remained very much confined to secondary schools, and even there it varied enormously in scope and intensity. Zhai Zhenhua, the young girl who had modelled herself on Lei Feng, dutifully denounced some of her teachers, but once the walls in her elite middle school in Beijing had been covered in posters, the pace of the revolution began to slacken.[28]

But where was the attack on the 'authorities within the party who take the capitalist road', those enemies 'nestling beside us' that so preoccupied the Chairman? In schools and universities, the work teams deflected most of the ire towards teachers and students considered to be 'black elements', using them as scapegoats or sacrificing a few local cadres to protect leading officials. They clamped down on anyone seen to voice a critical opinion of the party. In Zhengding, one of Gao Yuan's friends put up a poster denouncing the party secretary of the school, but the work team defused the assault by forcing the student to make a public apology. Similar incidents took place in other secondary schools across the country.

Perhaps the most significant confrontation occurred at Tsinghua University, where a bespectacled, heavily built student of chemical engineering named Kuai Dafu speculated publicly whether the 'power in the hands of the work team represents us'. Wang Guangmei, who had just joined the work team, declared that 'the rightist student Kuai Dafu wants to seize power'. A few days later, Kuai was denounced as a counter-revolutionary, humiliated along with dozens of his supporters in front of the assembled student body and locked up in his dormitory.[29]

Wang Guangmei interpreted the Cultural Revolution as a new version of the anti-rightist campaign that had followed the Hundred Flowers nine years earlier. She thought that her mandate was to expose teachers and students like Kuai Dafu who were opposed to the party. She was not alone in this conviction. Bo Yibo, the powerful vice-premier in charge of industry, instructed members of his work team in language uncannily reminiscent of the Hundred Flowers to 'trick the snakes into leaving their pit', suppressing them once they had revealed their true colours by speaking out. Liu Shaoqi gave similar instructions to members of the work team he was guiding himself at an elite middle school attached to Beijing Normal University: 'The leadership must learn to pick the right moment, waiting until most of the monsters have already exposed themselves, and launch the counter-attack in a timely manner. Those anti-party and anti-socialist elements within colleges and universities must be dragged out.' Liu even set a quota of 1 per cent for the number of students and teachers in schools and universities to be denounced as rightists, amounting to an astounding projected total of 300,000 victims for the country as a whole.[30]

Within weeks, more than 10,000 students in the capital alone had been branded as 'rightists'. In Peking University, scores were condemned as 'counter-revolutionaries' for parading and humiliating the president of the university on 18 June. A mutinous mood of open defiance against the work teams spread. In dozens of colleges and universities, the work teams were thrown out by radical students, only to be sent back in by Liu Shaoqi to quell the opposition.

The unrest was not limited to Beijing. After one of their schoolmates had been condemned as a rightist for putting up a poster calling the president of the Communication University a 'capitalist roader', students in Xi'an went on a hunger strike, sitting in silent protest opposite the party headquarters for three days in a row. When the provincial authorities refused to budge, students from other universities joined the protesters. Soon there were scenes of chaos, with nurses administering intravenous drips to children who had fainted from dehydration in the summer heat and students being rushed to hospital for emergency treatment. Students sent representatives to Beijing, prompting Zhou Enlai to intervene to break the impasse.[31]

In Lanzhou, a city along the upper reaches of the Yellow River, surrounded by loess hills in barren Gansu province, the work team broadcast a message warning students that all those who sent telegrams to complain to leaders in Beijing would be designated as counter-revolutionaries. The persecution was such that one student threw himself in front of a train, while another jumped from a building.[32]

Work teams also clamped down on factories. In the Shanghai Number Seventeen Cotton Textile Mill, a handsome young head of security called Wang Hongwen, soon to rise to glory as one of the Gang of Four, pioneered the Cultural Revolution by denouncing the use of piece rates rather than fixed wages to increase output. He and his followers stirred up discontent among the factory's 8,000 workers. By the end of June a work team was sent in to counter-attack, persecuting those who had spoken out. Several hundred workers were denounced as 'anti-party elements', while Wang was labelled a 'self-seeking careerist'.[33]

Liu Shaoqi was rapidly becoming the most detested leader in the country. His work teams were turning vast numbers of people into martyrs. Mao was ready to return to Beijing.

6

Red August

Mao had cultivated an aura of enigma, shunning the spotlight and travelling the country in great secrecy for months on end. Even his colleagues were not always sure where to find him. A popular ditty during the Socialist Education Campaign was 'Father is Close, Mother is Close, but Neither is as Close as Chairman Mao'. In reality the leader was a remote figure, never heard on radio, rarely seen in public.

On 16 July 1966, the Chairman signalled his return to public life, taking a celebrated swim in the Yangtze River. He used the strong current to float downstream and emerge on the other side of the river an hour later, 'with ruddy cheeks and buoyant spirit'. The news was broadcast all over the country, squashing rumours about his health. 'He showed no sign of fatigue,' the papers gushed, comparing the wind and waves to the black storm kicked up by imperialists, revisionists and reactionaries: China would triumphantly ride it out. Photos showed the Chairman standing on a boat, dressed in a robe and waving his hand. Mao penned a poem to mark the occasion. 'I care not that the wind blows and the waves beat; it is better than idly strolling in a courtyard.'[1]

Celebratory parades were organised with lanterns, drums and firecrackers. A swimming craze followed: how else could one brave the wind and waters and emulate the Chairman? In Beijing, 8,000 people, some of them soldiers in full uniform, swam across the water at the Summer Palace, a sprawling imperial domain with lakes, gardens and pavilions. In Shanghai, a floating lido appeared between the pontoons, designed for port workers keen to swim during their lunch break. In Zhengding, Gao Yuan and his friends were taken to a local river, where they entered the water in their gym shorts. They merely paddled around in the shallow end, but there were casualties elsewhere. In Nanjing, thousands flocked to the Xuanwu Lake in Nanjing each day after a section had been cordoned off and opened as an outdoor swimming pool on 17 July. Several people drowned every day.[2]

Two days after his swim, Mao was back in Beijing. In a further symbolic gesture, he refused to move back into Zhongnanhai but took up temporary residence in the Diaoyutai State Guesthouse, where the Cultural Revolution Group had established its offices. A day later, as Liu Shaoqi was summoned to Diaoyutai, Mao opened fire: 'I have been feeling deeply aggrieved since I returned to Beijing. The place is cold and cheerless. Some colleges have closed their gates. Some are even suppressing the student movement. Who is it who suppresses the student movement?'[3]

He sent out members of the Cultural Revolution Group to undermine the work teams. On her way back to Beijing, his wife stopped in Nanjing to warn the leadership that support for the work teams was not the same as support for the Chairman. 'Don't blindly put your faith in the work teams,' she explained. 'The power of those leaders who are fundamentally on our side should be strengthened, the power of those who are fundamentally against us should be seized.'[4]

Then, on 21 July, Chen Boda sent two members of the Cultural Revolution Group to visit Kuai Dafu, still under detention at Tsinghua University. It was a direct snub to Wang Guangmei, who had condemned Kuai as a 'rightist'. Two days later Madame Mao, flanked by Chen Boda, appeared at Peking University, declaring that they had come on the orders of the Chairman to 'learn from the students'. In a statement greeted with an outburst of cheering from a jubilant crowd, they overturned the verdict of the work team that one month earlier had condemned riotous students as 'counter-revolutionaries'.[5]

On 24 July, Mao, dressed in white pyjamas, received several party leaders in a large room on the ground floor of his residence in the Diaoyutai complex. He scolded them for 'fearing the masses' and 'suppressing the students'. He demanded that the work teams be dismissed.[6]

Work teams apologised and disbanded. In Zhai Zhenhua's elite school, they left 'without even a word of farewell'. Rebel students were exonerated. All of them embraced Mao as their liberator.[7]

The official announcement was made in the Great Hall of the People on 29 July 1966. Years earlier some 7,000 leading officials had assembled to confront the catastrophe unleashed by the Great Leap Forward. Now more than 10,000 students from schools and colleges crowded the premises. Kuai Dafu, released from his cell at Tsinghua University and ferried to the meeting by car, was fêted as a hero. Nie Yuanzi, now chair of a newly elected revolutionary committee at Peking University, basked in glory. Liu Shaoqi and Deng Xiaoping were forced to make a public self-criticism, taking responsibility for having organised the work teams in the Chairman's absence. Mao, sitting behind a curtain at the back of the stage, listened intently. When Liu admitted that they did not yet understand how to carry out the Great Proletarian Cultural Revolution, as they were 'old revolutionaries facing new problems', Mao snorted. 'What old revolutionaries? Old counter-revolutionaries is more like it.' At the end of the meeting, as the curtains parted, Chairman Mao unexpectedly stepped on to the stage, appearing as if by magic. The crowd erupted in a roar of excitement. 'I simply could not believe my eyes!' one student later wrote in his diary. As the Chairman paced the stage, slowly waving, his face impassive, the cheering audience started thundering out rhythmic chants: 'Long Live Chairman Mao! Long Live Chairman Mao!' Liu Shaoqi and Deng Xiaoping looked on in a daze. As the chants echoed throughout the auditorium, Mao left in triumph. Zhou Enlai trailed behind 'like a faithful dog'.[8]

Much as Peng Zhen had been forced to make an impossible choice when his vice-mayor Wu Han had come under attack months earlier, Mao's skilful manoeuvring left Liu Shaoqi in a predicament. Had he allowed the schools and colleges to erupt in demonstrations against the party, Mao could have accused him of letting counter-revolutionary forces run amok. When Liu decided instead to muzzle the most outspoken critics, the Chairman turned around and blamed him for 'suppressing the masses'.

A plenum was hurriedly convened in early August to endorse the Chairman's views. Many Central Committee members were absent, sensing trouble. Mao set the tone on the second day, accusing Liu of 'running a dictatorship' and 'aligning himself with the bourgeois class' during his absence from Beijing. 'Why do we talk about democracy all day long, and then when democracy finally arrives we fear it?' Still, many of the party elders failed to rally behind the Chairman with sufficient enthusiasm, prompting more ire from Mao, who accused some of them of being 'monsters and demons'. On 6 August, he called in reinforcements, much as he had done at the fateful Lushan plenum in the summer of 1959. Lin Biao was ordered back to the capital and asked to denounce Liu Shaoqi. He threw his full weight behind the Chairman, promising that the Cultural Revolution would 'turn the world upside down, whip up tempests and make huge waves', to the extent that it would prevent both the bourgeoisie and the proletariat from sleeping 'for six months'. On the final day of the plenum, as the Central Committee elected a new, all-powerful Politburo Standing Committee of eleven members by secret ballot, Lin Biao took over from Liu Shaoqi as number two and heir apparent.[9]

The most important statement issued by the Central Committee during the plenum was its 'Decision on the Great Proletarian Cultural Revolution', widely propagated on 8 August. It proclaimed that the main target of the attack was 'those in power within the party taking the capitalist road'. But as soon as the leadership had sanctioned the Cultural Revolution, real power shifted towards the Cultural Revolution Group. Mao had effectively captured the decision-making organs of the country.

The 'Decision on the Great Proletarian Cultural Revolution' became rapidly known as the 'Sixteen Articles', as it listed under sixteen headings the first guidelines on how to implement the Cultural Revolution. The document was read out over the radio in a deliberate, solemn tone: 'Trust the masses, rely on them and respect their initiative. Make the fullest use of big-character posters and great debates to argue matters out, so that the masses can clarify the correct views and expose all the monsters and demons.' In factories, offices and schools, people were stunned into silence, as they strained to catch every word broadcast through the loudspeakers. 'Be on guard against those who branded the revolutionary masses as "counter-revolutionaries",' the announcement continued. Everyone listening to the broadcast realised that the tide had just turned. Those members of the party who had tried to deflect denunciations made in big-character

posters over the summer by calling their accusers 'counter-revolutionaries'
now had the charge hurled back at them by the very voice of the party.[10]

The broadcast came three days after the Chairman had scribbled his
own big-character poster, entitled 'Bombard the Headquarters'. In pithy
and incendiary language, Mao denounced those 'leading comrades' who
had 'adopted the reactionary stand of the bourgeoisie' and had repressed
the 'surging movement of the Great Proletarian Cultural Revolution'. Mao
accused them of having 'encircled and suppressed revolutionaries' in a
reign of 'white terror'. His note would not be published for another year,
but it was leaked almost immediately.[11]

The very people who had been accused of being 'rightists' and 'counter-
revolutionaries' over the summer now closed ranks behind the Chairman.
Those who had been defamed and locked up by work teams turned the
tables against their erstwhile tormentors. In factories in Changsha, the
capital of Mao Zedong's home province of Hunan, workers put up posters as soon as the work teams withdrew, using the Cultural Revolution
to retaliate against their superiors for everything they had done wrong in
the past. They attacked party leaders for curbing their freedom of speech.
'They accused the leaders of taking home government property and using
influence to get scarce goods and special privileges. They denounced one
leader for insulting women by touching their shoulders when he spoke to
them, and another for wearing slippers to work and taking off his shirt
in the office.' The list of crimes grew longer by the day, with everything
apparently fair game.[12]

Not all work teams withdrew. In some cases they had the support of
workers who feared the chaos unleashed by the Cultural Revolution. In the
Number Seventeen Cotton Textile Mill, where Wang Hongwen and others
had been branded as 'anti-party elements', many of the employees sided
with the leadership, as the work team continued to direct the Cultural
Revolution.[13]

In order to keep abreast of the campaign and find out where one stood,
reading posters became essential. They soon moved out of the corridors of
offices, factories and schools to colonise every available space, into the ves-
tibules, up the lower walls of main buildings, then across pavements and
floors, and finally down from the roof in large slogans. Later that summer

even the vermilion walls of the Forbidden City were plastered with belligerent messages. 'Some were like bombs in their effect, exploding and clearing up a situation. Some were like bazooka shells, piercing armour and the thickest hide. Some were grenades, even squibs. Some were artful smokescreens.'

Many organisations started publishing their own bulletins or newspapers, reporting on the most recent developments. More than twenty broadsheets were distributed or sold near Tiananmen Square. As some of them had direct links to the leaders of the Cultural Revolution Group, they relayed privileged information unavailable in official newspapers. People roamed the capital, scanning the walls of the most important government units for new information about the direction of the campaign. As the Cultural Revolution unfolded, unpublished speeches, classified material, secret reports and internal government files made their way on to the streets. For the first time, everybody could obtain a glimpse into the inner workings of the party.[14]

But one group was more privileged than the others. When the radio broadcast the guidelines of the Cultural Revolution on 8 August, it pointed out that no measures should be taken against students at primary schools, middle schools, colleges and universities.

Mao went straight to the students, seeing in the young his most reliable allies. They were impressionable, easy to manipulate and eager to fight. Most of all, they craved a more active role. 'We have to depend on them to start a rebellion, a revolution. Otherwise we may not be able to overthrow those demons and monsters,' he confided to his doctor.[15]

On 1 August, he sent a personal note of support to a group of youngsters at a middle school attached to Tsinghua University. 'To Rebel is Justified!' the Chairman told them. Two months earlier, these students had established their own organisation, called Red Guards. They were not alone, as students elsewhere in the capital banded together to form groups called Red Flag or East Wind. All of them were inspired by Mao's widely disseminated letter to Lin Biao, in which the Chairman had urged the people to become one with the army, learning military skills in addition to performing their usual tasks – following the model established in Yan'an decades earlier. But the work teams did not tolerate the existence of any organisation established without official approval. In the years following liberation, civil society had gradually been brought under the thumb of the party. From independent political parties, charitable organisations, religious associations and chambers of commerce to trade unions, all were either eliminated or brought under the party's formal supervision. In schools and universities alike, the only organisations with recognised status were the communist party, the Communist League and the Young Pioneers. The work teams ordered the fledging Red Guards to disband.

Now, with the Chairman's blessing, Red Guards started popping up again. They pledged to defend Chairman Mao and his revolution to the death. Seeing themselves as his faithful fighters, they abandoned their normal clothes and started wearing army uniforms. A few managed to find military clothing from older family members. Chang Jung, as soon as she had enrolled, rushed home and dug out a pale-grey jacket from the bottom of an old trunk. It had been her mother's uniform in the 1950s. Others turned workers' trousers and cotton jackets into simple, baggy uniforms. Some were made to look vintage and worn. Overly fitted uniforms and shiny clothes in general were frowned upon as bourgeois. A leather belt, always handy to whip class enemies, was compulsory. A red cotton armband with gold characters reading 'Red Guard' completed the outfit.[16]

Not everyone was allowed to become a Red Guard. The youngsters praised by Mao for having first organised a Red Guard detachment belonged to an elite middle school administered by Tsinghua University. They were the children of high-ranking cadres and military officers, and they had learned through their parents that revisionists inside the party were opposing the Chairman. In other middle schools, too, the core of students who threw themselves behind the Chairman and formed gangs of Red Guards had parents who were party officials. They had been brought up in an environment dominated by political intrigue, and they had privileged access to classified information. Most of all, they were already well organised, having joined the many activities that had been offered during the Socialist Education Campaign, from military training in summer camps to shooting guns in rifle clubs. In a political climate that portrayed the world in terms of an endless class struggle, they felt inherently superior for belonging to the revolutionary class.

Many of them believed that only those with the purest family pedigree could become true Red Guards. They were the children of veteran revolutionaries, and they alone had the class background necessary to lead the Cultural Revolution. They were born red. 'We are born into this world only to rebel against the bourgeoisie and carry the great proletarian revolutionary banner. Sons must take over the power seized by their fathers. This is called passing on the power from generation to generation.' A couplet did the rounds, calling for the exclusion of anyone from a bad class background: 'If the father is a hero, his son is also a hero. If the father is a reactionary, his son is a bastard.' In Beijing, no more than one in five students from middle schools were eligible for membership of an exclusive club based on blood.[17]

Red Guards began physically attacking teachers and administrators the moment they heard of Mao's battle cry 'To Rebel is Justified'. On 4 August, three days after receiving Mao's letter of encouragement, the students at Tsinghua University Middle School forced the principal and vice-principal to wear labels denouncing them as 'Heads of a Black Gang'. Over the following days, the Red Guards took turns to beat them. Some of the students used a club, others preferred a whip or a copper-buckled belt. The vice-principal's hair was burned.[18]

The first death occurred in a girls' school administered by Beijing Normal University. Bian Zhongyun, the vice-principal, had already been tortured under the supervision of a work team in late June. The students had spat in her face, filled her mouth with soil, forced a dunce's cap on her head, tied her hands behind her back and then beaten her black and blue. Now that the work team was gone, the Red Guards were determined to rid the school of bourgeois elements. In the afternoon of 5 August, as they accused five of the school administrators of having formed a 'Black Gang', they splashed them with ink, forced them to kneel and hit them with nail-spiked clubs. Bian lost consciousness after several hours of torture. She was dumped into a garbage cart. When her body finally reached the hospital across the street two hours later, she was pronounced dead.

All along, members of the Cultural Revolution Group did the rounds, meeting one batch of Red Guards after another. Already on 28 July, Madame Mao had appeared at Peking University, telling the crowd that 'we do not advocate beating people, but what's so special about beating people anyway!' She offered a further insight: 'When bad people get beaten by good people, they deserve it. When good people get beaten by bad people, the credit goes to the good people. When good people beat good people it is a misunderstanding that should be cleared up.'[19]

More encouragement came on 13 August, as a mass rally was organised at the Workers' Stadium. In front of tens of thousands of students, five ordinary citizens who had threatened Red Guards a few weeks earlier were paraded on a stage and denounced as 'hooligans'. They were beaten and whipped with belts. Zhou Enlai and Wang Renzhong, presiding over the struggle meeting, made no attempt to stop the violence.[20]

In the following days, a wave of terror spread through the schools of Beijing. At Beijing's 101st Middle School, a prestigious institution where Mao and other central leaders sent their children, more than ten teachers were forced to crawl on a path paved with coal cinders until their knees and palms were burned. At the Beijing Sixth Middle School, across the street from Zhongnanhai, Red Guards wrote 'Long Live the Red Terror' on the wall of an interrogation chamber. Later they repainted the slogan with the blood of their victims.

But the biggest show of support came on 18 August, as more than a million young students spilled out on Tiananmen Square. The Red Guards had set off in groups a little after midnight and arrived at the square before daybreak. Some were issued with red silk armbands to replace their own homemade cotton ones. They waited anxiously in the dark. Then, as the sun started rising over the eastern end of the square, Mao came down from the rostrum, wearing a baggy army uniform. He mingled briefly with the crowd, shaking hands. A few hours later some of the students were selected to meet the Chairman and his colleagues from the Cultural Revolution Group. Lin Biao made a lengthy speech, appealing to the excited youngsters to destroy 'all the old ideas, old culture, old customs and old habits of the exploiting classes'.

The high point of the day came when a student named Song Binbin was given the special honour of pinning a Red Guard armband on the Chairman's sleeve. She was the daughter of a veteran general and student at the school where Bian Zhongyun had been tormented to death two weeks earlier. Song Binbin and other Red Guard leaders had personally reported the news to the Beijing Municipal Party Committee. As the cameras flashed, Mao asked her what the meaning of her given name was. When she replied that Binbin meant 'suave', the Chairman suggested that a more fitting name was Yaowu, 'be martial'. Song Yaowu shot to stardom.[21]

A wave of violence engulfed the capital after the rally on Tiananmen Square. At the Beijing Third Girls Middle School, the principal was beaten to death. The dean hanged herself. At another middle school near Beijing Normal University the principal was ordered to stand under the hot sun while Red Guards poured boiling water over him. New depths of horror were plumbed at another middle school, this one attached to the Beijing Teachers' College, as a biology teacher was knocked to the ground, beaten and dragged by her legs through the front door and down the steps, her head bumping against the concrete. She died after being further tormented for several hours. Then the other teachers, rounded up as so many monsters and demons, were forced to take turns and beat her dead body. At elementary schools, where the students were no older than thirteen, some teachers were made to swallow nails and excrement, others had their heads shaved and were forced to slap each other.[22]

The Red Guards also turned against some of their schoolmates. For years they had harboured deep resentment of students from bad family backgrounds who often performed well, having to rely on their marks rather than their status to succeed. Only two years earlier the Chairman had voiced his opposition to an education system he viewed as dangerously meritocratic, demanding that admission of children from 'exploiting families' be limited.[23] The Red Guards now craved a system of permanent discrimination. They were born red, their enemies were born black. Students from bad class backgrounds were locked up, forced to carry out heavy labour on campus, humiliated and sometimes tortured to death. Students from families that were neither 'red' nor 'black', for instance the children of clerks, office workers, technicians and engineers, were allowed to assist the Red Guards.[24]

Violence also spilled out on to the streets. One of the first targets of the Red Guards were the 'bourgeois intellectuals' accused of having spewed venom at the socialist system. For months the students had tracked Wu Han, Deng Tuo and their followers, poring over their essays, short stories, plays and novels for the merest hint of revisionist ideology. Now, at long last, they could take them to task. Deng Tuo was already dead, and Wu Han locked away in prison. But there were plenty of other targets. Tian Han, the dramatist whose play about a concubine had offended the Chairman, was repeatedly dragged on to an improvised stage with a heavy placard around his neck, forced to kneel and beaten, as the crowd cheered 'Down with Tian Han!'

Other prominent intellectuals were also targeted in a wave of violence. Lao She, one of the most celebrated writers and author of the novel *Rickshaw Boy*, had served as a lecturer at the School of Oriental and African Studies, University of London, in the 1920s. Like many others, he was keen to serve the new regime after 1949, but his background got him into trouble. A few days after the mass rally, he and twenty others were taken by lorry to the Temple of Confucius, a serene compound where hundreds of stone tablets, in the shade of ancient cypress trees, recorded the names of generations of scholars who had successfully passed the imperial examinations. Dozens of schoolgirls from the Eighth Middle School stood in two lines, forming a live chain. As the victims were pushed through the human corridor, they were pummelled by the Red Guards, screaming 'Beat the Black Gang!' Placards were then hung around their necks, stating their names and alleged crimes, as an official photographer recorded the event. The beatings continued for several hours. A day later, Lao She's body was found in the shallow end of a lake near his childhood residence. He had a collection of the Chairman's poems in his pocket.[25]

Ordinary people considered to be from bad class backgrounds were openly persecuted. The family of one of the victims denounced as 'hooligans' a week earlier at the Workers' Stadium were tracked down by Red

Guards. They lived near the lake where Lao She's body was found. The father, an impoverished elderly man named Nan Baoshan, was dragged on to the street and clubbed to death. His second son was beaten and locked inside his home, where he died of thirst a few days later.[26]

The local street committee had denounced Nan Baoshan and his family to the Red Guards. Throughout the capital, lists appeared on walls, signed by local party committees or police stations. They named people by age and class background. Sometimes their crimes were spelled out: 'Has been Dragging his Feet since Liberation'. More often they were simply labelled 'landlords', 'counter-revolutionaries' or 'bad elements'. 'Wanted' notices also appeared, as the Red Guards hunted down specific targets. In public parks, imperial gardens and ancient temples, there were scenes of victims being flogged with ropes, beaten with clubs or otherwise demeaned and tortured in front of cheering crowds. One member of the British consulate observed an old man shuffling out of a covered market, turned into a temporary prison by the Red Guards, with a denunciation hanging to his knees, a blackened face and blood on the back of his shirt. 'A close second to this spectacle was the sight of two old ladies being stoned by small children.'[27]

Zhai Zhenhua was one of the girls from an elite middle school who joined the Red Guards. The first time she saw a friend remove her belt to beat a victim until his clothes were drenched in blood, she recoiled. But she did not want to fall behind, so she persevered. At first she avoided eye contact with a human target, justifying the beatings by imagining how they were plotting the return of the old society. But after a few beatings she got the hang of it. 'My heart hardened and I became used to the blood. I waved my belt like an automaton and whipped with an empty mind.' Another Red Guard later remembered being taken aback by the explosion of violence in his school, although he soon acquired a taste for blood himself: 'When I first started beating people, I did not quite know how to go about it. I was weak. But soon enough I could hit harder than any other student: no matter how hard you hit, I will hit harder, like a wild animal, till my fists hurt.' Children were the most vicious. For a few, beating a class enemy to a pulp became a favourite pastime.[28]

Many of the targets listed by street committees and the police were rounded up and deported. The Red Guards tried to make the capital 'purer and redder', cleansing the city of class enemies. Old people were being marched through the streets with labels around their necks, their arms tightly bound with cord. Soon a stream of bedraggled humanity was seen at the railway stations in Beijing, as an estimated 77,000 victims, or just under 2 per cent of the total population, were transported to the countryside.[29]

The worst killings took place in the outskirts of the city. In Daxing, a county where the sandy soil produced sweet watermelons, the local cadres ordered the extermination of all landlords and other bad elements, including their offspring. Their justification was a rumour that class enemies were about to exact revenge, overthrow the local party branch and execute their erstwhile tormentors. A night of butchery followed, carefully co-ordinated across several people's communes. Party activists joined the local militia in locking their victims into their own homes or makeshift prisons. They were taken out one by one. Some were clubbed to death, others stabbed with chaff cutters or strangled with wire. Several were electrocuted. Children were hung by their feet and whipped. One eight-year-old girl and her grandmother were buried alive. More than 300 people were killed, including entire families and their children, as the killers wanted to make sure that there would be none left to take revenge years later. Most of the bodies were thrown into disused wells and mass graves. In one case the stench became so overpowering that the villagers had to dig out the bodies and throw them into a pond instead.[30]

An officer from the People's Liberation Army phoned Beijing to report the killings in Daxing, and a report was immediately sent to the Cultural Revolution Group. Nobody lifted a finger.[31] A week earlier, Xie Fuzhi, the minister of public security, had already instructed a group of police officers that 'We must support the Red Guards.' He enjoined the police to 'talk to them and try to make friends with them. Don't give them orders. Don't say it is wrong of them to beat up bad people. If in anger they beat someone to death, then so be it.' The speech was widely circulated.[32]

There are no accurate statistics about the number of victims in Beijing, but in late August more than a hundred people were killed every day.

One internal party document reports that, on 26 August, 126 people died at the hands of Red Guards; the following day, 228; the day after, 184; on 29 August, 200. The list goes on. According to a conservative estimate, by late September, as the first wave of violence abated, at least 1,770 people had lost their lives, not including those massacred in the outskirts of the capital.[33]

7

Destroying the Old World

The killings were mainly confined to Beijing, where members of the Cultural Revolution Group were in daily contact with the Red Guards. Still, there was plenty of violence in the rest of the country, as students took to heart Mao's battle call 'To Rebel is Justified'. Even before the mass rally on 18 August 1966, students from the Huadong Teachers University in Shanghai arrested more than 150 faculty members at their homes and paraded them on campus, forcing them to wear dunces' caps and heavy boards around their necks reading 'Reactionary Academic Authorities'. At the Fuxing Middle School, founded in 1886 by Elizabeth McKechnie, a missionary nurse whose motto was 'Seek Truth', students attacked some of their teachers with hammers. One of the victims suffered a fractured skull.[1]

The mass rally on Tiananmen Square further prompted students around the country into action. In Changsha, Red Guards started beating students and teachers from 'bad families' the moment they returned from their first meeting with Mao Zedong on Tiananmen Square. Further south, in Guangzhou, a teacher was forced to drink a bottle of ink. After he had been repeatedly kicked in the stomach, the ink he regurgitated was mixed with blood. He later committed suicide. In Xi'an a 'Red Terror Brigade' doused a teacher in petrol and set him alight.[2]

But these were isolated acts. Many students outside the capital, at this early stage of the Cultural Revolution, were still unsure just what level of violence would be tolerated.

The real founding act of Red Guards was a campaign to destroy all remnants of old society. On 18 August, appearing on the rostrum next to

Chairman Mao, Lin Biao had exhorted his youthful audience to go forth and destroy 'all the old ideas, old culture, old customs and old habits of the exploiting classes'. Feudal ideology had fettered people's minds for thousands of years, and now these cultural remnants were to be destroyed to ensure that the country's revolutionary colour would never fade. Tradition was the dead hand of the past trying to maintain its grip on the living, and it was to be smashed to smithereens. Sidney Rittenberg, an American who had thrown in his lot with the communist party before liberation and knew many of its leaders, was surprised by the fury of the message: 'Everything was smash, smash, smash. I could hardly believe what I heard. These people at the very top were truly planning to destroy everything they had built up over the past two decades, to smash and build something new.'[3]

Lin Biao's appeal was widely disseminated, and a day later Red Guards in Beijing put up posters boldly declaring war on the old world. 'We want to take to task and smash all old ideas, old culture, old customs and old habits. Barbers, tailors, photographers, book pedlars and others who are at the service of the bourgeois class, none of these are exceptions. We want to rebel against the old world!' High heels, fancy haircuts, short skirts, jeans, bad books, all of these had to be eliminated at once, the Red Guards proclaimed. Printers at the officially sponsored *China Youth Daily* churned out thousands of copies of these inflammatory speeches on 19 August. On the evening of 20 August, bands of Red Guards began roving through the streets of Beijing, attacking anything that smacked of the old order. They changed street names, plastering new revolutionary terms over the old signs. Shops providing services, for instance tailors and barbers, came under attack, as their owners were humiliated, sometimes beaten and forced to close down. By the morning of 22 August, the atmosphere had turned ugly, as the Red Guards started attacking ordinary people, forcibly cutting their hair, slashing narrow trouser legs, chopping off high heels. That very same day, the New China News Agency hailed the Red Guards as 'Mao's little generals', lauding their efforts to sweep away old culture. In a special broadcast, the Central People's Radio spread the news to the rest of the country. The result was a nationwide explosion from 23 to 26 August of Red Guard violence towards anything that smacked of the past. The aftershocks would be felt for months.[4]

———

In Zhengding, where Gao Yuan and his schoolmates had already spent an exciting summer persecuting their teachers, the moment they read in the *People's Daily* of the mass rally on Tiananmen Square each class set up its own Red Guards. Those who lacked a good class background were not eligible and walked off in shame. The successful ones put on torn strips of red cloth stencilled with yellow paint. The strips were not quite as elegant as the armband they had spotted on Chairman Mao in the newspapers, but they nonetheless gave them a new sense of importance. A day or two later they followed the news on how Red Guards had smashed old name boards in the capital. They decided to eradicate all traces of the old world in Zhengding, setting off towards the old quarter of the town with a red flag inscribed with 'Red Guard' fluttering at the head of their column. They copied what they had read and heard about the Red Guards in Beijing. They changed street names and attacked the lacquered signboards hanging over small shops. They deprecated pedlars selling their wares for being 'capitalist'. An old woman with bound feet was harassed, forced to stand motionless in the sun for four hours wearing a sign denouncing her as a 'prostitute'. But the biggest target was an ancient archway that symbolised feudal oppression. Thick ropes were attached around the top, the foundations were prized loose with crowbars and the structure was pulled down, reduced to a pile of broken stones. The onion dome of a local mosque posed an even greater challenge, and it took hundreds of Red Guards to bring it down. An old Muslim watchman with a wispy beard who tried to intervene was forced to wear a pig's tail, obtained from the local butcher, around his neck.[5]

Similar scenes played out across the country. In Xiamen, where Ken Ling had managed to join the Red Guards despite his bad family background, teams fanned out through the streets destroying everything old in their path, from ornamental brass knockers and antique shop signs to the dragon-shaped cornices on temples. Each team had its own red flag and marched in formation. Some of them beat drums and gongs, while others went about their business quietly and methodically, following a carefully prepared itinerary with all the addresses marked out by street committees. They gave haircuts to returned overseas students and cut long braids. A simple test was applied to stove-pipe trousers, a fashion also introduced by overseas students: if they were not wide enough to accommodate two bottles, the seams were slit open with a knife. Pointed shoes were confiscated, and high heels sliced off. There was nothing ordinary people could do: when the guidelines of the Cultural Revolution had been broadcast to the nation on 8 August in the so-called 'Sixteen Articles', the party had specified that no measures should be taken against students at primary schools, middle schools, colleges and universities. 'To Rebel is Justified,' the Red Guards cried.[6]

Zhengding and Xiamen were small cities, but an even greater outpouring of destruction took place in Shanghai, a city that had been administered by foreign powers before liberation and never quite managed to shed its image as a decadent, bourgeois stronghold. Every sign of the imperialist past came under attack, as Red Guards chipped, drilled and burned off ornaments from the solid granite buildings along the Bund – renamed Revolutionary Boulevard. Shops selling curios or flowers were smashed. Mattresses, silk, velvet, cosmetics and fashionable clothes, all condemned as bourgeois luxuries, were tossed out and carted away.[7]

More encouragement came from above. On 23 August, the *Liberation Army Daily*, under the thumb of Lin Biao, applauded the Red Guards: 'What you did was right, and you did it well!' The following day, another editorial enthused about the campaign, followed by a solemn pledge that the army would stand resolutely behind the Red Guards. 'Learn from the Red Guards! Respect the Red Guards!'[8]

Now that the army had given them full licence to turn the old world upside down, the Red Guards went on the rampage. Libraries were easy targets, as they worked their way through the stacks, in schools and on campuses, confiscating every volume that looked even vaguely feudal or bourgeois. Book burnings were common. Some were symbolic, with only a few books thrown into the bonfire. Others were conflagrations that lit up the sky for days on end. In Xiamen, the flames leaped three storeys high, as Ken Ling and his comrades fed the fire with sixty litres of kerosene. People came with chairs to watch the spectacle. Under a red sky, some onlookers crowded the roofs of surrounding buildings.[9]

In Shanghai, Red Guards destroyed thousands of books from the Zikawei Library, a scholarly repository of over 200,000 volumes started by Jesuits in 1847. Wen Guanzhong, a local student who had not been allowed to join the Red Guards, observed with interest that foreign books were much harder to burn, as they were protected by sturdy leather covers. In the Huangpu district, where the shopping street of Nanjing Road had been laid waste by the Red Guards, several lorries were working around the clock to take books to the local paper mill for pulping.[10]

Public monuments were assailed. In Shanghai, it took the Red Guards only a few days to demolish eighteen listed historical monuments, including the tomb of Xu Guangqi (1562–1633), the city's first Christian convert, who had collaborated with the Italian Jesuit missionary Matteo Ricci. Longhua Pagoda, the oldest temple in Shanghai and a towering 44 metres in height, fell victim to the hammers and ropes of the Red Guards. Three thousand ancient scriptures belonging to the temple were reduced to ash. The Confucius Temple, an ancient architectural complex located in a quiet public park, was razed to the ground. Red Guards also tackled St Ignatius Cathedral, next to the Zikawei Library, tearing down the spires and the ceiling before shattering its stained-glass windows. There were many churches in Shanghai, and a report later established that 'All the articles of worship inside Catholic churches have been destroyed.'[11]

There were scenes of Red Guards toppling the steeples of foreign churches or burning ancient pagodas in most cities. In Qingdao, where the churches had been packed in the years following Mao's Great Famine, the organ of St Michael's Cathedral was smashed with hammers, the windows shattered one after the other.[12] In Mount Hengshan, one of the five sacred mountains revered by followers of both Taoism and Buddhism, local cadres and Red Guards collaborated to take down every temple and statue, feeding a hungry fire for three nights.[13]

In a few places the assault on tradition was rebuffed. Qufu, the hometown and resting place of Confucius, had some of the largest compounds and family tombs in the country. Tens of thousands of descendants of the ancient sage had their final resting place in the Confucius Cemetery, a sacred compound with dozens of buildings surrounded by an ancient wall, overgrown with gnarled trees. Local Red Guards repeatedly tried to attack the premises, but the Qufu authorities managed to repel their assaults. Only after more than 200 Red Guards from Beijing had descended on the city were the tombs finally desecrated. Five female corpses, still well preserved, were tied together and hung from a tree. Chen Boda had personally wired his instructions, allowing the graves to be dug up but demanding that the main edifice be preserved as a 'museum of class education'.[14]

Other cemeteries were easier targets, in particular those belonging to foreigners. Shanghai, before liberation, was a metropolis half as big again as Moscow, with a larger foreign population than any other city except New York. It had some sixty-nine cemeteries with 400,000 graves, and 20,000 of these belonged to foreigners. Headstones were systematically smashed, crosses broken and memorial plaques and inscriptions obliterated with cement or smeared over with paint. Soon the local authorities reported proudly that 'except for the graves of a few revolutionary martyrs, all the tombstones have basically been completely overturned or smashed to pieces'. One exception was the Ji'an Cemetery, where many foreigners had been reburied in 1951. Guards on duty were able to protect some of the graves. The party intervened instead, deciding to level all tombstones dating from the pre-liberation era, since they were 'symbols of imperialism'.[15]

In Shanghai, as elsewhere, burials were almost immediately abolished by revolutionary decree in favour of cremation. Within weeks, a brand-new facility appeared in the suburbs, as burn teams worked around the clock to fill the crematoria. In Nanjing, where the authorities also banned burials, Red Guards smashed all the coffins confiscated from funeral parlours.[16]

Nationwide, in 1966 there were roughly 50,000 graves belonging to foreigners. More than half of these were destroyed during the Cultural Revolution. Many others were defiled, and only one in ten managed to escape undamaged.[17]

Local tombs also suffered. Among the victims was Hai Rui, the official who had been dismissed from office by the Ming emperor. Red Guards destroyed his resting place on Hainan Island.[18]

On 23 August, Red Guards attacked some thirty-six flower shops in Shanghai. Ornamental plants and flowers were considered wasteful and bourgeois, and in the following days Red Guards rampaged through flow-erbeds and hothouses in parks across the city. Elaborate rockeries and gold-fish ponds were smashed. Flowers at funerals were prohibited. Complex economic calculations were made to highlight the inherently exploitative nature of growing flowers, as one party hack concluded that the 3 million bunches of fresh flowers sold in Shanghai in 1965 had been cultivated on a surface large enough to produce a year's supply of grain for 3,000 members of the proletariat.[19]

Dogs had long since disappeared, denounced as a threat to public hygiene before they were hunted down in cities across the country in the early 1950s.[20] Now came a great cat massacre, as Red Guards did the rounds to eliminate the feline symbol of bourgeois decadence. Rae Yang, the fifteen-year-old student who had turned against her teacher in Beijing, tried to smuggle her pet out of the house, but Red Guards noticed some-thing moving in the bag she was carrying and guessed what was hidden inside. They grabbed the bag, swung it round and hit it against a brick wall. The cat mewed wildly. 'The boys laughed. It was fun. They continued to hit him against the wall.' Her brother started to cry and begged them to stop but nobody listened. Walking through the streets of the capital at the end of August, people saw dead cats lying by the roadside with their front paws tied together.[21]

Less successful was the attack on racing pigeons, a hobby introduced in the nineteenth century by foreigners. In Shanghai the first Homing Pigeon Club was opened in 1929, and soon local enthusiasts started developing pigeon breeds distinguished by their sense of direction, endurance and speed. By the time the city had been liberated, there were nine different pigeon clubs, all merged into one association under strict government control in 1964. As in Britain, the vast majority of its members were working people, and they kept an estimated 30,000 birds, although a further 20,000 were bred by independent fans with-out a licence. Their owners were accused of wasting precious grain that could sustain thousands of workers. Red Guards first issued an ultima-tum calling for their destruction within two days. Then they did the rounds, smashing some of the racks and lofts that dotted the roofs of Shanghai. The local authorities lent a hand by arresting hundreds of pigeon breeders in the ensuing months. Despite the pressure, pigeon breeding persisted, as people moved their birds away from public view.[22]

But the most frightful development by far was house searches, which started on 23 August and peaked in the following days. Pieces of paper with details of the targets – their name, age, status and address – were passed on to the Red Guards, sometimes by the local police, sometimes by street committees. The Red Guards searched the homes of people from bad class backgrounds for an ever growing list of suspect items: articles of worship, luxury items, reactionary literature, foreign books, concealed weapons, hidden gold, foreign currency, signs of a decadent lifestyle, portraits of Chiang Kai-shek, old land deeds, documents from the nationalist era, signs of underground activities or incriminating evidence of links with enemies of the regime.

Many of these victims had already been subject to systematic persecution since liberation. They were regularly denounced by the regime, paraded through the streets during every major political campaign, hounded from their jobs and forced to sell their possessions in order to eke out a living for themselves and their dependants. When the Red Guards who had ransacked the Zikawei Library turned up at the home of Wen Guanzhong, the boy who had watched as a bonfire consumed a pile of foreign books, they were astonished by what they saw. His father, who had been a general under Chiang Kai-shek, was in prison in Beijing. His mother had been driven to her death in 1955. Her wet nurse, treated like family, looked after Wen and his two brothers. The Red Guards found nothing but bare walls. There was nothing the Red Guards could take that had not already been pawned or bartered for food.[23]

Nien Cheng, on the other hand, lived in great comfort as the widow of the former manager of a foreign firm in Shanghai, the oil company Shell. The Red Guards turned up on the evening of 30 August, as she was reading William Shirer's *The Rise and Fall of the Third Reich* in her study. There were thirty or forty of them, led by two elderly men and a woman. 'We are the Red Guards. We have come to take revolutionary action against you!' a gangling youth shouted at her, as others dispersed in groups to loot her two-storey house. There was the sound of people walking up and down the stairs, followed by the tinkle of broken glass and heavy knocking on the wall. Crates in a storeroom were opened with pliers, curtains were torn down, mirrors smashed, rare antiques shattered. 'On the floor there were fragments of porcelain in colours of oxblood, imperial yellow, celadon green and blue-and-white.' In the bedroom, Red Guards hammered on the furniture. Bits of silk and fur were flying around under the ceiling fan, as garments were torn to pieces. Trembling with anxiety, Nien Cheng tried to intervene but was kicked in the chest. On the lawn outside, a bonfire was lit, as Red Guards tossed books into the flames. All along her street, smoke rose over the garden walls, permeating the air as the Red Guards burned piles of confiscated goods.

This was merely the beginning. A couple of weeks later, Red Guards arrived from Beijing, armed with leather whips. They were looking for hidden treasure in Nien Cheng's house, and they were far worse: 'They ripped open mattresses, cut the upholstery of the chairs and sofas, removed tiles from the walls of the bathrooms, climbed into the fireplace and poked into the chimney, lifted floorboards, got onto the roof, fished in the water tank under the ceiling, and crawled under the floor to examine the pipes.' The garden was turned into a sea of mud, as the flowerbeds were dug up and plants were pulled from their pots.[24]

Similar scenes were seen in many towns and cities across the country, as people scurried to dispose of compromising items before the Red Guards knocked on their door. In Beijing, Rae Yang's parents burned family letters and old photographs, flushing the ashes down the toilet. In Xi'an, Kang Zhengguo, a young man who was passionate about literature, hid some of his favourite books inside a large earthenware jar. The Red Guards tore up the other books and carted off pieces of furniture.[25]

Some targets of the campaign, knowing that they would be next, went to bed fully clothed, waiting for their turn. Every night there were terrifying sounds of loud knocks on the door, objects breaking, students shouting and children crying. But most ordinary people had no idea when the Red Guards would appear, and what harmless possessions might be seen as suspicious. They lived in fear.[26]

Driven by fear, spite or ambition, some people started informing on their neighbours. Rae Yang, herself a Red Guard, was approached by an

old woman who insisted that she and her friends raid the home of a prominent overseas Chinese. In Chengdu, two members of a street committee
turned up in Jung Chang's school, denouncing some of their neighbours
in grave and mysterious tones, as if they were on a grand mission. The Red
Guards found a partly naked woman kneeling in the middle of a room that
had already been turned upside down. The stench of faeces and urine per-
meated the air. The victim's eyes were bulging with fear and desperation as
she shrieked for forgiveness. The Red Guards found nothing. Outside the
door, one of the informers beamed with satisfaction. 'She had denounced
the poor woman out of vindictiveness.'[27]

Lorries heaped with works of art, musical instruments, linen cupboards and
other bourgeois belongings drove to and fro through every city, sometimes
blocking the traffic.[28] The plunder was collected and inventoried at a central
location in each city, much as the works of art confiscated by the Nazis in Paris
went to the Jeu de Paume. In Guangzhou, the Sacred Heart Cathedral, in the
very centre of the old town, was selected for this key operation. Modelled on
the Basilica of St Clotilde in Paris with imposing twin spires, it was vandalised
by the Red Guards before the municipal party committee decided to commandeer it as a sorting house. Mountains of furniture, books and clothes
were hoarded in one huge, cavernous space, while more valuable objects were
stored in two gatekeeper's rooms. There was a mound of silver rings, brace-
lets, necklaces, earrings, charms and pendants in one corner, while gold bars
were stacked separately against a wall. But what most struck one of the Red
Guards, in charge of a pushcart used to deliver the gold to the cathedral, was
a sprawling collection of musical boxes. 'It was the first time in my life that I
saw musical boxes, and there were a lot of them, over a hundred.'[29]

Meticulous inventories were kept, and many are still extant in the archives.
In Wuhan, the capital of Hubei where 20,000 homes were raided, the loot
included 319,933 silver dollars, over 3 million yuan in bank deposits,
560,130 yuan in cash, 679 antiques, 3,400 pieces of furniture, 8,439 sealed
boxes, 9,428 silver objects, over 91,000 pieces of porcelain, 798 watches, 340
radio sets, 8 nationalist flags, 22 rifles, 971.1 kilos of gold and 1,717 kilos of
silver. Across the province as a whole, where 1 per cent of all households were

raided, the value of the seized assets was estimated at 200 million yuan. The Red Guards collected more than 4 tonnes in gold alone.[30]

The biggest booty was probably in Shanghai, where Red Guards searched more than a quarter of a million households. Three million collectible antiques and art objects ended up in warehouses, not including jewellery and currency estimated at 600 million yuan.[31]

These lists, of course, reflected a mere fraction of the total. Nien Cheng had to beg the Red Guards not to destroy her collection of rare porcelain but donate it to the state instead. Red Guards had been enjoined to smash the old world, and they thoroughly enjoyed themselves with hammers, axes, crowbars, pliers and bats. Much besides books was consumed by fire. In Xiamen, the list of objects thrown into the flames included 'wooden ancestor tablets, old paper currency, brightly coloured Chinese-style dresses, men's suits, old signboards, movie tickets printed with the original names (now changed) of movie theatres, bamboo mah-jongg tiles, playing cards, foreign cigarettes, curios, antiques, scrolls with calligraphy, Chinese opera stringed instruments, Western violins'.[32]

And the loot was exposed to a plethora of thieving hands. It started with the Red Guards, who lined their pockets with money, jewellery and wristwatches, openly appropriating radios and bicycles in the name of the cause. 'The school dormitories suddenly became plush. Many students were enjoying themselves there with their loot.' There were also common thieves who impersonated Red Guards, doing the rounds to seize their share of the booty. Once the objects had arrived at the central storage, many vanished even before they were inventoried. In Xi'an a mere scribble on a piece of paper was handed to Red Guards who deposited their plunder in the City God Temple.[33]

But the biggest thieves were members of the Cultural Revolution Group. Much as Hermann Göring travelled to Paris twenty times, selecting the very best objects for his own personal collection from the Jeu de Paume, Kang Sheng built up an impressive collection of fine art by visiting the main storage centres around the country. There were prehistoric oracle bones, antique bronzes, ivory seals, precious paintings and more than 12,000 books. A cultured scholar and skilled calligrapher, deeply versed in the classics, Kang was particularly keen on rare rubbings from stone inscriptions, calligraphy scrolls and antique inkstones. Some of the artefacts amassed by Deng Tuo ended up in his possession, as well as the collections of around one hundred other scholars – all persecuted during the Cultural Revolution. Kang was not alone. On a single visit in May 1970, Kang Sheng, Chen Boda, Lin Biao's wife Ye Qun and four of her acolytes more or less emptied an entire warehouse. Kang Sheng and Jiang Qing also divided rare seals and inkstones among themselves.[34]

What the Nazis did not burn, they cherished, but the same could not be said of the Red Guards. The vast majority of the loot was left to rot. In Shanghai, some 600 confiscated pianos were distributed to kindergartens, but many other objects fared badly. This was particularly true of the 5 million books that somehow managed to escape the flames. Many were bundled together and dumped in an attic above a wet market on Fuzhou Road, a street where bookshops used to thrive. On Huqiu Road, once called Museum Road in honour of the Shanghai Museum, set up by the British in 1874, a million rare volumes were stacked up to the ceiling, attacked by vermin and the elements. The situation was worse in the suburbs. In Fengxian, where a new crematorium was opened in September 1966, antique calligraphy scrolls and paintings littered the floor of an improvised storage room, most of them wet, torn and mouldy.[35]

A belated attempt to rescue some of the loot was made by the end of 1966, as restrictions were imposed on the recycling or breaking up of antique bronze bells, ritual containers and statues.[36] A team of specialists from Beijing was put in charge of salvaging what remained, but they faced an uphill battle. Many priceless antique bronzes had already been melted down in foundries or sold off on the black market. Much of the porcelain was smashed to pieces. Still, the team managed to save 281,000 objects and 368,000 books.[37]

If the situation was bad in Shanghai, inland it was far worse. In Wuhan, there were no guards in the storage centres, and by 1968 most of the plunder had been stolen or was damaged beyond repair by vermin and humidity.[38]

———

A day after Red Guards had ransacked her home, a party official paid Nien Cheng a visit. He made a sweeping gesture encompassing the entire house, and asked rhetorically: 'Is it right for you and your daughter to live in a house of nine rooms with four bathrooms when there is such a severe housing shortage in Shanghai? Is it right for you to use wool carpets and have each room filled with rosewood and blackwood furniture when there is a shortage of wood and basic furniture for others? Is it right for you to wear silk and fur and sleep under quilts filled with down?' Nien was allowed to pack a suitcase before being confined to her room, stripped of all furniture but for a mattress and two chairs. Soon enough she was put under formal arrest and deported to a local gaol. Several working families moved into her house.[39]

The homes of people from bad backgrounds were divided up. Rae Yang, despite being a Red Guard herself, was unable to protect her own family. Her aunt, bedridden with diabetes, was moved into a pantry without windows. Six families from 'revolutionary backgrounds' moved into the compound, sharing the house among themselves. They dug up the garden, levelled the roses, turned several corridors into storage rooms and built makeshift kitchens in the courtyard, using salvaged material like broken bricks, plywood planks and pieces of asphalt felt.[40]

The bulk of the victims were ordinary people, but party members tainted by their links to disgraced leaders also suffered. On the campus of Peking University, a party stalwart who had boasted of his ties to Deng Tuo and Peng Zhen found a poster glued to the outside wall of his house. The announcement declared that he had to give up his living quarters to the proletariat. His family had to work feverishly through the night to move their possessions and clear enough space for two other families.[41]

The situation varied from place to place, but archival evidence from Shanghai gives an idea of the scale of the expropriations. A total of 30,000 families were forced to hand over their property deeds to the state. Many were allowed to retain a total living surface of 3 to 5 square metres per family, although rent was due. The vast majority of the victims were classified as 'bad elements exploiting the proletariat', being neither intellectuals nor administrators working for the party.[42]

Many more were hounded out of town, but not without first being beaten, spat upon and otherwise humiliated. Red Guards emulated their counterparts in Beijing, cleansing the cities of class enemies. In Shanghai there were harrowing sights of elderly people being frogmarched barefoot through the streets to the railway station, their clothes in tatters, with placards proclaiming their crimes hanging around their necks. A conservative estimate places the number of exiled victims in the country overall at 400,000.[43]

8

Mao Cult

The violent outburst against the old world lasted no more than a few weeks, but it had lasting consequences. A drab sense of uniformity set in soon after women who dressed fashionably had been tackled by Red Guards, their heads shorn in public and their faces smeared with lipstick. Long braids, deemed to be feudal, vanished, while makeup, however discreetly applied, was considered a remnant of the past. Men and women preferred plain clothing, with a preference for blue or grey cotton uniforms and black cloth shoes.

Barbers still opened, but offered nothing but proletarian haircuts (short back and sides). Restaurants served only cheap, plain meals. Hawkers and pedlars, selling everything from fruit, vegetables, candy, nuts, cloth, crockery and coal to rattan baskets, were banned once again. Bookstores offered very little beyond the Little Red Book and other writings of the Chairman. Whole categories of people became unemployed. In Nanjing, the number of jobseekers increased tenfold. There were florists, greengrocers, fruit sellers, cobblers, tanners, coppersmiths, papermakers, printers, photographers, painters, dressmakers, embroiderers, bookbinders, undertakers and others. Many were ruined because their shops were forced to close down, while others could no longer make ends meet. The vast majority were poor people.[1]

Entire branches of arts, craft and industry were wiped out. In Guangdong province alone, some 20,000 people had been employed to make artefacts now condemned as 'superstitious'. These products were worth 40 million yuan a year, and ranged from joss sticks to spirit money, burned at traditional funerals to provide the deceased with sufficient income in the afterlife. Only a third of the workforce was redeployed in different branches of industry, although even they fell into destitution, as they were often put on half-pay or deprived of the tools needed to carry out their new trade. Many were reduced to selling all their possessions, including their clothes and furniture. In a small town outside Shantou, south China's second biggest port before liberation and once a major exporter of embroidery, one in five had to survive on less than 3 yuan a month.[2]

The effects of the Cultural Revolution reverberated throughout the industrial sector. The labelling, packaging and contents of every single manufactured product, from toys, textiles, cosmetics and appliances to porcelain, had to be purged of all remnants of the feudal past. A pair of socks, a tube of toothpaste or an enamelled washbasin branded Fairy or Golden Pagoda was an insult to the proletariat. The State Council demanded strict compliance with the demands of the Cultural Revolution, but in Shanghai alone there were close to 6,000 products with a label or design evocative of the past.[3] It took years of overhauling to conform. Two years later, to take but one example, the China Textile Company still had a hoard of 20,000 quilt covers, not to mention 15,000 metres of silk, rendered useless by 'feudal' patterns.[4]

In many cases, an expedient solution was used: stickers with a warning were added to offending goods, while feudal or bourgeois brand names were obliterated with a large red cross, from toys and figurines to poker cards.[5] But this did not always satisfy the consumers, wary of being associated with objects that might be denounced by Red Guards. Sales dropped precipitously. A ceramic jar for chopsticks decorated with a mythical unicorn no longer attracted any buyers, but the same object adorned with revolutionary slogans sold out briskly, despite being twice as expensive.[6]

There were other issues. The works of fallen leaders such as Peng Zhen and Lu Dingyi had to be destroyed as early as August, but the blacklist of books containing 'political errors' grew longer by the month. An even bigger conundrum was Liu Shaoqi. As head of state, his calligraphy graced endless objects, ranging from pottery, porcelain and posters to stationery of every form and shape. As the Cultural Revolution unfolded, few Red Guards were willing to keep a diary with a slogan graced by his hand. In March 1967, the Central Committee ordered that all traces of the renegade be obliterated, but this left the authorities with a further problem.

The state generated endless commendations and awards to honour its meritorious citizens, not to mention the usual paperwork, from birth certificates to pension booklets. Many were marked by the former head of state. Disabled army veterans, for instance, complained that their official documents carried his photo on the front and his calligraphy on the back. The Ministry of Internal Affairs became so overwhelmed that it had to delegate the right to remove all offending pages to local representatives.[7]

The very landscape of proletarian culture became difficult to navigate. Shops were renamed, the most common names being Red Flag, Red Guard, The East is Red, Workers, Peasants and Soldiers, Liberation, The Masses, The People and Yan'an. In Shanghai more than a hundred were called Red Guard. Among 230 pharmacies, 200 had a duplicate name. Their windows were all the same. 'Mao's portrait occupies the central position surrounded by red bunting, quotations from his work and placards with important news items.' Their uniform appearance confused everybody.[8]

When Lin Biao, at the mass rally on 18 August 1966, had called upon the excited young students to strike down 'all the old ideas, old culture, old customs and old habits of the exploiting classes', he had also demanded that 'new ideas, new culture, new customs and new habits' be created, all of them thoroughly proletarian. What precisely constituted 'old culture' was vague enough, but it was even less clear how 'new culture' should be defined. Soon enough everybody understood that the only acceptable proletarian culture was the cult of Chairman Mao.

The most visible aspect of this cult was a rash of slogans. They went up everywhere. As one close observer noted: 'There have always been plenty of them in the past but all previous records have now been broken. Every stretch of clean wall must have its carefully inscribed quotation or tribute to Mao.' Some of the favourite slogans were 'Our Great Teacher, Great Leader, Great Commander, Great Helmsman' and 'Long Live Chairman Mao!' Shops, factories and schools were plastered with them, a few stretching across the top of entire buildings. Massive brick structures were erected at key points in Beijing, displaying slogans and quotations from the Great Leader. Others carried giant paintings of steely-eyed workers and peasants, determined to smash all capitalist roaders. Quotations were painted on the outside of buses, lorries, cars and vans. Trains had a mounted photograph of Mao on the front of the engine. Even bicycles had a little card with a quotation displayed on the front. Lorries careened through the streets with Red Guards, carrying their red plastic-backed book of quotations and brandishing it at each other like a revolutionary passport.[9]

In this new world steeped in red, all the senses were bombarded. Red Guards on temporary platforms called upon the people to join the revolution in shrill voices. Bystanders were harangued in fiery rhetoric peppered with quotations from the Chairman. High up in the skies, air hostesses on internal flights treated passengers to regular readings from the Little Red Book.

But the most fearful weapon was the loudspeaker. These had long been used in propaganda campaigns, but now they were switched on permanently, spewing out the same quotations – always at full volume. Red Guards read from the Little Red Book in police boxes, connected to loudspeakers on the streets. Gangs of youths paraded through the cities, belting out revolutionary songs praising the Chairman and his thought. The same songs were broadcast on radio, which in turn was connected to loudspeakers in courtyards, schools, factories and government offices. One favourite was 'When Sailing the Seas, We Depend on the Helmsman', another 'The Thought of Mao Zedong Glitters with Golden Light'. One foreigner was taken aback by what he called a 'ceaseless inferno of sound', but shrewdly pointed out that it had taught the population to hear without listening.[10]

Much of this new fervour was guided from above, not least by the People's Liberation Army, which was behind the promotion of the Little Red Book. On 27 August, for instance, a directive from Beijing demanded that only portraits of the Chairman be displayed on public occasions.[11]

But nobody wanted to fall behind in the cult of the leader. As the range of objects condemned as feudal or bourgeois expanded, ordinary people increasingly turned to the only politically safe commodities available – Mao photos, Mao badges, Mao posters and Mao books.

Demand vastly outstripped the quantity of products on offer. The *Selected Readings of Mao Zedong's Work* was a case in point. There were two formats for the general public. Edition A was designed for the more advanced reader, Edition B for people with a limited educational background. The Ministry of Culture determined that the print run of both editions had to increase from a combined total of 40 million to 60 million in 1966, but there was too little paper to carry out the plan. The production of all 'unnecessary books', including leisure magazines, was curbed, and only reprints of important political works were permitted, one example being Lei Feng's diary. Still it did not suffice to satisfy popular demand. So the official target for the production of machine-made paper shot up, reaching 500 tonnes in 1967. To balance the economy, the national production of soap was cut by 15 per cent.[12]

In Shanghai, seven new factories were built with a total surface area of 16,400 square metres, the size of about three football pitches, to keep up with demand for photos, portraits, posters and books. In Jiangsu province, industrial plants were refitted to print the Little Red Book. Factories making red ink worked around the clock but still ran dry.[13]

The books needed covers – nice, bright and red. The amount of plastic needed for the Little Red Book alone reached 4,000 tonnes by 1968. As early as August 1966, the Ministry of Trade curbed the production of plastic shoes, plastic slippers and plastic toys, as factories around the country geared up to contribute to Mao Zedong Thought.[14]

Posters were particularly popular. Children loved them. Anchee Min, a Red Guard, recalled that 'To be able to feel closer to Mao, I filled my house with posters.'[15] But here, too, customers were demanding. They had learned the importance of innuendo during the campaign against Wu Han and Deng Tuo, and scrutinised every product for defects that might carry a political connotation. Close to a million posters of the Chairman were withheld after buyers complained that a small, faintly printed character that read 'pickpocket' appeared on his shoulder. The Bureau for Public Security immediately investigated, but concluded that it was the result of a mechanical error. Another poster, depicting the Chairman at a mass rally of Red Guards in Beijing, appeared to have a double 'x' run through a strand of his hair. Rumours started circulating. Customers, always wary of the ubiquitous counter-revolutionary, returned the poster to the shops.[16]

There were other issues. The regime decried anything that smacked even remotely of capitalism, but how should objects carrying the image of the

Chairman be priced? It was more than a philosophical conundrum. Even in a command economy where all the decisions were made by the state, the price of a similar object varied widely. Take a simple plaster bust of the Chairman standing eighteen centimetres high. Customers complained that different department stores in Shanghai charged different prices. A fixed price of 0.37 yuan was introduced, but then some shops started offering discounts, bringing back price differentials that looked suspiciously similar to those of the market economy.[17]

The profit motive was even more ubiquitous when it came to the Mao badge. These badges were extremely popular, and were often used by Red Guards to individualise an otherwise uniform outfit. But here, too, the planned economy struggled to keep up with popular demand. In Shanghai, seventy-five factories worked overtime to churn out 15 million badges a month. Wuhan made about 6 million, but Nanjing only managed a million. It asked for an extra 90 tonnes of pure aluminium to treble its production in 1967. By 1968, the national output stood at more than 50 million badges per month.[18]

It was not enough, and a thriving black market emerged to compete with the state. Some government organisations produced badges for their own members, but expanded their operations into a legal twilight zone, lured by the profit motive. Underground factories appeared, entirely devoted to feeding the black market. They competed with state enterprises for rare resources, stealing aluminium buckets, kettles, pots and pans. Such was the demand that even the protective layer of aluminium used on expensive machinery in factories was ripped away to feed the badge frenzy.[19]

The illegal markets themselves were hardly hidden from view, a few of them attracting crowds of over 10,000 punters, spilling over on to the streets and blocking the traffic. In Shanghai the authorities counted more than thirty of them, mainly located near railway stations and docks. The coveted objects were bartered for goods or sold to the highest bidder. Local officials decried these capitalist activities as 'extremely disrespectful towards our great leader', but there was not much that they could do, since Red Guards and other revolutionary organisations policed the markets. In Shanghai a special taskforce of 500 agents was set up, and they prosecuted hundreds of speculators. Most of them escaped with a caution, although more than twenty entrepreneurs were arrested, including one Zhou Abao, who oversaw a criminal gang involved in selling hundreds of kilos of aluminium to a dozen government units.[20]

There were thousands of different badges, a few fashioned crudely from perspex, plastic or even bamboo, some carefully crafted with hand-coloured porcelain, the majority with an aluminium base and a profile image of Mao in gold or silver, invariably looking to the left. Like the Little Red Book, the badge became a symbol of loyalty to the Chairman, and was worn just above the heart. People from bad backgrounds were not allowed to wear them.[21]

Badges were the most hotly traded pieces of private property during the first years of the Cultural Revolution, open to every form of capitalist speculation. Red Guards became expert at recognising the relative value of different badges, and traded them among themselves or used them as currency when they travelled the country. Xu Xiaodi had more than a hundred. When one of her most prized specimens was stolen on a crowded bus in Beijing she cried inconsolably. But the biggest collectors were higher up. Ye Qun, Lin Biao's wife, amassed thousands of them, presenting her collection to the Chairman on the occasion of his seventy-third birthday on 26 December 1966.[22]

Since so many badges were made illegally, accurate estimates are impossible to reach, but at the height of the revolution some 2 to 5 billion badges had been produced across the country. The amount of aluminium diverted away from other industrial activities was so excessive that in 1969 Mao intervened: 'Give me back my aeroplanes.' The fad declined rapidly, and largely ceased after the death of Lin Biao in 1971.[23]

9

Linking Up

The violence subsided in late August 1966. In Shanghai, a rumour spread that the municipal authorities were displeased with the Red Guards, and the city began to quieten down. There were still bands of students marching through the streets, singing revolutionary songs and clashing cymbals, but the spark of enthusiasm had died. Many of the slogans started to peel off the walls and windows. Shops opened their doors again. Nien Cheng, like so many other victims of the house raids, contemplated the damage around her.[1]

In Beijing, where most of the killings took place, public acts of violence by Red Guards began to abate in the first days of September and then seemed to cease altogether. The police were in charge again. People were busy sprucing up the city for the National Day celebrations on 1 October.[2]

The lull did not last. The flames of the revolution had to be constantly rekindled, and on 31 August another mass rally was organised in Beijing. This time the Chairman called upon the Red Guards to apply their revolutionary experience to other parts of the country. On 5 September, the State Council announced that travel, board and accommodation would be free for all Red Guards.[3]

Months earlier, after the *People's Daily* had exhorted the nation to 'Sweep Away All Monsters and Demons!', the Chairman had already suggested that students be allowed to travel to Beijing to take part in the Cultural Revolution. But as the work teams dispatched by Liu Shaoqi took over, any attempt to liaise with the authorities in the capital was viewed with a baleful eye. In Lanzhou, the work teams took pre-emptive action by warning that all those who expressed their grievances to Beijing would be treated as 'counter-revolutionaries'. In Xi'an, where students rallied in support of a schoolmate denounced as 'rightist' by staging a hunger strike in front of the provincial party committee, a delegation of students had managed secretly to make its way to Beijing to seek the support of Zhou Enlai.

In early August, the trickle of petitioners travelling to Beijing became a flood, as people sought to have the verdicts passed by work teams over-turned. Over a thousand students approached the party headquarters in Zhongnanhai every day, asking for an audience with a party leader. Some were from local schools and universities, but others hailed from the prov-inces. A few of the first students to seek redress in the capital came from Tianjin, a large city port over a hundred kilometres to the south-east. They marched side by side, singing revolutionary songs and reading quotations from the Little Red Book. Defying wind and rain they persisted, until news of their march reached the Cultural Revolution Group. A special train was sent to bring them to the capital. Others followed their lead. Chen Boda met the Tianjin students on 16 August, two days before the first mass rally on Tiananmen Square, and applauded those who had 'braved strong winds and heavy rain' to come to the 'proletarian revolutionary capital'. He demanded that they take the Cultural Revolution back to their home regions.[4]

There were compelling reasons for offering free travel to Red Guards. It had taken Mao more than a year of political manoeuvring to break Peng Zhen's hold on the capital. But the Chairman suspected that many other party leaders were running similar 'independent kingdoms' around the country. How could the Cultural Revolution succeed if the main targets, those 'power holders within the party who take the capitalist road', were safely ensconced in their fiefdoms far away from Beijing? All of them were hardened, wily leaders who had honed their survival skills during decades of dog-eat-dog politics. Many deflected the violence away from themselves by encouraging the Red Guards to raid the homes of ordinary people from bad family backgrounds, stigmatised as social outcasts.

A few even turned the Red Guards against their enemies. In Changsha, the mayor fancied himself as a minor version of the Chairman, appearing in a military uniform to perform his own review of the local Red Guards. In the ranks were the sons and daughters of local party members, middle-school students proud to have been born red and eager to attack the enemies of the party. When university students organised their own demonstration, attacking the municipal party committee for harbouring 'capitalist road-ers', the mayor denounced them as 'rightists' bent on overthrowing the party. Violent clashes soon followed, as the mayor used Red Guards against other Red Guards.

Similar confrontations occurred elsewhere, as revolutionary students were converted into protective organisations. In Fuzhou, the capital of Fujian, the provincial leader Ye Fei, a veteran general who was born in the Philippines to a Chinese father and a Filipina mother, presided over a mass rally on 21 August, appearing in front of 20,000 Red Guards with a red armband prominently displayed on his sleeve. But further south, in Xiamen, Ken Ling and his fellow Red Guards soon tired of smashing up old temples. They wanted to hunt down the 'capitalist roaders' within the party ranks. Urged along by a senior adviser who had stayed on after the work team had been disbanded, they found a target in the provincial head of the Education Department. Her name was Wang Yugeng. A short, plump woman with a double chin and reddish face, Wang happened to be Ye Fei's wife. She seemed untouchable, but the senior adviser passed on incriminat-ing evidence. Determined to confront her, Ken and some 300 other Red Guards converged on Fuzhou, where Wang addressed a mass rally.

They were vastly outnumbered, as the stadium where the rally was being held had been stacked with thousands of supporters of the provincial party committee. A scuffle broke out after one of Ken's allies seized the micro-phone and denounced the meeting as a cover-up. After Wang Yugeng had been hurriedly led off stage by security guards, an ugly fistfight broke out as her local supporters turned on her opponents, who were forced to beat a hasty retreat. Three days later, on 29 August, Ken and his rebels were back with reinforcements, as more than a thousand protesters organised a hunger strike on the square in front of the provincial party committee. Among them were Red Guards who had travelled all the way from Beijing. They called themselves 'rebel Red Guards', in opposition to the 'royalist Red Guards' who stood by the provincial party committee.

To protect itself, the provincial party committee whipped up support from some 20,000 local party activists and factory workers. Since workers were banned from joining Red Guard organisations, they formed squadrons of Scarlet Guards instead, harassing their opponents for days on end. Local cadres supplied the Scarlet Guards with food and water. Rumour had it that they received a special allowance and a hard hat from the provincial party committee, as factories stopped production to allow workers to join in the demonstrations.

On the afternoon of 5 September, the same day that transportation, food and lodging became free for Red Guards, Ken's rebel protesters were joined by more than 30,000 rebel Red Guards, converging on Fuzhou from all parts of the country, clamouring for Ye Fei's dismissal. The city descended into chaos, as the two factions fought each other in the streets.[5]

Similar scenes occurred in many other parts of the country. In Shanghai, the lull that had developed after 26 August lasted only a couple of days. Red Guards from Beijing and Tianjin began descending upon the city, bringing more chaos and violence. On 4 and 5 September they besieged the party headquarters, demanding to see Cao Diqiu, the mayor who had taken over after Ke Qingshi's untimely death. Calling Cao a 'capitalist roader', they were determined to hunt him down.[6]

Mao wanted his young combatants to spread the fire of revolution to every corner of the country. The flow went in two directions. Red Guards from Beijing and Tianjin crisscrossed the country, cranking up violence and laying siege to party headquarters where 'capitalist roaders' were ensconced. Revolutionary youngsters from the provinces, on the other hand, made their way to Beijing, where they learned the ropes, studying the Cultural Revolution and meeting with members of the Cultural Revolution Group. The Chairman himself reviewed millions of Red Guards. After each mass rally, batches of radicalised students left the capital, ready to take the revolution back home.

In early September, Red Guards from the provinces invaded Beijing. Many arrived by bus, some from places as remote as Wenzhou, a once prosperous treaty port 1,400 kilometres south of Beijing. As many as thirty coaches from Shanxi alone could be seen parked on the main boulevard simultaneously. Even more travelled on trains, with carriages crammed full of young passengers.[7]

Schools and colleges around the country selected delegates to be sent to the capital, who set off with great fanfare to the local railway station, equipped with a canvas shoulder bag, an aluminium flask, a tea cup, toothbrush and towel, and of course the ubiquitous Little Red Book, tucked away in a pocket or rolled inside a quilt. Their most treasured possession was a formal letter of introduction, duly stamped by the local committee in charge of the Cultural Revolution, to be presented at reception centres in each city where the Red Guards intended to stay. Some delegates were given blank forms with an official seal, to be used in case of emergency.

Only students from a good class background were allowed to travel. The first question in China was always 'What is your class background?', and the form was no different. But a few people managed to slip through the net. Wen Guanzhong, the young man who lived near the Zikawei Library in Shanghai, had maintained a good relationship with some Red Guards in his school. They agreed to let him go and introduced him as a member of the 'Revolutionary Masses' in his travel document.[8]

Red Guards left in high spirits. They sang revolutionary songs on the train, played cards or told each other stories. There were boisterous food fights, as some of the excited youngsters threw orange peel and eggshells at one another.

But as more delegates got on board, space soon ran out. They occupied every available inch, sitting on each other's laps, on the backs of the seats and on the small tables dividing pairs of seats. 'Some squatted in the aisles, others lay on the luggage racks, and still others had squeezed into the lavatories.' When trains came to a halt in the countryside, local ruffians walked up to the windows, feigning interest in the revolutionary cause. Just as the train started to move, they would snatch the watches from their wrists, grab bags hanging out of the windows and even whisk glasses off people's noses. Some of them pulled knives. When Ken and his schoolmates travelled to Shanghai, several hundred beggars forced their train to a standstill at a small railway station in Zhejiang province. They used iron bars to pry open the doors and smash the windows, trying to force their way inside. Some hung on to the windows when the train began to pull out, or tried to seize hold of passengers inside, screaming 'Let's die together!'⁹

Food soon ran out, but in any case nobody wanted to eat or drink more than the bare minimum. The toilets were always full, and no one wanted to leave the train at stops to relieve themselves for fear of never being able to get back on again. It was easier for the boys, who would pull down their trousers and urinate out of the window while the train was moving. But it was misery for the girls. A bad smell spread, as urine mixed with sweat, vomit and excrement. Some carriages became so wet that Red Guards used their knives to pry open a hole in the floor. Trains became moving prisons.

Tensions flared, especially on long journeys, as trains moved at a snail's pace, taking many days to reach the capital from the south. Sometimes wooden baggage racks collapsed under the weight of dozens of people. Doors were locked, and sick or injured passengers had to be passed on to security troops on the platform through the windows. Red Guards started fighting each other for space. Fistfights broke out between rival groups. Ordinary passengers took advantage of the chaos to force their way aboard without tickets.

As travelling youngsters spilled out of trains in their thousands every day in Beijing, all wearing red armbands and speaking mutually unintelligible dialects, the railway station became a vast transit camp. Huge slogans welcomed them as 'Chairman Mao's little guests'. In the middle of the night, searchlights illuminated the square in front of the station. Loudspeakers blared out instructions, directing new arrivals to the reception rooms in a corner of the station, a Soviet-style structure with two clock towers, topped by curving roofs of glazed tiles. There were rows of students sleeping in their quilts. Every available space in Beijing was pressed into service, as Red Guards were sent in batches to makeshift dormitories in universities, schools, hotels and even government offices.

Gao Yuan and his schoolmates were sent to Beijing's elite 101st Middle School. Within an hour they learned a valuable lesson: the school's Red Guards, who weeks earlier had forced teachers to crawl on cinders, treated them like country bumpkins, refusing to have anything to do with them.

They were taken on another ride, ending up in a primary school near Drum Tower, where they slept on straw mats on the floor of the auditorium.[10]

Jung Chang was luckier, as her group was assigned to Tsinghua University, one of the most prestigious in the country. Ken and his friends were also billeted there, sleeping in a large classroom on the eighth floor. The stench was overwhelming. Many Red Guards had no change of clothes and did not bathe for weeks on end. The quilted covers, passed from one delegation to the next, were rarely washed, and the toilets down the corridor were overflowing, spreading sewage over the tiled floor. 'Even today I can still smell the latrines,' Jung recorded.[11]

Beijing was stretched to breaking point. At the peak of the campaign there were 3 million visitors in the city on top of a permanent population of 7.7 million. Food was commandeered from the surrounding countryside to feed the capital. Chaos set in. One rebel worker, arriving from Shanghai at the offices of the powerful All-China Trade Union in the middle of the winter, was shocked when he saw the floors covered in rubbish and a flow of excrement, frozen solid by the cold. He wondered: 'What is this? Is this hell or hallowed revolutionary ground?'[12]

The Red Guards complained, but none apparently spared a thought for the cleaners – referred to in communist parlance as the 'proletariat' – who had to sort out the mess, forced to plunge their arms down toilets to unblock the sewage. In Shanghai the situation was made worse by visitors who were unfamiliar with sitting toilets and squatted on them instead. When several cleaners refused to carry on, complaining that the stench made them vomit, they were told that 'what stinks is not so much the excrement as your own ideology'.[13]

Fights were frequent, and not just over ideology. There was great friction between Red Guards from different parts of the country, and quarrels broke out over food, living quarters and theft, which was endemic. One of the many officers deployed by the army to help with the logistics of looking after hundreds of thousands of youngsters noted that they tended to behave when under strict supervision, but attacked each other as soon as they were left to their own devices. Some fights involved dozens of Red Guards, who went for each other with fists and belts. On his first morning at Tsinghua University, Ken walked past a student with a broken skull who had been thrown from the fourth floor. Nobody seemed to care.[14]

Travel in the capital was free, and many students did the rounds, transcribing entire texts in their notebooks when reading big-character posters outside government buildings and on university campuses. In some of the ministries, mat screens were erected to provide more space for hanging posters. Electric lights were hung in front of every screen, so that people could come and read at night.

The Red Guards also queued up, sometimes for hours at a stretch, to buy Mao badges. A thriving black market competed with beleaguered shops. Among the pine trees on the south side of Tiananmen Square, ten small photos of the Chairman could be traded for one badge. But as the weather gradually turned cold in November, many students were reluctant to leave their heated rooms until noon. Some had no money to spend, and little interest in the revolution. They were there to eat, sleep and pick the occasional fight.[15]

There were mass meetings with members of the Cultural Revolution Group, talks by leading officers from the People's Liberation Army, and even classes in military training. But, most of all, the Red Guards had come to Beijing to see the Chairman. After the two mass rallies of 18 and 31 August, a further six reviews of Red Guards were held in Beijing. By the time the last one took place on 26 November 1966, Mao had appeared in front of 12 million Red Guards.

The Chairman initiated the mass rallies to ignite the spark of revolution. But by October they had become a necessity. Despite repeated warnings that they could not remain in the capital for ever, the Red Guards refused to leave until they had seen the Chairman. Mao had to review them by the million. In the end, when even the giant square in front of the Forbidden City could no longer contain them, he rode through the city in an open jeep, reaching 2 million students in one fell swoop.

Preparations for each rally started early, as Red Guards were marched in groups or ferried by a fleet of 6,000 lorries to the square in the middle of the night. The rallies were never announced in advance, and students who were unlucky enough to have just washed their only set of clothes had to go along soaking wet. Some marched for hours. Security guards searched the students for dangerous articles such as knives and metal objects, including keys. One soldier confiscated a hairpin, insisting that it could be used to assassinate the Chairman. The students were ordered to sit in rows, each group having an allocated position. As the hours went by, many of them dozed off, leaning their heads against others. Puddles of urine started to appear, as nobody could reach the latrines.[16]

Time seemed to stand still, but after hours of waiting word spread through the ranks: 'Here he is! Here he is!' People jumped up, standing on their toes, craning their necks, seeking a glimpse of the Chairman. They surged forward, shouting 'Long Live Chairman Mao!' Not all managed to see the Great Helmsman. One student who had walked to the square with wet clothes on his back could just make out the leader in the distance. The Chairman was not as tall as he had imagined. On the other hand, the Red Guard who had been in charge of delivering confiscated gold to the cathedral in Guangzhou saw the Chairman very clearly. He had a pair of binoculars with him, filched a month earlier during a raid on a bourgeois family.[17]

Many were ecstatic. Some would remember the moment they saw the Chairman as the highlight of their lives. Jung Chang, disappointed at catching no more than a glimpse of the Chairman's back, his right arm steadily waving, already knew what the girl standing next to her would say, as the sentence had been publicised endlessly by press, radio and television after every mass rally in Beijing: 'I am the happiest person in the world today. I have seen our Great Leader Chairman Mao!'[18]

But propaganda documentaries of the mass rallies, showing hysterical Red Guards waving the Little Red Book, projected a deceptively uniform image. Wang Rongfen, a student of German at the Foreign Languages Institute, attended the first mass rally in Tiananmen Square on 18 August. She could not help but feel that the keynote speech given by Lin Biao resembled Adolf Hitler's orations at the Nuremberg rallies. A month later she sent the Chairman a letter, pointing out that 'the Cultural Revolution is not a mass movement. It is one man with a gun manipulating the people.' The nineteen-year-old student was arrested and sent to prison for thirteen years.[19]

She was hardly alone. Liu Wenzhong belonged to a Shanghai family ostracised as 'counter-revolutionaries'. He was schooled at home by his elder brother. While other students were taking part in the Socialist Education Campaign, he was taught to respect human rights and cherish democracy. He referred to the Chairman as a despot even before the Cultural Revolution began. On Tiananmen Square he stood a mere 30 metres away from Mao, close enough to see the mole on his chin. He was overcome by a sense of dread while those around him cheered.[20]

Ken, on the other hand, had grown cynical enough to wonder whether the fat man with the slightly disdainful look, staring ahead in the distance as he stiffly raised his arm, was a double. Ken had seen scenes in the movie theatres of Red Guards cheering, jumping and shedding tears. No matter how hard he tried, he could not bring himself to match the excitement. 'It all seemed like an act with each one imitating the other.' He felt slightly nauseated.[21]

The cameras captured the rallies, but not their aftermath. The Red Guards had been warned to tighten their shoes, but as they surged forward, thousands still managed to lose their footwear during each rally. They were collected and dumped in huge heaps in a nearby stadium, where students in flimsy socks could be seen poking around trying to retrieve a matching pair.[22]

The final rally was a disaster. Held at an airfield on the outskirts of the capital on 26 November, it was followed by a stampede. As a crowd of 2 million people rushed towards the only available exit, they levelled wheat fields, bent trees and pushed mud huts out of their way. Those who tried to bend down to pick up their belongings or tie their laces were trampled underfoot. A wooden bridge over a stream collapsed, followed by piercing screams. Panic spread, as waves of people were pushed into the stream, forced to wade through the shallow water. Most of it was soaked up by the cotton trousers of the crowd, leaving behind nothing but an expanse of mud. After crossing the stream, the Red Guards started to disperse, but many were now barefoot. In the freezing winter cold, every step hurt. Ken managed to grab a pair of torn cotton plimsolls. Amid scenes of pandemonium, military lorries filled with clothes, socks and shoes sped up and down the only road. Some carried mutilated bodies.[23]

Of the many lessons the Red Guards learned during their visit to the capital, one stood out: they discovered the generosity of the state. In Beijing queues of students borrowed money and ration coupons. All that was needed was a name and a school affiliation. With no proof of identity required, many Red Guards gave fake names, scattering as soon as they had attended a rally. Instead of taking the revolution back home, they started touring the country. Li Shihua, a Red Guard from Anhui province, put it in a nutshell: 'Everywhere there were reception centres for Red Guards, and food, accommodation and travel were all free; when would such a great opportunity present itself again?'[24]

Li and his friends had little interest in politics. Soon after they had cheered the Chairman on Tiananmen Square, they set off for Wuhan. They were asked to attend a mass meeting held in a giant stadium, where provincial boss Zhang Tixue, just like Ye Fei in Fuzhou, appeared in army uniform to defend the provincial party committee. Song Yaowu, who had shot to fame when she pinned an armband on the Chairman's sleeve during the first mass rally in Beijing, appeared by his side. But as soon as they were allowed to leave, they set off for the East Lake, where Mao had hunkered down before his celebrated swim in the Yangtze River. They visited the Yellow Crane Tower, a sacred Taoist site by the river which had so far survived furious assaults by Red Guards. They marvelled at the imposing Yangtze River Bridge, watching in awe as trains and cars crossed the river on two separate levels. They went on to Changsha, Nanchang, Hangzhou, Shanghai and Nanjing, borrowing clothes and even emergency cash from reception centres around the country. When some of them arrived back home, they were laden with gifts for family and friends. Little did they know that the bill would follow a few years later. They were among the few in their school who had naively given their real names when touring the country, and the sums of money borrowed were subtracted from their meagre salaries as they worked in re-education camps.[25]

Some students spent months crisscrossing the country, while others became homesick and returned to their families after a couple of weeks. Zhai Zhenhua and her friends set off from Beijing to visit the Three Gorges, where the Yangtze River was forced through steep cliffs and tall mountains. But the boat from Shanghai to Wuhan moved slowly against the current and took a full three days. She and her friends were confined to third-class bunk beds, peering through a porthole. All they saw was muddy water and a monotonous shoreline. She gave up on the Three Gorges and travelled back by train from Wuhan.[26]

Li Shihua and Zhai Zhenhua travelled with friends, and developed deep, lasting bonds on the road. But a few set off alone. Wen Guanzhong, who had managed to obtain a letter of introduction from Red Guards in Shanghai, explored the capital and toured the country. He made fleeting friendships, but moved on swiftly, as he feared that his travelling companions might discover his true class background.[27]

Most students were red tourists, seizing the opportunity to visit the hallowed grounds of revolution of which they had read so often in school. Columns of Red Guards could be seen in Yan'an, all of them eager to explore the cave dwellings where Mao and his fellow revolutionaries had found shelter after the Long March. The Chairman's birthplace in Shaoshan, Hunan province, was similarly overrun by Red Guards, queuing to see the yellow mud-brick house where he had grown up, the school he had attended and the Orange Islet, a narrow river island covered with citrus orchards where the Chairman had sunbathed in his youth.

Another revolutionary site was Jinggang Mountain, where Mao and his ragtag army of a thousand men had set up their first peasant soviet in 1927. The mountain plateau in Jiangxi province was remote, poor and densely wooded. Young people kept on pouring in, triumphant and excited at having reached the cradle of revolution after weeks of travelling. But the local villagers were unable to cope. By December, more than 60,000 Red Guards were arriving every day. A month later, there were thirty times more visitors than locals. The holy ground soon turned into a disaster area, forcing the People's Liberation Army to drop food parcels and medicine by helicopter. A convoy of a hundred lorries was sent to evacuate the area.[28]

Inspired by the Long March, when the Red Army had been forced to retreat from the Jinggang Mountain in 1934–5, trekking all the way north to Yan'an, Red Guards set off on foot in Long March teams. On 22 October 1966 the Cultural Revolution Group encouraged the practice, seeking to reduce the pressure on a transportation system close to collapse. The students followed in the footsteps of the Red Army, striving to experience every hardship their predecessors had suffered to prove themselves worthy inheritors of the revolution. A red banner bearing the name of the Long March team was sometimes held by a Red Guard walking in front of the group. Some young pilgrims attached small boards to their backpacks, inscribed with quotations from the Chairman, so that those following behind could read.[29]

Jinggang Mountain was a disaster, but other small villages along the most popular routes also suffered, as hospitality stations in people's communes had to provide food and shelter. In Hunan there were roadside stands where flasks could be filled with boiled water, while rice was served from wooden barrels. In Jiangxi, on the other hand, the villagers could no longer accommodate the growing number of Red Guards. There were arguments between the students and the locals, as station workers were accused of failing to support the Cultural Revolution.

Even in the cities the strain could be felt, as hard-working people came to resent the way that self-righteous students outstayed their welcome. In Chengdu, Li Zhengan was a poor woman whom sheer destitution had forced to place her four-year-old daughter with another family during Mao's Great Famine. The adoptive family did not like the girl, forcing her to work and confiscating most of her food ration. Li took her child back home after discovering that she was starving and covered in lice. Now, seven years later, her daughter was one of those commandeered to help at a hospitality station, washing the bedding used by Red Guards. The work was tough for the eleven-year-old, who suffered from poor health and severe rheumatism. Having scrimped and saved her entire life, barely able to feed her own family, her mother could not understand why the government wasted so much money on free travel and board for students. Many echoed her sentiments. In Beijing, one of the officers in charge of looking after 12 million visitors could only wonder at the immensity of the cost incurred by those who ultimately had to foot the bill, namely ordinary people. Free board and travel was only abolished on 21 December 1966.[30]

———

Red Guards travelled for free, and so did a host of microbes, viruses and bacteria. Of the many diseases that thrived in the overcrowded, unhygienic conditions brought about by revolutionary youngsters, meningitis was the most lethal. An inflammation of the protective membranes covering the brain and spinal cord, it was spread through coughing and sneezing. Lack of ventilation in crowded trains and dormitories helped it achieve epidemic proportions.

The disease first appeared in Beijing in August 1966, reaching a peak there a few months later. The alarm was raised, and the Central Committee duly informed, but no preventive measures were taken, as nothing was allowed to impede revolution. At first, students infected in the capital carried the disease to major cities along the railway network, where meningitis developed into an epidemic in November. Then, as students were encouraged to spread the revolution on foot, the disease was transmitted from the cities to the villages. Although free travel was abolished in December, many Red Guards continued to enjoy their newfound freedom. From December 1966 to February 1967, when the Cultural Revolution Group finally called on all Red Guards to go home, meningitis became prevalent along all the major railway routes. At this stage, however, so much of the country was in the grip of the Cultural Revolution that even basic medical supplies such as facemasks were in short supply. As a result, many nurses and doctors treating meningitis patients became infected in their turn.[31]

Most hospitals could not afford facemasks, let alone the drugs used to treat the disease. Scarce financial resources were being channelled into the Cultural Revolution, and the Red Guards paralysed much routine government work. As early as 1964 the Ministry of Health had been thrown into turmoil when Mao accused it of serving the leadership rather than the people. By the autumn of 1966, it was besieged by Red Guards, determined to bring to account the 'capitalist roaders' hiding inside.

The United States offered medical help, but China did not respond. In February 1967, the shortages of antibiotics were such that the government was forced to turn to pharmaceutical companies in Western Europe and Asia, purchasing several hundred metric tonnes of medicine. Control centres were established to co-ordinate nationwide efforts to prevent and treat the disease. But it was too little, too late. By the time the situation had been brought under control, more than 160,000 people had died.

Rebels and Royalists

Red Guards were proud of their class background, and they tried to keep their ranks pure. When students started to pour into the capital in the last week of August 1966, control squads met them at the station. Thousands of youngsters who belonged to bad families were ejected. Wang Guanghua, a Beijing Sixth Middle School student from a 'capitalist family' who had responded enthusiastically to the Chairman's call to bring revolution to other parts of the country, was kidnapped by a control squad after returning home in late September, and tortured to death for travelling without permission from his school's Red Guards.[1]

But as the weeks went by, the grip of the old Red Guards on the Cultural Revolution loosened. From the beginning, there had been furious debates about who could join their ranks. One of the most discussed documents was a speech given by a Red Guard named Tan Lifu. The son of a high-ranking official, he spoke passionately about the need to keep those who were not born red out of Red Guard organisations. Millions of copies of his speech, delivered on 20 August in Beijing, were printed at all levels of local government, and soon found their way on to every campus. However, in some schools the sons and daughters of local cadres were in the minority. In Xiamen, many of those who became Red Guards in the Eighth Middle School were born 'black'. They were strongly opposed by schoolmates from a revolutionary background, who accused Ken and others of trying to subvert the revolution and inflict 'acts of class revenge' on the proletariat. But these critics were outnumbered.[2]

In Fujian province, it was the Red Guards from Xiamen Eighth Middle School who spearheaded the attack on the provincial party committee, travelling all the way to Fuzhou to confront Ye Fei and his wife Wang

Yugeng. In Changsha, it was the university students labelled as 'rightists' who confronted the local party machine. In many parts of the country, divisions appeared between those who dared to question the local leaders and those who rallied to their defence. Soon they were called 'rebels' and 'royalists' or 'conservatives'. Many of the rebels were born 'black'.[3]

The balance of power shifted in October. In Fuzhou, where rebels demonstrated before the provincial party committee, a telegram was sent to the Central Committee in Beijing, denouncing the hunger strike as a counter-revolutionary act organised by hooligans with backing from Taiwan. Many other beleaguered party organisations likewise asked for help from the central authorities. Beijing's answer came on 3 October in an editorial published in the party journal *Red Flag*, edited by Chen Boda: 'The power holders inside the ranks of the party who take the capitalist road are a small bunch of counter-revolutionary revisionists. They raise the red flag in order to fight the red flag. They are like Khrushchev. At the first opportunity, they will plot to usurp the party, the army and the state. They are our most dangerous and principal enemies.' The editorial then denounced those who were following a 'bourgeois reactionary line'.[4]

Two weeks later, Chen Boda for the first time named Liu Shaoqi and Deng Xiaoping as the main targets of the Cultural Revolution. He contrasted the 'bourgeois reactionary line' they had been following with Mao Zedong's 'proletarian revolutionary line'. Everywhere, Chen explained, the masses should educate and liberate themselves. He took aim at Tan Lifu's bloodline theory, which he denounced as reactionary. Chen Boda savaged the popular couplet 'If the father is a hero, his son is also a hero,' calling it feudal and 'completely against Marxism and Mao Zedong Thought'. Tan Lifu, who had been catapulted to stardom months earlier, was now accused of opposing the Cultural Revolution. Mass meetings were organised on campuses across China to criticise him. Much as millions of copies of Tan Lifu's speech had been distributed in August, Chen Boda's talk was now widely disseminated, on instructions from the Chairman.[5]

It was a turning point in the Cultural Revolution, as the very meaning of the terms 'red' and 'black' began to shift. Those who were born red suddenly found themselves in the wrong camp, as their parents were denounced as followers of the 'bourgeois reactionary line' promoted by Liu Shaoqi and Deng Xiaoping.

Virtually overnight entire Red Guard organisations were suddenly born 'black', as they discovered that their families were labelled as members of a 'Black Gang' plotting to usurp power. Now they became the targets of the revolution they had so fervently supported only weeks earlier. In order to protect their reputations and help their parents survive the onslaught, erstwhile radical youths turned into conservatives, keen to defend the status quo.[6]

Chen Boda's interpretation of Mao's mass line generated huge enthusiasm among students from backgrounds considered to be less than revolutionary. At long last they could now fully participate in the revolution. Those from families that were neither 'red' nor 'black' – they were often described as 'grey' – became rebel Red Guards. Young people from bad backgrounds finally had an opportunity to regroup against their erstwhile tormentors, the old Red Guards. They, too, joined Mao's crusading army against the party establishment. By November, rebel Red Guards were common. Jung Chang remembers meeting an attractive, slim girl with velvety black eyes and long eyelashes on a train full of Red Guards. She was surprised by the quiet confidence with which the girl told her that she was from a 'black' background. It looked as if Chairman Mao was giving ordinary people the courage to stand up and rebel against the red elite.

The rise of the rebels coincided with a shift in the targets of violence. Local party authorities had so far managed to deflect the thrust of the Cultural Revolution away from themselves, unleashing the Red Guards on to ordinary people, turned into scapegoats for belonging to the wrong class. Now a growing army of rebels laid siege to party leaders suspected of following the 'bourgeois reactionary line'. In Fuzhou, the balance of power shifted away from the provincial party committee. Red Guards from Tsinghua University, Peking University, the Aeronautics Institute and other campuses travelled south to lend a hand. The rebels fanned out to seize strategically located buildings, schools and offices. They requisitioned dozens of vehicles, creating a mobile force that was dispatched across Fuzhou to bolster rebel positions against the opposition. Much of the local population was divided into two camps, leaning either towards the rebels or towards the royalists. Since propaganda was paramount, loudspeakers were mounted in the post office and department stores at key intersections of the city, in order to drown out the messages broadcast by the opposition. Meanwhile, behind the scenes, teams travelled up to Beijing, meeting with Chen Boda to complain that Ye Fei and the provincial party committee stood behind Tan Lifu's class theories to oppress the rebels.

A few days later, on 1 November, the rebels seized control of the party headquarters. Ken and his friends stormed Ye Fei's residence. The provincial leader, who was being served breakfast by two servants, turned pale as the Red Guards entered his dining room. He was paraded through the streets in the following days, and soon sent out an appeal for help to Han Xianchu, the local army commander. Han, a gaunt man with a maimed left hand fixed in the shape of a chicken claw, refused to intervene. By the end of the year, Ye had fallen from grace. Han took over as leader of the province.[7]

That very same day yet another editorial of the *Red Flag* appeared, this one entitled 'Victory for the Proletarian Revolutionary Line Represented by Chairman Mao'. It dealt a fatal blow to Red Guard organisations branded as 'royalist' or 'conservative', and accused leading party members of 'treating the masses as if they were ignorant and incapable': 'They shift the targets of attack and direct their spearhead against the revolutionary masses, branding them "anti-party elements", "rightists", "pseudo-revolutionaries", "pseudo-leftists but genuine rightists" and so forth.'[8]

The result of the editorial was a rush to join rebel organisations, as few people wished to be seen as supporters of the 'bourgeois reactionary line'. But the ranks of the revolutionaries now went far beyond mere students, whether or not they were born red. People everywhere joined the Cultural Revolution, trying to better their lot. In Xi'an, Kang Zhengguo could feel 'their pent-up rage spilling out like water rolling over a dam'. Temporary factory workers demanded permanent jobs; youths who had been sent to the countryside wanted to return to the cities; laid-off government employees called for reinstatement. All of them blamed the 'bourgeois reactionary line'. 'Now that the leaders had been pronounced fair game, nobody was afraid to lash out at them any more.'[9]

It looked like a people's revolution. Just as Mao had incited students to rebel against their teachers months earlier, he now unleashed ordinary people against their party leaders. In doing so he tapped into a deep pool of resentment. There seemed to be no end to the number of people who harboured grievances against party officials. Across the country the population was organised into self-contained work units under the thumb of local cadres, and in every unit there were those who became rebels – from farmers, workers, teachers and shop assistants to government clerks.

The country was a giant pressure cooker. Seventeen years earlier, when the communists had conquered the country, many ordinary people had accepted liberation with a mixture of fear, hope and resignation. There was widespread relief that the civil war had come to an end. The proclaimed values of the regime, including equality, justice and freedom, were genuinely appealing, and the party tirelessly trumpeted the New Democracy, a slogan promising the inclusion of all but the most hardened enemies of the regime. Above all, the communists promised each disaffected group what it wanted most: land for the farmers, independence for all minorities, freedom for intellectuals, protection of private property for businessmen, higher living standards for the workers.

One by one, these promises were broken, as a whole range of real or imagined opponents were eliminated with the unwitting help of the enemies of tomorrow, those who were cajoled into co-operating with the regime. By 1957, basic liberties had been curtailed, including the freedom of speech, the freedom of association, the freedom of movement and the freedom of domicile. Everything that stood between the state and the individual had been eliminated, as entire categories of people – from farmers and intellectuals to monks – had become state employees working in government units at the beck and call of local cadres. In the following years, Mao's Great Famine not only consumed tens of millions of people in the countryside, but also extinguished whatever hope most ordinary people had for a better future – with the exception of a small band of true believers.

In the years following the catastrophe, the party reasserted its control over the population through the Socialist Education Campaign. In the words of one political scientist, 'the state ruled society more thoroughly than during any other equivalent length of time'.[10]

In order to cope with the colossal economic losses of the Great Leap Forward, a ruthless policy of cutting labour costs was pursued, undermining the livelihoods of many urban residents. In 1955, in order to prevent large numbers of villagers from seeking shelter in the cities, Zhou Enlai had expanded the household registration system, used in the cities since 1951, to the countryside. Like the internal passport in the Soviet Union, it tied the distribution of food to the number of people registered in each household, effectively preventing villagers from moving around. But it also divided people into two separate worlds, classifying them as either 'city dwellers' (*jumin*) or 'peasants' (*nongmin*). Children inherited this status through their mother, meaning that even if a village girl married a man from the city, she and her children remained 'peasants'. People in the countryside were treated like an hereditary caste deprived of the privileges that the state granted most city dwellers, namely subsidised housing, food rations and access to health, education and disability benefits.[11]

After the famine, in order to reduce the burden on the state further, large numbers of urban residents were dispatched to the countryside, where they lost their status and all the associated benefits. This policy began in 1961 and 1962, when more than 20 million people were driven from the cities and left to their own devices in people's communes across the country.[12]

This was the opening of a deliberate effort to decrease the number of permanent workers entitled to state benefits. In Shanghai, Cao Diqiu – the man who would become the beleaguered mayor of the city after Ke Qingshi's premature death in 1965 – ordered factories and enterprises to employ more temporary workers. People with secure jobs were relocated to remote villages, while farmers were recruited instead during the slack winter months. They were assigned to the most demeaning jobs at much lower pay than their permanent counterparts. On the eve of the Cultural Revolution, approximately one-third of all workers nationwide were on temporary contracts thanks to state efforts to whittle away welfare expenditure.[13]

China, in short, was still mired in the catastrophe unleashed by the Great Leap Forward. Demands for improved working conditions, higher wages, better health care and increased benefits were common. Vast disparities existed between workers described in communist parlance as the 'proletariat'. At one end of the salary range there were union workers and technicians who received a range of benefits dating back to the early days of liberation. Some factories provided their workers with major amenities, including large dining halls, clinics, libraries, table-tennis facilities, lounges, schools for children and generous pensions of up to 70 per cent of wages on retirement. At the bottom of the scale there was a vast, dark underworld of impoverished workers on temporary contracts, hired and fired at will without any fringe benefits, some of them working on giant construction projects without any basic rights, living in crowded, insanitary dormitories. In between these two extremes many workers complained of poor housing, low wages, excessive discipline and the widespread use of overtime without compensation.[14]

Tensions further increased during the Cultural Revolution. In June and July 1966, workers had joined the students in writing big-character posters to denounce the 'monsters and demons' who, according to the official guidelines, had oppressed the working people. They needed little encouragement, and soon disgruntled employees took to task the local cadres who wielded so much power over their lives. In the Guangming Watch Factory in Shanghai, the party secretary found posters in every corridor accusing him of corruption and nepotism. In other factories too, some leaders were accused of being 'despotic emperors', and employees demanded that they step down. Some of the more militant protesters formed Combat Teams. They linked up with like-minded agitators in other factories, raided offices to dig up incriminating evidence against their leaders and accused the management of being 'royalists' who produced nothing but fake self-criticisms. On a single day in August, more than 400 factory cadres were paraded in dunces' caps through the streets of Shanghai.[15]

In Shanghai over a million workers participated in the Cultural Revolution over the summer.[16] But despite the outpouring of discontent, some work teams managed to deflect the brunt of the attack away from themselves on to ordinary workers. Across the country as a whole, work teams stigmatised many ordinary people as 'counter-revolutionaries' and 'rightists', leaving a permanent blot in their personal dossiers that would blight their careers.

When Mao called on 'the masses' to 'educate and liberate themselves' in October, he was seen as a liberator. The *Red Flag* editorial of 1 November lambasted 'royalist' leaders for branding the revolutionary masses as 'anti-party elements' and 'rightists'. It also demanded that the dossiers compiled by work teams be destroyed and their verdicts overturned.[17]

Overnight the victims of the work teams were vindicated, as the world was turned upside down. It seemed that the misfortunes of those persecuted over the summer had come to an end. At first rebel Red Guards forced party committees in some schools to turn over all the dossiers and publicly dispose of them. Ordinary people soon tried to emulate them, storming party offices, rummaging through storage rooms, tracking down their personal dossiers and burning them in public.[18]

Before long, the victims of earlier campaigns started clamouring for justice. They included party members who had been punished or expelled from the ranks. They, too, demanded redress and joined the attack on the 'bourgeois reactionary line' of Liu Shaoqi and Deng Xiaoping. Liu Shaoqi, after all, was the man responsible for a vicious purge of the party during the Socialist Education Campaign, when 5 million members had been punished. And Deng Xiaoping had overseen the anti-rightist campaign of 1957, when hundreds of thousands of people had been labelled as 'rightists' and deported to labour camps.

There was a long list of discontents, as ordinary people used their newly acquired freedoms to protest. Factories, both big and small, started printing their own bulletins and newspapers, relishing their newly found freedom of publication. Hundreds of associations were spontaneously established in Shanghai alone, as people were finally granted the right to assemble in the name of the 'great proletarian democracy'. No longer requiring official permission to undertake a trip, people left their jobs in droves to make their way to the local party headquarters. In Shanghai, some 40,000 workers returned from the countryside to demonstrate their discontent. Some of them occupied Shanghai Mansions, a luxury art deco block of apartments opened in 1936 and reserved for the top leadership after 1949.

Others staged a hunger strike in front of the Labour Bureau. Many joined the rebels laying siege to the municipal party committee.[19]

There was hardly a work unit where some form of rebel opposition did not appear. In some cases the revolution was limited to a few inflammatory posters, but elsewhere it developed into pitched battles between different factions. In most cases, the rebel workers faced deeply entrenched opposition. Factory leaders were well organised, attuned to political campaigns and tempered by years of revolutionary experience. Some of them were veterans of the Long March. They presided over a tightly controlled network of support, which ranged from the factory party committee, its political department and representatives of public security down to floor managers and workshop superintendents. There were party activists among the workers, as well as trade union members who stood firmly behind the old order. Temporary labourers, by definition, could be fired at any time, but even rank-and-file workers faced a range of retaliatory devices at the disposal of the party administration. They could be transferred to a different job, be moved to a factory far away in the countryside, have their benefits cut or be forced out of their subsidised housing. The rebels clamoured for justice in the name of proletarian democracy, but so did the factory leaders, who were savvy enough to join the campaign to denounce the 'bourgeois reactionary line'. Everybody criticised Liu Shaoqi, while proclaiming loyalty to Chairman Mao. Everywhere the red flag went up. To show their commitment to the Cultural Revolution, the factory managers established their own mass organisations, lavishly funded, well organised and stacked with reliable followers. Workers were now fighting workers.[20]

Both factions appealed to Beijing. In Nanjing, where scuffles broke out across all sectors of industry, irate party officials phoned or petitioned the higher authorities in writing, complaining of counter-revolutionary plots and mounting economic losses as many factories were brought to a standstill. Rebel workers, in turn, sent delegations to protest against their party leaders. The scale of the unrest was enormous: from the Nanjing Machine Tool and Electrical Apparatus Factory alone, a third of its 185 workers made their way to the capital by the end of October to air their grievances.[21]

Many protesters converged on the All-China Federation of Trade Unions, a seven-storey building near Tiananmen Square. The place was soon teeming with representatives from all parts of the country. They complained about wage inequities, insecure employment, health hazards and lack of social and political rights. 'They were a strangely quiet crowd, but their felt injustice hung menacingly over the city.' On 26 December, as Mao Zedong turned seventy-three, representatives of a newly forged nationwide alliance of temporary workers met with Jiang Qing and other members of the Cultural Revolution Group in the Great Hall of the People. Jiang Qing applauded them: 'Chairman Mao is backing you!' She urged them to attack the contract system, which she saw as a capitalist system instituted by Liu Shaoqi and his cronies to cut state costs at the expense of the proletariat. She personally denounced the minister of labour. 'Let him become a temporary worker!' Yao Wenyuan quipped. A larger meeting followed at the Workers' Stadium, as one enraged demonstrator after another appeared on stage to denounce exploitative working conditions, decrepit housing and a starvation diet. Many of them went on to camp in front of the Ministry of Labour.[22]

In her inflammatory speech at the Great Hall of the People, Jiang Qing ordered the Ministry of Labour to reinstate all workers, permanent and temporary, who had been fired since 1 June 1966 as a direct result of their criticism of enterprise leaders. Their salaries were to be paid retrospectively. Her decision was published the same day by the *People's Daily*, along with an injunction further prohibiting local cadres from exacting any form of revenge against workers who participated in the Cultural Revolution. That evening, celebrating his birthday with members of the Cultural Revolution Group, the Chairman gave a toast: 'To the unfolding of a nationwide civil war!'[23]

––––––––

Compared to the students, who had been catalysed into action over the summer, the entrance of the workers into the revolution was a much slower process, but one that would have equally far-reaching consequences. Nowhere was this more evident than in Shanghai, the base from which the Cultural Revolution had been launched a year earlier.

When Red Guards from Beijing had laid siege to the offices of Mayor Cao Diqiu in early September, thousands of loyal workers had been mobilised to rebuff their demands. It appeared to be a stalemate, as neither side managed to gain the upper hand. But after the *Red Flag* editorial of 1 November, accusing leading party members of 'directing their spearhead against the revolutionary masses', rebel workers joined the fray. In the Shanghai Number Seventeen Cotton Textile Mill, where months earlier the work team had labelled Wang Hongwen a 'self-seeking careerist' for stirring up discontent among the factory's workers, a rebel organisation was established. Wang took the lead: 'What if the Public Security Bureau finds out, declares us counter-revolutionaries, and arrests us? Are you afraid or not? I'm not afraid! I'm determined to rebel!'[24]

A midnight raid was carried out on a fabric shop, where bolts of red cloth were commandeered to make armbands. On 9 November, the organisation popularly known as the Red Workers was formally inaugurated on Cultural Plaza, the former Canidrome in the French Concession where greyhound races had once been hosted. Mayor Cao Diqiu spurned the event, referring to the rebel workers as the 'dregs of humanity'. Right after the inaugural event, more than 20,000 workers marched to the city hall, demanding that their organisation be recognised. As the protesters waited for hours in the pouring winter rain, news of a telegram sent by Zhou Enlai did the rounds: 'If the Shanghai Municipal Committee does not want to see you, come to Beijing. I will see you!' It was a rumour, but it caused a rush to the railway station. Over a thousand workers forced their way on to an express train bound for Beijing, but the railway authorities shunted it off on to a siding some twenty minutes out of Shanghai. The rebels refused to get off the train. Some lay down on the tracks, holding red flags. When local officials organised hot water and buns for the passengers, some of the food was thrown out of the window: 'We do not wish to eat this revisionist food!'

After transportation between Shanghai and Nanjing had been paralysed for thirty hours, the deadlock was finally broken by Zhang Chunqiao, the brooding man who as director of propaganda in the Shanghai party machine had helped Jiang Qing a year earlier. Now a member of the Cultural Revolution Group, he was sent by military plane to sort out the dispute, bringing with him a message from Chen Boda. Standing in the back of a lorry in the heavy rain, he addressed rebels through a loudspeaker, urging them to return to Shanghai.[25]

The rebels won the day, gaining official recognition from Beijing. A mass rally was held a few days later under the auspices of Zhang Chunqiao, comfortably ensconced in a suite of rooms at the Peace Hotel on the Bund.

The party machine now changed tack, organising their own force to keep the rebels in check. They were better funded and much larger in number than the Red Guards. By the middle of December, Shanghai looked like a city under siege, as massive battles were staged between hundreds of thousands of Red Workers and a million Scarlet Guards. One of the bloodiest clashes took place on Kangping Road on 30 December, as 100,000 rebels armed with iron pipes, clubs and bamboo poles launched an assault on 20,000 of their opponents guarding the municipal party committee. Wang Hongwen personally led the charge, which caused close to a hundred casualties. On Zhang Chunqiao's instructions, Scarlet Guard offices in factories around the city were ransacked, armbands were confiscated and several hundred leaders were rounded up.

In an attempt to whittle down support for the rebels, factory administrations started awarding special bonuses to outstanding workers, agreeing to wage increases, issuing travel vouchers and granting windfall bonuses. They turned the editorial of the *People's Daily* published on Mao's birthday to their own advantage, attempting to mollify the ranks of the opposition by acceding to some of their demands. There are no complete statistics, but according to one study some 38 million yuan were withdrawn from the banks, nearly twice the usual amount, in the first week of January 1967 alone. The amount of money sent in the direction of the rebels was such that a run on the banks followed, as people were afraid that they were going under. A shopping spree ensued, soon superseded by panic buying, as it was feared that shops would run out of daily necessities such as charcoal briquettes and cooking oil.[26]

Chaos extended into the countryside, as tens of thousands of villagers entered the city to join the rebels. In some fields around Shanghai, only the women and the elderly were left to till the fields. With blocked ports, paralysed railway stations and a workforce fighting the revolution,

Shanghai was threatened by critical shortages. Although the city needed 3,500 tonnes of grain a day, by New Year's Eve there were not enough provisions to cover a week. Coal reserves could keep the city warm for no more than five days.[27]

The deadlock was broken on 3 January 1967, as a northern wind brought bitterly cold weather with sleet icing up the streets. Red Guards and rebel workers, wearing safety helmets and armed with iron bars, stormed two of the biggest newspapers, assuming control of the city's propaganda machine. Others took over the municipal television and radio stations. A few days later all the major thoroughfares into the city were barricaded. Wang Hongwen, leading tens of thousands of rebels at a mass rally, stormed the city hall, knocking over the two brass lions that flanked the building. A huge red flag was raised to deafening cheers from the crowd. Factory sirens hailed the proletarian victory. On 11 January Mao dealt a fatal blow to the old order by sending a congratulatory telegram to the Red Workers. The entire nation, he wrote, should learn from Shanghai and seize power from those who followed the 'bourgeois reactionary line'.[28]

To 'seize power' became the motto of the day. As the Chairman put it in an editorial published by the *People's Daily* on 22 January, praising what was now called the 'January Storm' in Shanghai: 'If you have power, you have everything. If you don't have power, you have nothing . . . Unite yourselves, form a great alliance and seize power! Seize power!! Seize power!!!'

Enter the Army

The Chairman enjoined the masses to unite and seize power in order to sweep away the capitalist roaders who stood in the way of the proletarian revolution. But party leaders were deeply entrenched, adept at deflecting the opposition and able to harness mass organisations to their own advantage. In many cities across the country, rebels and royalists had fought each other to a stalemate. Meanwhile, the 'revolutionary masses' themselves were hardly united. Even in Shanghai the Red Workers were not a disciplined army at the beck and call of Zhang Chunqiao and Wang Hongwen, but a fragile alliance of rebel outfits with very different allegiances from a wide variety of backgrounds. The moment the red flag went up over the municipal party committee, different constituencies started jostling for power and fighting each other.

The Chairman applauded the January Storm, but it had come at great cost, wrecking the local economy as hundreds of thousands of workers went on strike or became caught up in protracted battles that lasted for months on end. The chances of a red tide quickly washing away all followers of the 'bourgeois reactionary line' in the rest of the country were remote.

There were other issues. Mao did not trust the security apparatus, built up over many years by Luo Ruiqing, who had been minister of public security for a decade before becoming chief of staff in 1959. The Chairman was determined to smash the police, prosecutors and courts, which were all infiltrated by class enemies. A first step towards this goal was the public humiliation of Luo. Unable to walk after his suicide bid months earlier, he was carried to the Workers' Stadium in a basket, his left leg in bandages. For two days, on 4 and 5 January 1967, one delegation of Red Guards after another appeared on stage to voice their hatred, raising the audience's fury to fever pitch. Photos of Luo, forced to assume the jet-plane position by two soldiers, were widely disseminated.[1]

Instead of relying on the police, tainted by their association with the old order, the State Council turned to soldiers to assume some of the more urgent tasks of law enforcement. Banks were under huge pressure, forced in some cases to remit funds to mass organisations, and on 11 January soldiers with machine guns started appearing on their premises. The following day, soldiers were ordered to take over public security at radio stations, prisons, wharves, granaries and key bridges across the country.[2]

In a separate development, an entire province joined the revolutionary camp a few weeks after the January Storm in Shanghai. But it was hardly a revolution from below. Liu Geping, deputy governor of Shanxi province and a close associate of Kang Sheng, was in Beijing when Wang Hongwen stormed the city hall in Shanghai. Kang urged him on, telling him that the Chairman supported the rebels and hoped to see a whole string of similar revolutions across the country. Liu hurried back to Taiyuan, Shanxi's provincial capital, and with the support of one of the provincial military commanders put up a big-character poster announcing a rebel seizure of power. They faced opposition from their colleagues, but on 20 January the commander wrote to ask Lin Biao for his support. A mere sign from the country's second-in-command tipped the balance of military power. On 25 January the *People's Daily* celebrated the country's second power seizure.[3]

A similar request for assistance reached the Cultural Revolution Group on 21 January. In Anhui province, some 200,000 rebels were about to denounce the provincial party committee at a mass meeting, but feared that without military support they would fail in their bid to seize power. Months earlier, on 5 September 1966, the armed forces had been expressly instructed to stay out of the Cultural Revolution. Now the Chairman scribbled a note to Lin Biao: 'The military must be sent to support the broad masses on the left.' The army, Mao believed, had been asked not to intervene in the earlier stages of the Cultural Revolution, but this neutral attitude was 'fake'. Lin Biao agreed. Two days later, on 23 January, the army was ordered to send troops wherever the proletarian left asked for help.[4]

Before joining the Cultural Revolution, the army managed to wrangle major concessions out of the Chairman. Some military chieftains had become victims of the Red Guards, and there was widespread revulsion at the way in which several of them had been humiliated for hours on end in struggle meetings, beaten and forced to adopt the jet-plane position. In December 1966, Peng Dehuai, the marshal who had confronted the Chairman over the famine at the Lushan plenum in 1959, was hunted down in Sichuan and brought back to Beijing by a team of Red Guards acting on Jiang Qing's orders. Peng's ordeal was predictable. Like Luo Ruiqing, he was dragged out of prison to face interminable struggle meetings. One bystander remembers seeing him in an open lorry, surrounded by Red Guards. He was attempting to keep his head defiantly high, but a puny student kept on hitting him on the neck, trying to force him to bow in submission. 'I watched with horror. Here was a man who had fought all his life for the revolution, a man whom everyone in China knew, almost as a legend. If even he had no protection in this anarchy, then what of us ordinary people? I felt myself choking and I wanted to cry.'[5]

What also sent ripples through the military ranks was the treatment of He Long, a flamboyant, legendary marshal whose signature in the early guerrilla days had been a butcher's knife. He was senior to Lin Biao, and enjoyed widespread support in the army. In December dozens of Red Guards tried to track him down, although Zhou Enlai managed to shelter him in his personal residence.[6]

Several other marshals, including Xu Xiangqian and Ye Jianying, joined together and demanded that order, first of all, be restored within the military. Lin Biao, keen to protect his own power base in the military, acceded to these demands, submitting a document to the Chairman drafted in consultation with the army veterans. In essence, it shielded the army from assaults by rebel groups. The document contained a further trump card, granting the army the right to take 'resolute measures' against proven counter-revolutionaries and counter-revolutionary organisations.[7]

Mao had little choice. Neither the Red Guards nor the rebels had so far been able to unseat the 'capitalist roaders inside the party ranks'. The army was the only force capable of pushing through the revolution and bringing the situation under control. But by allowing the armed forces to decide who constituted the 'true proletarian left', the Chairman opened Pandora's box.

Less than a week after rebel workers had stormed the Shanghai Radio Station, the army took over. It was not welcome, but there was very little a loose aggregation of rebel groups could do. More restrictions followed. On 22 January all parks were closed by revolutionary decree to forestall their potential use by counter-revolutionaries. Cinemas were shut. The museum closed. The Great World, an amusement arcade renamed East is Red, was locked. People were still allowed to walk along Nanjing Road, but on 24 January more than a dozen lorries trundled down the main high street loaded with soldiers who chanted slogans and waved the Little Red Book. Three days later pamphlets were airdropped over the city, explaining that the People's Liberation Army was the most important tool of the Cultural Revolution and all genuine revolutionaries should support it.[8]

Zhang Chunqiao, with full backing from the Cultural Revolution Group, started eliminating his erstwhile allies, who were now contenders for power. He stressed discipline and obedience, reading out instructions from Lin Biao. Raids were launched against former supporters. A detachment of soldiers was sent to Fudan University to occupy the offices of a rival organisation. A raft of directives ordered people from revolutionary organisations to return to work. On 29 January the Cultural Revolution Group sent a telegram in support of Zhang, accusing some rebel leaders of having 'turned the spearhead of struggle' against him.[9]

Zhang Chunqiao's day came on 5 February, as a large rally was organised in People's Square to establish the new 'Shanghai People's Commune'. The name echoed the Paris Commune, a revolutionary government that briefly ruled France's capital in 1871 after the country's defeat by Germany. The commune loomed large in the socialist imagination, and was celebrated by Marx as a model of participatory democracy. Mao himself was an admirer of the Paris Commune. It was a bright Sunday afternoon, warm and cloudless, and thousands of scarlet, yellow and green banners went up. Small balloons with pennants were fired in canisters from several mortars. Those who watched the balloons float off could not fail to notice heavily armed troops on top of a number of buildings overlooking the square.[10]

'We have the mighty People's Liberation Army standing on our side,' Zhang declared, flanked by Yao Wenyuan. His first decree was to order the army and the police to 'resolutely suppress active counter-revolutionaries who undermine the Great Cultural Revolution, the Shanghai People's Commune and the socialist economy'. Half of the rebels stood defiantly outside, excluded from the inauguration.[11]

Zhang was jubilant. But just as Zhang did not want to share power with other rebels, the Chairman was not about to delegate the city to him. There was no congratulatory telegram from Beijing. A few weeks later, the Chairman reflected: 'If every province, city and region were called a people's commune, we would have to change the name of our country from People's Republic of China to People's Commune of China . . . Then what about the party? Where would we place the party? Where would we place the party committee? There must be a party somehow! There must be a nucleus, no matter what we call it.'[12]

In the early hours of 25 February the Shanghai People's Commune quietly changed its name to the Shanghai Municipal Revolutionary Committee. Cleaners had been busy all night, and by morning the word 'Commune' had almost completely disappeared. 'Revolutionary committees' were the new fad, and they would spread in the following eighteen months. They were supposed to be a show of unity between three major groups, namely rebel representatives, loyal party cadres and army officers. In reality they were dominated by the army.[13]

In many parts of the country, the army attempted to impose order. Few military leaders were impressed by the rebels, who responded to the call to 'seize power' by storming government premises, ransacking party offices and taking over newspapers and radio stations. Government officials denounced by the rebels had colleagues and friends in the military, and many of them were veteran revolutionaries devoted to the party. In the eyes of most army commanders, rebel organisations were dominated by individuals from dubious class backgrounds, the very people they had fought against in the revolution before 1949. They suspected that many of them were controlled by counter-revolutionaries, who used the Cultural Revolution as a pretext to attack the party and vent their resentment against socialism.

Violent clashes occurred in several provinces. In Shihezi, a major transportation hub in Xinjiang, the Muslim-dominated province where the country's first atomic test had been carried out in October 1964, the military sided with the old order in a concerted assault on rebel organisations, portrayed as remnants of the nationalist party and bad elements. By the end of January 1967, dozens of people had been mown down by machine guns.[14]

In Changsha in August 1966, tens of thousands of protesters had been branded as 'counter-revolutionaries' and 'rightists' after the mayor had used Red Guards to fight Red Guards. Since the Cultural Revolution stipulated that students could not be targeted, the bulk of the victims at the time were ordinary people. One rebel group, which named itself after the river that flows through the province, agitated on their behalf. The Xiang River Group gained an astonishing following all over Hunan, claiming a membership of 1 million by early 1967. It was a loose coalition, acting as an umbrella for a variety of smaller organisations that had mushroomed after Mao had called on the masses to 'educate and liberate themselves' in October. People flocked to join their ranks – workers, teachers, shop assistants, even government employees and local cadres who saw a change in the wind.

Energised by the January Storm in Shanghai, the Xiang River Group tried to seize power in Changsha. But unlike the Red Workers in Shanghai, it did not have a powerful backer in Beijing. When a group of disgruntled veterans affiliated with the Xiang River Group assaulted a local command post, they alienated the military, who portrayed the incident as an armed uprising of counter-revolutionary elements abetted by ex-convicts. Chen Boda personally ordered a crackdown. Martial law was proclaimed. A massive manhunt was organised by the army, as tens of thousands of students, teachers, workers and army veterans were hunted down. Schools and factories were converted into prisons. In a scenario that would become all too familiar, a rival rebel group actively assisted the army in hunting down their competitors for power.[15]

In Fujian, where the military commander Han Xianchu had taken over from Ye Fei, the rebels were in close touch with the military, regularly visiting the headquarters to play ping-pong and basketball or watch propaganda movies. But here, too, a split occurred, as some mass organisations denounced the military command as adherents of the 'reactionary bourgeois line'. They demanded that Han step down. Rumours started circulating, claiming that Chen Boda was secretly encouraging the rebels to attack Han Xianchu.

Further south in the province, after the call to seize power Ken Ling and the rebels succeeded in beating the municipal party committee and its defenders. They established the Xiamen People's Commune, taking their lead from Shanghai. Within days, entire sections of the local government fell in line, handing over power to the rebels. The royalists had the backing of the local police, and soon both camps were fighting each other over control of the three-storey Public Security Bureau. Rebel workers lent a hand, storming the compound and attacking the police, ripping off their badges and knocking off their caps. Uninvited, powerful local gangs joined the fray. They loathed the police more than anyone else, and they had excellent fighting skills. More than a hundred people were injured. Local people rejoiced, some of them rushing to help, bringing baskets of oranges and lining the streets to cheer the rebels.

It was a strategic mistake, as Han Xianchu and the provincial military command condemned the attack. The military in Xiamen intervened, ordering the rebels to surrender. Hundreds of people were arrested and tried in public on the square before the Workers' Palace of Culture, where the rebels had established their headquarters. Ken Ling was on a blacklist and fled the province.[16]

The worst confrontation took place in Qinghai, the barren province to the east of Xinjiang, dominated by steppe and desert. After weeks of skirmishes between rebels and royalists, the deputy commander of the military sent his troops on 23 February to quell an organisation that had seized control of the main newspaper. At first all the loudspeakers attached to the office block housing the newspaper were shot down. A barrage of gunfire followed, killing all those who defended the entrance to the building. The army had prepared several flamethrowers, but these turned out to be unnecessary as the rebels were unarmed. All resistance crumbled. The army took less than twenty minutes to storm the premises. More than a hundred people were killed in the assault, including a seven-year-old girl crying by the side of her injured father. The bodies were hastily buried in a mass grave. When the deputy commander telegraphed his report to Ye Jianying in Beijing, the marshal complimented him. Lin Biao and Mao Zedong, eager to protect the army, did not intervene. In the following week some 10,000 people were arrested, many of them tried as 'counter-revolutionaries' and sent off to the gulag. As one historian of the Cultural Revolution has observed, the crackdown was more violent than any of the killings perpetrated by warlords or foreign powers during the republican era.[17]

Rebels were also condemned as 'counter-revolutionaries' and violently suppressed by the army in other provinces, such as Hubei, Guangdong, Sichuan and Inner Mongolia. Xu Xiangqian and Ye Jianying, the army veterans who had managed to have the army officially shielded from assaults by rebel groups in late January, were in the ascendant. In mid-February they identified a further opportunity to consolidate their power against the Cultural Revolution Group.

Mao, by late January, was increasingly annoyed with the group headquartered at the Diaoyutai State Guesthouse. Its members were squabbling among themselves. Kang Sheng and Chen Boda could not stand each other. Jiang Qing had an imperious style and tended to overshadow her colleagues. Despite massive logistical support, the group seemed disorganised and tended to take matters into its own hands without sending regular reports to the Chairman. Zhang Chunqiao, for one, had gone out on a limb by inaugurating the Shanghai People's Commune without any form of consultation.

The irritated Chairman, in a meeting he summoned on 10 February, thought it time to bring the group down a peg or two. He accused its members of political inexperience and told them that they were arrogant. He termed Chen Boda an 'opportunist' who in the past had tried to exploit the divide between himself and Liu Shaoqi. Mao turned on his own wife:

'As for you, Jiang Qing, you have great aspirations but not an ounce of talent, and you look down on everyone else.' It was a bruising encounter. 'It looks to me like it's still the same as it was before. You don't report to me, you block me out!'[18]

When the army leaders learned of this outburst, they sensed an opportunity to reverse the course of the Cultural Revolution. At a meeting of the central leadership the following day, Ye Jianying laid into Chen Boda, who was still shaken from the Chairman's accusation. 'You have made a mess of the government, a mess of the party, a mess of the factories and the countryside! And still you think it's not enough, you are determined to make a mess of the army as well!' Xu Xiangqian banged the table and mentioned the rebel leader from Tsinghua University: 'What do you want? For people like Kuai Dafu to lead the army?'

Five days later, at a second session, the marshals went further. Tan Zhenlin, who had been the Chairman's most faithful agricultural aide during the Great Leap Forward, was scathing when Zhang Chunqiao mentioned the masses: 'What masses? Always the masses, the masses. There is still the leadership of the party! You don't want the party's leadership, and all day long you keep on talking about how the masses should liberate themselves, educate themselves and free themselves. What is all this stuff? It's all metaphysics!' He flew into a rage: 'Your aim is to purge the old cadres. You are knocking them down one by one, until there is not a single one of them left.'

The most inflammatory comments came from Chen Yi, the feisty and outspoken minister for foreign affairs who had conquered Shanghai in 1949. He pointed out that during the Yan'an days in the Second World War, Liu Shaoqi, Deng Xiaoping and Peng Zhen had professed to be the most enthusiastic supporters of Mao Zedong Thought while he and the other military veterans around the table had been taken to task. Khrushchev, too, had embraced Stalin when he was still alive.

As the brawl between the two groups developed, Zhou Enlai said very little, making sure that he could not be implicated in any of the more extreme comments made by the marshals. When Tan Zhenlin was about to storm out of the session, Zhou pounded the table, demanding that he return to the meeting.[19]

The outburst was nothing less than a collective assault by military leaders on the Cultural Revolution. It was a turning point, one in which the very fate of the Chairman's vision was at stake. Never before had such a powerful group directly attacked a campaign initiated by Mao himself. If the marshals prevailed, Liu Shaoqi and Deng Xiaoping could soon make a comeback, exacting revenge for all the humiliation they had endured and wrecking the reputation of the Chairman.

Mao considered his position carefully and realised that he needed to gain the support of two people to outmanoeuvre the opposition. Lin Biao was easily won over. Mao quoted Chen Yi's comments about how Khrushchev had been Stalin's most faithful follower, which could be interpreted as a direct swipe at Lin's position as heir apparent. Chen Yi's attitude indicated that Lin did not have widespread support in the higher echelons of power. Mao further cemented his relationship with Lin by reaching out to his wife, asking Ye Qun to join the Cultural Revolution Group.

But the key was Zhou Enlai. He could have tilted the balance of power towards the marshals by rallying to their cause. But the premier had made his career by vowing never to antagonise the Chairman. He had not intervened to restrain the meeting, but he had also tactically withheld any explicit support. Mao ordered the Cultural Revolution Group to stop circulating any document critical of the premier.[20]

Having secured the support of the two most important players behind the scenes, the Chairman summoned a meeting in the early hours of 19 February with leading members of the party. In a vituperative encounter, he bullied the marshals into submission. He ranted at length, declaring that the meetings at which the military leaders had attacked the Cultural Revolution Group were targeted at him personally and at Lin Biao. As Lin Biao was absent from the meeting, he warned his wife: 'Comrade Ye Qun, you tell Lin Biao that he is not safe either. Some people are trying to seize his power and he should be prepared!' Mao vowed to oppose anyone who undermined the Cultural Revolution Group, which had made errors amounting to 'no more than two or three per cent' when compared to their achievements. In an echo of the bombastic threats he had made at the Lushan plenum in 1959, Mao vowed to take to the mountains and start a guerrilla war together with Lin Biao. 'You say that Jiang Qing and Chen

Boda are no good. Well, let Chen Yi become the head of the Cultural Revolution Group! Arrest and execute Chen Boda and Jiang Qing, send Kang Sheng into exile. I, too, will step down!' Everyone present was stunned. Kang Sheng later confided that he had never seen the Chairman so angry. 'He was in a proletarian rage.'[21]

Struggle meetings against Tan Zhenlin, Chen Yi and Xu Xiangqian followed, all of them chaired by Zhou Enlai, in the very room in Zhongnanhai where they had led the attack on the Cultural Revolution Group and where they had been granted their military titles years earlier. All opposition collapsed. The standing committee of the powerful Politburo, which for years had dominated the party, became paralysed. The Cultural Revolution Group now ran the show. Zhou had to obey Madame Mao. 'From now on you make all the decisions,' he grovelled, 'and I will make sure that they are carried out.'[22]

On 8 March, Marshal Ye Jianying invited the deputy commander of Qinghai who had used troops to put down rebels to Beijing. The People's Liberation Army had its own venue where the military elite could meet behind closed doors to hammer out important deals, namely a Soviet-style hotel in the west of Beijing. In the Capital West Hotel, built in 1964, the deputy commander was fêted as a model in crushing counter-revolutionary insurgencies. For three days, he proudly explained his pacification methods to military leaders from other regions, who were keen to learn how to contain the rebels. But Mao, who had gone along with the suppression of rebels in Qinghai for several weeks, now intervened. Ye Jianying and Xu Xiangqian were forced to write their own self-criticisms, accepting that their handling of the situation in Qinghai had been a serious error. The deputy commander and his allies were thrown into prison. The rebels in Qinghai were hailed as martyrs.[23]

But the role of the army did not diminish. On 19 March, the Military Affairs Commission, now firmly in the hands of Lin Biao, asked the army to exert control, taking over the running of government units from schools and factories up to huge administrative entities such as ministries and entire provinces. Over the following months some 2.8 million soldiers left their barracks to occupy key positions across the country, closely shadow-ing the party and state structures. A few days later, Kang Sheng explained what military control meant: 'Military control is autocratic rule. You obey me in everything. You put out a public notice in which you announce that you obey me.'[24]

The military team that arrived at Zhai Zhenhua's school in March did not bother to hold a meeting with the Red Guards. They simply gathered the students and announced that the Red Guards had helped the work teams in pushing the bourgeois reactionary line. They had persecuted stu-dents from bad class backgrounds instead of directing their fire at capitalist roaders. The students were asked to rise up against them, as the Red Guards were forced to confess their errors in class. From revolutionary leader, Zhai became a revolutionary target overnight. A new group of student leaders emerged, supervised by a platoon leader. Zhai was cast aside.[25]

In Zhengding, thirty-six soldiers with backpacks marched into Gao Yuan's school. For the first time since September, the students actually sat together in the same room, exchanging stories about their adventures travelling around the country. The officer in charge brought a sense of order to the class, making sure that the students were roused before dawn, compelling them to practise drill formations on the sports field each day. Much time was spent studying Mao Zedong Thought.[26]

It seemed as if the revolution was coming to an end. The students who had run amok were all back in class, subjected to a regime of strict mili-tary discipline. Workers were back at their posts. Rebels who had been caught on the wrong side of the political divide were asked to return to the Chairman's 'proletarian revolutionary line' after making a self-criticism. Unity was praised, as the propaganda machine trumpeted a great alliance between the military, the revolutionary cadres and mass organisations that would surge ahead and sweep away all factional differences. In the capital, posters and slogans were removed from buses, and shop windows were scraped clean. It was springtime, and a few young couples even dared to walk hand in hand. People sat outside in the sun on their doorsteps, a few playing badminton in the side-streets.[27]

It was a fragile truce. Even in Shanghai, firmly under the thumb of Zhang Chunqiao, getting students back to class after half a year of mayhem was a challenge. There was the sheer extent of the damage inflicted on school buildings. Less than half of them had managed to avoid major destruction, and one in five had to be completely written off. Many had broken doors, shattered windows and damaged roofs, not to mention the tables, chairs and blackboards that had been smashed up. Even where classes were resumed, education was intermittent. A few opened their doors for only two or three hours a week. Some of the students did not turn up. In the Ningbo Road Primary School and the Nanjing East Road Primary School, schoolchildren had formed gangs with names like 'Tokyo' or 'Field Army', roaming the neighbourhood in search of public property to vandalise. They stole light bulbs, telephones, microphones and bicycles from their own schools, as well as locks, windowpanes and cables. A few smoked and gambled. They beat people up, sometimes for a fee (the going rate in March 1967 was 10 yuan per victim). Fear reigned among the teachers, who continued to be spat at by some of the more rebellious students. Excrement was thrown at them from the upper floors.[28]

The peace did not last. The Chairman had sought to dampen down the revolutionary fires, forcing the different rebel factions across the country to unite under the single command of the army. But he did not want to extinguish the revolution.

In April he shifted the balance of power towards the rebels. First, a new directive introduced limits on the power of the military to stigmatise people as counter-revolutionaries and arrest them arbitrarily. Victims who had been arrested for having stormed military district commands were to be rehabilitated. This had already happened in Qinghai. Now the Cultural Revolution Group wanted to rescue other rebels from the hands of the military. In Sichuan, where the People's Liberation Army had arrested over 100,000 people after rebels had besieged the military command in Chengdu for a full week in February, some 28,000 victims were released from prison.[29]

The *People's Daily* began praising the 'revolutionary young generals', telling them that they had been following the correct line all along and should resolutely fight against the forces of revisionism. But the most important command came from the Military Affairs Commission under Lin Biao. On 6 April it prohibited the army from firing on rebels, disbanding mass organisations or retaliating against those who raided military commands.[30]

These documents were widely copied, circulated and posted. The situation was reversed within days. Rebel organisations that had been disbanded by the army were revived. People who had been labelled 'rightist' or 'bad elements' became hopeful. Students took to the streets again, shouting 'To Rebel is No Crime!' In some schools they were given armbands and paraded the streets. Other rebels followed, including workers and government employees. Rumours circulated that army commanders openly shielded capitalist roaders and colluded with them to establish independent kingdoms. The rebels were needed once again. Many of them were jubilant, embracing the Chairman as their saviour and supreme commander.[31]

A day after the army had been prohibited from using violence against rebels, the *Beijing Daily* opened fire on Liu Shaoqi, who had been under house arrest since his fall from grace in August 1966. On 10 April, Kuai Dafu, acting on detailed instructions from Jiang Qing and Zhou Enlai, assembled a crowd of 300,000 at Tsinghua University to humiliate Wang Guangmei, the 'stinking wife of China's Khrushchev'. A number of female Red Guards forced her to put on a tight-fitting dress with a high neck and slit skirt as well as high-heeled shoes. It was the attire in which she had appeared in Indonesia during a goodwill mission in 1963. A necklace made of ping-pong balls further mocked the pearl jewellery she had worn to make herself 'a whore with Sukarno'. She shivered as she was being pushed around on the stage, tripping in her shoes, her hair tousled. The audience went wild, as people tried to climb on each other's shoulders for a better view. Posters appeared the next day, accompanied by caricatures of Wang tottering on the stage in her improvised dress and fake necklace.[32]

The propaganda machine spewed out rants against the former head of state. The campaign was intended to unify the rebel organisations and help direct their fire at Liu and his agents in the party machine. In Zhengding, students were given copies of an article from the party journal *Red Flag* that criticised Liu Shaoqi. Gao Yuan and his schoolmates began to write posters attacking the officially designated target. 'It was a fine show of unity against a common enemy.'[33]

But the alliance was too frail to last. Instead of following the cues from Beijing, victims in many parts of the country sought retaliation against their erstwhile oppressors. Many of them had spent weeks in crowded, insanitary prisons, where they had been humiliated, beaten and forced to confess. They had been fed a starvation diet. They wanted revenge. They attacked rival factions and turned against the military, whose hands were now tied. This was true not only for provinces where the army had sided with the old order. In Shanxi, where Kang Sheng and his puppet Liu Geping had engineered a rebel coup from above, many of those persecuted as 'capitalist roaders' were spoiling for a fight. The result was a new tide of violence.[34]

Riots against the army broke out across the country, as rebels demanded that the military release their comrades still in custody, rehabilitate those labelled as 'counter-revolutionaries' and apologise for the suppression of mass organisations. The Cultural Revolution entered a new phase, as students, workers and government employees split into two factions, those who relied on the army and those who opposed it. Both sides claimed to represent the true revolution, although often they were hard to tell apart.

The situation on the ground was further complicated by the fact that the army itself was divided. At the very top, a line ran between Lin Biao and his supporters on the one hand and the veteran marshals on the other. The heir apparent had scored a huge victory when the Chairman had crushed the marshals in late February. It almost looked like a coup within a revolution, as Lin's followers benefited from the fallout inside the army. But Mao was wary of his second-in-command, and made an attempt at reconciliation with the marshals in April. They, too, should be part of his grand plan for unity, the Chairman told the old soldiers. He promised that they could make an appearance on the rostrum in Tiananmen Square for the annual parade on May Day.[35]

As different mass organisations embraced different army units in each province, the daily battles between factions began turning some cities into battlegrounds. In Xiamen, Ken and his faction came out of hiding and sided with an anti-aircraft artillery regiment sent by the Fuzhou Military

Region. Their opponents embraced the Thirty-First Army Corps and the local military command instead. Each faction reinforced the buildings under their control with barbed wire. There was round-the-clock surveillance, as raids against each other were staged at night. The weapons now included knives, clubs, javelins and crude spears improvised by tying scissors to the end of a wooden pole. Lime, sulphuric acid and pesticide were also used, spread through fire hoses. The combatants routinely wore rattan and metal helmets, stolen from the fire brigade. Special training grounds were set up to practise scaling walls and crawling through barbed-wire fences. There were planning rooms to pore over military strategy, often with the help of military advisers or retired security personnel. There were departments for external affairs, finances, transportation and security, as each faction started shadowing the state in its attempt to rule the city.

At first, both factions clashed without any direct involvement of the military. But many rebels were keen to avenge their previous persecution, and soon there were direct assaults on the army. Ken and a thousand students from his Eighth Middle School raided the offices of the local military command, smashing the dishes and bowls of the soldiers who were eating lunch. They seized protective gear and seven vehicles. Restrained by standing orders forbidding them to open fire, the soldiers did not intervene.

Word went around that Jiang Qing and Chen Boda supported the rebels. The skirmishes increasingly polarised the city, as members of each faction did the rounds, inciting people to cut electricity wires, poison the water supply or otherwise harass neighbours who supported the opposition. Entire suburbs became no-go zones for people on the wrong side of the divide.[36]

A similar scenario unfolded in other parts of the country. In Zhengding too, the conflict moved beyond the school walls, as entire organisations and work units began to align themselves with one faction or another. Gao Yuan's faction was supported by a missile-engineering institute directly under the command of the General Staff Headquarters in Beijing. Their opponents were backed by the local military command in Shijiazhuang, an austere, modern railway hub just south of Zhengding where factories had shot up with Soviet assistance in the 1950s. Gao Yuan, like Ken Ling in Xiamen, became deeply involved in urban guerrilla warfare, as buildings were seized, enemy leaders kidnapped and prisoners exchanged. Skirmishes took place at night around strategic strongholds, often against invisible enemies, as the sound of muffled running and occasionally the crash of shattering glass punctuated the silence. Every casualty only increased the blood debt, contributing to a cycle of revenge and renewed violence.

By mid-July, the opposition had been forced to retreat to a building controlled by the Public Security Bureau. Gao and his friends set up giant catapults to shoot bricks into the compound, while loudspeakers on rooftops blared out propaganda. They had their own arsenal, where weapons were forged from high-carbon steel with the help of a blacksmith. A few students also made body armour from steel plate. As they prepared for the final assault, a figure holding a red flag emblazoned with her organisation's name appeared at a window on the third floor in the enemy camp. It was a schoolmate of Gao, but she was on the wrong team. 'I would rather die than surrender to you,' she screamed, before throwing herself from the windowsill. The red flag unfurled as she shouted 'Long Live Chairman Mao!' 'Her body lay perfectly still, enfolded in the flag.' A white flag was soon raised inside the compound, as all resistance crumbled.[37]

Even more ferocious battles took place in provincial capitals. In Sichuan, the lines were drawn between Li Jingquan and a couple popularly referred to as the two Tings. Li was a radical leader who had enthused about collectivisation, exclaiming at one point that 'Even shit has to be collectivised!' He had been one of Mao's most faithful supporters during the Great Leap Forward. After he had been presented with a report from the provincial security bureau claiming that some 8 million people had starved to death in Sichuan between 1958 and 1961, he compared the Great Leap Forward to the Long March, in which only one in ten soldiers had made it to the end: 'We are not weak, we are stronger, we have kept the backbone.'[38]

But Li Jingquan had allied himself with Liu Shaoqi during the Socialist Education Campaign. It was he who had presided over the demise of the entire leadership in neighbouring Guizhou province in 1964. The Chairman sided instead with Zhang Xiting and her husband Liu Jieting. Both had worked in an army unit that had participated in the invasion of Tibet in 1950, and were later posted in Yibin, a wealthy port city surrounded by bamboo forests along the Yangtze in southern Sichuan. They used their positions to engage in endless persecutions and political vendettas, and caused widespread starvation across the county. Critics of the famine were silenced. Their abuse of power was such that they were expelled from the party in 1965. But they appealed to a close friend in Beijing, namely Chen Boda. He introduced them to Jiang Qing, who recognised them as kindred spirits. The two Tings were rehabilitated in March 1967 and empowered to organise a Sichuan Revolutionary Committee.[39]

In April and May, hundreds of people were wounded in fierce battles between the two factions in Chengdu. Jung Chang saw processions of tens of thousands of rebels carrying the bloody corpses of people killed in the confrontations. Her own father, who had incurred the wrath of the two Tings, was arrested, denounced and paraded through the streets. Fighting was more vicious than elsewhere because the city was a centre for the arms industry. Some of the workers used hand grenades, automatic rifles, mortars and rocket-propelled grenade launchers.

This was true at the Sichuan Cotton Mill. Li Zhengan, whose eleven-year-old daughter had been made to clean the bedding for Red Guards, was asked to join the dominant faction in the mill or have her already meagre salary slashed even further. In the morning she washed clothes; in the afternoon she pulled bodies from the rubble. Ambulances ferried the injured to the hospital.[40]

The Cultural Revolution Group tried to impose its will on the provinces, but its mandate was limited. Even after Li Jingquan had been dismissed, the fighting continued. Much as Liu Shaoqi had installed his followers in the upper echelons, Li Jingquan had placed his people in key position of power. The two Tings were frail, even with Mao's backing. In Yibin, there was brutal fighting with guns, hand grenades, mortars and machine guns, dividing the army even further.

No one wanted to give up. Those on both sides were fuelled by mutual hatred, but also by the belief that they, rather than the opposition, were faithful followers of the Chairman. Most of all, the rebels and the royalists were fighting for their own political survival. They were defending their past choices. Many of the students, workers and cadres involved in the Cultural Revolution had been forced to make rapid choices in extraordinarily confused circumstances. The situation changed constantly, with bewildering reversals in fortune dictated by the whimsical policies emanating from Beijing. People drifted towards different sides of the divide, ending up fighting their own friends, colleagues and even family members. And all of them realised that if they were exposed, the victors would brand them as 'rightists' and 'counter-revolutionaries'. At best they would be driven out of their work units and lose all their benefits, forced to eke out a living on the margins of society. At worst they would be sent to the gulag. They were fighting for their own survival. As one historian of the Red Guards has observed, they were trapped in a cycle of violence and the prospect of losing had become unthinkable.[41]

The Arms Race

By June 1967 China was in chaos. From Dalian in the north to Guangzhou in the south, many freight workers and longshoremen no longer turned up in the country's main ports. Each day, an average of 138 ships had to be berthed and unloaded, but more than half had to wait at anchorage for a month. In Manchuria, the industrial powerhouse of the country, scores of factories relying on shipping stopped production. In Shanghai, the revolutionary committee was forced to turn schools, temples and other public spaces into makeshift storage rooms, as hundreds of lorries tried to clear 400,000 tonnes of abandoned freight. In Chongqing, the army had to intervene, tackling the backlog in the inland port.[1]

Trains were congested. Even though free travel for Red Guards had been abolished more than half a year earlier, streams of rebel delegations went to the capital, seeking redress or petitioning the party. Rows of people wrapped in their quilts could be seen sleeping outside the huge, brass-studded gates of the State Council, waiting to see Zhou Enlai. But, most of all, factional fighting paralysed entire trunks of the railway system. Hardly a day went by without some section of the national network falling victim to one mass organisation or another. On 16 May, over a hundred rival Red Guards fought each other while trying to board a freight train in Shanghai, forcing all traffic to a standstill for many hours. The following day a different group of rebels blocked a train bound for Hangzhou. Across the city, there were 'railway guerrilla troops' who specialised in breaking windows, assaulting passengers and beating up conductors.[2]

Crime was rampant, even by the standards of the time, when beating a 'capitalist' or raiding the home of a 'revisionist' was deemed a revolutionary act. In Shanghai, petty thieves could be found near markets, wharves, stations, shops and parks. In May 1967 the police arrested six times as many pickpockets at the North Railway Station as a year before. Robberies were on the increase, with most of the culprits young people, many of whom had acquired a taste for crime during the glorious days of red August.[3]

Mob justice took over, as a few cases reported from Shanghai illustrate. On 28 May 1967, an apprentice was beaten to death by a crowd, allegedly for having 'humiliated' a girl. The following day, rebels arrived at the house of Zhao Ada, knocked down his door, took him, his son and his daughter into custody and beat them up for being 'hoodlums'. Zhao, an ordinary factory worker, died of his injuries. Later that week, a recently released prisoner who approached a woman on the Bund was beaten to death by Red Guards, who were cheered on by a crowd of onlookers. On 11 June, a mob killed a man accused by his second wife of having abused her six-year-old daughter. People started using the Cultural Revolution to right personal wrongs, exact retribution for past injustices or set up vigilante teams to impose their own version of justice.[4]

The revolutionary upsurge, meanwhile, was apparently heading nowhere. Instead of leading to unity between rebels, revolutionary cadres and the army, the movement was splintering further, producing ever more hostility and outright violence. Rather than support the revolutionary left in a final push for victory, the army was trying to fend off constant attacks by mass organisations suppressed by the military in the past. Most of all, since February only one new area had been liberated from the clutches of the reactionary bourgeois line, namely Beijing. A revolutionary committee was inaugurated with much fanfare in April, welcoming among others Nie Yuanzi, the author of the first big-character poster in Peking University in May 1966.

The revolution was failing to proceed according to plan. But since the Chairman was infallible, failure could only be the result of faulty execution. Some among the central leadership favoured a return to order, others advocated a more militant approach. Even before these tensions were resolved, events in Wuhan changed the parameters of the revolution, ushering in an arms race that would lead to a whole new level of violence.

———

Wuhan, along with Nanjing and Chongqing, is called one of China's three furnaces. Located at the confluence of two major rivers, studded with lakes, it is frequently flooded by heavy rain and engulfed by stifling heat and humidity during the summer. Wuhan is also a busy inland port and transportation hub, transformed into a base for heavy industry in the 1950s. Mao visited the city at the height of the Great Leap Forward in September 1958 to inaugurate a giant iron and steel combine built with Soviet help, looking on as the molten iron from the first firing flowed out of the furnace.

In Wuhan, as elsewhere, sporadic fighting between the two main factions had continued for months, marked by lethal bursts of violence as thousands of combatants clashed with crowbars and homemade weapons. The old order had the upper hand, as the party leaders were protected by a citywide organisation of office employees, skilled workers, party activists and militiamen, boastfully called the Million Heroes. The rebels were a coalition composed of iron and steel workers, students and Red Guards from Beijing. In June they were under siege and threatened with complete annihilation, as the Million Heroes commandeered lorries to assault their stronghold across the Yangtze River Bridge, where the Wuhan Iron and Steel Company was located. Dozens of defenders died as the rebel headquarters were captured.

Chen Zaidao, the regional military commander, openly backed the Million Heroes. Determined to crush the opposition, he took little notice of Lin Biao's command in April, which prohibited the army from firing on rebels or disbanding their organisations.

Zhou Enlai flew to Wuhan on 14 July, keen to transmit orders from Beijing on the status of rebel organisations directly to the local leaders. He was joined in the evening by the Chairman, who was touring the south of the country on his private train. That same day other delegates were summoned to Wuhan to help with the negotiations, including Xie Fuzhi, the minister of public security who had urged the police to support the Red Guards in August 1966, and Wang Li, a suave man with a bankerly appearance who was used to travelling the country and cutting deals on behalf of the Cultural Revolution Group.

Zhou and his emissaries declared their support for the rebels in a series of stormy meetings with the top brass from the regional military command. There was great resistance, but in a private meeting Mao managed to convince Chen Zaidao that it was time for a self-criticism. Chen, loyal to the Chairman, gave in. Zhou flew back to Beijing, believing that the crisis had been resolved.

It was a premature move, as Chen Zaidao was unable to control the tense situation in the city. As rumours spread that the Million Heroes had become the target of a delegation headed by Xie Fuzhi and Wang Li, angry soldiers turned up in the evening at their hotel on the East Lake. In the early hours of 20 July, they dragged Wang to the military headquarters, where an enraged crowd beat him, tore out clumps of his hair and broke his ankle.

Lin Biao, who had a longstanding loathing for Chen Zaidao dating back to the civil war, when the military leader of Wuhan had served under Xu Xiangqian, sensed an opportunity to deal another blow to the veteran marshals who had opposed him in February. He played up the incident, sending one of his followers, Qiu Huizuo, with an alarmist letter endorsed by Jiang Qing, warning the Chairman that his life was in danger. Mao was furious, suspecting Lin of using him as a pawn in his own game, but went along after having spoken to Zhou Enlai, who had hurried back to Wuhan. The Chairman was escorted by air force fighters to Shanghai. Chaos descended on Wuhan, as bridges were closed, communication routes blocked, strategic buildings occupied and the airport seized. Sirens sounded over the river, while loudspeaker vans blared slogans denouncing the rebels. Lorries careened through the streets, as the Million Heroes attacked their enemies throughout the city.

Li Zuopeng, deputy commander of the navy, was already in Wuhan to protect the Chairman. He was reinforced by airborne divisions from neighbouring Hubei province. Xie Fuzhi and Wang Li were rescued in a rebel operation and smuggled out of the city two days later.

Lin Biao immediately denounced the Wuhan incident as a 'counter-revolutionary revolt'. The Chairman summoned all the Wuhan leaders to go and explain themselves in the capital, where the moment they landed they were surrounded by soldiers carrying rifles with fixed bayonets. They were questioned in a marathon meeting at the Capital West Hotel lasting six hours. Wu Faxian, commander-in-chief of the air force and protégé of Lin, was put in charge, shouting down and even slapping Chen Zaidao. Xu Xiangqian, his patron, was accused of standing behind the rebellion.

Outside, a million people marched in a great rally, welcoming Xie Fuzhi and Wang Li as martyrs of the revolution. Slogans denouncing the mutiny blared from loudspeakers: 'Down with Chen Zaidao!' On 27 July, a new team of military leaders close to Lin Biao took control over Wuhan, forcibly disarming the units that had suppressed mass organisations. The Million Heroes collapsed. The rebels celebrated the 'second liberation of Wuhan', persecuting tens of thousands of their enemies.[5]

When the Chairman had met Zhou Enlai and Wang Li on 18 July during his visit to Wuhan, he had toyed with the idea of arming students and workers. A week later, Wang and the Cultural Revolution Group under Madame Mao penned an editorial for *Red Flag* entitled 'The Proletariat Must Take Firm Hold of the Gun'. Published on 1 August, it called on mass organisations to seize weapons, invoking historic words from the Chairman: 'If we do not seize the barrel of the gun, if we do not use the revolutionary armed forces to oppose the counter-revolutionary armed forces, people will never be able to liberate themselves.' China's Khrushchev, the article went on, had placed his henchmen Peng Dehuai and Luo Ruiqing inside the People's Liberation Army to usurp power. Much as a handful of capitalist roaders must be pulled out of the party, a handful now needed to be dragged out of the army.[6]

That very same day, the Ministry of Defence held a banquet to celebrate the fortieth anniversary of the People's Liberation Army. The acting chief of staff Yang Chengwu gave the evening's speech, referring to Peng Dehuai and Luo Ruiqing as counter-revolutionary revisionists. The applause from the top brass was weary, their faces expressionless. But Jiang Qing enlivened the evening, rising from her seat with Ye Qun, the wife of Lin Biao, to walk among the younger generation of delegates with glass in hand. Dressed in a neatly pressed military uniform, a cap on her short wavy hair, she toasted the revolutionary rebels and young cadets, seated away from the centre of the dining hall. Neither woman spared a glance for the colonels and generals gathered for the occasion.[7]

The *Red Flag* editorial hailed Lin Biao as the most faithful follower of the Chairman. Lin used the call to arms to beef up the credentials of Wu Faxian, Qiu Huizuo and Li Zuopeng, the three men who had assisted him in his takeover of Wuhan. All three had served under Lin Biao in the

Fourth Field Army during the civil war, but had come under fire from the rank and file in the early months of 1967. Lin now denounced their attackers, demanding that the left be armed since 'bad people are fighting good people'. It was another shot aimed at his opponents inside the army, the 'handful of capitalist roaders' who were usurping power: 'This revolution is a revolution against the ones who carried out the revolution.' Together with Huang Yongsheng, the military leader in Guangdong, Wu Faxian, Qiu Huizuo and Li Zuopeng would soon become the heir apparent's 'four guardian warriors'.[8]

The *Red Flag* editorial was nothing short of a call for civil war. The revolutionary task was no longer to seize government power, but to seize military power. As the announcement was read over the radio, rebels throughout the country began assaulting arsenals and military commands in their search for weapons. A tidal wave of violence engulfed the country, as Madame Mao and Lin Biao worked in concert to increase their power.[9]

One of the first major battles took place in Shanghai. Days after the Chairman had arrived from Wuhan, Zhang Chunqiao requested that the workers be allowed to set up their own militias. Mao acquiesced. On 4 August, Wang Hongwen, the man who had led the assault on the city hall in January, assembled a small army of 100,000 workers armed with rattan hats and iron rods. Their target was a rebel faction that acted as a magnet for people holding a grudge against Zhang Chunqiao and Wang Hongwen – rebels excluded from power, students condemned as rightists, workers forced to disband their organisations. They were ensconced at the Shanghai Diesel Engine Factory, a sprawling complex set up with Soviet help a decade earlier. A crane was used to smash the metal gates, while bulldozers levelled the mighty brick wall surrounding the compound. Teams of fighters rushed through the breach, fanning out to capture the buildings one after the other in a carefully planned military operation. All opposition was crushed. Many of the rebels were beaten black and blue, a few left for dead by the wayside. Over a thousand people were injured, and eighteen died. Mao, after watching footage of the battle, complimented Wang Hongwen on his victory.[10]

It was only the start. Soon the workers in Shanghai acquired light weapons and anti-aircraft artillery. By 1970, they had grown to a force of 800,000 militants, many of them equipped with semi-automatic weapons manufactured in local factories.[11]

Armed battles were much more vicious elsewhere. Like the assault on the Shanghai Diesel Engine Factory, all were engineered from above. In Changsha, where a loose coalition of rebels under the Xiang River Group had been declared 'counter-revolutionaries' and brutally crushed months earlier on Chen Boda's personal order, on 10 August an urgent directive from Beijing overturned the verdict. Before the assembled provincial leaders, a representative of the People's Liberation Army solemnly read out a telegram from the Cultural Revolution Group declaring that the Hunan Military Command had erred in attacking the rebels. The army was to support the Xiang River Group, since it alone represented the true left. The provincial leader was declared a 'capitalist roader', and the Cultural Revolution Group replaced him with the party secretary of Shaoshan, Mao's birthplace.[12]

Hua Guofeng had built a huge memorial hall in Shaoshan dedicated to the Chairman three years earlier. Not unlike the Confucius Temple in Qufu, the complex included the former residence of the Chairman, the tombs of his parents, his private school, several ancestral temples and the obligatory statue. The Chairman was impressed. In June 1967 he had dispatched Zhou Enlai to negotiate Hua's release from the hands of a rebel organisation. Now that he was in charge of the province, his first order of business was to crush the opposition. The Forty-Seventh Army was there to help. It had served under Lin Biao as part of the Fourth Field Army.

Power shifted overnight, as rebels attacked their erstwhile oppressors. They were exacting revenge, storming strongholds belonging to their opponents, smashing the windows, tearing down the broadcast system, burning papers and beating captives with leather belts. Ordinary people were having a field day, taking out their anger on the party activists, model workers and loyal cadres who had sided with the old order to make their lives so miserable.

But soon the rebels started fighting among themselves, as they could not agree on which military faction they should support. They squabbled over the apportionment of power, as some of them were not given seats on the provisional party committee. Old comrades became sworn enemies, as people started battling for the right to wield power in the name of Chairman Mao. The guns distributed by the Forty-Seventh Army no longer sufficed. They stole from the local militias, broke into arsenals and attacked military bases. They had grenades, bayonets, machine guns, cannon and anti-aircraft missiles. In the stifling summer heat, bullets whistled past in the streets, sirens wailed in the distance and lorries sped by. A curfew was imposed, but even in daytime ordinary people out to buy food risked being hit by stray bullets if they went too close to some of the strategic buildings guarded by armed fighters. 'People crisscrossed their windows with tape to prevent their shattering as the city shook with explosions and gunfire.' Mortars were fired by inexperienced rebels. Some of the shells went astray, exploding on roofs, landing on the road or smashing into buildings. The night sky flashed. In daytime it glowed orange.[13]

Rebels used their weapons to secure dwindling food supplies, which were severely affected by a paralysed transportation system. There were endless cases of raids on grain shops. In August one on Panxi Lane, just off People's Road in central Changsha, was robbed repeatedly, losing several tonnes of rice. Lorries would come to an abrupt halt in front of the shop, allowing armed rebels to jump off the back and commandeer sacks of grain 'in support of the war'.[14]

Ordinary people took advantage of the civil war to pursue their own personal vendettas, and not just against their neighbours. Tens of thousands of villagers lived in Changsha without a permit. They beat up the civil servants in charge of the household registration system and ransacked their offices, prizing open chests of drawers in the hunt for documents. On twenty occasions that summer villagers pulled out a gun. In one case a disgruntled man brandished a revolver and shouted, 'I will shoot anyone who tells me that I cannot have a residence permit!' The scale of the unrest was unprecedented. In a single municipal district, in a mere ten days an estimated 2,600 people took part in similar incidents.[15]

Jiang Qing and Lin Biao were busy fomenting revolution across the country. In Gansu, one of the country's poorest provinces, their target was Wang Feng, a party leader who had taken away responsibility for agricultural management from the people's communes in the wake of Mao's Great Famine and given it back to the villagers. In 1960 Xi Zhongxun had recommended him. Wang Feng's position was increasingly precarious after the fall of his two other mentors, namely Peng Zhen and Deng Xiaoping. Wang became one of the first people whom the Chairman labelled a 'counterrevolutionary revisionist' during the Cultural Revolution.[16]

In Gansu, as in Hunan, the local military and the regional command were split. The country was divided into thirteen military regions, each covering two or three provinces, and named after the city where their headquarters were based. There were also provincial armies, subordinate to the military regions. The Lanzhou Military Region was a strategically vital part of the country, close to Xinjiang and Tibet. But the provincial army was also stationed in Lanzhou, and it was loyal to Wang Feng. Despite repeated instructions from Zhou Enlai, its commander refused to turn against his provincial boss. In May and June 1967, fierce confrontations tore the city apart. As elsewhere, a bewildering diversity of mass organisations tended to coalesce into two opposite factions. All were convinced that they were the true followers of Mao Zedong, but their opinions as to the loyalty of the local leaders were divided. One faction denounced Wang Feng and embraced Zhang Dazhi, the commander in charge of the Lanzhou Military Region. Its opponents saw Zhang Dazhi as the 'Chen Zaidao' of Lanzhou. They sided with Wang Feng and the provincial army.[17]

On 3 August, Beijing recognised the faction behind the Lanzhou Military Region as the 'true left'. Coming a mere two days after *Red Flag* had called on the proletariat to 'take firm hold of the gun', this was followed throughout the province by assaults on arsenals and weapon factories. In Tianshui a group of Red Guards stormed a dynamite factory, absconding with hundreds of kilos of explosives. They used machine guns and mortars in their pursuit of revolution. In Pingliang all roads in and out of the county seat were blockaded. 'City residents have nothing to eat, all factories have ground to a halt and shops are closed,' one report noted. Thousands of people turned against the army, including hundreds of children armed with improvised weapons. In Heshui prisoners in a labour camp banded together, assaulting their guards and ransacking the offices in search of weapons.[18]

In Lanzhou everyone seemed to be joining the fray. Workers lashed screwdrivers on to spear shafts. Stones were hauled in baskets on to the roofs of buildings around the city. Even waiters and cooks in the main hotel gathered around an anvil in the kitchen to make weapons. Opponents pursued each other in broad daylight. A mob surrounded one man, stabbing him with improvised javelins until he collapsed in a pool of blood. An old man running a small shop had a spear driven through his stomach. The streets were littered with bodies.[19]

All along, Kang Sheng provided detailed instructions to Red Guard delegations in private meetings in Beijing. On 10 August, he undermined Wang Feng, enjoining his audience to support the Lanzhou Military Region and ignore those who denounced its leader Zhang Dazhi as a local 'Chen Zaidao'.

But the leaders of the Cultural Revolution Group were not simply obedient followers of the Chairman. They used the campaign to settle their personal scores. In a one-party state, personal relations were far more important than ideology. Mao Zedong was not alone in easily taking offence, carefully noting every slight and using court politics to wreak revenge on his unwitting victims many years later. Madame Mao, decades earlier, had been left seething with resentment, forced to refrain from political activities the moment she married the Chairman. As head of the Cultural Revolution Group, she obsessively pursued family feuds and personal vendettas. The merest slip of the tongue in her presence could have fatal consequences.

Kang Sheng, too, was wilful and vindictive, excelling at concocting entirely fictitious accusations against his enemies. In September 1966, he wrote to the Chairman to express his suspicions of sixty-one leading party members who had surrendered to the nationalists in 1936 but had been allowed to recant by Liu Shaoqi. Liu Lantao, who had been Wang Feng's mentor as first secretary of the north-west, was one of them. Mao initially rejected what would become known as 'the Case of the Sixty-One Traitors', but in March 1967 changed his mind. In the following months Red Guards investigated some 5,000 cadres, encouraged by Kang Sheng to ferret out hidden traitors in the party ranks. Several were hounded to their deaths.[20]

In his meeting with Red Guards from Lanzhou, Kang pointed his finger at an erstwhile colleague who had crossed him in the early 1950s. 'You should get rid of Sha Tao,' Kang said, explaining that he was a spy who had changed his name and worked under Liu Shaoqi before liberation. One week later, Sha Tao was dragged out by the Red Guards in Lanzhou and beaten up. He lingered in gaol for six years, interrogated regularly about his connections with other suspects. He survived the ordeal, and an inquiry years later cleared his name.[21]

People now had weapons, and members of the Cultural Revolution Group encouraged them to fight in the name of revolution. In Chongqing, some Red Guards even managed to equip three gunboats with artillery cannon, clashing in August with a small fleet of ships manned by their opponents who opened fire with machine guns.[22] In Guangxi province, rebels raided freight trains with armaments in transit from the Soviet Union to Vietnam. On 19 August alone, thousands of anti-aircraft bullets were seized, fuelling the factional warfare.[23]

But the event that captured most foreign headlines was the burning of the British mission on the night of 22 August 1967. For months Red Guards had laid siege to the embassies of countries denounced as revisionist and imperialist. Earlier that year, a wall of hatred had started to surround the Soviet embassy, as crowds of self-righteous Red Guards blockaded the building, trapping 170 Russians inside. East European and even Western diplomats ran the gauntlet daily, insulted, spat upon and pushed around when bringing supplies of vodka, beer, bread and soup to their beleaguered colleagues. At one point, the Russians even filled their swimming pool with water, fearing that the municipality would cut off their supply. At night, the crowd lit bonfires, casting grim shadows of Soviet leaders lynched in effigy.[24]

In front of the Kenyan embassy, a straw figure with blackened face was hanged, dangling on the gate for many months. The Indonesian and Mongolian embassies were under permanent siege.[25]

All foreigners who expressed less than absolute loyalty became targets, but none attracted as much attention as the British. The reason was to be found some 2,000 kilometres south of the capital, in the crown colony of Hong Kong. The city had become a watching post for the outside world after the bamboo curtain came down on China in 1949, but in May 1967 violence spilled across the border from the mainland. Hong Kong was shaken out of its spectator status. A strike at a plastic-flower factory in Kowloon quickly developed into a major public disturbance, joined by thousands of picketing workers. Many of them lived in shared cubicles in crowded tenements in Kowloon, with street upon street of tall, dilapidated buildings. Revolutionary youths took to the streets to demonstrate against the colonial authorities, waving the Little Red Book and chanting revolutionary slogans. As tensions rose, protesters started throwing stones and bottles at the police, who responded with clubs and tear gas. Soon crowds began erecting barricades in the streets, overturning cars and setting fire to a double-decker bus.

The local communist party initially orchestrated the trouble, but Beijing soon came to the rescue, alleging that the British were committing 'fascist atrocities' in Hong Kong. The British chargé d'affaires in Beijing, a placid, much decorated Second World War officer called Donald Hopson, was summoned to the Foreign Ministry and presented with an ultimatum, including a demand that all those who had been arrested be released and compensated for their time in prison. London refused to answer.

Mass rallies in support of the protesters were organised in Guangzhou and Beijing. In Hong Kong posters went up demanding 'Blood for Blood'; others screamed 'Stew the White-Skinned Pigs'. Tens of thousands of students and workers went on strike. Loudspeakers blasted propaganda from the Bank of China, while a dozen newspapers loyal to Beijing churned out inflammatory literature. But the campaign failed to garner wider support. Hong Kong was a city built by wave after wave of refugees from the mainland, and few among the working population of 1.5 million had any illusions about communism. By the end of June, the strike had begun to run out of steam.

Then, on 8 July, across the white demarcation line that split the small fishing village of Sha Tau Kok into British and Chinese sectors, some 300 armed protesters stormed the police post. First the police were pelted with stones and bottles, but after a while a machine gun started stuttering across the border, fatally mowing down five policemen on the British side. The incident rekindled the violence, and riots soon paralysed much of Hong Kong.

A curfew was imposed, as the police started raiding suspected centres of communist activity. Protesters retaliated with a spate of bomb attacks on police stations and government buildings. By the end of July, bombs, mixed with many decoys, had been planted in theatres, parks, markets and other public venues, severely disrupting routine life. Many were home-made devices, crudely put together by extracting gunpowder from fire-crackers. But a few were lethal. One was wrapped like a gift, killing Wong Yee-man, a seven-year-old girl, as well as her brother aged two. Bomb-disposal experts defused as many as 8,000 devices. On 24 August, Lam Bun, a popular radio presenter fiercely critical of the communists, was trapped in his car by a death squad posing as road-maintenance workers. He and his cousin were doused in petrol and burned alive. Many other prominent figures who had spoken out against the demonstrators received death threats.[26]

All along, there were rumours in Hong Kong that Beijing was massing troops along the border and preparing to take back the colony. But the Chairman had a very shaky grip on the campaigns he unleashed, and in any event the communists needed the city as a banking platform and win-dow on the rest of the world. The British possession depended critically on the water supply from the mainland, which provided 45 billion litres a year. The tap was never turned off.[27]

But after the Wuhan incident, the pressure on the British mission in Beijing increased. The real target, however, was not Britain, although ostensibly the Red Guards clamoured for retaliation after the colonial authorities had suppressed the demonstrators in Hong Kong. Members of the Cultural Revolution Group were targeting Zhou Enlai, whose posi-tion had been severely weakened after the Chairman had taken the veteran marshals to task in February. Zhou, his back against the wall, had sided with Mao, but was overshadowed by Jiang Qing as a result. Soon, incrimi-nating evidence about the premier began to be leaked. In Beijing, posters went up denouncing him as a representative of the 'bourgeois reactionary line', and urging his overthrow. The most damaging document came from

Tianjin, where rebels unearthed a newspaper article from the early 1930s, which claimed that he had resigned from the communist party.

The rebels sent their findings to the Chairman via Jiang Qing. Bristling with confidence, she was ready to expose Zhou, demanding that he come forward with a full confession. On 19 May, Zhou appealed to the Chairman, sending him a lengthy dossier to show that the newspaper item was a hoax planted at the time by his enemies. Mao, instead of shrugging off the incident, circulated Zhou's appeal to every member of the Cultural Revolution Group. They now had a weapon they could use any time they wished to crush Zhou Enlai. But the Chairman, always keen to play off one faction against another, had no desire to get rid of his premier. By the end of May, he had instructed Chen Boda to circulate a public note to Red Guards prohibiting them from finding fault with Zhou Enlai.[28]

The Wuhan incident further strengthened the hands of the Cultural Revolution Group. On 7 August, Wang Li, his foot in a cast, appeared at the Diaoyutai State Guesthouse to call on radicals from the Ministry of Foreign Affairs to seize power. Chen Yi, who was minister of foreign affairs, was already under siege by thousands of Red Guards at his home in Zhongnanhai. On 11 August he was forced to appear at a mass meeting where he was accused of wishing to capitulate to imperialists, revisionists and reactionaries. Wang Li's speech also encouraged a more confrontational tone towards the British in Hong Kong. On 20 August, the same day that Wong Yee-man and her little brother died, the British chargé d'affaires was given an ultimatum demanding that a ban on all communist publications in Hong Kong be lifted. The diplomatic note expired two days later.[29]

As the ultimatum became public, radical students started putting the British mission under pressure. On the morning of 22 August, a foreigner based at the Institute for Foreign Languages saw some of his students walk down the tree-lined street next to the school 'with the happily expectant air of summer picnickers'. They were carrying cans of gasoline. By lunchtime the crowd outside the British mission was so large that the twenty-two diplomats and support staff had been trapped inside.[30]

In the early evening, Polish diplomats tried to warn their British counterparts that Red Guards were rolling barrels of oil towards the mission, but the phone lines had been cut. Still unable to leave, some of the foreigners settled down for a game of bridge with Donald Hopson, while others watched Peter Sellers in *The Wrong Arm of the Law*. Outside, searchlights illuminated the building. At 10.00 p.m., a firework rocket was launched from the Ministry of Foreign Affairs. The crowd, which had been quiet and orderly, sitting down in tightly packed ranks, rose as one and started pushing angrily through a small cordon of soldiers who had linked arms in front of the gates. They roared into the compound and swiftly overran the building. Those trapped inside managed to withdraw behind a heavy metal door in the registry, reinforced by filing cabinets and an enormous brass lectern dating from 1900, when hundreds of foreigners had taken refuge in the British embassy, besieged for fifty-five days by the Qing army and a secret society of peasant fighters called the Boxers.

Flames appeared outside the registry, lapping at the wooden shutters outside the windows. Smoke entered the room, which was now plunged into darkness. Amid the sound of frantic shouting, blowing whistles and breaking windows, the insistent pounding of a battering ram could be heard. It broke through the brickwork and created a small hole in the wall. A hand grasping a flashlight appeared through the aperture. By now, as the smell of smoke was spreading, it became clear that surrender was the only option.

The party emerged through the emergency door to be met by a flurry of blows. Some were swept along by the mob and beaten on the back and shoulders. It was a restrained beating: the blows were painful but not crippling. Photographs were taken, but here too the ritual followed meticulous rules. The head of the victim had to be pulled up by the hair or forced down while the arms were held tight by two men. In the mêlée, a few managed to reach the Finnish embassy opposite the mission. Others went into hiding. Soldiers herded the remaining members of the party towards a side road, moving them away from the crowd and eventually leading them to a lorry. It was a beautiful, still night. Flames from the burning building could be seen from several kilometres away. Long months of house arrest followed for the mission staff.[31]

It was the beginning of the end. The Cultural Revolution Group had gone too far. The following day, Zhou Enlai deflected criticism away from the Ministry of Foreign Affairs by sending a copy of Wang Li's speech to the Chairman, who was still in Shanghai. Mao thought long and hard, and then gave his decision to Yang Chengwu, the acting chief of staff, to be relayed back to Beijing. The Chairman declared that Wang Li and several other members of the Cultural Revolution Group were 'bad people' out to wreck the revolution. 'Report this to the premier alone. Have them arrested and let the premier handle the situation.' Power shifted back from the Cultural Revolution Group to Zhou, as the next phase of the Cultural Revolution began.[32]

13

Quenching the Fires

Wang Li was denounced in a secret meeting lasting eleven hours, chaired by Zhou Enlai. For good measure, his entire family including his in-laws were dismissed as nothing more than a 'burrowful of black trash'.[1]

Wang Li, as well as two other members of the Cultural Revolution Group, took the fall for the burning of the British mission. The Chairman used the occasion to distance himself from the split developing within the army. He had made a point of reaching out to the veteran marshals in April 1967, calling on them to participate in his grand plan for unity. But they had come under pressure again after the incident in Wuhan, as a hunt ensued for smaller 'Chen Zaidao' figures inside the army. On 1 August, *Red Flag* had called on the proletariat to 'take firm hold of the gun', proposing that a handful of traitors be dragged out of the military. Mao realised that the damage done by the slogan was reaching dangerous proportions. He was wary of Lin Biao, who exploited the campaign to consolidate his grip on the army. The heir apparent used the fall of Chen Zaidao to place his own followers in charge of the Wuhan Military Region. A few weeks later, the Lanzhou Military Region declared its support for the Cultural Revolution Group. In Hunan, the Forty-Seventh Army, which in the past had served under Lin Biao, was asked to assist the rebels. And it was not merely the delicate balance of power inside the army that risked being upset. In several parts of the country, violent clashes occurred between different factions, each with their own links to the military.

The Chairman saw the danger. In Shanghai, he scrawled 'Save our Great Wall' along the incendiary *Red Flag* editorial. It was the term he used for the People's Liberation Army. Respect for the army became the motto of the day. On 5 September, Jiang Qing, the very person who had encouraged an attack on the army a month earlier, told the rebels in stark terms that nobody had the right to steal weapons from the People's Liberation Army. She warned them that the soldiers had been instructed to shoot back. Her speech was printed and widely circulated to signal the new party line. The same day, the Chairman signed a decree authorising the army to use self-defence against rebel organisations in an effort to end factional fighting. It was a signal of strong support for the People's Liberation Army, praised as a 'peerless people's army' led by 'our great leader Chairman Mao'.[2]

A stream of editorials and announcements followed, as the Cultural Revolution Group tried to quench the fire it had kindled a month earlier. The Chairman toured the country, visiting areas where the fighting had verged on civil war and calling for a great alliance of all revolutionary forces. 'There is no reason whatsoever for the working class to split into two irreconcilable organisations,' the Chairman concluded. His statement was repeatedly broadcast to the entire nation as part of a Great Strategic Plan that called for all factions to unite under the banner of proletarian discipline.[3]

The revolution was in retreat. In Beijing, posters were scraped from walls, windows and pavements to prepare for National Day on 1 October. 'No description can convey to those who have not seen it for themselves an accurate picture of the extent to which the poster-writers had submerged this city in a sea of paper,' one resident noted. After days of scrubbing, the walls were almost clean. Only official slogans and posters were now allowed, and they proclaimed the importance of unity, work and support for the People's Liberation Army. On university campuses, loudspeakers blasted the same message day after day: 'Unite Together!', 'Among Workers There Can Be No Fundamental Contradictions!'[4]

On 1 October, in a great show of co-ordinated unity, half a million soldiers marched across Tiananmen Square, led by an enormous, silver-coloured, plastic figure of Mao pointing the way forward. They were fol-lowed by hundreds of thousands of citizens, forced to march together, many in contingents with members from opposed factions. The rostrum was packed with figures from the army. The old marshals occupied promi-nent positions next to the Chairman, including Chen Yi, Xu Xiangqian and Ye Jianying.[5]

Red Flag, the magazine which had become the mouthpiece of the Cultural Revolution Group, fell silent. Jiang Qing stepped back, and then left Beijing altogether to seek rest in Hangzhou. By the end of 1967, the Cultural Revolution Group was in a state of virtual eclipse. Zhou Enlai took centre stage, spending most of his time negotiating behind the scenes, trying to unite different factions into the much publicised great alliance. The Chairman had now set a deadline for revolution, deciding that revolutionary party committees should be established everywhere by the end of 1968. The goal was no longer to be achieved through violent power seizures, but through peaceful negotiation. One batch of squabbling delegates after another arrived in the capital, as the premier tried to hammer out compromises in the Great Hall of the People between the different factions vying for a seat on the new revolutionary committees.[6]

A third faction appeared, popularly referred to as the 'free and unfettered'. This was the party of the disaffected, and it was deliberately apolitical and leaderless. Its ranks were filled with members of mass organisations who quietly withdrew from factional warfare. They came from all sides of the political spectrum, but had one thing in common, namely disillusionment with politics. By the end of 1967, Ken Ling found it difficult to gather enough people to hold a mass meeting in Xiamen. Where thousands had proudly displayed their weapons over the summer, no more than a few hundred still responded to the call. 'At the various headquarters the staff thinned out, and eventually entire offices became deserted.'[7] People had become more cynical. There was weariness, if not distaste, about the fighting, political or otherwise. Boredom and lethargy also set in. The Cultural Revolution had dragged on too long. Any sense of excitement had vanished. Those who had once agitated in the name of revolutionary justice were less sure about the mutual invective, the torture and the killings. Some found sleeping at night difficult.

Disaffected students spent time helping with family chores, reading novels or playing cards and chess. It was a relatively unconstrained life, but one marked by boredom. The parks had been vandalised, libraries were closed, and clubs of any kind prohibited. 'There were virtually no books, no music, no films, no theatre, no museums, no teahouses, almost no way of keeping oneself occupied – except cards, which, though not officially sanctioned, made a stealthy comeback.'[8]

Some started playing music or assembling transistor radios at home. Leisure activities condemned as 'bourgeois' enjoyed a revival. In Xi'an, Kang Zhengguo and some of his friends found a pile of phonograph records in the Great Mosque, located in the Muslim quarter of the provincial capital. Kang took recordings of Russian folk songs back home. 'For the people I knew, this period was a miniature renaissance, a touch of spring in a cultural wasteland.'[9]

Kang also quietly obtained a variety of books, including some of the great classics of Chinese literature. One such was an unexpurgated edition of *The Golden Lotus*, an erotic novel set in the Northern Song dynasty and depicting the sexual adventures of a wealthy libertine. Unfortunately some of the key pages were missing. Zhai Zhenhua, who joined the ranks of the unfettered the moment her Red Guard organisation expelled her in March 1967, obtained reading material from the school library. The building was boarded up, as most of the windows had been shattered, but some of the planks were loose enough to be moved to one side. Students had never been allowed to roam around the bookshelves before the Cultural Revolution. Now she had her pick of all the forbidden books. Her favourite was a biography of Marie Curie.[10]

Others travelled. People got on their bicycles and started exploring the countryside. A few took to the road, drawing on the lessons learned during the dizzy heights of free travel a year before. But they stayed clear of historical sites associated with the communist party, heading for nature instead. Song Yongyi, a student who earlier that year had joined a rebel group fighting Zhang Chunqiao, hitchhiked from Shanghai to Huangshan, a strikingly beautiful mountain range in south Anhui with hot springs, pine forests and rugged granite peaks vanishing into clouds. He and his friends paid their way by bartering Mao badges.[11]

Students were not the only ones to withdraw from politics. Some rebel workers, too, drifted into a life of seemingly carefree leisure, as lax discipline at work left those tired of politics with plenty of spare time. In Nanjing, Fang Zifen joined a circle of friends who all shared a bad class background. They enjoyed talking about music, literature and cinema. Like Kang Zhengguo, they found a stash of records confiscated by Red Guards during the house raids a year earlier. Tchaikovsky and Mozart were their favourites. They also organised excursions to some of the historic sites at Purple Mountain, where Chen Zhigao had swallowed a vial of cyanide in May 1966.[12]

A few joined gangs. There was a thriving underworld in the cities, as professional criminals vied with sworn brotherhoods of like-minded youngsters, attracting orphans, juvenile delinquents, fallen Red Guards, children whose parents had been sent to re-education camps and villagers hiding in the city. Many of these gangs replicated the party hierarchy with a command structure divided into several ranks. Most were miserably poor, but at least their members seemed to live 'beyond political life', more or less free of the ceaseless campaigns of the Cultural Revolution.[13]

But as factional violence started abating and the army increasingly assumed power, those few realms of relative freedom came to an end. Weapons were turned in, students returned to school, and workers went back on full shifts.

Cadres suspected of 'revisionism' were given a chance to remould their thoughts and rejoin the ranks of the great revolutionary alliance – under the supervision of the army. In Changsha, where the military had brought a gory summer of fighting to an end, batch after batch of suspect cadres were sent to the city's party school to attend Mao Zedong Thought study classes while their cases were being investigated. Many saw this as a chance to prove themselves and were relieved to be protected from the endless parades and struggle meetings to which mass organisations had subjected them.[14]

As the prestige of the party waned, so the cult of Mao increased. Everywhere study classes in Mao Zedong Thought were convened. The People's Liberation Army had stood behind Mao Zedong Thought years earlier, and now it used the cult of its leader to impose order and discipline. The cult of personality, as Lin Biao phrased it, would unite 'the entire party, the entire army, and the entire people'.

A new campaign called the Three Loyalties and Four Boundless Loves was launched in March 1968. It brought the worship of Mao to new heights, requiring absolute loyalty to the Chairman, his thought and the proletarian revolutionary line. In schools, offices and factories, altars were set up to Chairman Mao. Large characters reading 'The Red Sun in Our Hearts' were cut out in bright, shiny red paper, forming an arc over a picture of the Chairman. Sun-rays emanated from his head. One office worker remembers that:

> Every morning we would stand in front of this with our Little Red Books and read aloud a few passages. Then waving the Little Red Book we would say three times, 'Great Leader, Teacher, Helmsman Chairman Mao, May You Live Ten Thousand Years' and 'Good Health Forever to Vice-Chairman Lin Biao!' It struck me as absurd, almost like a religion. Most of us felt that way, as I was to discover after the Cultural Revolution. At the time, however, no one in their right mind would dare say so openly, let alone discuss it.[15]

In newly opened classrooms, too, everything except the Little Red Book was in short supply. Gao Yuan and his schoolmates had to assemble before the Chairman every morning and every evening, chanting slogans, singing songs and waving the Little Red Book. It was a welcome respite from the bloody wars that factions had fought in Zhengding over the summer, and soon some of the students started taking the campaign in a new direction. Chairman Mao quotation contests became popular. The very same students who had learned how to seize buildings, kidnap enemies, torture captives, forge weapons and fire guns were now trying to outdo each other in mastering the Little Red Book. One student could recite all 270 pages without missing a word. Another could come up with the correct citation when prompted with any page number from the red book. Gao did not do very well, but managed to impress his peers with his flawless recitation of the Chairman's poems. Before long, people were trading quotations in everyday situations, replacing small talk with words of wisdom from the Chairman.[16]

In the capital miniature shrines went on sale, with three leaves in the form of a triptych. The centre had a portrait of the Chairman, while the outer panels carried quotations. These cult objects took the place of the old family altar at home, as people met the gaze of the Chairman the moment they woke up and reported back to him in the evening.

There was even a loyalty dance, consisting of a few simple moves with outstretched arms from the heart to the Chairman's portrait. The dance was accompanied by the song 'Beloved Chairman Mao'. On television, entire evenings were devoted to ritual song and dance. A giant bust usually occupied the centre of the stage, producing rays that throbbed and flickered with electricity, as if light and energy poured forth from the godhead.[17]

Statues of Chairman Mao, usually in death-white plaster, became ubiquitous in classrooms, office lobbies and meeting rooms. Life-size statues appeared in every vestibule and corridor. Outdoors, on university campuses and city parks, towering monuments portrayed him with his right arm outstretched to acknowledge homage from the masses. In Chengdu, the city where the first armed confrontations had taken place in April, an ancient palace gate in a central location was blown up with dynamite to make room for a giant statue. Special lorries, called 'loyalty lorries' with red silk ribbons like a float in a parade, shipped the white marble from the mountains. At the quarry, groups of sweating workers discarded all machinery to work with their bare hands in a show of loyalty to the leader.[18]

Government units vied with each other in displaying better, taller and more expensive statues. In 1968, more than 600,000 of them were dotted across the institutional landscape of Shanghai. Many were made of plaster, but reinforced concrete, aluminium and tinplate, besides marble, were also used. Some towered above pedestrians at a majestic fifteen metres, others stood at a more modest three metres. Scarce resources were expended in the informal competition, and in 1968 the city used 900 tonnes of tinplate alone. The Steel Institute, rather predictably, turned to stainless steel to erect its monument at a cost of 100,000 yuan. Another unit diverted close to 40 tonnes of concrete, originally earmarked for the construction of a storage room, to erect its sculpture.[19]

The demand for posters, portraits, altars, busts and statues dedicated to the leader seemed endless, but the production of cult objects was fraught with danger. A wrong stroke of the brush, a faltering hand on the plaster, any seemingly innocuous mistake could have lasting political consequences. Artists, like everybody else, were state employees, and they were envisaged as empty vessels who linked the people to their leader by faithfully reproducing his image. There were plenty of snoops and snitches ready to denounce an artist for wittingly or unwittingly introducing a personal touch into the portrayal of the Chairman. In Shanghai, ordinary people put pen to paper to complain of the 'adverse political influence' of poorly executed portraits of the Chairman. Chen Suzhen, seeking security in numbers, wrote a petition signed by his colleagues from the Hygiene Department to complain about 'insufficiently solemn and earnest' representations of their leader. Apparently such paintings 'make people feel deeply aggrieved when they see them'.[20]

There were serious consequences for artists. Zhang Zhenshi, a famous portrait painter who created one of the most reproduced images of Mao, was viciously beaten up because one of his works depicted the Chairman with his face slightly inclined in the wrong direction. Shi Lu, a painter, woodblock printer and calligrapher from a family of wealthy landowners, was taken to task for his 1959 painting in which he had placed the Chairman in front of a cliff, suggesting that the leader had no way forward. In 1967, Shi was locked up for three years.[21]

As a result, few professional artists were willing to risk their careers by churning out the endless icons requested by the market. The gap between supply and demand was exploited by enterprising individuals, often from politically dubious class backgrounds. Fang Zifen, who spent his leisure time discussing classical music with friends in Nanjing, executed large murals for government units that could not afford more established artists. Rather than being paid in cash he was offered room and board. A large work took up to twenty days, a smaller one a full week. The job gave him plenty of time to read.[22]

Xiao Mu was another outcast from a bad class background who ironically thrived thanks to the cult of personality. An intellectual condemned as a 'rightist' for having spoken out during the Hundred Flowers a decade earlier, he and his team earned up to a thousand yuan a month painting large slogans on government walls. They were paid by the character, and they literally turned entire towns red. He briefly tried his hand at sculpture, but it was a much riskier affair, as reject products had to be hidden in a burlap sack and dumped at night in a lake. Frightened of being accused of besmirching the Chairman, after a couple of days he abandoned the project.[23]

The campaign cooled in March 1968. After the burning of the British mission in August 1967, the Chairman had ordered a retreat. The Cultural Revolution Group had gone too far, calling for a purge inside the army and encouraging rebels to seize weapons. It paid the price, as Mao purged several of its members. The last one to fall was Qi Benyu, a radical theorist and frequent contributor to *Red Flag*. He was arrested, tried and sent to prison in January 1968. But while Mao wished to protect the army and restrain factional violence, he had no desire to jettison the Cultural Revolution altogether. He was alarmed by the speed with which the army was taking over the reins of power, and wary of its skill in promoting Mao Zedong Thought as a cover for its own authority. The revolutionary party committees which were being set up across the country were heavily dominated by army officers. They looked uncomfortably like military governments, concentrating real power in the hands of the army.

Many of these committees were dominated by regional officers faithful to the veteran marshals. While Lin Biao had scored a big victory over the summer, placing some of his allies in key positions in several military regions, his authority over the army was far from absolute. After the fall of Luo Ruiqing, Lin Biao himself had recommended Yang Chengwu, the acting chief of staff who had shuttled back and forth between Zhou Enlai and the Chairman in September. But after February 1967 Lin Biao started having doubts about Yang, as the acting chief of staff began siding with Zhou Enlai in trying to protect some of the older marshals. Yang accompanied Mao on his long trips throughout the country, but was evasive when asked by Lin Biao to report what the Chairman had said.[24]

Another potential threat came from Fu Chongbi, the Beijing Garrison commander. Like Yang Chengwu, his loyalties were with the old marshals, and throughout the Cultural Revolution he had used his troops in the capital to protect army generals from rebel attacks. His men were responsible for providing security for the top leaders. They guarded Lin Biao's residence and the Diaoyutai State Guesthouse, where the Cultural Revolution

Group had its offices. If ever the old guard were to attempt a coup, he would be one of the keys to power.[25]

In November 1967, Yang wrote an editorial calling on the nation to 'establish the absolute authority of Mao Zedong Thought in a big way and a special way'. The Chairman fired a warning shot in the form of a brief note sent on 17 December to Lin Biao, Zhou Enlai and the Cultural Revolution Group. The Chairman indicated that all authority was invariably relative. He tried to shore up the credentials of the Cultural Revolution Group. By the end of January 1968, Jiang Qing came out of her retreat, meeting with representatives of rebels from around the country. On 15 March, she hinted darkly at the danger of 'rightism', which she saw as the 'principal danger'. A few days later, flanked by Lin Biao's wife Ye Qun, Kang Sheng, Chen Boda and Wu Faxian, she explained to delegates from Zhejiang that 'rightist split-tism has raised its head from last winter to the present'.[26]

A week later, on 22 March, Fu Chongbi, Yang Chengwu and a political commissar in the air force were purged. Jiang Qing alleged that the Beijing Garrison commander had conspired to assault her headquarters with armed forces under the direction of the acting chief of staff. Huang Yongsheng, the military leader in Guangdong, took over from Yang Chengwu. He was one of Lin Biao's 'four guardian warriors'. Another loyal follower of the heir apparent took command of the capital's garrison.

Effusive praise for Jiang Qing followed from Lin Biao and Zhou Enlai two days later. She played an 'outstanding role', she had 'great creative power', she had 'great merits' and she was a 'great proletarian fighter'. 'We should all learn from her!' Zhou Enlai enthused at a meeting of the top brass in the Great Hall of the People. Extreme deference followed from other leaders. Prolonged tributes appeared in newspapers. On 7 April the *People's Daily* took the step of describing Lin Biao as well as Jiang Qing as Mao's 'closest comrades-in-arms'. Bookshops apparently started taking orders for the 'Selected Speeches of Comrade Jiang Qing', although the book never appeared.[27]

———

The hopes of the rebels were revived the moment Yang Chengwu was arrested. In Zhengding, Gao Yuan began dreaming of a change of fortune.

His enemies had long boasted that the local military command who backed them had a direct link to Yang Chengwu. They had now lost their most important spokesman. But he was soon disappointed. The county revolutionary committee was dominated by officers from the local military command. One of his classmates, the leader of the opposition, became vice-chairman.[28]

Throughout the country there were repercussions, as 'counter-revolutionary double-dealers' who had followed Yang Chengwu were hounded in Shandong, Liaoning and Shanxi provinces. Factional fighting, which had flickered on and off across parts of the country, blazed with renewed fury in Hunan, Sichuan, Guangdong and Guangxi. But the situation became even more bewildering as the Chairman fostered competing military factions in the country. He needed the heir apparent to push through the Cultural Revolution, but he was also wary of his growing power. Many of Lin Biao's loyal supporters came from the Fourth Field Army. Mao instead propped up the Fourth Front Army, led by Marshal Xu Xiangqian, and the Second Field Army, which had served under Deng Xiaoping. He used generals from the local military to contain Lin Biao.

One such was Xu Shiyou. A burly, gold-toothed man dubbed the 'monk general' because he had enrolled as an apprentice monk in a Shaolin temple before joining the communists in the mid-1920s, Xu had served in the Fourth Front Army under Zhang Guotao. Mao clashed with Zhang during the Long March, and a brutal purge of the Fourth Front Army was carried out in Yan'an. Xu Shiyou was accused of heading a 'counter-revolutionary clique', but Mao redeemed him, personally removing his shackles. Xu denounced his erstwhile leader as an 'opportunist' and 'adventurer' and devoted the rest of his career to serving the Chairman. He was as loyal as a dog from the pound. In 1954 he became commander of the Nanjing Military Region. He despised the Red Guards, calling them bandits who disrupted social order, and showed contempt for the radical ideologists gathered around Jiang Qing. He became a target of rebels in 1967 and had to go into hiding. Mao, again, intervened. Mao knew that the strategically vital lower Yangtze River would be under his control with Xu Shiyou, who stood next to the Chairman at the National Day parades in Beijing on 1 October 1967. When after months of protracted negotiations between different factions a provincial revolutionary committee was finally formed in Nanjing, Mao made sure that Xu was the top man. Xu promptly proceeded to tighten his grip by targeting his former opponents and potential rivals.[29]

An even more critical region from a military point of view was Guangxi province, which shared a 600-kilometre border with Vietnam. Neighbouring Guangdong, with its powerful air force and naval base, was under the leadership of Huang Yongsheng. Whoever controlled both provinces could build up a power base in the south and challenge the capital. Like every other province, there were two main factions in Guangxi. One group stood behind the provincial head, a local man named Wei Guoqing. Wei was born into a Zhuang family, an ethnic group common in Guangxi, and had joined the communists at the age of sixteen. He had risen through the ranks under Deng Xiaoping and was close to the Second Field Army. A weak coalition of rebels opposed him. Wei Guoqing had the backing of the provincial army, but the regional military command was in the hands of Huang Yongsheng in Guangzhou. In February 1967, following the Chairman's order to 'support the left', a unit from the Fifty-Fifth Army closely associated with Lin Biao's Fourth Field Army was dispatched into Guangxi to reinforce the rebels. They were soon joined by Wu Jinnan, the deputy secretary of Guangxi. Both factions fought ferociously, each backed by different troops. Zhou Enlai stood by Wei Guoqing. In June Kang Sheng even denounced Wu Jinnan as a traitor. But after the Wuhan incident in July, Wei Guoqing, in turn, was attacked as the 'Chen Zaidao' of Guangxi province. Both sides now openly seized weapons from the army. They assaulted freight trains shipping armaments to Vietnam. Bloody battles took place over the summer. On 22 July, in the provincial capital Nanning 300 people were killed in a clash involving tens of thousands of fighters.[30]

Interference from above turned factional strife into a full-blown civil war. Zhou Enlai and Lin Biao were waging a proxy war, each trying to place his own men in the revolutionary committee that would dominate Guangxi. By the end of 1967, mortars, machine guns and napalm were used in the military battles for control of key cities in the province. But the balance of power started shifting towards Wei Guoqing. On several occasions, Mao slipped in a word in his favour. After Wei had offered a self-criticism in November, the Chairman declared that Wei had merely made a 'few mistakes' which could easily be corrected. A few months later, Zhou Enlai offered to send a battalion to help Wei Guoqing crush the rebels. Troops from the Fifty-Fifth Army started quietly withdrawing, leaving the rebels to their fate. By March 1968, large-scale massacres were claiming thousands of rebel victims.[31]

On 3 July 1968, Mao finally intervened, condemning the factional fighting in Guangxi as an attempt by a 'small group of class enemies to sabotage the dictatorship of the proletariat'. He ordered an immediate end to the violence. Wei seized the opportunity to persecute his opponents, giving the order that they be eliminated in a 'force 12 typhoon against class enemies'. In Nanning, where the rebels had several strongholds on Liberation Road, an entire district came under sustained fire. After two weeks of heavy bombardment by mortar and cannon, more than 2,000 houses in the area were reduced to rubble. Thousands of rebels were locked up in makeshift prisons. Many were interrogated and tortured. More than 2,000 were later executed. A group of twenty-six prisoners were shot on the spot by soldiers in front of a photographic studio. Unable to dislodge several thousand rebels hiding inside a concrete bomb shelter, the military opened the floodgates of a nearby river to flush them out. So many bodies were strewn across the city that corpses were tossed into coalmines and ditches. A team of cremators, divided into eight groups, was busy for weeks burning more than 600 bodies. Large amounts of formaldehyde and other disinfectants were used to clean up the shelter, but the stench of putrefying flesh lingered for many weeks in the hot, humid summer.[32]

As monsoon rain swelled the main rivers running through Guangxi, thousands of bodies were carried along, moving past rice fields and karst mountains to end up in the Pearl River, not far from Hong Kong, some 500 kilometres downstream from Nanning. Here they joined the bodies of victims in Guangzhou, where factional fighting also raged that summer. Police in the British crown colony fished dozens out of the harbour, many of them trussed up and badly mutilated. Passengers on the ferry to Macau saw corpses floating among the flotsam and jetsam carried downstream from the mainland.[33]

Across the entire province of Guangxi, as many as 80,000 people were killed that summer. The local militia joined forces with the army to hunt down alleged rebels and political outcasts. In Liujiang, some of the victims were decapitated in public, their heads displayed with a note reading 'counter-revolutionary'. In one people's commune, where rumours circulated about an imminent counter-revolutionary plot in which landlords would come and claim back their land, some sixty people were frog-marched to an abandoned field and forced to kneel as their heads were smashed with hammers.[34]

But the worst violence occurred in Wuxuan, an old market town set among soaring limestone mountains. A river runs through the town. A long flight of flagstone steps leads to its bank, where large, flat rocks were used as a butcher's block. Zhou Shi'an was one of the victims. He was a 'bad element' who had been sentenced to seven years in prison for having stolen a sack of rice during Mao's Great Famine. He returned home from a labour camp in the middle of the Cultural Revolution, during which his younger brother had headed a rebel organisation. 'This is Zhou Wei'an's elder brother. He wants to take revenge for his brother!' one of the persecutors cried. His brother had already been sliced up, his head and one of his legs displayed in the market. Now came Zhou Shi'an's turn, as his chest was cut open with a five-inch knife. He was still alive. A local boss extracted his heart and liver. Other villagers followed suit, stripping the victim to the bone. In total more than seventy victims were cannibalised in Wuxuan.

There was a hierarchy in the ritual consumption of class enemies. Leaders feasted on the heart and liver, mixed with pork and a sprinkling of local spices, while ordinary villagers were allowed only to peck at the victims' arms and thighs. After several teachers had been sliced up in a middle school, a crowd carried away chunks of flesh in bags dripping with blood. Students cooked the meat in casseroles sitting on top of small, improvised brick barbeques. The deputy director of the school's revolutionary committee, who oversaw the butchery, was later expelled from the party, but was proud of his actions: 'Cannibalism? It was the landlord's flesh! The spy's flesh!' One subsequent investigation listed all the ways in which people had been killed in Wuxuan, including 'beating, drowning, shooting, stabbing, chopping, dragging, cutting up alive, crushing and hanging to death'.[35]

On 26 August 1968 a new revolutionary committee was finally set up in Guangxi province. The founding ceremony took place amid much fanfare, including the unveiling of a large, marble statue of the Chairman. A congratulatory telegram arrived from Beijing.

When Mao had blamed factional strife in Guangxi on 'class enemies' and 'counter-revolutionaries' and had demanded an immediate halt to the violence in his directive dated 3 July 1968, his words were directed at rebels across the nation. Although his pronouncements were widely disseminated, in parts of the country the violence continued unabated. On 24 July a new command was issued, demanding that all rebels comply with the 3 July directive and lay down their weapons. In the following days, to propagate the new party line, the Chairman sent into the universities massive Mao Zedong Thought propaganda teams formed by workers.

On 27 July, some 30,000 workers from more than sixty factories approached Tsinghua University, waving copies of the 3 July directive and shouting 'fight with words, not with weapons'. They met stiff resistance from hard-core remnants of the Red Guards, armed with sub-machine guns, rifles and even a makeshift tank. The students opened fire and killed five workers, wounding many more. The majority of students, by now, had deserted their campuses. Those still holding out had become lost in a seemingly endless cycle of factional strife that had taken on a life of its own. But their ranks had been replenished with the arrival of hundreds of rebels from other provinces. Some had managed to escape from Nanning, where Wei Guoqing had laid siege to Liberation Road. Kuai Dafu, the fiery leader who had stood up to the work team two years earlier, now proclaimed that a 'black hand' had sent the workers to crush his revolution.[36]

Kuai and four other Red Guard leaders were summoned to a meeting at the Great Hall of the People. Days earlier, on 25 July, Zhou Enlai and Kang Sheng had met separately with rebels from Guangxi, accusing them of working on behalf of class enemies. Kang Sheng had grilled them: 'What rumours have you come to spread in Beijing? What black meetings have you attended? What black activities have you conducted? Which black headquarters provide you with instructions?' Chen Boda had interjected: 'Do you think Tsinghua University can solve your problems? Kuai Dafu should not be too arrogant. Do they understand what Marxism is, what Mao Zedong Thought is?'[37]

At the Great Hall of the People, Mao was flanked by Jiang Qing, Lin Biao, Zhou Enlai, Ye Qun, Kang Sheng, Xie Fuzhi and other members of the Cultural Revolution Group. Facing them were five of the most power-ful commanders of the Red Guards, including Nie Yuanzi, by now also vice-chair of the municipal revolutionary committee. Kuai Dafu was late, still embroiled in the fighting at Tsinghua University. The Chairman set the tone, mocking Kuai's claim that a black hand was behind the propa-ganda team sent to his campus. 'I am the black hand! Kuai Dafu did not come, but he should have come to arrest me!'

Mao accused the rebels of deliberately ignoring his directive of 3 July:

> There are those who say that the directive about Guangxi only applies
> to Guangxi, the directive about Shaanxi only applies to Shaanxi, and
> they do not apply here. Well, let me issue a directive for the whole of the
> country right now: whoever still continues to rebel, attack the People's
> Liberation Army, sabotage transportation, kill people or set fire to prop-
> erty is a criminal. If there is a small number of people who do not listen
> and refuse to reform, then they are bandits, they are nationalists, they
> are trying to encircle us, and if they persist then we will have to exter-
> minate them.[38]

On 5 August, exactly two years after the Chairman had declared 'Bombard the Headquarters' in his own big-character poster, he sent a bas-ket of mangoes to the workers of the Mao Zedong Thought propaganda team at Tsinghua University. The mangoes were a gift to Mao Zedong from Pakistan's foreign minister, on an official visit in Beijing. The following day the propaganda machine went into overdrive. Newspapers reported the jubilation and excitement of the workers. They cheered with joy and wept with gratitude, pledging their loyalty to the Chairman by chanting his quotations. Everyone understood the message, even Nien Cheng, the widow of the former manager of Shell whose house had been raided several times by Red Guards. Reading the *People's Daily* from her cell in the Number One Detention House in Shanghai, she realised that the mangoes were a clear and eloquent warning to the students not to resist the disciplinary actions of the propaganda team. It was a signal that the workers were back in charge. If the message was not clear enough, Yao Wenyuan penned an article providing the theoretical underpinning of the last stage of the revolution. It was entitled 'The Working Class Must Exercise Leadership in Everything'.[39]

It was the end of the Red Guards. After a last impassioned round of accusations and counter-accusations, the incessant din of loudspeakers on university campuses ceased. A blissful silence settled over Beijing. The students now looked grim, marching behind portraits of the Chairman out of habit rather than conviction. Mao had suspended the Cultural Revolution.[40]

Over the next couple of weeks, propaganda teams marched into universities and schools all over the country. They were formally called 'Worker and Peasant Propaganda Teams for Mao Zedong Thought', although the teams included no farmers and only a few workers. They were composed of military men in civilian clothes and loyal party cadres.

With the propaganda teams came mango mania. At Tsinghua University one of the sacred mangoes was pickled in a jar of formaldehyde, to be displayed for all to see. Soon plastic and wax replicas appeared, as millions of workers queued up to catch a glimpse of the mango reliquary. In the oilfields of Daqing, close to the border with Siberia, the visit was compulsory, and all workers were taken in unheated buses in the middle of the winter at minus 30 degrees Celsius to see the national treasure. Everybody knew that these were wax imitations, but nobody said anything. Mangoes appeared on badges, pencil boxes, sweet wrappers, quilt covers, washbasins, mugs and trays. Giant ones were paraded in floats on National Day on 1 October. A film entitled *The Song of the Mango* appeared.[41]

On 7 September 1968, standing on the rostrum in Tiananmen Square, Zhou Enlai announced an all-round victory. Revolutionary committees had been established in all provinces and major cities. 'Now the whole country is red . . . Now we can declare that through repeated struggles during the past twenty months we have finally smashed the plot of the handful of top party persons in authority taking the capitalist road – counter-revolutionary revisionists, renegades, enemy agents and traitors headed by China's Khrushchev to restore capitalism – and fulfil the great call issued by our great leader Chairman Mao.' A month later Liu Shaoqi was formally expelled from the party and declared a 'renegade, traitor and scab hiding in the party and a running dog of imperialism, modern revisionism and the nationalist reactionaries who has committed innumerable crimes'.[42]

16 July 1966, Mao Zedong swims in the Yangtze to signal his determination to carry through the Cultural Revolution.

Thousands follow the Chairman's example.

Mao Zedong and Lin Biao drive through an enthusiastic crowd of Red Guards on Tiananmen Square, Beijing, on 18 August 1966.

Mao Zedong and Lin Biao review more than a million Red Guards from the rostrum on Tiananmen Square, 18 August 1966.

Song Binbin pins a Red Guard armband on the Chairman's sleeve as they stand on the Tiananmen rostrum, 18 August 1966.

The party secretary of Harbin has his face blackened, is forced to wear a dunce cap and has a placard placed around his neck for being a 'black gang element', 26 August 1966.

A building covered in big character posters extolling the Cultural Revolution, Guangzhou, 1966.

People read posters, anonymous denunciations and news bulletins to keep up with the Cultural Revolution, Beijing, August 1966.

Official parade in Beijing to mark National Day, 1 October 1966.

Late 1966, a propaganda squad of Red Guards and students brandishes copies of the *Little Red Book* to spread Mao's thought.

The army distributes Mao's *Little Red Book*.

A group of Red Guards parades through a village with portraits of Chairman Mao, 1967.

26 April 1967: Leading members of the Cultural Revolution Group, including, from left to right, Zhou Enlai, Jiang Qing (Madam Mao), Chen Boda and Kang Sheng.

Two leaders of a rebel faction are denounced in public, January 1967.

Execution of people condemned as 'counter-revolutionaries' on the outskirts of Harbin, 5 April 1968.

A young boy paints a slogan over wall posters.

Hospital patients make their morning pledge of loyalty to Mao's picture, October 1968.

People watch on as soldiers make their pledge of allegiance, October 1968.

The villagers of a commune just outside Harbin pin some 170 badges on the cap and uniform of a model soldier, April 1968.

March 1973: model worker Guo Fenglian visits an air-raid shelter project, as the country hunkers down in anticipation of a major war.

1973, Hui county, Henan province: work to build a tunnel.

Young students exiled to the countryside join local villagers to work on a terraced field, Baiquan county, November 1975.

China mourns Mao Zedong's death, September 1976.

PART THREE

The Black Years (1968–1971)

14

Cleansing the Ranks

When, on 7 September 1968, Zhou Enlai proclaimed that the whole country was drenched in triumphant red, he also called for a great cleansing of the class ranks. It was time to settle accounts. A campaign to ferret out traitors and renegades had been unfolding for many months, and now came to the forefront. It would dominate the lives of ordinary people and party members alike, as millions were persecuted from the summer of 1968 to the autumn of 1969.

The campaign had its origins in the Case of the Sixty-One Traitors, concocted by Kang Sheng in March 1967 to convince the Chairman that dozens of the most senior members of the party had been renegades who had surrendered to the nationalists in the 1930s. Mao used the case to accuse Liu Shaoqi of treachery, a charge that carried the death penalty. More than 5,000 cadres were investigated in the following months, with some hounded to their deaths.

On 5 February 1968 the situation escalated, as the leadership circulated a report on how more than a hundred renegades and double-dealers related to the Sixty-One Traitors had been uncovered in Heilongjiang province alone: 'Liu Shaoqi, Deng Xiaoping, Tao Zhu and their accomplices Peng Dehuai, He Long, Peng Zhen, Luo Ruiqing, Lu Dingyi, Yang Shangkun, An Ziwen, Xiao Hua and others, all of them renegades and counter-revolutionary revisionists, have hidden within the party, usurped important posts in the party and government organs and formed a renegade clique.' The directive demanded that the archives of enemy and puppet governments before liberation be examined so that hidden enemies, secret agents, and people with links to foreign powers as well as counter-revolutionaries could be unearthed and expelled from the party ranks.[1]

A month later, on 18 March, as Jiang Qing appeared with members of the Cultural Revolution Group at the Great Hall of the People to explain how 'rightism' was the new enemy, Kang Sheng went further. 'The big task of the Cultural Revolution is to drag out traitors and secret agents hidden inside the ranks of the party.' Liu Shaoqi, he announced, was a traitor who had first surrendered to the nationalists and the Japanese. His wife Wang Guangmei was a secret agent of the United States, Japan and the nationalists. 'Peng Zhen is a big renegade. Peng Dehuai is a spy and a traitor. Luo Ruiqing is a secret agent who never joined the communist party.' He Long was a bandit. Lu Dingyi was a secret agent on the payroll of Chiang Kai-shek. Tan Zhenlin ('we now have proof!') was also a turn-coat. As Kang Sheng was about to reach the end of his stunning indict-ment of former leaders of the communist party, Jiang Qing leaned forward to shout 'Down with Deng Xiaoping!' Kang promptly added that Deng Xiaoping was a deserter. The targets of the Cultural Revolution were no longer 'capitalist roaders' or even 'revisionists', but secret agents operating in the service of the enemy.[2]

In May, the Chairman officially gave his seal of approval to the cam-paign. He read a report on a printing plant in Beijing, where troops from the Central Guard Unit had followed the 5 February circular and managed to uncover more than twenty enemy agents who had wormed their way into the party after liberation. 'Of all the material of this kind that I have read, this one is the best written.'[3]

The Chairman delegated the task of ferreting out enemy agents to the new revolutionary committees. They used the campaign to eradicate their own enemies. In schools, factories and government offices, revolutionary committees set up their own prisons and established their own prosecuting committees, acting as judge, jury and executioner.

Real and imagined enemies had to be periodically expelled from the ranks. The history of communism is, after all, a history of endless purges. But this campaign differed qualitatively from its predecessors. The Cultural Revolution had battered the party, the government and the army. The Chairman had disliked the sprawling machinery of the one-party state, with its overlapping jurisdictions and conflicting interests. He aspired to a more responsive chain of command, one in which his orders could be carried out instantly and without question. The upshot was the revolutionary committees. Dominated by the army, they concentrated unprecedented power in a few hands. Generals headed roughly half of all the revolutionary committees at the provincial level. The people's republic, by the summer of 1968, increasingly resembled a military dictatorship.

The timing varied from place to place, but the campaign to cleanse the party ranks was in full swing between the summer of 1968 and the autumn of 1969. Spies were uncovered everywhere. In Shanghai, where underground organisations had flourished from the 1920s, thousands of members who had clandestinely joined the party before liberation were cross-examined. Since the communists and their enemies had played a lethal game of deceit and double-dealing, with agents switching loyalties, planting evidence or using false names for more than two decades, plenty of scope existed to trump up charges of treachery. A total of thirty-nine enemy organisations were uncovered, and more than 3,600 people were detained and persecuted. Those who had joined the party or worked for the government after the communists conquered the city were also interrogated. In total, some 170,000 people were harassed in one way or another. More than 5,400 committed suicide, were beaten to death or were executed.[4]

There were victims in the upper echelons of power as well. Of the twenty leading officials who had dominated the municipal party committee before the Cultural Revolution, all but three were denounced as 'traitors, spies and capitalist roaders'. However, the vast majority of victims were ordinary people with no party affiliation. Anyone with a foreign link in their past became suspect. Since the metropolis before 1949 had had a larger foreign population than any other city except New York, and more foreign investment than either London or Paris, almost everybody above the age of thirty was implicated. The Shanghai Conservatory, for instance, was established in 1929 by a graduate from the Geneva Conservatory of Music. Within a decade it had flourished into a world-class institution, attracting international staff of the calibre of Alexander Tcherepnin, a Russian-born composer and pianist. Chen Youxin, chairman of the Orchestra Department and one of the first Chinese to join the Shanghai Municipal

Orchestra, jumped from the roof of a skyscraper. Shen Zhibai, chairman of the Chinese Music Department, also committed suicide. By the end of 1968, more than a dozen people from the conservatory had been driven to their deaths.[5]

Anyone who had ever been involved in foreign trade was suspect. Nien Cheng was dragged out of the Number One Detention House to be confronted by former members of staff, assembled at struggle meetings carefully choreographed by party leaders. Former friends were denounced as 'foreign intelligence officers'. A woman employed as her secretary, one of the many Russians who had found refuge in Shanghai after the Bolshevik Revolution of 1917, was unmasked as a double agent for Britain and the Soviet Union. People were relentlessly threatened, pressured, interrogated and finally degraded, forced to level the most fantastic accusations against their erstwhile colleagues. 'The sum total of the accusations was an amateurish attempt at a spy drama without a convincing central theme, beginning or end,' Nien noted acerbically. A former chief accountant of Shell, visibly overcome with emotion, confessed in a faltering voice that he was a spy who had been promised a large sum of money by Nien if he would work for the enemy. In prison, Nien was grilled for days in an interrogation room decorated with a portrait of the Chairman. During these long sessions, as Mao stared down at her, Nien detected a smirk of malevolent self-satisfaction in his face. The worst period of her incarceration had just begun.[6]

In Beijing some 68,000 people were unmasked over the summer of 1968. More than 400 victims were beaten to death.[7] In secondary schools and universities, teachers were no longer persecuted by Red Guards, but by the Mao Zedong Thought propaganda teams. The question was who, among the many people denounced during the Cultural Revolution as 'black gang members' or 'counter-revolutionaries', would be allowed to teach again, and who was truly an enemy. In order to cleanse the ranks and sort out friend from foe, teachers, cadres and students were forced to move into dormitories, where they lived together under constant mutual supervision. Influential intellectuals were first singled out for public criticism, then others were investigated.

The criteria used to identify a class enemy were vague. It was enough to misread a passage from the Little Red Book during a study session to be accused of a counter-revolutionary offence. But soon enough it became apparent who the real targets were. At Peking University, where Nie Yuanzi had denounced the leadership in her big-character poster in May 1966, all those who in the past had been close to the disgraced president were singled out. 'It was becoming clear that the propaganda team's unspoken goal was the permanent destruction of a whole group of teachers and cadres formerly esteemed by Lu Ping,' the president of the university who had been denounced as a close associate of Mayor Peng Zhen. At one point a quiet man who was an expert in experimental phonetics was declared a counter-revolutionary in the middle of a study session. Everybody was stunned. The team leader used the occasion to announce triumphantly that even a person who had never spoken about political matters could be an enemy in his heart, and such inner convictions could no longer be concealed from the proletariat.[8]

The pressure was too much for some to handle. At Peking University, twenty-three people committed suicide. One drank insecticide and another jumped from a window, but most of the victims hanged themselves. In the History Department, a Marxist historian and committed member of the communist party who had devoted his life to the revolution took an overdose of sleeping pills with his wife. They were found lying side by side on their bed, their clothes neatly arranged, with peaceful expressions on their faces. The body of a lecturer in ancient history accused of being a spy was discovered in an office, covered in lacerations. One administrator committed suicide. Similar stories could be told of departments across colleges and universities in the capital and elsewhere.[9]

By the spring of 1969 the total number of victims in Beijing reached 100,000. These were 'diehard capitalists', 'reactionary capitalists', 'spies', 'traitors', 'counter-revolutionaries' and 'reactionary intellectuals', but the vast majority were social outcasts, those condemned to dwell at the bottom of society by virtue of a bad class background.[10]

In every province, revolutionary committees settled old scores, sometimes charging their enemies with imaginary crimes, occasionally finding scapegoats to fill a quota, invariably using the campaign to crush the local population. Although the bulk of suspected class enemies were uncovered in the cities, county seats did not lag far behind. Across Hebei, more than 76,000 people were incarcerated as the authorities uncovered enemy organisations. In Qiuxian county, over a thousand victims, or roughly 1 per cent of the population, were locked up. Forty houses were commandeered in the main town, since local prisons could not hold all the inmates. Some were detained for a week, while others stayed for many months. Many were accused of belonging to a 'New Nationalist Party' controlled from Taipei, the capital of Taiwan. Torture chambers sprang up across the county, as confessions were extracted from the victims under duress, implicating ever more people. Hundreds of homes were raided and ransacked for incriminating evidence, floorboards torn up, walls demolished. The head of the revolutionary committee had a simple saying: 'Kill a batch, arrest a batch and handle a batch.' More than 700 people were hounded to their deaths and 1,316 crippled or maimed for life. Meanwhile, half the population lived in abject poverty, as agriculture was neglected and output plummeted. A subsequent inquiry revealed that the entire affair was a complete invention.[11]

Other branches of the 'New Nationalist Party' were discovered in Hebei. In one village alone, over a hundred suspects in Weixian county were hung from beams and beaten. Some were tied together with wire that pierced their ears. In the Baigezhuang state farm, a sprawling labour camp with 100,000 inmates, established in 1956 outside the province's port of Tangshan, hundreds of victims were hauled to an interrogation room where 'seventy torture methods' were used to extract confessions. More than 130 people died. Some of the bodies were never recovered, even after the case had been thrown out a few years later.[12]

Although the campaign was guided from above, people from all walks of life took the opportunity to settle grudges or right past wrongs. In Shijiazhuang, the drab railway hub just south of Zhengding where Gao Yuan's enemies had had the upper hand, an average of thirty-eight denunciation letters reached the party headquarters every day in May 1969, twice as many as usual. In Xinle, in addition to the daily post, a throng of people turned up at the county revolutionary committee personally to inform on their neighbours or colleagues. In Cangzhou, also in Hebei, a vigilante group of twenty elderly women systematically checked the status of all the residents on Victory Road. Their aim, they stated, was to find out 'if there were suspicious people'. Their search yielded a lonely man who had so far managed to hide his status as a former landlord.[13]

———

There were over 2,000 counties across the country, and in each of the vast majority of these more than a hundred people were beaten to death or driven to suicide during the campaign to cleanse the class ranks. In some cases the body count reached four to five hundred victims. In Guangdong province as a whole, one estimate puts the number of unnatural deaths at 40,000.[14]

Border regions like Guangdong were more prone to violence than others, and not only because they seemed to harbour so many more unreliable elements living in close proximity to countries considered to be hostile. They were home to many ethnic minorities who were suspected of divided allegiances. In Yunnan, a subtropical province sharing a border with Vietnam, Laos and Burma, the regime classified a third of the population as belonging to 'minority nationalities', quite a few of whom had historically straddled the frontier, moving in and out of the country. Kang Sheng viewed the region with deep suspicion, and accused the provincial party secretary Zhao Jianmin of being a 'hidden traitor' and 'nationalist spy'. Xie Fuzhi, the minister of public security who had run the province until 1959 and had plenty of personal scores to settle, abetted him.

In January 1968, at a meeting in the Capital West Hotel, Kang Sheng pointed a finger at Zhao Jianmin: 'I rely on my forty years of revolutionary experience, and I have a feeling that you harbour deep class hatred towards Chairman Mao and the party leadership.' With these words, a campaign was started to root out Zhao's network of spies in Yunnan. Tens of thousands of people were implicated. Some of these were ethnic minorities. Shadian, a predominantly Muslim town close to Vietnam, was declared a counter-revolutionary stronghold, and hundreds of people were arrested, humiliated, tortured and locked up. Across the province, by 1969 the witch-hunt had resulted in 17,000 deaths and 61,000 people who were crippled for life.[15]

Inner Mongolia also came under suspicion. Spanning more than a tenth of the country's landmass, it bordered Mongolia and the Soviet Union.

Much of it was a plateau covered by loess, sand deposits and grasslands. In 1947, with strategic support from Stalin and the Red Army, the communist party had managed to seize control of the region, proclaiming an Inner Mongolia Autonomous Region. The Chinese Communist Party absorbed members of the Mongolian People's Party, established years earlier by a Soviet-trained Mongol named Ulanfu.

Ulanfu, who went by the nickname of 'Mongolian Khan', became leader of the province. But in the aftermath of Mao's Great Famine, as the extent of the devastation caused by radical collectivisation became clear, he started to distance himself from the Chairman, using harsh words to condemn the Great Leap Forward at the Seven Thousand Cadre Conference in January 1962. In Inner Mongolia, he relaxed his control over the collectives, and largely sidestepped the Socialist Education Campaign spearheaded by Liu Shaoqi. As the slogan 'Never Forget Class Struggle' became all the rage, Ulanfu expressed doubts over the very existence of class differences: 'In the minds of most herdsmen, there are no classes, and it is subjective to impose them.' In June 1966, he was summoned to Beijing for six weeks of gruelling meetings. On 2 July, Liu Shaoqi and Deng Xiaoping took turns to accuse Ulanfu in harsh terms of every conceivable crime, from 'using production to replace class struggle', 'promoting ethnic splittism' and 'establishing an independent kingdom' to 'revisionism' and 'opposing Chairman Mao'. Ulanfu disappeared from view.[16]

Kang Sheng and Xie Fuzhi revisited the whole affair in early 1968, as they launched a campaign of terror against former members of the Mongolian People's Party, set up by Ulanfu in the 1930s, who were now suspected of being spies and traitors. Most of its members had been ordinary Mongol farmers and herdsmen, and they bore the brunt of the campaign. Torture chambers appeared across the province, as around 800,000 people were incarcerated, interrogated and denounced in mass meetings. The methods used against the victims plumbed the depths of horror, even by the standards of the Cultural Revolution. Tongues were ripped out, teeth extracted with pliers, eyes gouged from their sockets, flesh branded with hot irons. Women were sexually abused, their breasts, belly and lower parts singed with canes heated in the fire. Men were lashed on the back with leather whips, the flesh torn so badly that the backbone was sometimes exposed. A few people were burned alive.[17]

Although less than 10 per cent of the population were Mongols, they constituted more than 75 per cent of the victims. In some areas, almost every one of them was rounded up. At the railway bureau in Hohhot, all but two of the 446 Mongol employees were persecuted. Large swathes of the Mongol elite – cadres, managers, scholars, technicians – were wiped out. The Mongolian language was banned from all publications. Estimates of the total number of deaths range from 16,000 to 23,000. It looked like genocide. The main instigator of the massacres was Teng Haiqing, a general who headed the provincial revolutionary committee. In May 1969 the Chairman ordered him to halt, but he was never brought to justice. Inner Mongolia was placed under military control. The province was dismembered, with most of its territory integrated into neighbouring provinces.[18]

Up the Mountains, Down to the Villages

The campaign to cleanse the class ranks was about spies, renegades and traitors who had wormed their way into the party before the Cultural Revolution. It did not generally affect young people. When Zhou Enlai had appeared at the rostrum in Tiananmen Square on 7 September 1968, hailing the revolutionary committees, he had envisioned something very different: students should 'go down to the country's factories, mines and villages to learn from the masses'.[1]

In schools and campuses, students spent the autumn studying under the auspices of the Mao Zedong Thought propaganda teams. But on 22 December 1968 came the official decree: 'We have two hands, let us not laze about in the city,' declared the *People's Daily*. The Chairman ordered students to go down to the countryside to be re-educated by the peasants.[2]

Over the following months, the towns and cities were emptied of young people. Millions of students would be transported to remote regions in the countryside in the following decade. In Beijing, columns could be seen marching towards the railway station, stretching as far as the eye could see, banners waving, brass bands playing, faces bright with anticipation. The station was crowded with students, parents and friends, 'some stepping onto the train with handbags and washbasins, others holding onto windowsills to talk to those inside'. Loudspeakers blasted revolutionary songs, one of them with lyrics from the Chairman's Little Red Book: 'The world is yours, and also ours. But it is, in the final analysis, yours. You young people are full of vigour and vitality like the eight or nine o'clock sun in the morning. You are our hope.' Zhai Zhenhua had heard the excerpt a hundred times before. It had filled her with pride. But on the day of her departure to Yan'an the words rang hollow. 'The world is ours?' she asked herself. 'Bullshit!'[3]

Many had already left voluntarily after Zhou Enlai's call to learn from the masses in September. They were genuine believers and loyal followers of the Chairman. Some thought that this would be the true test of their generation, since they were the red inheritors of the revolution and leaders of tomorrow: they could steel themselves in the countryside and further the revolutionary cause.

Students sent to military farms in Xinjiang, Inner Mongolia and Manchuria were proud to join the People's Liberation Army. Gao Yuan felt that he was finally fulfilling his destiny when he was recruited to join the army. His winter uniform was made of the best cotton. 'I admired myself in a big mirror. Never had I had such fine clothes. Now, short of a red star, I was a true soldier.'[4]

Other volunteers were driven by a vision of pastoral bliss. The countryside was pictured as a site of great beauty and plenty for all. Rae Yang, the student from Beijing who had tried to save her cat from her fellow Red Guards, had high hopes for the Great Northern Wilderness, the popular name given to Manchuria: 'In my mind it was a mysterious and exciting place. Vast stretch of virgin land. Boundless pine forest on snowy mountains. Log cabins. Campfires. Hunting and skiing. Wild animals. Hidden enemies. Spies sneaked across the border from the Soviet Union at night.'[5]

In some cases students had been so enthralled by the idea of direct contact with the peasants, the backbone of the revolution, that they set off on their own even before the campaign had officially started. Xu Xiaodi and her friend, both aged sixteen, rode on their bicycles to Daxing county from Beijing to do manual labour for 30 cents a day in the summer of 1968. The experiment ended after a month, as rumours started circulating in the village about the restoration of capitalist labour relations.[6]

Those with fewer illusions were simply bored, having been confined to their dormitories for months on end. They, too, yearned for something new.

But there was also resistance. Exile to the countryside was supposed to be permanent. Students had to hand in their registration card at the police station and could no longer legally reside in a city. They lost all the perks and privileges associated with urban residency, not to mention the trauma they underwent of permanent separation from family and friends.

In Hunan, between a quarter and half of all students who received their marching orders feigned ignorance in the hope that the campaign would blow over. Many parents refused to lose their children to the countryside, pleading with local cadres or pulling strings with their superiors. They rushed to find employment for their offspring in local government units or factories before they could be transported to rural areas. This happened with four out of every ten students in Qiangyang county. Others doctored their identity papers or faked the names of their children. A few parents were openly defiant: 'My daughter is being persecuted and transported to the countryside because of my political mistakes. But I am no counter-revolutionary, and if you want my daughter to leave for the countryside you will have to clear my name, or else she will not spend one single day away from home, even if I have to buy grain on the black market to feed her, so let's see what you are going to do about it!'

And families were not alone. There were many mass organisations, set up during the Cultural Revolution, that maintained links with their former members and now tried to help, hiding some of the students in the city. Some cadres even refused point blank to comply with the policy: 'I would rather carry out conscription work ten times over! I will never send young students to the countryside.'

The students themselves resisted, especially once news about real life in the countryside started filtering back to the city from the first batches of sent-down students. 'Alive I will not go to the countryside, dead on a stretcher I will,' in the words of one rebel.[7]

As soon as Rae Yang arrived in Manchuria, her illusions were shattered. There were no snow-capped mountains and primeval forests in the area she had been sent to. Instead she found a huge swamp infested by millions of mosquitoes. They were big and bloodthirsty, biting through her working clothes. Work started at six in the morning in the fields, seven days a week, and the food was barely adequate. She had to trudge through the mud, one foot deep, to cut soybean with a sickle. Rae had to do battle with her own body, pushing herself to the very limit. 'This is the test, the trial, the firing line,' she thought, fearful of collapsing in the fields. She did not wash at first, as there was no public bathhouse or private bathroom. After nits had hatched in her hair, she learned how to clean herself in a tin basin in the dormitory, naked in front of all the others. Even washing clothes was a chore, as water had to be drawn from a well and carried back on a pole. It was ice cold.[8]

She was lucky. Many students did not have a roof over their head. In Hubei, this was the case for roughly half of all exiled students, as many lived in caves, abandoned temples, pigsties or sheds. In Hunan province, three out of four students had no fixed abode. Some were forced to wander from place to place every few weeks, while others only managed to get hold of a dilapidated shed exposed to wind and rain. Officially they arrived in their allocated village with a housing subsidy, but the local cadres often confiscated this. When the authorities tried to remedy the housing shortage by providing funds for timber, village leaders used these instead to construct coffins. In one case a family buried a relative and after a few days dug up the coffin, handing the planks back to the student.[9]

Furniture was scarce. In the drive to increase steel output during the Great Leap Forward, villagers had cut down trees, using the timber to feed backyard furnaces. In Hunan, lush woods had been denuded, replaced by bare mountains. Near Changsha, a once dense forest had been turned into a vast expanse of mud. By the time of the Cultural Revolution, the province was far from having recovered from the effects of deforestation, and timber remained a rare commodity. Even in the cities, buying a bed was a challenge, forcing some people to sleep on the floor. In Tianmen, a county in Hubei, some students went without a bed or a mosquito net, 'and some do not even have a pot and a bowl'.[10]

In rural areas, keeping a fire going was a problem, let alone building furniture. Villagers were always on the lookout for brushwood. Chaff, left over after threshing the grain, was also used for fuel. In the Qiuling region, where the mountain was called Bare Mountain since it had sustained a savage assault during the Great Leap Forward, the villagers had to forage for twigs up to 8 kilometres away from home.[11]

Hunan was no exception. In Shandong, lack of fuel worsened with the onset of the Cultural Revolution, as the amount of coal made available to ordinary people was cut by one-third. In the winter of 1968–9, as young students were being sent to the countryside, some villagers burned their own furniture and then the thatch on their roofs to stay warm. In Laixi small bridges were taken down and chopped up for kindling. Pigs died of hunger because the fodder was used as fuel.[12]

Food was also scarce. The villagers had a hard time simply looking after themselves, never mind feeding extra mouths. Mao's Great Famine was largely over by 1962, but famine continued to reduce tens of millions to a starvation diet. Even in the cities food was insufficient. In Nanjing, by the spring of 1966, just before living conditions deteriorated again with the Cultural Revolution, meat was still rationed and the only vegetables to be found on the market were mouldy or spoilt. The Yangtze River flowed past the city's western gate, but people still had to queue for fish. Fistfights broke out over fruit, as only 3 to 4 tonnes reached the market each day, averaging a few grams per person.[13]

Conditions in parts of the countryside were far worse. When Ken Ling and his classmates travelled through Anhui and Shandong in the autumn of 1966, they had repeatedly seen beggars and vagabonds. The fields were barren, and trees had been stripped of bark. 'From time to time we saw corpses by the tracks.' Accurate statistics do not exist, but in the case of Shandong province alone, 10 million people lacked food in the spring of 1966. In Cangzhou, thousands suffered from famine oedema, as parts of their bodies swelled from water retention. Having sold all their belongings, including their own clothes, many took to the roads to beg. In Juancheng, some of the famished sold their own children. A year later, 14 million people were starving in the province. Throughout the Cultural Revolution, for many villagers hunger was never far away.[14]

Most students were taken aback by the sheer destitution they discovered in the countryside. Wen Guanzhong, who came from a home near the Zikawei Library in Shanghai, was sent to Siping, a region in Manchuria bloodied by ferocious battles during the civil war. His family had been forced to barter all their possessions for food, and they used to huddle together for meals on the bare floor, but nothing had prepared him for the abject poverty he found in the countryside. The villagers lived in huts built of grass, straw and mud. When it rained the huts disintegrated, melting into the dirt. Whole families had only one set of clothes, hiding inside stark naked. Whatever food there was came teeming with maggots and flies.[15]

Numbers provide a sense of scale that is often lacking in personal interviews and reminiscences. In many parts of Hunan, up to three-quarters of the exiled students lacked food. Across the Hengyang region, where 17,000 young people were confined to the villages, 83 per cent went hungry.[16]

Zhai Zhenhua, exiled to a cave in Yan'an, the cradle of revolution where only two years earlier eager Red Guards had queued up to visit the Chairman's childhood dwelling, had cornbread and a dish of potatoes and pickled cabbage every day. Meat was rare, and vegetable oil used sparsely.[17]

A student exiled to Manchuria survived on a diet of boiled cabbages, potatoes and beets. She did not see oil once in the first five months after her arrival. With the onset of winter, as temperatures plunged to 40 degrees below zero, the canteen served nothing but a salty broth with a few vegetable leaves. Across the Great Northern Wilderness, hard work combined with poor diet caused nine out of every ten female students to suffer from menstrual problems.[18]

Other diseases were common. In Jiangxi and Yunnan, probably the worst provinces for exile, one in six students sent from Shanghai suffered from a chronic disease, ranging from liver infection to heart disease. Those banished to the north of the country suffered from goitre, caused by prolonged lack of iodine. Some diseases were so debilitating that the victims could no longer work, falling into a spiral of illness, malnutrition and underperformance.[19]

Morbidity rates are hard to come by, but in Hunan cases of premature death among educated youngsters were described by one team of investigators as 'ceaseless'. There were reports of poisoning and drowning, not to mention suicide. Violence was endemic, and some students became embroiled in village politics. They were found dead by the roadside. In production teams run by the military, discipline was strict and physical punishment common. In Yunnan alone, many young students were beaten by soldiers, three of them to death.[20]

A few wrote to protest about their conditions. One young man in Hunan remembered his pride at being selected to work in the countryside in 1969. 'And now? I simply while away the days. I have lost interest in books and newspapers, and I have lost any concern for the fatherland's future or man-kind's dreams. I merely get through the motions by mechanically eating, working and eating again, as if I have become a mere beast working to earn a living.' Another young student felt so marginalised by the villagers that he repeatedly demanded that the authorities back in his home town give him a life sentence in a labour camp instead (he clearly had no idea of what life was like behind bars). Zhai Zhenhua hated her life, which she described as an 'unwanted, pointless existence': 'My country could not find any better use for us but dumped us all like dirt in the countryside. The peasants did not need us; we were their burden and only gave them trouble.'[21]

Work, especially for those enrolled in production units run by the army, was excruciating at first, but the sheer tedium of daily life also became a challenge. As Rae noted about her swamp in Manchuria, 'there was no TV, no movies, no library, no ping-pong, no chess, no poker'. Some of the stu-dents managed to get hold of books, while others put together transistors, listening to foreign radio. A few went hunting for wild dogs or scavenged for plants, berries and nuts. Others banded together, stealing food from the fields at night.[22]

Girls were vulnerable. Those enrolled in military production units or sent in batches to the countryside found safety in numbers, but many were alone, helpless, bewildered and often at the mercy of village leaders. Sexual abuse was common in a one-party state that rewarded male bullies, but now displaced students found themselves at the very bottom of the pecking order in the countryside, more vulnerable than ever. In a brigade in Fuyang county, Anhui, six young women were molested. Two of the victims committed suicide, and one lost her mind.[23]

Some victims took their cases to the higher authorities, alone or in groups. From Huanggang, Hubei, came a letter signed by ten young women who explained that from the moment that they had arrived in the countryside all of them had been harassed and molested. Several became pregnant and were forced to marry their rapists. But generally few girls complained. When they did, they were ignored at best, although many were ostracised even further by the villagers. A few were even accused of having abetted rape through 'improper behaviour'.[24]

In any event, the local response was at best half hearted. A few perpetrators were shot in Hunan in 1971, but as the authorities noted, 'in some places the rape and forced marriage of young women is considered to be part of normal sexual relationships'. Blaming local culture, of course, was a way of evading responsibility. Nobody in the higher echelons of power wished to query the Chairman's wisdom of having young students from the cities undergo 're-education by the masses'.[25]

It was Mao who had decided to send millions of young people into exile in 1968, and it was Mao who partially redeemed them in 1973. He signalled his concern in a personal response to a letter from Li Qinglin, a school teacher in Fujian who wrote to the Chairman about the appalling conditions his son was enduring in the countryside. The Chairman generously sent the man 300 yuan: 'Comrade Li Qinglin, the issue you wrote about seems ubiquitous around the country and needs to be solved as a whole. Please accept this 300 yuan. I hope it can help you to some degree. Mao Zedong.'[26]

A flurry of activity followed. Emergency meetings were held in Zhongnanhai, chaired by Zhou Enlai, whom the Chairman implicitly blamed for the state of affairs. Cases of rape suddenly came to light across the country. In Hubei, a systematic investigation conducted in Tianmen county, located a mere 60 kilometres to the west of Wuhan, revealed that between 1969 and 1973 more than 200 young women had been molested, raped or otherwise 'destroyed', to use the report's terminology. Some were as young as fourteen. Li Xiannian, the vice-premier who had been party secretary of the province for many years, personally wrote in the margin of the report: 'I'm afraid that in Hubei it's not just Tianmen county, what about the other counties?' Since there were more than forty counties in Hubei, by extrapolation from these figures at least 8,000 women had been abused in that province alone.[27]

Similar reports reached the capital from other parts of the country. In Liaoning province 3,400 cases of assault or rape were uncovered. The leadership was outraged. 'The Ministry of Public Security should act! Don't be soft-hearted!' Zhou Enlai exclaimed. 'Kill the bastards, otherwise we can't appease the people!' cried Li Xiannian. The following year, over 500 people were sentenced for molesting, attacking or raping young students in Hubei. Seven were sentenced to death.[28]

Conditions improved somewhat, but the campaign did not abate. Every year a million young students were sent into exile. Even after the Chairman's death, many of them could not leave the countryside. Some had married, and others were unable to obtain an urban residency permit. In total, from 1962 to 1978, some 18 to 20 million students were banished from the cities.

———

The students were not the only ones to be sent to rural areas. As soon as the bamboo curtain came down in 1949, the new regime had started emptying the cities of entire categories of people described as a threat to social order and a drain on public resources. Prostitutes, paupers and pickpockets, as well as millions of refugees and disbanded soldiers, were sent to the countryside, which became the great dumping ground for all undesirable elements. In the intervening years, as the household registration system imposed strict controls on the movement of people, a sometimes deadly game of cat and mouse developed. The most effective strategy for survival in the countryside was to leave the village and migrate to the city. The authorities needed cheap labour, so often they turned a blind eye to the incomers. A vast underclass was created, relegated to dirty, arduous and sometimes dangerous jobs. Migrant workers had no secure status, and risked expulsion back to the countryside at any time. Once in a while, a purge would cleanse the cities of people without proper documentation. Those who were caught were sent back to their villages, while hardened recidivists were dispatched to the gulag.

In 1958, at the height of the Great Leap Forward, as targets for industrial output were ceaselessly revised upwards, more than 15 million villagers moved to the city. But three years later, with the country bankrupt, 20 million people were deported back to the countryside.[29]

When, on 7 September 1968, Zhou Enlai had announced that students should go up the mountains and down to the villages to learn from the great proletarian masses, he had also urged the party to cleanse the class ranks and 'streamline the administration', sending superfluous staff back to join production in the countryside. Millions of people had used the chaos of the Cultural Revolution to find their way to the city, and now the premier indicated that the time for their deportation had come.[30]

The scale of the transportations was staggering, by far surpassing what had happened under the Red Guards in the summer of 1966, when nationwide some 400,000 people from bad family backgrounds had been hounded out of the cities. From Shanghai alone, up to 1975, roughly a third of a million people were removed, not including 950,000 students. In some cases, in smaller cities, the number of ordinary people banished to the countryside actually exceeded exiled students by a factor of two to one. In the single county of Lingling, a hilly part of southern Hunan where several rivers converged, 35,000 city dwellers were dispersed throughout the countryside compared to 17,000 students. In Hengyang, by the Dongting Lake, there were 30,000 ordinary people in exile, twice as many as banished students. Nine out of ten teetered on the edge of starvation, having to make do with a mere 12 kilos of unhusked grain a month, equivalent to less than 1,000 calories a day, far below the 23 to 26 kilos required to provide 1,700 to 1,900 calories per day, an amount international aid organisations consider the bare minimum for subsistence.[31]

Entire families were deported, regardless of their ability to survive. Huang Ying, condemned as a 'counter-revolutionary', aged sixty-one, was sent off with his mother-in-law, wife and daughter. Liu Sucai, a hunchback, had a wife who suffered from a learning disability, leaving him in charge of their four children aged four to fourteen. He was unable to make ends meet in the countryside, where hard labour earned most villagers barely enough food to survive on their own, let alone feed entire families. Liu was not an isolated example. In roughly one-fifth of all families in exile in Hunan, the main provider was unable to earn enough work points to look after others, whether children, sick people, the disabled or the elderly. In many cases, people with no experience of farming – pedlars, artisans, mechanics, clerks, teachers – were simply dumped in the countryside, left to fend for themselves and their dependants.[32]

Class background mattered a great deal in the socialist state, but ultimately the inability to earn a living was a far greater stigma. Destitute members of society, in other words, were treated like pariahs. The economy was in the doldrums, and the state wanted to reduce the number of people who represented a drain on its resources. In many parts of the country the most vulnerable categories of people were sent into exile. In Tangshan, the medium-sized city port of Hebei, tens of thousands of unemployed people and vagrants were removed.[33]

In Shanghai the authorities even envisaged reducing the population by one-third. As early as April 1968, all retired workers and those on sick leave were ordered back to the countryside without pension or medical support if they lacked the proper class credentials. A year and a half later, after more than 600,000 people had been deported, including students and other undesirable elements, a new plan proposed to increase the number of people earmarked for removal to a total of 3.5 million. Half of all medical workers were to be sent off, as well as all unemployed and retired people. Those suffering from a chronic illness were added to the list. Even prisons were to be relocated outside the city limits. The plan was never fully implemented, but for years the population of Shanghai stagnated around the 10 million mark.[34]

Cadres who had strayed from the path were also to be re-educated in the countryside, and they were sent to May Seventh Cadre Schools. Much of the Cultural Revolution was fuelled by a vision first developed in Yan'an during the Second World War, when everybody had been asked to fuse with the collective in war and work alike, becoming simultaneously soldier, worker and student. On 7 May 1966, Mao had written to Lin Biao to extol the Yan'an model, encouraging people to learn alternative skills and contribute to production. Exactly two years later, to mark the occasion, Heilongjiang province established a labour farm called the 'May Seventh Cadre School' in the countryside, where 'capitalist roaders', 'revisionists' and other wayward officials were to work, live and rehabilitate themselves. On 30 September, the Chairman gave the experiment his seal of approval, pronouncing that 'sending vast numbers of cadres to work in the countryside provides them with an excellent second chance to study'. Less than a week later, the *People's Daily* extolled the May Seventh Cadre School, call-ing on the whole country to emulate Heilongjiang's example.[35]

Cadre schools appeared everywhere. Peking University, where teachers and cadres had been forced to move into dormitories, studying together under the watchful eye of the Mao Zedong Thought propaganda teams, joined the trend and selected a muddy stretch of reclaimed land near the Poyang Lake in Jiangxi province. It was a stark and desolate landscape, with vast expanses of wild grass evenly covered in yellow sand as far as the eye could see. Here, more than a thousand kilometres south of the capital, the propaganda teams could observe troublesome intellectuals and suspect cadres in a carefully controlled environment. Those who demonstrated their loyalty to the Chairman could be recalled to the city, while stubborn elements would be condemned to permanent exile. Only the most reliable teachers and cadres who had survived the campaign to cleanse the party ranks were allowed to remain on campus.

The rehabilitation centre in Jiangxi consisted of nothing but four tem-porary sheds in the middle of a wasteland. Everything had to be built from scratch, including more permanent housing, as bamboo posts were lashed together with wire and makeshift walls erected, made of woven strips of bamboo plastered with mud. Ropes were used to dry clothes. The roofs leaked, and washbasins had to be placed beneath the worst drips. To stay dry when it rained, people slept under plastic sheets tied to a bamboo frame. More permanent brick structures gradually appeared, each brick being cut with a spade from hard clay, mixed with water, forced into rec-tangular wooden moulds and then baked in a kiln.

The cadre school was run by the military, and everybody was enrolled into a squadron of ten people, ten squadrons, in turn, constituting a com-pany. Discipline was strict, the work regime relentless at nine or ten hours a day, seven days a week. Company leaders always found new ways of test-ing people, assigning outdoor labour when it was raining or demanding that bricks be moved from one location to another for no good reason. They saw it as their duty to make life as miserable as possible, since other-wise the very goal of re-education through labour could not be achieved. Military drills were organised, sometimes in the middle of the night. There were also obligatory study sessions, when teachers and cadres assembled in the morning to study the Chairman's thoughts.

Here were some of the country's most eminent scientists, physicians, engineers and philosophers, far away from their laboratories and offices, forced to do hard physical labour, shovelling mud, baking bricks, collecting twigs or hauling manure. On one occasion, a mathematician trained in Cambridge and a physicist with a doctoral dissertation from Moscow University attempted to slaughter a pig. They botched the affair, the animal breaking free, spurting blood everywhere. Still, there was no lack of true believers, as some of the victims shared the conviction that they had to become more productive members of society. Yue Daiyun agreed with the goals of the propaganda team, and conceded that she 'rarely felt resentment at the way we were treated'. Others welcomed a simple life away from the tribulations of the Cultural Revolution.

Not all showed such equanimity. Nie Yuanzi, her face sallow and expressionless, was no longer fêted as a rebel hero, but given the task of emptying heavy buckets of urine every morning. Her sworn enemy, Peng Peiyun, once the powerful assistant party secretary under the university's president, was assigned the same strenuous work. The propaganda team was keen to destroy their power. In cadre schools across the country, leaders from all the factions that had appeared during the Cultural Revolution were crushed.[36]

Most cadre schools were completely cut off from the rest of society. There were occasional trips to local markets, or forays into town to purchase provisions and collect mail, but the exemplary workers, peasants and soldiers they were supposed to emulate were nowhere to be seen. Nor was all the hard labour they carried out particularly useful. They could not even sustain themselves, and cadre schools had to be heavily subsidised with regular rations of grain, edible oil, vegetables and meat.

Most of all, compared to the many batches of ordinary people and students deported to the countryside with no hope of ever returning to their homes, the government officials sent back to school were relatively sheltered. And their numbers were far smaller. In Gansu, by the spring of 1970, fewer than 20,000 people lived in cadre schools, representing roughly 5 per cent of all party officials. By comparison, half a million students were banished to the countryside. In Hebei, just over 32,000 cadres were undergoing re-education in the countryside. Like others across the nation, most of them were allowed to return to their posts in the autumn of 1970.[37]

16

Preparing for War

Sparsely covered with birch trees and brushy undergrowth, Damansky Island is less than 2 kilometres long and at most 800 metres wide. Called Zhenbao in Chinese, or 'Treasure Island', it sits low in the Ussuri River that marks the riverine border between China and the Soviet Union. Manchurian red deer, which shed their reddish summer coat for thick brown-grey hair, sometimes roam across the frozen river. The island was the subject of a territorial dispute, and endless incidents flared up in the area, as border patrol guards, outfitted in white winter uniforms, would fight each other with boat hooks, bear spears and spiked sticks. On a few occasions, a column of lorries would pull up on the Chinese side of the river and hundreds of troops would dismount, warming up for a fight as martial music blared from loudspeakers.[1]

The clashes did not involve heavy weapons, but this all changed when simmering tensions reached a flashpoint in March 1969. On 2 March, in the early hours of the morning, dozens of armed Chinese soldiers crossed the ice and occupied the island, shooting at the border post on the other side of the river at point-blank range. Mortars from the People's Liberation Army shelled enemy positions. The crossfire lasted for several hours, until Soviet reinforcements arrived and deployed missile launchers to crush their opponents.

Two weeks later, on 15 March, thousands of troops clashed again on Damansky. But this time the Soviets were better prepared, deploying dozens of tanks and armoured vehicles to repulse the attack. Hundreds died in combat.

For months, China had prepared for battle in order to regain the initiative in the border conflict. The entire operation was supervised from the

Capital West Hotel in Beijing. A special telephone line linked the hotel to the troops on the Ussuri River. Zhou Enlai made all the key decisions. But after the battle of 15 March, the Chairman intervened: 'We should stop here. Do not fight any more!' Mao had achieved his aim, which was to put the Soviet Union on notice and use the incident to ratchet up the tension at home.[2]

As soon as the confrontation was over, the propaganda machine started beating the war drum: 'Prepare for War!' became the motto of the day. The Chairman, never one to shy away from hyperbole, announced that the country should be on standby to 'fight a great war, an early war, and even a nuclear war'.[3]

Two weeks later, the long-awaited Ninth Party Congress opened in Beijing. At last, the Chairman was able to reverse the decisions made by the Eighth Party Congress in September 1956. Thirteen years earlier, the delegates had quietly dropped all references to the Socialist High Tide, Mao's failed attempt to rush the country into collectivisation in 1955. Half a year after Khrushchev's denunciation of Stalin in February 1956, they had also deleted all references to Mao Zedong Thought from the constitution and denounced the cult of personality.

The Chairman used the militant atmosphere created by the border clashes to impose strict conditions of secrecy on the delegates, who were flown to the capital by night on specially chartered military planes. They were instructed not to communicate with anyone about the congress.[4]

Lin Biao delivered the main political report, drafted by Zhang Chunqiao and Yao Wenyuan under close supervision from the Chairman. It praised the Cultural Revolution and promised unrelenting vigilance against class enemies. Zhou Enlai, in turn, gave a paean to 'the deputy supreme commander of our proletarian headquarters', asking that Lin Biao be officially named as Mao's successor. A new constitution laid down that 'Marxism-Leninism Mao Zedong Thought is the theoretical basis guiding the party's thinking.' Mao Zedong Thought was reaffirmed as the country's guiding ideology.

On the last day of the congress, the 1,500 delegates were asked to elect a new Central Committee. Voting was carefully manipulated. A list of candidates had been prepared, equal to the number of available positions, and all of them were guaranteed election unless their names were crossed out by more than half of the delegates. The clashes along the border served to strengthen a military bid for power, and more than a third of all candidates came from the army, navy and air force. Jiang Qing, together with the wives of Kang Sheng, Lin Biao and Zhou Enlai, was also among the new members, although a secret investigation was later launched to find out which ten delegates had failed to endorse her. But over the summer her Cultural Revolution Group began to wind down its operations, ceasing altogether in September 1969.[5]

With Lin Biao at the height of his power, the country was militarised even further. In the months following the clashes at Damansky Island, the country was fully mobilised for war. But then, in the middle of August 1969, came retaliation. In Xinjiang, at the opposite end of a 7,000-kilometre border separating both empires, more than 300 Soviet soldiers backed by two helicopters and dozens of armoured vehicles launched a surprise attack, striking deep inside enemy territory and eliminating a Chinese frontier squadron.

The confrontations on Damansky Island earlier in March had unsettled the leadership in Moscow. It was alarmed at the prospect of the People's Liberation Army attempting a large-scale incursion into Soviet territory. Some hardliners within the Soviet party even argued for the need to eliminate the 'China threat'. *Red Star*, the main organ of the Soviet military, published an article promising to deal the 'modern adventurers' a crushing nuclear blow. Having reclaimed the initiative with their surgical strike in Xinjiang, the Soviets began hastening preparations for war. Five days later, in Washington, the Soviet embassy asked the Americans how they would react to a Russian attack on a Chinese nuclear facility. The US ignored them. All along, the official Soviet mouthpiece *Pravda* appealed to the world to understand how dangerous China had become. It seemed as if all-out war between the two nuclear powers was imminent.[6]

The Chairman was stunned. He had not anticipated that the Soviets would contemplate going to war. Unlike the disputed border in Manchuria, where the Ussuri and Amur rivers created a natural boundary, vast stretches

of the frontier along the arid deserts of Xinjiang were only vaguely demar-
cated. The nuclear testing ground of Lop Nur was not far away. In addition, despite a relentless programme of colonisation resulting in millions of
Chinese settlers being relocated in the region, the majority of people there
were still Uighurs, Kazakhs, Kirghiz, Tadjiks and other ethnic groups, who
resented attempts to collectivise their herds and longed for genuine independence. In 1962, at the end of Mao's Great Famine, more than 64,000
people, including families with children and their meagre possessions, had
fled across the border into the Soviet Union.[7]

Soviet troops in the region were not only far superior, but were backed
up by medium-range missiles. Only a few years earlier, in January 1966,
the Soviet Union had concluded a treaty of mutual assistance with Ulan
Bator, stationing an army in Mongolia, which directly abutted Xinjiang.

The spectre of war hung over Beijing. Despite the slogan 'Prepare for
War', the country was far from ready, damaged by years of chaos caused
by the Cultural Revolution. Lin Biao now asked that military expenditure
be doubled. On 28 August, the Central Committee ordered a military
mobilisation in the provinces and regions bordering the Soviet Union and
Mongolia. It put the country on red alert, demanding that the population
be prepared for a large-scale Soviet invasion.

Behind the scenes, in a dramatic retreat from past intransigence, Beijing
agreed to discuss the border issue with the Soviets. But even after Kosygin
had made a number of diplomatic concessions designed to lower the tension, Lin Biao and Mao Zedong remained deeply suspicious. Moscow's
peace gesture was seen as a smokescreen designed to cover a future attack.
The panic was such that when, on 20 October, a Soviet delegation was
scheduled to arrive in Beijing to discuss the border issue, all party and
military leaders were ordered to leave the capital. Mao sought refuge in
Wuhan. Only Zhou Enlai remained, moving into an underground command centre in the suburbs with the army's general staff. On 17 October,
Lin Biao issued a 'Number One Order' from a bunker in Suzhou, putting
all military units on high alert. One million soldiers, 4,000 planes and
600 ships moved to take up strategic positions across the country. On 20
October, nothing happened.[8]

Although the transportation of whole categories of people had already started in September 1968, including families from bad class backgrounds, villagers without permission to reside in the city, workers on temporary contracts, retired people, invalids, young people and large numbers of cadres, the spectre of a Third World War was used to accelerate the removal of millions of people to the countryside. A drive was conducted to ferret out those who had returned from the countryside illegally, while the wives and children of employees sent to May Seventh Cadre Schools and the families of those sent to the countryside for permanent resettlement were now banished. In Guangdong and Fujian, long lines of refugees could be seen, clutching baskets and bags containing mosquito netting, enamel washbasins and cooking utensils.[9]

Those who remained behind were asked to prepare for war. In Shanghai and other cities, booklets were distributed to the population explaining the trajectory of bombs which were propelled forward by planes rather than dropped vertically; how to take cover in the event of a nuclear strike; how to dig trenches; how to shoot at an aircraft with a rifle; what part of a building to shelter in; how to give first aid; how to fight a fire; and how to recognise foreign combat aircraft. Hoardings appeared with the markings and silhouettes of Soviet and American aircraft and helicopters.[10]

Every city was soon pasted with anti-Soviet and anti-American posters. Cartoons on the Bund in Shanghai depicted Brezhnev poking his head through a flowery screen to engage in peace talks while secretly holding a match, ready to light a gigantic rocket gripped between his bare toes. Another showed President Nixon egging on his Soviet counterpart while covetously caressing a globe.[11]

Not everyone believed the propaganda. There was no lack of people who realised that the border skirmish had been used to ratchet up tension at home and corral the local population. One opinion survey in the city of Handan, Hebei, revealed that some residents wondered what all the fuss was about, since only a few shots had been exchanged. But others panicked. Among those who feared the onslaught of a Third World War, some fled to the countryside. Others stayed put, selling all their possessions to enjoy a final feast of wine and food in the countdown to Armageddon. Elsewhere in the province some villagers feared yet another requisition of their livestock and slaughtered all the pigs. In a few places the prospect of war sparked panic buying, as shops were emptied of batteries and candles.

A few rejoiced. Counter-revolutionary slogans were posted, predicting the fall of the communist party. In one county, an underground group issued a call to arms to the local population, asking that 'We must co-ordinate our movements with the United States and the Soviet Union in our attack on Beijing!' Here and there, flares went up, presumably to help the enemy in its advance. Some hotheads even volunteered to work for the enemy. One such was Feng Guiyuan, who defiantly declared that 'When troops from the Soviet Union come, I will go out there and welcome them.' Others started planning for life after communism. In Wanquan county, Ma Yu'e, the wife of a landlord, took her children to see the house that had been wrenched from them during land reform twenty years earlier.[12]

Sheer desperation also played a role. From her cave in Yan'an, Zhai Zhenhua, the once idealistic student who had emulated Lei Feng, now secretly wished for war. 'War brings disaster but also opportunity. I would rather die heroically on the battlefield than live the hopeless life I had been given. And if I didn't die, things in China would definitely change for the better after the war, I thought. This was crazy, of course, but I was living in a crazy time.'[13]

However, most people quite literally followed the drill. Factory workers, government employees and even schoolchildren were trained in civil defence. In Shanghai, children were seen parading in formation and throwing themselves on the ground, covering their eyes at the blast of a whistle. Another signal from their leader and they jumped up to resume their march, often with great relish. Others marched in time with dummy rifles. In Beijing, young people staged mock street battles with wooden guns, each of the combatants wearing pieces of paper on their chest to identify them as friend or foe. Soldiers instructed new recruits in how to handle firearms. Searchlight practices became frequent in the evening.[14]

Appeals went out for blood donations. But most of all, people were asked to contribute by digging trenches and air-raid shelters. The Chairman called on the people to 'deeply dig caves, extensively store grain'. Already in June 1965, Mao had proposed that 'the best way would be to dig shelters underneath houses, roughly a metre deep. If we connect all the houses with tunnels, and each household digs its own shelter, the state will not have to incur any expenses.' In an apocalyptic vision reminiscent of the battle of Stalingrad, when the Germans fought over individual streets in ferocious hand-to-hand combat with the Russians, he wanted each city to be ready for street fighting. Speaking to a foreign visitor in June 1970, he explained that all buildings would be linked by a network of tunnels, as the people would retreat into shelters to hide, study, practise shooting and harass the enemy.[15]

In the capital the Chairman got what he wanted. For more than a year, Beijing was covered in mounds of earth and 'almost unbelievable numbers' of bricks, as a frenzied wave of construction took place. Inside department stores and government offices, deep holes were dug, with access to a sprawling underground world of narrow corridors and bunkers served by electric lifts. On Tiananmen Square, huge hoardings went up, hiding cranes and pile drivers, as the army was entrusted with the mammoth task of linking up the Great Hall of the People with the maze of tunnels.[16]

Where construction work was supervised by engineers and the military, rapid progress was made, and eventually the capital boasted an underground city covering an area of 85 square kilometres. It came with restaurants, clinics, schools, theatres and factories, and apparently even had a roller-skating rink. Some shelters had gas-proof hatches and radiation-shielding steel doors 30 centimetres thick. Grain and oil were also stored underground, while mushrooms that required little light were grown on special subterranean farms.

Some of the excavations were carried out in conjunction with work on the metro, which had started a few years earlier. On 1 October 1969, to mark the twentieth anniversary of the founding of the People's Republic, trial operations were started on the first line, which ran from military barracks in the suburbs to the Beijing Railway Station.[17]

Accidents were frequent, especially where desultory citizens followed the commands of local cadres with no knowledge of geology or even basic engineering. The Yan'an spirit, after all, hailed the collective wisdom of the masses, while specialist knowledge was scorned as bourgeois. In many smaller projects, the excavated soil was removed in wheelbarrows and emptied in the streets. Heavy rain turned it to sludge, causing bicycles to slip, carts to tip over and gutters to clog up and overflow. In Puxi, a district in Shanghai, eight streets were lined with over a hundred heaps of excavated earth, debris and putrefying waste, weighing an estimated 30,000 tonnes. With everything mud-splattered, it resembled a clean-up operation in the aftermath of a devastating typhoon. Similar scenes could be seen in many streets all across the nation.[18]

Since geological surveys were carried out only on major construction projects, there were plenty of cases of damage to housing. In the Huangpu district, dominated by the Shanghai International Settlement until it was handed back to the republican government in 1943, the foundations of a dozen houses were so badly undermined by tunnelling that they caved in or were ripped open. Fatal accidents occurred when badly reinforced shelters collapsed, burying some of the workers alive. This happened regularly. Since schoolchildren were also compelled to take part in the digging, they sometimes ended up being suffocated to death when excavation sites caved in.[19]

People were also asked to contribute bricks. In a reminder of the Great Leap Forward, when improvised backyard furnaces appeared across the country in response to a call to double the steel output, makeshift brick kilns went up in every town and city. The idea was that the excavated mud could be turned into bricks, which could then be used to reinforce the underground shelters. In Beijing, where mud kilns appeared next to giant piles of earth, there was a quota of thirty bricks per person. Perhaps predictably, the bricks had anti-Soviet slogans printed on them. In Shanghai, as one report enthused, 'people took the initiative to tear down their own chicken sheds and fish tanks, and some even took the bricks used to prop up their beds and furniture, reinforce their walls, elevate their stoves or pave their floors'. People also donated coal to operate the improvised kilns, which apparently produced 7 million bricks – not counting those salvaged or scavenged from existing structures.[20]

Fatalities were less keenly inventoried than bricks, although they must have been frequent, as some of the kilns, built of sand, stone, fire clay or bricks, keeled over or exploded. When Shanghai tried to establish a new record in brick production in the run-up to National Day in 1971, one of these devices in the Putuo district imploded, burying or injuring twelve people. Makeshift kilns posed a lethal hazard until the mid-1970s.[21]

Beijing led a competition to build the country's most extensive under-ground network. Shanghai did not lag far behind, with an elaborate honeycomb of subterranean tunnels that could reputedly hold 2.5 million people. In the six main cities of Hebei province, more than a million people could be sheltered. By the end of 1970, the country's seventy-five largest cities boasted enough underground shelters to hold 60 per cent of their populations. Most were dug by hand.[22]

Strategic mountains were riddled with tunnels, some of them wide enough for several buses. The one blasted through Langmao Mountain, just outside Shandong's provincial capital of Jinan, was 8 metres wide and 7 metres high, leading to an underground storage facility designed to hold more than 10,000 tonnes of grain. Near by, deep inside Wanling Mountain, an underground parking lot could accommodate 200 military vehicles. Even in barren Gansu province, deep inside the hinterland, close to a million square metres were dug by the end of 1970. In Yan'an, so remote and isolated from the rest of the country that Mao had picked the place as his wartime base in the fight against Japan decades earlier, Zhai Zhenhua and some of the best workers from the village had to shovel their way through a loess mountain.[23]

It was a gargantuan effort, and most of it was wasted. In a carefully choreo-graphed visit to the capital's shelters in November 1970, the US journalist Edgar Snow was taken through narrow corridors to a brand new bunker, where he received a telephone call from Prince Sihanouk, also in Beijing after his overthrow in a military coup in his native Cambodia. But the war never took place. Once the warren had been completed it quickly faded into obscu-rity, colonised by fungi and vermin. Eventually many of the tunnels were blocked up. The network was deemed a military secret, and access prohibited to the very people who had built it with their own bare hands.[24]

Almost every adult and child in the country took part in building shelters. The war scare helped create much-needed national unity after all the politi-cal infighting of the Cultural Revolution. It kept people busy. Evacuating the cities, digging trenches and stockpiling food helped conquer factionalism.

Always a fastidious student of Stalin, the Chairman realised that one of his erstwhile master's most serious mistakes – besides his failure to spot

Khrushchev as his future nemesis – was the lack of a comprehensive evacuation programme in the event of a large-scale invasion. Only after the Germans had launched Operation Barbarossa in June 1941, sending a hundred divisions across the border in the largest military operation in the history of warfare, was a Council for Evacuation appointed. In an unprecedented logistical undertaking, more than 1,500 of the most important factories were dismantled and shipped eastwards. As trains moved 2.5 million soldiers to the front over the summer, industrial machinery was taken to the east on their return. Finding sufficient buildings in which to house the evacuated factories – in the Urals, Central Asia and Siberia – was another challenge, and much of the material remained locked up in warehouses until the spring of 1942. It was an immense task, but it represented only a fraction of the 32,000 factories captured by the Germans. Despite their belated efforts, the Russians lost 40 per cent of their population and much of their industry.[25]

Mao was determined not to make the same mistake. Before Khrushchev's downfall in October 1964, as tensions between China and the Soviet Union peaked with endless belligerent statements from both sides, the Chairman wondered whether Moscow could attack his country. 'Is it possible that the Soviet Union might dispatch its troops to occupy Xinjiang, Heilongjiang or even Inner Mongolia?' At the same time, the Americans were escalating their involvement in the Vietnam War. Mao's answer was to build a Third Front in the hinterland, far away from the land and sea borders most likely to come under attack in the event of war.[26]

The Third Front aimed at nothing less than the building of a complete industrial infrastructure in the country's interior. Between 1964 and 1980 a colossal programme was carried out to move some of the country's factories to the most remote and inhospitable areas in the hinterland, far away from the populated plains in the north of the country and along the coastline. Sichuan province, often referred to as a natural fortress with its mountain chains rising high above its fertile basin, was the centre of the Third Front. But other mountainous regions, stretching from Shaanxi and Hubei down to the elevated plateau straddling Yunnan and Guizhou, were also selected for development. In some cases entire factories were dismantled and moved, but more often than not only a portion of an urban plant's machinery and workforce was relocated inland.[27]

Other facilities were built from scratch. At Panzhihua, a forbidding and barren region with large mineral resources in the south of Sichuan, a huge iron and steel complex emerged after 1965. Tens of thousands of construction workers were sent from all over the country, to dig coalmines, lay rail tracks and build power plants. The railway alone, tunnelling through hundreds of kilometres from the new steel city to both Chengdu and Kunming, cost 3.3 billion yuan. One member of the Youth Corps was part of the first contingent to move to Panzhihua in 1965: 'We didn't have anything, not even coal to cook with, and the hills were covered only in scrub brush that was hardly fit for burning . . . We wandered around with just one set of clothes, a wide-brimmed hat to protect us from the sun, and a canteen. As for transportation, we had nothing but our own two feet.' But no amount of hardship could stand in the way of the Third Front. The impatient Chairman told the Ministry of Mining and Industry that 'I cannot sleep until we build the Panzhihua iron and steel mill.' Concerned about the lack of capital, he donated the royalties of the Little Red Book and his other writings to the cause.[28]

In 1965, the hand of the state redrew the boundaries of the new city, bringing under its administrative purview more than 80,000 villagers from several surrounding communes. They were worked hard. The mortality rate reached an astonishing 13 per cent. A harsh environment, military discipline and the great haste with which the plan was carried out were only part of the problem. As one historian of the Third Front has noted, in Panzhihua and elsewhere there was barely any preparatory work. Sites were simultaneously selected, designed and built, in an ad hoc manner that demanded constant remedial measures to correct costly mistakes.[29]

From 1966 to 1968, much of the work on the Third Front ground to a halt with the Cultural Revolution, and transport disruptions intermittently stopped work at Panzhihua. But a new wave of investment came after the March 1969 clash at Damansky. Hundreds of thousands of temporary workers were used in human-wave tactics to link other parts of the hinterland through a railway grid. At the height of the campaign, as the regime used the war scare to whip the workforce into a frenzy, up to two labourers were used for every metre of track.

Across the hinterland, up in the mountains, hundreds of factories were built. The Number Two Automobile Plant in Shiyan, deep inside western Hubei, received help from more than 140 factories and research institutes. Many plants related to the Number Two were scattered across the region, producing tyres, rubber, paint and automobile parts. Some were located in narrow valleys, others in giant caves hollowed out from the mountains. Transportation was often impossible, despite the new railway lines.[30]

The Third Front brought some 600,000 workers to the region, pushing the total population to 4 million. The pressure was unbearable. In Shiyan itself, a mere 500 shop assistants had to serve 200,000 people. They followed a capricious routine, selling only a limited range of items on any given day. On a Monday morning, for instance, they would sell plastic shoes, but only in size 38. Customers wanting the next size up had to come back the following day. Those who managed to obtain a pair were considered lucky. Shortages were such that some workers in the new factories had no shoes at all. Bulbs, thermos flasks, towels, socks, tinned food and washbasins were also in short supply. There was only enough cable to connect 6 per cent of the telephones. In the main street of Yuan'an, a county seat, a single bulb dangled disconsolately along a stretch of a hundred metres. But workers at the Third Front still enjoyed priority over local villagers. Those living in proximity to the new factories saw their already paltry living standards plunge even further, as everything was drained away to fuel the war effort. Some hamlets did not even have matches, and others lacked the nails required to repair simple water wheels.[31]

Food was also an issue, compounded by the deliberately remote location of many of the Third Front factories. In some canteens, for instance near the Number Two Automobile Plant, the diet varied between plain dumplings and radish soup. Vegetables were in short supply, and often the workers had nothing but a little soy sauce to add to their buns or dumplings. Meat was a luxury, rarely seen except to celebrate the Lunar New Year.[32]

Western Hubei was part of the remote hinterland, but similar problems afflicted even more developed parts of the country. The First Front was the border and coastal areas, stretching from the industrial belt in Manchuria to major coastal cities such as Tianjin and Shanghai on the east coast. The Second Front was the rest of the country, and it, too, was pressed into war preparation, as factories from the cities relocated no more than a few hundred kilometres inland. In parts of Handan, less than 500 kilometres from Tianjin in southern Hebei, the workers in new factories only ever ate a thin broth with a few pickles on the side. 'What we earn is socialist money, what we eat is capitalist food,' some of them observed, commenting on the cost of the food in the canteen. There were no shops, as the factories were placed strategically deep inside the countryside. The workers bartered with local villagers for cigarettes. More substantial purchases, for instance a pair of shoes, demanded an expedition to the county seat some 30 kilometres away.[33]

The scale of the Third Front was staggering, as about 1,800 factories were set up in the hinterland to prepare for war. As one scholar has noted, since about two-thirds of the state's industrial investment went to the project between 1964 and 1971, it constituted the main economic policy of the Cultural Revolution. At best, it put in place the rudiments of a transportation system in the hinterland. But even a well-planned and carefully executed project on this gargantuan scale would have been extremely costly, given its remote and scattered location as well as the difficult terrain up in the mountains and along narrow valleys. It was done in great haste, at breakneck speed, in a climate of impending apocalypse. 'Nearly every project about which we have information ran into substantial additional costs and delays because of inadequate preparatory work,' writes one specialist on the Third Front. The first furnace of molten steel was eventually smelted in Panzhihua in July 1970, but three other steel mills were still under construction in the 1980s. The design of the mill at Jiuquan, in Gansu province, was changed six times, but despite more than a billion yuan in investment it produced steel only after twenty-seven years. Vast amounts were wasted on other projects. Several economists have calculated that the Third Front cost the country hundreds of billions in forgone output alone, as the high priority of the Third Front starved other parts of the country of much-needed investment. It is probably the biggest example of wasteful capital allocation made by a one-party state in the twentieth century. In terms of economic development, it was a disaster second only to the Great Leap Forward.[34]

Learning from Dazhai

On the last day of the Ninth Congress in April 1969, delegates were asked to elect a new Central Committee. Among the successful candidates was an illiterate villager with deeply tanned, leathery skin and week-old stubble. His name was Chen Yonggui, and all the delegates would have recognised his trademark white terrycloth turban, which he wore tightly wrapped around his head to ward off the sun. Six years earlier, after his village had been destroyed by a flood, he had refused all government aid, instead encouraging his brigade to transform itself into a grain depot by sheer strength of will. Dazhai, located on a sterile plateau of loess in north China, soon attracted Mao Zedong's attention. On 26 December 1964, to mark Mao's birthday, Chen Yonggui was invited to share a meal with the Chairman in Beijing, where the slogan 'In Agriculture, Learn from Dazhai' was launched. This saying was to define agricultural policy for the next fifteen years, much as the Third Front determined what happened in industry.

Dazhai illustrated one of the Chairman's most cherished notions, namely that man could overcome nature. Most of all, it stood for self-reliance. Chen Yonggui insisted on the principle of the 'three no's', refusing state grain, state funds and relief materials.

Self-reliance was not a new notion. Already during the Great Leap Forward, the Chairman had seen the substitution of labour for capital as the key to rapid industrialisation. The country's greatest asset, he had declared, was a workforce numbered in the hundreds of millions of people. The people, after all, were the only motive force in history. Collectively, so propaganda went, they could accomplish in a matter of months what their forefathers had done in thousands of years. Villagers became footsoldiers in a giant army, herded into people's communes where their lives were organised along military lines, at the beck and call of local cadres.

The experiment resulted in a catastrophe, but the notion of self-reliance flourished, especially after scores of large-scale projects were cancelled and the Soviet Union froze transfers of high-end military technology. By 1964, China had few friends, and the country's isolation only deepened two years later with the onset of the Cultural Revolution. Self-reliance became a convenient rationale for leaving people to their own devices. They were told to rely on their own strength, as abundant labour, once again, was meant to replace scarce capital. Dazhai became a model, as villagers were asked to transform arid land into fertile fields – without aid from the state.

––––––––

Surrounded by dried gullies and steep hills in an isolated corner of impoverished Shanxi, some 350 kilometres south-west of Beijing, Dazhai became the Chairman's model commune. The village drew hundreds of thousands of visitors a year, many of them keen to absorb the revolutionary lessons of self-reliance, struggle against nature and radical egalitarianism. There were endless posters showing Chen Yonggui working in the fields among the villagers, transforming the barren mountainside into terraced farmland. There were newspaper articles, magazine stories and feature films, following the villagers through their daily routines, as they planted apple, walnut and mulberry trees, raised silkworms and honey bees, looked after chickens and fat pigs, all without government subsidies. In Dazhai, the propaganda showed, every villager was provided with free education and medical care. By 1968, some 1.3 million people had visited Dazhai, which now had an auditorium, a special dining hall and a hotel with real plumbing to accommodate all the tourists – including foreign dignitaries and high-powered delegations from fraternal countries.[1]

Dazhai, in effect, was a return to the Great Leap Forward. Everything in Dazhai was collectivised. The very slogan that had launched the Great Leap Forward – 'Greater, Faster, Better and More Economical' – was resurrected by the *People's Daily* in its call to follow the 'Dazhai Road' in February 1964. The frenzy that had accompanied the Great Leap Forward was reproduced in the Dazhai model, as villagers were expected to work not only during the day, but through the night as well, come rain or snow. Material incentives were spurned as capitalist, replaced by political zeal and endless propaganda, as loudspeakers were installed at work sites to broadcast music and songs while the villagers took a break. Much as people were forced to tackle one infrastructure project after another during the Great Leap Forward, from water conservancy projects during the winter to steel production over the summer, the Dazhai model enjoined them to move hills, dig tunnels and build canals in selfless dedication to the greater good. 'Battle Hard for Three Years to Change the Face of China' was the slogan in 1958; in 1964 it was 'Work Hard, Diligently and with Extra Energy, and Build our Village into a Dazhai-Like One in Three Years'. 'Learn from Dazhai' was spelled out with large stones on thousands of hillsides across the country, the same way huge slogans praising the Great Leap Forward had been carved into mountainsides years before. Chen Yonggui himself marched under the banner of the Great Leap Forward, making sure that every portion of private property was collectivised. There were no private plots in Dazhai, even though they had been reintroduced across the country after 1961.

But Dazhai remained no more than a vision during the two first years of the Cultural Revolution. In 1958 the Chairman had ensured that the party stood united behind the Great Leap Forward. In 1966, he was busy undermining his colleagues, unleashing the people against his real or imagined enemies within the party ranks.

Not that there was a lack of true believers among the Red Guards. The Cultural Revolution, after all, had started off with a campaign against 'Khrushchev-like revisionists' who were 'taking the capitalist road'. During red August, when Red Guards appeared in all major cities, some radical students had gone to the surrounding countryside to attack all remnants of 'capitalism'. In Nanjing, for instance, on 18 August 1966, the very day Lin Biao appeared in Tiananmen Square to call for the destruction of the old world, they forcibly collectivised all private plots belonging to farmers in the suburbs.[2]

More violence followed in the ensuing months, but in the countryside it generally remained confined to villages located close to the main towns and cities. In Zhengding, Gao Yuan and his friends were marched by the military to a cluster of hamlets about an hour away along the main road, only to find that the local leaders had already taken all bad elements to task. Former landlords, rich peasants and other class enemies had to get up earlier than everybody else and sweep the streets. 'They were easily recognisable, for they all wore black armbands with their status described in white characters.'[3]

In other parts of the countryside, Red Guards vandalised temples, felled sacred trees and burned old almanacs, together with anything else that smacked of superstition. Here too, however, the majority of villages that experienced revolutionary violence were located near cities, along railway lines or adjacent to major roads. Vast swathes of the countryside were only superficially affected by the turmoil gripping towns and cities.

The Chairman himself realised that the revolution could be carried out only if a steady supply of food reached the cities. He had no intention of turning the countryside upside down. On 14 September 1966 the regime limited the Cultural Revolution to county seats and larger cities, and no students or Red Guards were allowed to foment disorder in the villages. As Zhou Enlai put it to a delegation of Red Guards, 'we have to carry out revolution, but we also have to produce, otherwise what will we eat?'[4]

Still, as large parts of the country descended into civil war in 1967, members of all factions tried to recruit more combatants from the surrounding countryside. In Shuangfeng, Hunan, some villagers were asked to converge on the county seat and take to task the royalist faction. They were paid 20 cents in addition to their usual work points. Many cheered wildly and dressed in their best clothes, as if they were going to a festival. They took their savings with them. Once they had turned up to denounce the party committee, they started drifting away. Some went shopping for a new towel or a small mirror.[5]

In other parts of Hunan, the factional fighting spilled over into the countryside with more tragic results. As we have seen, on 10 August 1967 the Cultural Revolution Group overturned the verdict pronounced earlier against a loose coalition of rebels in Changsha. They were called the Xiang River Group, and had supporters throughout the province. A few days later, invigorated by recognition from Beijing, their followers in Daoxian county managed to deal a crushing blow to their opponents, a powerful group backed by local officials and the militia. Violence followed in the countryside, as members of the defeated faction spread rumours of an impending apocalypse. They alleged that the Xiang River Group consisted mainly of bad elements, including the sons and daughters of former land-lords, rich peasants and counter-revolutionaries, who were about to rise in a rebellion closely co-ordinated with Chiang Kai-shek, set to attack the mainland with his nationalist troops. In the following weeks, close to 5,000 people were butchered for their wrong class background. Some of the victims were mere infants. Daoxian was exceptional, but according to one specialist on collective killings in the countryside, during the Cultural Revolution more than 400,000 people were systematically exterminated in villages across the country. The perpetrators were not young Red Guards, but neighbours killing neighbours.[6]

Much of this violence was confined to a small number of provinces, mainly Guangdong, Guangxi and Hunan. And even there, many villages merely went through the routine of holding denunciation rallies of bad elements, who were paraded through the streets with dunces' caps, rather than organising systematic killings under the supervision of the local militia. Compared to the Great Leap Forward, when tens of millions of people had been beaten, worked and starved to death, the first years of the Cultural Revolution largely bypassed the countryside.

But villagers did not simply sit back idly and watch the chaos unfold in the cities. They, too, had a long list of grievances. Foremost among these was the radical collectivisation of the Great Leap Forward. Bricks, furniture and tools had been commandeered in the rush to build collec-tive canteens. In some people's communes almost every form of private property had been abolished, including the clothes on people's backs. Pots and pans were confiscated to prevent villagers from preparing meals out-side the canteens. Entire rows of houses were destroyed, to make fertiliser, build dormitories, relocate villagers, straighten roads, make room for a better future or even punish their occupants. Household implements and farming tools were thrown into backyard furnaces to increase the country's steel output, producing nothing but useless heaps of slag. Livestock had declined precipitously, not only because animals were slaughtered for the export market but also because they died of disease and hunger. Burial sites were flattened to make space for more agriculture, with headstones used for irrigation projects. In order to extract compliance from an exhausted workforce, local cadres resorted to coercion and systematic violence.

Even after the power of the people's communes over villagers had been weakened in the wake of Mao's Great Famine, villagers continued to resent the state's monopoly of the sale of grain. They sought to regain control over their own harvest. They wished to own the land. They longed for a return to freedom of movement, curtailed by the introduction of the household registration system in 1955. They wanted to trade.

In parts of the countryside the chaos of the Cultural Revolution provided villagers with an opportunity to reclaim some of the freedoms they had lost under communism. Since most government officials were embroiled in the political turmoil emanating from the capital, some of them fighting for their own survival, few systematic surveys of the countryside were carried out, but revealing glimpses can be gleaned from the party archives. A comprehensive survey of thirty counties across Shaanxi province showed that more than two-thirds of all local markets operated without any formal supervision. The state had simply melted away. The scale of the trading that took place in parts of the countryside could be enormous. In Yinzhen and Sanqiao, two villages a mere stone's throw away from the provincial capital, the black market in timber alone amounted to some 30,000 yuan a day. Windows, doors and coffins were sold in so brisk and lucrative a fashion that the commerce blocked traffic. Teams of up to a hundred villagers cut down trees in the mountains, operating entirely outside the state plan. The trend had started in the summer of 1966, as the Cultural Revolution kept the local authorities busy.[7]

In the county seat of Yaoxian, over 10,000 people went to market each day, as streets were crowded with the hustle and bustle of traders. Some of this was allowed, but large quantities of rationed items were also sold, in flagrant contravention of the state monopoly on grain, including an estimated 2.5 tonnes of sweet potatoes and several hundred kilos of peanuts a day. Up to eighty bicycles changed hands on any market day. Dozens of itinerant pedlars and local traders operated without any permit. In Fuping county some markets were entirely unregulated, as unlicensed doctors, itinerant dentists and private butchers offered their services for a fee. There was a lively market in joss paper, outlawed in 1966, not to mention batteries, bulbs, dyes and coal.[8]

In Fuping, as elsewhere, the black market had thrived during Mao's Great Famine, but vanished in the following years, as the economy slowly recovered. It reappeared in parallel with the Cultural Revolution, as the transportation system was stretched to the limit by Red Guards, choking off the local economy. But instead of trading on the sly, vanishing at the first sight of a police agent, many black marketeers had now grown bold, openly resisting arrest. Market inspectors were powerless to intervene, overwhelmed by crowds of sympathetic onlookers who gathered as soon as they questioned one of the traders. Some pedlars banded together, resisting any attempt by government officials to interrupt their trade. In Baoji, an irate mob beat to death one supervisor.[9]

Shaanxi was a poor province in the hinterland, but similar activities also thrived in the middle of coastal cities in the grip of the Cultural Revolution. In Guangzhou, entire underground factories were dedicated to the black market. The merchandise offered went far beyond rationed or forbidden goods such as grain and incense. Anyone with sufficient cash could buy petrol, gold, weapons, ammunition, detonators and dynamite.[10]

People in the countryside also used the political turmoil to clamour for larger private plots. Evidence, again, is difficult to come by, but in the spring of 1967 some cultivators in Dingbian county, Shaanxi, doubled their private holdings. Each household was normally allowed to keep only a few animals, but here too farmers pushed their luck, acquiring flocks of up to fifty sheep. In Ankang, some villagers left the people's communes altogether, striking out on their own or seeking their fortune in the city. The trend was significant enough in some villages to amount to decollectivisation.[11]

Decollectivisation was not limited to a few isolated places. In Gansu too, some people's communes were broken up, while villagers used their newfound freedom to double their private plots and expand their livestock. In parts of Jiangsu province, villagers demanded that temples and ancestral halls confiscated by the state be returned. In Shanxi some people divided up all collective property, slaughtering livestock and selling the meat on the private market. So worried was the central government that in February 1967 the *People's Daily* enjoined the population to be vigilant against counter-revolutionary forces in the countryside who were seeking to 'destroy the socialist economy' and 'seize power from the hands of the revolutionary people'. What was at stake was spring ploughing, one of the most important activities in the countryside. Whole regions had lost interest in the sowing season. Across Guanzhong, a fertile region along the lower valley of the Wei River, the local cadres were so powerless that the army had to intervene. They even printed 6 million leaflets and scattered them by plane, here and elsewhere in Shaanxi, enjoining the population to return to collective farming.[12]

But the party was not about to do battle with the peasants. In March 1959, in response to reports that people in the countryside were hoarding grain, the Chairman had ordered that up to a third of the crop be seized, far above previous rates of procurement. He demanded that regions that failed to fulfil their quota be reported. Mao even made an extra 16,000 lorries available to carry out the task. 'He who strikes first prevails, he who strikes last fails' became the motto of the day, as cadres rushed to reach the grain before the villagers could eat it. Forced requisitions were one reason behind the famine that ensued.[13]

Eight years later, in May 1967, villagers were once again reported to be hiding grain. But the Chairman did not make the same mistake. He turned weakness into a strength, demanding that grain be stored widely in the countryside, increasing self-reliance among the villagers. As he put it, 'When peasants fail to report the crop fully and hide the grain, they are storing the wealth among the people.' Zhou Enlai even added that 'peasants will always be peasants', explaining that 'every time the situation improves a little, they move back towards capitalism . . . They have been working on their own for thousands of years, whereas collectivisation is only a few years old, so the influence of the individual economy is very big.' The regime did not impose higher requisitions, but instead reduced the amount of grain that could be sold back to the countryside. Self-reliance, in the spirit of Dazhai, meant that the state would not help with extra grain.[14]

———

The countryside's turn came in 1968. Where revolutionary committees took over, order was soon restored. In Zhejiang, the Twentieth Army carried the day, closely supported by Wu Faxian, commander-in-chief of the air force and protégé of Lin Biao. The military ran the province from January 1968 onwards, purging countless numbers of people who had sided with the opposition.[15]

One of their first acts was to impose the Dazhai model. In order to 'thoroughly smash the evil plot by China's Khrushchev to restore capitalism in the countryside', the Twentieth Army sent a delegation of a hundred cadres to learn from Chen Yonggui in Shanxi. They, in turn, spread the spirit of self-reliance to every people's commune in the province. Posters went up, followed by newspaper articles, radio announcements and documentary films. War was declared on capitalism in the countryside.[16]

Over the next two years, a further 30,000 cadres and farmers were sent to Dazhai, all expenses paid. Many came back fully converted. By the end of 1969, more than 200 villages were hailed as model collectives. Zhejiang, like other provinces, acquired its own Dazhai, called Nanbao. The village was flattened by a flood in July 1969, but instead of relying on state handouts, the people from Nanbao, under the leadership of party secretary Li Jinrong, fought back. They rebuilt their houses, repaired the paddy fields and went all out to achieve economic independence. On 3 June 1970 the *People's Daily* praised Nanbao as a paragon of the principle that 'man can conquer nature'. More than 1.6 million people from Zhejiang alone came to visit Nanbao.

But some places got carried away. In their eagerness to recollectivise the economy, some cadres abolished private plots and even slaughtered private animals. Across the province, a quarter of all production teams reverted to the radical collectivisation of the Great Leap Forward by handing over responsibility for accounting to the brigade, the second tier of organisation in the countryside, placed between the people's commune and the team. This meant that the villagers lost control over income distribution. In some counties this was true for an astounding 80 per cent of all production teams. Simply gathering firewood or raising a buffalo was now denounced as 'capitalist'.[17]

Similar scenes could be observed in other parts of the country, as the military forced through the Dazhai model from 1968 onwards. In Gansu province, where Wang Feng and Liu Lantao were accused of having followed the 'capitalist road', private plots covering a total surface of more than 77,000 hectares were returned to the collectives, equivalent to roughly a third of all private holdings. In some counties, for instance Linzhao, Yumen and Subei, 'all private plots have been entirely taken back'. In some villages every tree and household animal was once again returned to collective hands.[18]

With the wave of recollectivisation came the usual modes of popular resistance, as farmers tried to slaughter their cattle and fell the trees before these could be taken from them. As news spread that the people's communes were attacking the 'evil wind of capitalism', villagers chased their pigs between mudbrick houses, their screams echoing through the streets. In Hunan, 'every courtyard became a slaughterhouse and every man's hands were bloody', as the villagers secretly smoked and salted the meat, stowing it away in earthenware jars.[19]

There are examples from other provinces. In Longyao county, Hebei, private plots only ever accounted for 6 per cent of all holdings, but by 1969 every last bit of land was grabbed back by the collectives. In Zhengding county, where Gao Yuan and his friends had done battle during the Cultural Revolution, in the summer of 1968 the entire countryside seemed to revert to the Great Leap Forward. Villagers who kept a pig or a sheep were denounced as 'capitalists', and all incentives to produce fertiliser were abolished. Every tree was deemed collective property. In parts of the province, responsibility for many key decisions was moved from the villagers to the larger collective. Sideline occupations, traditionally pursued by villagers in their spare time, were banned. A few cadres went so far as to confiscate all tools that did not contribute directly to the collective economy.[20]

With recollectivisation came a renewed emphasis on grain for the state, as 'Take Grain as the Key Link' became the main slogan. As in the days of the Great Leap Forward, everyone in the countryside was enjoined to produce grain. Alternative crops, whether or not they were better suited to the terrain, were abandoned. Fruit trees, tea bushes and medicinal plants were cut down. Vegetables were spurned. Prairies better suited to grazing were converted to cropland, sometimes after the cattle had been slaughtered. Plots with thin topsoil were covered with vast amounts of fertiliser.

No matter how barren or inhospitable the land, hard work would conquer nature, and grain would be wrenched from the earth.[21]

Terraced fields appeared in the most unlikely places. Much as Chen Yonggui had filled ravines and terraced slopes in Dazhai to produce more grain, the country was to 'Get Grain from the Mountaintops, Get Grain from the Lakes'. Neither climate nor topography mattered, as lakes were filled, forests cleared and deserts reclaimed in desperate attempts to emulate Dazhai, from the Mongolian steppes to the swamps of Manchuria. Dogmatic uniformity was imposed across the country. In one extreme example of slavish emulation, local cadres even decided to build hills on a flat plain – simply so that they could be terraced like Dazhai.[22]

The campaign intensified after Chen Yonggui had been elected to the Central Committee, and reached its peak between August 1969 and September 1971. The Dazhai model was now linked to the war effort, as every region was pressured to increase its yield and store the surplus.

In Yan'an, Zhai Zhenhua had to help build a terraced field against the loess mountain. It kept the villagers busy all year round, except when the soil was frozen in winter. In Chongqing, a woman remembered how she and the other villagers were forced to open up wastelands in the mountains for cultivation. Nobody resisted for fear of being denounced. 'So we built terraces on the mountain, and carried earth and fertiliser. On every spare metre of earth, we tried to grow grain. But the mountain was never suitable for growing grain. It's only good for trees.'[23]

Terraces were built on steep slopes, regardless of the erosion caused by rain and floods. Some hillsides were cut down straight to the bedrock. Others collapsed at the slightest downpour and had to be maintained all year round, demanding ever greater amounts of topsoil.

Grassy plains, too, were converted, although many suffered from salinisation, caused when dry earth is artificially irrigated. Lack of rainfall allows the soluble salts contained in the irrigated water to accumulate in the soil, severely reducing its fertility. Here is how one enemy of the state, sent to the gulag to reclaim wasteland, described the fields of Ningxia province:

On the land before me abandoned fields stretched in all directions. Now covered with a thick layer of salt, they looked like dirty snowfields, or like

orphans dressed in mourning clothes. They had been through numerous storms since being abandoned, but you could still see the scars of
plough tracks running across their skin. Man and nature together had
been flogged with whips here: the result of 'Learn from Dazhai' was
to create a barren land, on whose alkaline surface not a blade of grass
would grow.[24]

In the Bashang prairie near Zhangjiakou, too, sandstorms turned great
stretches of grassland into an expanse of brown sand. Further away from
the capital, in Qinghai province, some 670,000 hectares of green pastures
were converted into cropland. Desertification soon degraded the environment beyond recovery.[25]

Lakes were drained, rivers dammed and wetlands reclaimed, all in the
name of Dazhai. In Hubei, hundreds of lakes vanished. The largest one,
lying between Hubei and Hunan, was depleted from an original 560,000
hectares to 282,000. In Yunnan, the Dianchi Lake, China's sixth largest,
sheltered by a mountain range dotted with temples, pagodas and pavilions, with corridors and caves chiselled from the rocks by Daoist monks
in the nineteenth century, was taken in hand by hundreds of thousands of
people, mobilised by the army to fill the wetlands in the spring of 1970.
Boulders were blasted from the mountains and dumped into the lake in
an effort to turn it into farmland. The project was supervised by the head
of the provincial revolutionary committee. At daybreak the army marched
the villagers to the lake and expected them to dig ditches, pile earth, carry
gravel and build paddy fields, doing much of this by hand. An atmosphere
of impending war was used to intensify the pressure, as teams competed
against each other in trying to reach ever higher targets. Ultimately the
reclaimed soil proved too soft and soggy for planting. More earth was
added, but the yield remained dismally low. Much of the ecological balance was permanently damaged, with the lake's transparent blue water
turned into a brown scum that killed off many local species. Where the
catch of fish had been over 6 million tonnes in 1969, ten years later it had
fallen to just over 100,000 tonnes.[26]

Across the country the army intervened, determined to promote
the Dazhai model. It whipped up the workforce, using the villagers as

footsoldiers to increase output. In a state farm run by the army in Manchuria, everyone awoke at the whistle at 3.30 in the morning. Nobody wanted to lag behind, fearful of being accused of not supporting Chairman Mao. Everyone's performance was recorded, and those at the bottom of the scale were denounced in public struggle meetings. Nanchu, a young student from Shanghai, carried wicker baskets heaped with manure to the fields, pushing herself to move as fast as possible. Perspiration soaked her clothes, and some salty sweat froze at the corners of her mouth in the deep winter, but she did not slow down. Soon the cold turned her soaked clothes into a frozen armour, rattling with every movement. Surviving the campaign became everyone's primary concern: 'With sore backs, aching muscles and weary bones, we persevered stoically for several months.'[27]

Local cadres, too, pushed the workforce to the very limit. They were keen to create a local miracle, determined to turn their village into the next Dazhai and be invited to Beijing to see Chairman Mao. As one villager put it, 'Learning from Dazhai was the continuation of the Great Leap Forward.'[28]

Like the Great Leap Forward, the campaign to Learn from Dazhai was a gigantic exercise in deception. Dazhai itself was a sham, its model villagers the reluctant actors in a play written by the Chairman. The miracle harvests were fake, obtained by inflating the figures and borrowing grain from other villages. The People's Liberation Army built much of the irrigation system. Far from being self-reliant, Dazhai received huge subsidies and other forms of aid from the state. What happened in Dazhai was replicated throughout the country, as vast amounts of labour, energy and capital were lavished on showcase projects, from the steel mills at Panzhihua to the reclaimed wetlands of Dianchi Lake. As one eminent scholar of the campaign put it, 'Rarely has there been a historical moment in which political repression, misguided ideals, and an absolutist vision of priorities and correct methods coincided to achieve such concentrated attacks on nature, environmental destruction, and human suffering.'[29]

More Purges

Between the summer of 1968 and the autumn of 1969, the newly established revolutionary committees had set out to cleanse the ranks of the party, using their power to get rid of their own opponents. The official line was that enemy agents, traitors and renegades had wormed their way into the very institutions established by the party, concealing their past misdeeds by professing to follow the proletarian revolutionary line. The campaign was about past betrayals by party members, and did not generally affect those who were too young to have experienced the corrupting influence of capitalism before liberation. Students were sent instead to the countryside to be re-educated by the peasants.

But plenty of questions still arose about the political reliability of people who had been born after liberation, given the complexity of factional strife and the bewildering diversity of mass organisations that had sprung up at the height of the Cultural Revolution. As the campaign to cleanse the ranks started winding down by the end of 1969, a new movement was launched to ferret out a younger generation of hidden enemies. Beijing alleged that there existed a counter-revolutionary organisation going under the name of 'May Sixteenth', reminiscent of the date in 1966 when the Chairman had circulated a notice to announce that Peng Zhen had turned the capital into a citadel of revisionism.

The 16 May Circular was the inner-party document that had launched the Cultural Revolution, but it remained restricted until it was published a year later on 17 May 1967. In the original notice, the Chairman pointed out that other revisionists, besides Peng Zhen, 'are still trusted by us and are being trained as our successors'. Some Red Guards interpreted this as an indication that Zhou Enlai was about to fall from power. Posters went up branding the premier a 'counter-revolutionary double-dealer' and a representative of the 'bourgeois reactionary line'. Jiang Qing took the lead in trying to expose the premier.[1]

The Chairman intervened, protecting his faithful servant. A few months later, in early August, attacks on the premier were again repudiated, and a witch-hunt started for May Sixteenth elements, denounced as members of a counter-revolutionary organisation. The hunt escalated after the burning of the British mission on 22 August, as detailed charts were produced to claim that a well-organised conspiracy existed at all levels, with underground members in virtually every sector of the state and the army. Zhou Enlai used the purge to retaliate against some of his own enemies inside the Cultural Revolution Group, bringing down several prominent supporters of Jiang Qing, including Wang Li, the man who had encouraged young radicals to seize power in the Ministry of Foreign Affairs. Zhou Enlai cleverly turned Yao Dengshan, a firebrand inside the ministry, into a scapegoat for the burning of the mission, accusing him of being a 'core member' of the May Sixteenth group. Dozens of others fell from power.[2]

But the height of the campaign did not come until two and a half years later. On 24 January 1970, Zhou Enlai appeared in the Great Hall of the People to address the danger posed by the underground organisation. May Sixteenth, he explained, was merely the name of an extraordinarily complex clandestine organisation, which was 'a hodgepodge of foreign imperialists, revisionists and reactionaries, hidden counter-revolutionaries, nationalist spies, renegades inside the party ranks, traitors, capitalist roaders, revisionist elements, as well as landlords, rich peasants, rightists and bad people who have not reformed themselves'. Two months later, on 27 March, a circular extended the search to anyone who had contravened the party line by committing a 'leftist' or a 'rightist' error. Inside the Ministry of Foreign Affairs, the institution with the closest ties to Zhou Enlai, more than a thousand followers of the May Sixteenth conspiracy were discovered in the spring of 1970, accounting for roughly half of all staff.[3]

Members of the counter-revolutionary organisation seemed to be everywhere. Millions were implicated, as revolutionary committees used the conspiracy as an excuse to get rid of anybody who had spoken out during the Cultural Revolution. In Nanjing, where the 'monk general' Xu Shiyou held sway, the campaign targeted some 27,000 victims out of a million residents. Xu disliked the rebels intensely, persecuting them vehemently as counter-revolutionaries. He questioned important suspects himself, slapping one major general in the face in order to extract a full confession. More than a third of all faculty members at Nanjing University were persecuted. Hundreds were imprisoned, and twenty-one hounded to their deaths. In the Nanjing Forestry School, nine out of ten teachers were victimised. People who had heeded the call to join the Cultural Revolution were at risk, including students who had travelled to Beijing, Red Guards who had denounced party officials, rebels who had participated in power seizures and, most of all, any person who had ever opposed Xu Shiyou.[4]

Song Erli was one student who had made the mistake of writing a big-character poster against Xu Shiyou at the height of the Cultural Revolution. His university was controlled by the military, and the army ran the state farm he was sent to after graduation. He was compelled to write one self-criticism after another, but in early 1970 he was transferred back to a 'study class' – also administered by the military – that was set up to uncover May Sixteenth elements. The study class turned out to be a prison, and an army officer gave him a long list of names of students and teachers suspected of being conspirators. 'At first I thought that this campaign was very strange. I had never heard of this May Sixteenth group. I said I had heard nothing about it. But what was even stranger was that I saw my comrades one after another confess. Every confession had to be made at a mass meeting in front of the whole study class.' In the end the list of suspects encompassed every member who had ever spoken out against the army. In a strange twist of fate, even rebels who had joined a faction in favour of Xu Shiyou ended up being accused of treachery. 'Because they were rebels. The army doesn't like rebels.'[5]

The campaign was not confined to Nanjing. Across Jiangsu province people were persecuted as counter-revolutionaries. By one account, the number of victims was twenty times higher than those labelled 'anti-rightists' in 1957 in the wake of the Hundred Flowers. A popular ditty did the rounds: 'May Sixteenth are Everywhere, Among Family and Friends'. In Wuxi, the confessions of thirty suspects were broadened to implicate no fewer than 11,000 victims. Here, as elsewhere, the accused were forced to supply the names of other members. Under torture they provided lists of imaginary suspects, and the numbers mushroomed. In some government units every member of staff was arrested.

Across the entire province, the campaign affected more than a quarter of a million people. Over 6,000 suspects were injured or beaten to death during interrogation sessions. Some of those accused preferred to commit suicide rather than denounce others. One woman jumped from a window, strangling herself with a sheet. In death she was still condemned for betraying the party. Her colleagues were forced to attend a denunciation rally and go on stage, one after the other, confessing that she had introduced them to the underground group.[6]

Jiangsu was ferocious, but other provinces where army commanders still faced opposition also used the campaign to eradicate their enemies, real or imagined. In Guangxi, where Wei Guoqing had unleashed the army against the rebels, scores of people were rounded up. In Shanghai, anyone who had ever opposed Zhang Chunqiao ended up in prison. The movement was the final act in the persecution of people who had risen during the Cultural Revolution. Statistics are difficult to obtain, but as many as 3.5 million people were implicated across the country.[7]

On 12 November 1969, a month after his expulsion from the party, Liu Shaoqi died in solitary detention. He had become too weak to get out of bed, but nobody would help him wash, change his clothes or use the toilet. He was covered in bedsores, haggard, his hair long and unkempt. Although he suffered from muscle atrophy in his legs, the guards insisted on tying him down with gauze strips for fear that he might commit suicide.[8]

After his arrest in 1967, he had been beaten repeatedly in mass denunciation meetings and denied medicine for his diabetes. He also suffered from pneumonia, but was kept alive until the Ninth Party Congress. The Chairman had put Zhou Enlai in charge of Liu's case, and the premier denounced his erstwhile colleague as 'a criminal traitor, enemy agent and scab in the service of the imperialists, modern revisionists and the nationalist reactionaries'. After Liu's body had been cremated, the premier toasted the completion of his task at a small banquet.[9]

But there were still plenty of other revisionists and counter-revolutionaries who could undermine the party. Zhou Enlai wrote to the Chairman to point out that resolute measures should be taken against a minority of counter-revolutionaries who were sabotaging the country's preparations for war. The Chairman agreed. On 31 January 1970, the Central Committee called for a strike against all 'counter-revolutionary activities', which were defined in such a way as to encompass almost anything deemed 'destructive'. A week later, on 5 February, it issued a directive demanding that 'corruption', 'speculation' and 'waste' also be resolutely eliminated. This proclamation was equally vague, providing no legal definition of any of these terms, meaning that almost every economic activity taking place outside the planned economy could be criminalised, from selling an egg on the black market to using excessive edible oil in the canteen. These two campaigns lasted from February to November 1970 and largely overlapped, being referred to as the 'One Strike and Three Antis'. Behind the communist jargon lay a ruthless attempt to attack ordinary people who could not be indicted for belonging to the May Sixteenth conspiracy.

Millions had their lives destroyed. In Hubei alone, 173,000 suspects were investigated for 'counter-revolutionary activities', while a further 207,000 were prosecuted for graft, speculation or waste. Although the campaign was supposed to last only ten months, in 1971 the revolutionary committee again persecuted 107,000 'counter-revolutionaries', as well as 240,000 people accused of an economic crime. By the time Lin Biao died in September 1971, the total amounted to an astounding 736,000 cases. Even if some suspects were eventually cleared, this meant that roughly one in fifty people, in every village across the province, fell victim to the campaign.[10]

Like the May Sixteenth conspiracy, many of the charges were trumped up. A good example is a group of rebels who had launched a journal called the *Yangtze Tribune* in 1967. They were radical communists, and a few modelled themselves on the young Mao Zedong. They yearned for a return to the Great Leap Forward, and at the height of the Cultural Revolution they carried out an experiment in militant communism in the countryside just outside Wuhan. They abolished all production teams, making sure that authorities higher up in the people's commune controlled everything related to production. All privately owned livestock had to be surrendered. Collective canteens, abandoned after Mao's Great Famine, were restored. Private buildings were torn down, and the villagers herded into collective dormitories. The experiment met with strong resistance, and the local military soon brought it to an end.

The fate of the rebels associated with the *Yangtze Tribune* was sealed once the Chairman demanded an end to factional violence in July 1968. Within weeks, the provincial revolutionary committee in Wuhan declared their publication to be 'extremely reactionary', and several of its members were arrested. But the scale of persecution escalated one year later in September 1969, after Beijing had characterised the *Yangtze Tribune* as 'a hotchpotch manipulated by a handful of renegades, spies and counter-revolutionaries from behind the scenes'. While no more than a dozen members had ever belonged to the initial group, across the province thousands were now hounded. In 1971, as part of the campaign to strike hard against counter-revolutionaries, no fewer than 15,000 followers of the *Yangtze Tribune* were tracked down, the vast majority having never even heard of the publication.[11]

But most of the victims had very little to do with the factional politics of the Cultural Revolution. In 1971 alone some 89,000 victims of the campaign against counter-revolutionaries in Hubei were people belonging to bad class backgrounds. As elsewhere, they bore the brunt of the campaign. Any expression of discontent with the party, whether real or imagined, was enough to land a social outcast in hot water. Some were accused of having poked a hole in a poster of the Chairman, others of writing reactionary slogans. People who listened to foreign radio broadcasts were arrested. Hundreds of fictive underground organisations were discovered, accused of 'liaising with the enemy'. This included disgruntled citizens who had contacted relatives in Hong Kong and Macau or had written letters to *Pravda*, the mouthpiece of the Kremlin.[12]

Very few culprits were shot. The majority ended up in a 'study class' for re-education, closely supervised by a propaganda team, while hardened cases were sent to the gulag. Even at this stage some people showed a remarkable willingness to confront power. When one man was sent to a class for re-education, he said, 'You can hold your class for three years, I will be stubborn for three years. Hold it for six years and I will be stubborn for six.'[13]

Not everyone was so resilient. Whether the endless harassment, the brutal interrogations or the fantastic nature of the accusations the authorities concocted were responsible, some victims felt they had no future worth living for. In just the first six weeks of the campaign across all Hubei, more than 600 people committed suicide.[14]

Hubei may have seemed exceptional, but the numbers were similar in Gansu. Within the first three months of the campaign, more than 225,000 people were denounced, equivalent to 1.5 per cent of the entire population. By the end of 1970, the total had spiralled to 320,000, equivalent to one in fifty people. Some towns carried out co-ordinated raids, arresting hundreds of people in one fell swoop. This happened in Pingliang, where 393 victims were swept up in a single day.[15]

As in Hubei, the suicide rate was high. Complete statistics are unavailable, given that much of the reporting was haphazard and local authorities were keen to downplay the figures. But by October 1970 more than 2,400 people had ended their lives. In the single county of Jingchuan, forty-five people killed themselves in less than a month.[16]

As elsewhere, endless 'counter-revolutionary' organisations were brought to light. In Chengxian county, sixteen members of a Democratic Party were uncovered, while nine of the chief organisers of a National Salvation Party were arrested in Hezheng. By May 1970, the authorities boasted that more than 2,000 counter-revolutionary cliques, gangs and conspiracies had been broken up. Even the head of the provincial revolutionary committee, at this stage, started advising prudence in prosecuting these organisations, since some were entirely fictitious.[17]

Local authorities were eager to outdo each other, vying to discover ever more cases to demonstrate their dedication to the Cultural Revolution. In Wuwei, a city on the ancient silk road bordering Inner Mongolia, so many doctors were arrested that the main hospital was almost forced to close down. Five medical experts were accused of being 'counter-revolutionaries'. One was found guilty of 'liking freedom'. Another was accused of having listened to a foreign radio station in 1963. A third had been overheard singing a reactionary song in 1966. Even children who had scrawled a slogan on a wall were denounced and paraded through the streets. Such was the pressure to produce results that sometimes a verdict was overturned no fewer than a dozen times in less than three weeks. The liberal use of manacles, shackles and bare fists helped to achieve results and meet quotas.[18]

In the countryside, the Learn from Dazhai campaign promised prosperity and abundance to all those who laboured collectively on the land. The campaign against graft, speculation and waste was the tool revolutionary committees used to enforce this vision. Across the country, the 'Three Antis' was directed at millions of ordinary people who had quietly exploited the chaos of the Cultural Revolution to advance their own economic freedoms. From poor villagers who had enlarged their private plots to ordinary people who had bought some vegetables from the black market, the campaign crushed those accused of following the capitalist road.

In Hubei, they represented 447,000 out of the 736,000 victims who had been harassed by the authorities from February 1970 to October 1971. They made up 169,000 of the total of 225,000 suspects taken to task in the first three months of the campaign in Gansu. In a single town of more than 4,000 people in Wushan county, the authorities suspected roughly one in four of having participated in the black market, some of them selling from stalls, others hawking their goods. It would have been impossible to arrest one-quarter of all the people, but forceful measures against a few prominent targets sufficed to exact compliance from the local population.[19]

These targets, yet again, were people from bad class backgrounds. If not persecuted as 'counter-revolutionaries', they were accused of being the 'black hands' behind the revival of capitalism in the countryside. In Wushan, where scores of people were involved in the black market, the authorities homed in on fifty 'landlords', 'rich peasants' and other class enemies. This was not an isolated example. In all Gansu, the provincial authorities calculated, there were precisely 122,223 people with bad class labels, many of whom were undermining the collective economy. In Lanzhou, the provincial capital, the official press shrilly accused them of subverting the road to socialism. 'In some places, a handful of landlords, rich peasants, counter-revolutionaries, bad elements and rightists who are not yet remoulded are frantically opposing and undermining the collective economy of the people's communes in an effort to take the capitalist road. Capitalist tendencies and the evil, counter-revolutionary wind of economism in the rural areas are still seriously undermining socialist production.'[20]

From other provinces came similar calls to wipe out all bad elements. In Yunnan, the authorities condemned the monsters and demons who were guilty of corruption, embezzlement, speculation and the neglect of collective farming.[21]

Social outcasts were persecuted for the slightest infringement of the planned economy. But the ranks of the administration were also cleansed of those indicted for following 'capitalist methods'. In Hezheng and Guanghe counties, Gansu, they accounted for one in ten of all government employees. Similar purges took place in other provinces. In Hebei, 45,000 cadres, or one in six of those active in the bureaucracy overseeing trade and commerce, were viewed as suspect and were subjected to a full investigation. Thousands were demoted, dismissed or arrested.[22]

Nobody knows how many people fell victim to the purges that followed the Ninth Party Congress in April 1969. The hunt for May Sixteenth elements alone may have implicated as many as 3.5 million people. But by far the most ferocious campaign was the 'One Strike and Three Antis', which was so vague as to suit the purposes of any revolutionary committee determined to dispose of its enemies. If the numbers from Hubei and Gansu are representative of the country as a whole, then as many as one in fifty people were denounced at some point or another, equivalent to 16 million people out of a total population of more than 800 million. Not all of those brought to the attention of the authorities ended up being condemned as 'counter-revolutionaries'. In many cases, only a fraction were actually found guilty. And of those, few were shot. In the bloodshed that had followed liberation in 1949, executions had come in the hundreds of thousands. From October 1950 to October 1951, the regime eliminated somewhere between 1.5 and 2 million people. Although the killing quota was fixed at one per thousand, in many parts of the south it was more than double that. But twenty years later, revolutionary committees handed out death sentences more sparingly, with victims counted in the tens of thousands. In Gansu, by April 1970, just over 200 people had been shot, representing less than 1 per cent of all those denounced for one crime or another. Seven times as many suspects killed themselves.[23] The point of these purges was not physically to eliminate the regime's enemies, whether real or imagined, but to intimidate the greatest number of people possible. The objective was to produce a docile population by transforming almost every act and every utterance into a potential crime.

19

Fall of an Heir

Liu Shaoqi's body was cremated in great secrecy, in the middle of the night, under a false name. Since he was described as a 'highly contagious patient', only two workers were present to handle the cremation.[1] His death was never publicly announced during Mao Zedong's lifetime, but soon enough the wrangling to decide who should replace him as head of state began.

As heir apparent, Lin Biao would have been justified in thinking that he should occupy the post. But he must have been wary of appearing overly ambitious, and may not even have wanted the position for fear of upsetting the Chairman. In Chinese, the formal title of the leader of the party and of the head of state alike was 'chairman'. Lin Biao knew that there could be only one Chairman.

Mao himself loathed the endless ceremonial duties demanded of a head of state and did not want the job, from which he had resigned in 1959 in Liu Shaoqi's favour. When, ten years earlier in 1949, the chief of protocol had suggested that the Chairman conform to international convention and wear a dark suit and black leather shoes, he had been fired. He subsequently committed suicide during the Cultural Revolution. The Chairman enjoyed his freedom, and was not about to be hemmed in by schedule, routine or ritual.[2]

On the other hand, Mao was increasingly suspicious of Lin. After the leadership had vacated the capital in a panic in October 1969, fearing a surprise attack by the Soviet Union, the heir apparent had issued a 'Number One Order' from a bunker in Suzhou, putting the military on red alert. A million soldiers had moved forward to take up strategic positions around the country, backed up by thousands of tanks, planes and ships. The order was soon rescinded, as it became clear that someone along the command structure had jumped the gun and failed to clear it with the Chairman, who was furious at being sidestepped. What precisely went wrong is unclear, but Mao must have realised just how easily his second-in-command could take control of the army and possibly one day turn it against him.

Much as the Chairman needed Lin Biao, he had tried to contain his growing influence over the years by fostering competing factions inside the army. But the heir apparent had triumphed at the Ninth Party Congress. The entire country was becoming militarised in an atmosphere of impending war with the Soviet Union or the United States. The army took over the government and ran the economy. Lin Biao enjoined the whole country to study Mao Zedong Thought, which in effect meant that everyone was learning from the army. Mao himself was constantly surrounded by soldiers, and he suspected that they reported everything to their superiors. His hostility towards the grip the military had on his own life was turning into animosity towards Lin Biao and his generals.[3]

Mao carefully manipulated the issue of the office of head of state against his chosen successor. He was suitably vague in refusing the post for himself, fuelling speculation that he expected his underlings to grovel and insist that he accept. He also dangled the position before the heir apparent, trying to gauge his reaction. Lin insisted that the Chairman should fill the post.[4]

Soon enough two factions emerged. Lin Biao, buttressed by his followers Li Zuopeng and Wu Faxian, the two generals who had helped seize control of Wuhan in the summer of 1967, insisted on a state chairmanship. Always the sycophants, they also demanded that the constitution include a statement that the Chairman was a genius who had creatively and comprehensively developed Marxism-Leninism. Zhang Chunqiao and Kang Sheng, two of the most senior members of the Cultural Revolution Group, were against the office. They also objected to the use of the term 'genius', which was taken from Lin Biao's foreword to the Little Red Book. Both camps believed that they knew best what the Chairman wanted.

The issue came to a head when the Central Committee met in the summer of 1970. Lin Biao asked the Chairman for permission to address objections to the use of the term 'genius' at the start of the conference. Mao saw an opportunity to trap Lin, and encouraged him to do so, throwing in a few deprecatory comments aimed at Zhang Chunqiao and his own wife Jiang Qing. Lin spoke for an hour, eulogising the Chairman.

The following day the conference participants discussed an essay entitled 'On Genius', compiled by Chen Boda. Chen was the nominal head of the Cultural Revolution Group, but he loathed Kang Sheng and felt threatened by his rival's longstanding relationship with Jiang Qing. His star was on the wane, and he had thrown in his lot with Lin Biao soon after he was declared the official successor to Mao Zedong at the Ninth Party Congress.[5]

Chen had been a ghostwriter for the Chairman since the Yan'an days, and many party leaders assumed that the tract reflected the party line. Realising that Zhang Chunqiao was the main target, they attacked him indirectly by demanding that 'plotters' and 'counter-revolutionaries' who still denied the Chairman's genius be expelled from the party. Mao remained aloof, watching from a distance. Soon there were enthusiastic calls for Mao and Lin to become chairman and vice-chairman of the state.

The Chairman now had enough to spring his trap. The heir apparent was spared, but at a special session Mao denounced Chen Boda as a sham Marxist and a long-time enemy spy. He put a halt to all discussion of his genius. He demanded that Lin Biao's generals, who had spearheaded the attack on Zhang Chunqiao, make their own self-criticisms. None was judged satisfactory, and they were left in limbo after more rebukes from the Chairman.

Over the following months Mao placed trusted figures in the top echelons of the army to keep an eye on Lin Biao's generals. He reorganised the Beijing Military Region, suspending two leaders from their posts. Chen Boda was further excoriated as a 'traitor, spy and careerist'. Lin Biao's power was on the decline, Jiang Qing's was on the ascent.

———

Chen Boda's fall from grace was only made public months later, but people who knew how to read between the lines had an inkling that something had gone awry. He was number four in the leadership, but his name was missing from the usual lists of important leaders in the newspapers. There were oblique references to a 'sham Marxist', which could only point to someone renowned as an exponent of the communist faith.

But the clearest signal that a dramatic shift in policy was taking place came on 1 October 1970. Each year National Day was celebrated with processions in all major cities, as hundreds of thousands of workers, peasants and students marched in serried ranks, shouting slogans, waving red flags and holding aloft portraits of the Chairman. Mao himself, surrounded by leading party officials, reviewed the annual parade from the rostrum above the Gate of Heavenly Peace in Tiananmen Square. There were special stands for foreign dignitaries and diplomats who, like everyone else, noted who stood next to the Chairman. For the first time ever, an American was given that honour. Chen Boda was nowhere to be seen.

Several months after the event, on 25 December, a photograph of Edgar Snow standing by Mao Zedong's side was splashed over the front pages of every major newspaper. In January 1965, on the eve of the Cultural Revolution, the Chairman had used the veteran journalist to let it be known to the outside world that Chinese troops would not cross the border into Vietnam as long as the United States did not attack China. Now he sent another signal, namely that major changes were afoot in relations with the imperialist camp.

Already after the Ninth Party Congress in April 1969, the Chairman had hedged his bets and asked a team of experts to devise an alternative to Lin Biao's model of a people's war in foreign policy. The task was kept secret and assigned to Chen Yi, Ye Jianying, Xu Xiangqian and Nie Rongzhen, the veteran marshals who had opposed the Cultural Revolution in February 1967. They were given free rein to think outside the box. As war with the Soviet Union loomed after the August 1969 surprise attack in Xinjiang, the marshals came up with a bold plan: play the American card. They favoured exploiting the antagonism between the two superpowers by opening up to the United States. Their assessment was at loggerheads with that of Lin Biao and his generals, who viewed the United States as an enemy on a par with the Soviet Union.[6]

A similar shift in thinking was taking place on the other side of the Pacific. Richard Nixon, the newly elected president, distrusted Moscow far more than Beijing and realised that China had to be brought into

the international system. In January 1969 he scribbled a note that read
'Chinese Communists: Short range – no change. Long range – we do not
want 800,000,000 living in angry isolation. We want contact.'[7]

Other considerations motivated the Americans. In April 1970, China
hosted a 'Conference in Solidarity with the Indochinese People' in
Guangzhou chaired by Prince Sihanouk, overthrown a month earlier by a
Cambodian general close to the United States. The conference brokered an
alliance between communist forces in Vietnam, Laos and Cambodia, creating a new Indochinese revolutionary front. Five days later, President Nixon
extended the war beyond Vietnam's borders, entering Cambodia with a
military operation dubbed 'Total Victory'. But instead of wiping out communists ensconced across the border once and for all, the invasion turned
the Vietnam War into a Second Indochina War. Soon the Americans were
looking to China for assistance in extricating themselves from the quag-
mire. They, too, hoped to exploit the clash between the two communist
giants to isolate North Vietnam's main backer, namely the Soviet Union.[8]

Both sides, in any event, had for some time sought to resume talks at
the ambassadorial level. These attempts collapsed after Operation Total
Victory began, but towards the end of 1970 tensions eased. One week
before the photograph of Mao and Snow was released on 25 December,
the Chairman told the journalist that he would be happy to meet Nixon,
'either as a president or as a tourist'.

Secret negotiations took place to agree on an agenda, complicated by
the Taiwan issue, as Chiang Kai-shek was an ally of the United States.
But concessions were made. In early April 1971, the Chinese table-tennis
team was sent to Japan to take part in an international tournament. Three
of the country's best players had committed suicide during the campaign
to cleanse the class ranks in 1968, but now the team was instructed by
Zhou Enlai to put 'friendship first, competition second'. In Nagoya, they
extended an invitation to the US team to visit China. A few days later, nine
American players and several officials crossed the bridge from Hong Kong
to the mainland, spending a week playing friendly matches, and visiting
the Great Wall and the Summer Palace.[9]

The Forbidden City, just opposite the Great Hall of the People, was still
off limits to the ping-pong players, but a week later several foreign parties

were permitted to visit – the first such occasion since 1967. Likewise for the first time since 1967, a group of seventy diplomats were taken on an official tour of the country in a special train, visiting large iron and steel works, hydroelectric power stations, tractor factories and model production brigades.[10]

There were other signs of a relaxation towards foreigners. The disdain and abruptness that they usually encountered when dealing with party officials were apparently gone. Some cadres were even affable. Across the border from Hong Kong, where only years previously shots had been fired, they were unusually cordial. At the trade fair in Guangzhou, one of the main points of commercial contact between state officials and the outside world, lectures on Mao Zedong Thought were suspended. Portraits of the Chairman were removed from hotel rooms and anti-American slogans toned down. The city was tidied up.[11]

Local residents, of course, were banned from the trade fair, as a huge discrepancy existed between the variety of food and clothing on display for the export market and the paucity of goods available in the shops. Still, ordinary people could feel the wind of change. A flicker of hope was kindled the moment Edgar Snow appeared next to the Chairman. Nien Cheng, still lingering in the Number One Detention House, became quietly excited and hopeful, if a little apprehensive: 'That communist China might move closer to the West seemed too good to be true.' Outside the prison walls, on the streets of Guangzhou, Shanghai and Tianjin, fewer people pinned badges on their clothes. On some trains crisscrossing the country, portraits of the Chairman were quietly removed.[12]

Soon after the visit by the ping-pong team, Henry Kissinger was invited to Beijing. Dazzled by the prospect of dealing with the Middle Kingdom, Nixon's national security adviser came laden with gifts. His country was bound by treaty to Taiwan, but Washington was ready to drop its ally, promising full diplomatic recognition of the People's Republic of China. Kissinger indicated that the United States would help China obtain the Chinese seat at the United Nations. He lavished praise on the Chinese leaders, and even offered to provide highly classified information, including details of the United States' bilateral negotiations with the Soviet Union. 'We tell you about our conversations with the Soviets; we do not tell the

Soviets about our conversations with you.' Kissinger was so awed that he somehow failed to ask for substantial reciprocal concessions.[13]

The trip was kept secret, but on 15 July 1971 Nixon appeared on national television to reveal the preparatory work done by his national security adviser and announce his own impending trip to China. The news sent shockwaves around the world, as the balance of the Cold War shifted away from the Soviet Union. In Beijing, Mao gloated that the United States was 'changing from monkey to man, not quite a man yet, the tail is still there'.[14] He had reduced the leader of the most powerful nation on earth to a mere emissary seeking an imperial audience.

As the United States and China held secret talks, the split between the Chairman and his heir apparent continued to widen. After Mao had shown his hand in the summer of 1970, undermining his successor by denouncing his theory of genius, he fell ill with pneumonia. Doctors prescribed antibiotics, but Mao suspected that Lin Biao was trying to poison him. 'Lin Biao wants my lungs to rot,' he complained. The situation dragged on, but the relationship had broken down. It was a political impasse.

There were other issues besides personal distrust. Lin Biao had always led a reclusive, secretive existence, shunning the limelight. He often called in sick, suffering from a series of real and imagined diseases. Mao once sneeringly referred to the marshal as the 'forever healthy'. From the summer of 1970, Lin became increasingly inactive, relying instead on his wife to read party documents and do his work. He skipped important meetings. Mao became disillusioned. Lin Biao made a rather unimpressive heir apparent.[15]

By August 1971, the Chairman's distrust reached the point where he started musing aloud about which of the regional commanders would be loyal to Lin Biao in the event of a rebellion. Most of the heir's supporters were in Beijing. Mao embarked on a tour of the south, whipping up support from military leaders in Wuhan, Changsha, Hangzhou and Shanghai. He never mentioned Lin by name, but spread the message that someone had been in a hurry to take over as head of state a year before, and was now trying to split the party and seize power for himself. 'There is someone who says genius appears in the world only once in several hundred years, and in China such genius has not come along in several thousand,' he quipped. 'There is somebody who says he wants to support me, elevate me, but what he really has in mind is supporting himself, elevating himself.'

A month later, at dusk on 12 September, the Chairman's train pulled back into Beijing. Hours later, at about 2.30 the following morning, a British-built Trident crashed in Mongolia. Debris was strewn over a wide stretch of steppe, but the local police soon lined up the charred bodies of eight men and one woman. 'Fire had left most of them naked save for pistol holsters and belts,' recalled Tuvany Jurmed, one of the first police officers to arrive at the crash site.[16]

What exactly happened remains shrouded in mystery, although rumours soon began circulating that Lin Biao had tried to flee to the Soviet Union after the failure of a plot to assassinate the Chairman.

The hand behind the alleged plot to dispose of the Chairman was the heir apparent's twenty-five-year-old son, an officer who despite his relative youth wielded considerable influence in the army, thanks to the protection of Wu Faxian, commander-in-chief of the air force. Lin Liguo knew that his father's position was under threat and understood court politics sufficiently well to realise that the Chairman took no half-measures when it came to his enemies:

> Is there a single political force which has been able to work with him from beginning to end? His former secretaries have either committed suicide or been arrested. His few close comrades-in-arms or trusted aides have also been sent to prison by him . . . He is paranoid and a sadist. His philosophy of liquidating people is either to not do it or to do it thoroughly. Every time he liquidates someone, he does not desist until he puts them to death. Once he hurts you, he will hurt you all the way; and he puts the blame for everything bad on others.[17]

Lin Liguo and several close colleagues had devised a half-baked plan to eliminate the Chairman, including attacking his special train with flame-throwers, bombing the train from the air or dynamiting a strategic bridge. Lin Liguo informed his sister Doudou of the plot, but she was opposed to it, believing that any attempt to challenge the Chairman would have dire repercussions for her father. On 8 September she leaked information to two guards responsible for Lin Biao's security.[18]

No assassination attempt was ever carried out. It is unclear whether or not the Chairman got wind of the plot, but at about midnight on 8 September he cut short his tour of the south and suddenly ordered his train to return to Beijing. After a brief stop in Nanjing to meet his loyal follower Xu Shiyou, Mao arrived back in the capital four days later. Immediately after his train had entered the station in the outskirts of the capital, he met with several leaders of the Beijing Military Region, including the two men whom less than a year before he had inserted into the top echelons of the army to watch the generals faithful to Lin Biao. Security was beefed up around Beijing, and the Chairman hunkered down in the Great Hall of the People.

That very same day, fearing that Mao would move against his father, Lin Liguo flew back to Beidaihe, where his family was ensconced in a villa overlooking the Bohai Sea. He wanted his parents to flee. 'To where?' asked his sister Doudou. 'Dalian, or Guangzhou, or Hong Kong. Anywhere, depending on the situation.' But their father refused to budge. Pale, thin and unshaved, his eyes sunken, for months he had known what was in store, and seemed prepared to accept his fate passively.[19]

Doudou realised that the escape plan was hopeless, and tried to protect her father by alerting the central security forces. She was devoted to Lin Biao, but had a strained relationship with Ye Qun. Zhou Enlai was informed by telephone that evening, but no attempt was made to prevent the family from boarding the plane. Lin Liguo and his mother helped the heir apparent to dress, and around 11.30 in the evening they dragged him into a car, rushing off towards the local airport, some forty minutes away. Soldiers holding guns let them pass. Troops had also been dispatched to the airport, but they did not intercept the group either. Panic broke out as the car reached the Trident. As the family and their entourage clambered on board, Lin Biao's wife insisted that they take off immediately, even though the plane had not been fully refuelled. There was no navigator, radio operator or co-pilot on board.

Shortly after the plane disappeared into the sky, the region was plunged into darkness. In Beijing, Zhou Enlai had grounded all planes nationwide and ordered the runway lights to be turned off. The plane flew north, but being short of fuel it did not travel very far, crashing in Mongolia.[20]

The moment the plane disintegrated, Lin Biao's 'four guardian warriors' began to destroy all evidence of their connections with his family, burning photographs, letters, notebooks and telephone logs. Huang Yongsheng, Wu Faxian, Qiu Huizuo and Li Zuopeng were removed from their posts on 24 September. Zhou Enlai set up a special investigative group to look into the Lin Biao affair. A purge of his followers in the army lasted until May 1973 and claimed hundreds of victims, including prominent political commissars and military leaders in almost every province.[21]

The veteran marshals who had taken Lin Biao and the Cultural Revolution to task in February 1967 felt buoyant. They wasted no time in denouncing their former comrade-in-arms. Chen Yi, always outspoken, lambasted his 'sinister conduct, double-dealing, cultivation of sworn followers and persistent scheming'.[22]

Rumours of Lin Biao's demise began circulating after the parade on 1 October 1971 had been cancelled. Nien Cheng, from her prison in Shanghai, was astonished to find that the morning broadcast on National Day failed to mention the customary celebrations. That very same day, a guard made the rounds of all the inmates to collect their Little Red Books. She returned Nien's copy that evening, but with Lin Biao's foreword torn out.[23]

Soon everybody knew of the alleged plot. Those who listened to foreign radio picked up the news from abroad. Dan Ling, who as a sixteen-year-old had carried a banner flag to welcome the People's Liberation Army in Beijing in 1949, had been condemned as a counter-revolutionary during the Cultural Revolution and banished to the countryside in Manchuria. A village accountant invited him to his house, tuning his radio in to several stations. A Japanese news broadcast covering the death of Lin Biao came through loud and clear.[24]

Whether they overheard foreign radio or were told in party meetings, everyone was shocked. The Chairman was supposed to be infallible, and for years Lin Biao had been presented as his closest comrade-in-arms and designated successor. For Dan, who had so enthusiastically joined the party in his youth, the Japanese news report was the 'best political education' he ever received. It destroyed whatever faith he still possessed in the system. Nanchu, the young woman sent to a state farm in Manchuria, wondered why she should believe in the Chairman if his best pupil did not. 'The pillar of spiritual certainty had completely crumbled inside me. The belief in communism and my unwavering faith in Mao had collapsed.'[25]

Many felt relief. Lin Biao had not been a popular figure. But, most of all, people realised that his death marked the beginning of the end of the Cultural Revolution. One translator who attended a meeting at which an official announcement was made thought 'the sigh of relief was almost audible'. Nonetheless, people reacted very differently. Some felt revulsion, others betrayal. One young woman banished to the countryside remembers that, when she heard the news, she thought her universe had shattered: 'I was shaking. I did not know what was going to happen next.' But her closest friend, also a student in exile, saw hope and instead rejoiced.[26]

The Chairman, too, was shaken. His health took a dramatic turn for the worse. Gone was the beaming and spirited leader who relished political struggle. Mao was depressed and took to his bed, lying there for weeks on end. He suffered from a chronic cold, swollen legs and an irregular heartbeat. He walked with a shuffle, revealed by cameras when he met the North Vietnamese premier a little more than two months after the incident.

But Zhou Enlai was pleased. 'It's best that it ended this way,' he told Mao's doctor. 'A major problem has been settled.'[27]

The bodies of Lin Biao and Ye Qun were never returned to China. They were buried in Mongolia, but then exhumed with those of the other crash victims by a team of forensic specialists from Moscow. Like all top Chinese leaders, Lin Biao had spent considerable time receiving medical treatment in the Soviet Union. The Russians wanted to make sure they had their man. The heads of two of the bodies that had gold teeth were severed and boiled in a cauldron to remove the flesh and hair. The bone structure of one of them matched the marshal's medical record perfectly. The two skulls were taken to Moscow and stored in the KGB archives.[28]

PART FOUR

THE GREY YEARS (1971–1976)

20

Recovery

After spending nearly two months in bed in a state of depression, mulling over his options, the Chairman was finally ready for his next move. He wanted a reconciliation with the veteran marshals pushed aside during the Cultural Revolution. They were still in disgrace. Chen Yi, who had insinuated in February 1967 that Lin Biao was no better than Khrushchev, died of colon cancer on 6 January 1972. The Chairman woke in the middle of the afternoon on the day of his funeral and suddenly decided to attend the ceremony, slipping on a silk robe and a pair of leather sandals. At the funeral parlour he consoled Chen Yi's widow. He blinked his eyes and made an effort to wail. Soon everybody in the room was crying.

After the funeral, other military leaders were restored to their former positions. Chen Zaidao, the general from Wuhan denounced by Lin Biao as a 'counter-revolutionary mutineer', was allowed to preside over official occasions. Yang Chengwu, who had been acting chief of staff before his purge in March 1968, was reinstated. 'Yang Chengwu, I understand you,' Mao wrote, describing him as a victim of Lin Biao. Luo Ruiqing, the chief of staff who had jumped feet first from a window after a gruelling interrogation session in 1965, also had his name cleared. 'Lin Biao falsely accused Luo Ruiqing,' the Chairman said. 'I listened to Lin and dismissed Luo. I was imprudent to listen so often to his one-sided views. I have to criticise myself.' Mao pretended to have been duped all along by a perfidious schemer now gone.[1]

Besides a reshuffling of the top brass, there were other promising indications of a new dawn. Signs of relaxation had followed ping-pong diplomacy in the spring of 1971, and in the first weeks of 1972 entire cities were being spruced up. The reason was simple: Nixon was coming to China.

Whole districts in the capital were scrubbed down in preparation for his visit. Posters were removed, anti-American slogans toned down. Some of the street signs dating from the Cultural Revolution were painted over, as Red Guard Street reverted to its old name of Horse and Mule Street. Doorways and windows along the main roads to Zhongnanhai, Diaoyutai and Tiananmen Square glistened with fresh paint. Rows of trees, some more than three metres tall, were planted by crane at the entrance of the park by the Temple of Heaven. Soldiers still guarded all the main compounds, but their bayonets were gone.[2]

Shanghai, too, received a facelift. According to one observer, more paint was used in a few weeks than the city had seen in twenty-two years. Yuyuan Garden, a sprawling park with pavilions, halls and cloisters built by a wealthy government official in the sixteenth century, had hundreds of doors that were stripped and given a new coat of paint. Many shops changed their names back to pre-Cultural Revolution days. Colours besides red were introduced, with signboards allowed in sky blue, cream and apple green. Variations in calligraphy, so far dominated by Mao's flamboyant handwriting, were encouraged.

Slogans and posters dating from the Cultural Revolution were taken down in a carefully co-ordinated campaign, street by street, district after district. It took a small army of women to scrub out a massive slogan with three-metre-high characters opposite the Peace Hotel proclaiming 'Long Live the Invincible Thoughts of Chairman Mao'. New slogans appeared, welcoming the 'Great Unity of the Peoples of the World'. All references to the Chairman were removed from window displays.[3]

Statues posed a problem. They were numerous and potentially dangerous, as bits of plaster regularly fell on to pedestrians. In one district alone, some 2,000 of them presented a threat to the public. In front of the Shanghai Exhibition Centre, the Chairman's giant arm, boldly extended into an open-hand salute, had come crashing down. Thousands of statues were removed, discreetly sent off to gypsum factories for recycling.[4]

Popular demand for small-sized statues of the Chairman also collapsed. Soon enough, the basements of department stores were packed with tens of thousands of plaster and enamel busts, staring into the void.[5]

Parks were spruced up. In Shanghai more than 300 hectares of green space had been converted for industrial use since 1966, but now the *Liberation Daily* proclaimed that parks were the new face of socialism. Work was carried out on hundreds of parks and gardens badly damaged during the Cultural Revolution. In Fuxing Park, opened in 1909 with flowerbeds, fountains and pavilions, every lamp that had been smashed by the Red Guards was repaired. Zhongshan Park, where the original gate had been dismantled as a sign of imperialism, was restored to at least part of its former glory. The main road to the site of the First National Congress of the Communist Party of China, in the former French Concession, was tidied up, as stunted and diseased wingnut trees were pruned or replaced.[6]

The Chairman, too, was primped and preened. His health had further declined following his impromptu visit to Chen Yi's funeral, and after a brief collapse he was put on a regimen of antibiotics, digitalis and diuretics. His condition improved rapidly. He started practising sitting down and getting up, and received his first haircut in more than five months. Emergency medical equipment was hidden behind potted plants, ready to be assembled within seconds should anything go wrong.[7]

The meeting with Nixon on 21 February 1972 was a success. It was scheduled to last for fifteen minutes, but went on for more than an hour. A week later, a communiqué was issued from Shanghai in which both nations pledged to work towards full diplomatic recognition.

Coming in the wake of the Lin Biao incident, Nixon's visit had huge propaganda value. It was widely interpreted as an admission of defeat by the United States in its attempt to isolate China. Kim Il-sung, leader of North Korea, was reportedly jubilant, saying that 'Nixon went to Beijing waving the white flag!' As propaganda explained, people used to fear imperialism, but now they could see the United States as it really was, namely a paper tiger.[8]

The prestige of the Soviet Union also suffered a blow, as Nixon's visit set off a chain reaction. Leaders of countries from Europe, Latin America, Africa and Asia flocked to Beijing, seeking recognition. The visit of the Japanese prime minister Kakuei Tanaka was another triumph for Mao. Although Japan was the most important ally of the United States in Asia, Tokyo was told of the Shanghai communiqué only fifteen minutes before it was broadcast. It was a breach of trust whose effects would be felt for many years.

The United States did less well from the talks.[9] Diplomatic recognition, despite the promises made in Shanghai, was not achieved until six years later. Nixon had also hoped that the rapprochement would achieve some sort of compromise over Vietnam. But China was even more determined to help its allies in Indochina. Its support for the murderous Khmer Rouge in Cambodia never wavered. In the following years America's predicament in Indochina worsened.

The Lin Biao incident drastically undermined the role of the military, despite the rehabilitation of the veteran marshals. Years before, in the early months of 1967, more than 2.8 million soldiers had been asked to support the revolution, closely shadowing the party and the state. But in August 1972 the People's Liberation Army went back to its barracks.

The Chairman had little choice but to turn to the party officials denounced as 'capitalist roaders' during the Cultural Revolution. They replaced the army officers, who quietly withdrew from the civilian administration. Ulanfu, the revisionist leader of Inner Mongolia, was returned to power, even though his province was much reduced in size. Li Jingquan, who had lost out against the two Tings in Sichuan, was rehabilitated. Twenty-six other provincial leaders took up where they had left off. As the *People's Daily* put it, 'We should remain convinced that more than 95 per cent of our cadres are good and fairly good, and that a majority of those who have committed errors are able to change.'[10] By the end of 1972, most of the government administrators and party cadres still in May Seventh Cadre Schools were back at their desks.

But the power and prestige they had once wielded were gone. Many of them had been badly damaged by the political infighting of the Cultural Revolution, not to mention the endless purges that had followed the establishment of revolutionary committees under the watchful eye of the military. The old guard lived in fear of committing yet another political mistake, having experienced enough violent shifts in court politics to realise that the climate could change abruptly at any time. Many were keen to demonstrate that they had been fully re-educated and 'were able to change'. They were not about to propose ideas that strayed from rigid communist orthodoxy.

The limits of the recovery were particularly evident when it came to the economy. It remained moribund. The priority given to the Third Front was reduced, since the immediate threat of war no longer existed after the rapprochement with the United States, but massive resources were still being diverted towards heavy industry. Steel targets were cranked up, leading to constant power shortages and strict rationing of energy. In Hubei, in February 1973, top party leaders and foreign experts were the only ones to receive a regular supply of electricity. Half of all street lights in Wuhan were regularly switched off.[11]

Many state enterprises continued to suffer from low productivity. The soldiers in the Mao Zedong Thought propaganda teams were gone, but the Cultural Revolution had undermined the standing and credibility of the old cadres who replaced them. At best they managed to keep the paper flow moving, at worst they remained paralysed by fear of the next political campaign. Apathy set in among the workers, who over the years had refined a whole range of techniques to resist pressure from above. They knew how to steal time, slacking and shirking on the job. Discipline was lax. Some people used the factory facilities to wash their clothes, others played poker as soon as the manager on duty turned away. Some pilfered factory goods, distributing them to family and friends or bartering them on the black market.[12]

The quality of the output produced by a disenchanted workforce was dismal. In some factories in Guangdong a mere third of all products, from fans and cameras to tractors, conformed to production standards. In other factories in Shaanxi, the proportion of faulty goods reached 50 per cent. The quality of china was so bad that shop assistants in department stores would routinely tap each porcelain bowl with a spoon to check for flaws.[13]

State property was also damaged through sheer carelessness or wilful neglect. In Hankou, one of the largest transportation hubs in central China, freight workers often threw cardboard packages from a height of three metres, shattering the contents. 'The management does not care and neither do we,' they responded when a newly hired worker queried the practice.[14]

The exact dimensions of the problem are hard to identify, if only because transparency and accounting were not among the prime virtues of the planned economy. In Gansu province one in six state enterprises operated at a deficit in 1972. The total losses incurred by the industrial sector had increased by more than a third in the year following Lin Biao's death as a direct result of lower productivity and what was referred to as a 'chaotic administration'. The situation did not improve. Three years later, in 1975, one in four ran at a loss.[15]

In Shaanxi province, one out of every three factories was in the red. Few cadres running the state enterprises seemed concerned about the cost of their products, their only concern being the fulfilment of state-imposed output targets. For each 100 yuan in fixed assets, just over 160 yuan worth of goods were churned out in 1966. By 1974, this amount had plummeted to a mere 84 yuan. The waste was enormous. The Xi'an Cable Company alone had 1,700 tonnes of reject products, valued at 4 million yuan, piled high in the backyard.[16]

As the state continued to view heavy industry as a priority, consumer goods were neglected. The inability of the planned economy to fulfil even the most basic demands of the population had reached surreal proportions during the years of military dictatorship under Lin Biao, when the inherent inefficiencies in capital allocation had been compounded by rigid insistence on self-reliance. The Learn from Dazhai campaign forced entire provinces to cut off many of their old trade connections and sink into economic autarky. Even the production of something as simple as a button became problematic. Before the Cultural Revolution, clothes made in Xinjiang were sent to Zhejiang, where whole villages specialised in the button industry. These national networks were closed down, as textile factories were forced to produce everything locally. The result was shortages for everybody.[17]

Xinjiang did not only suffer from a shortage of buttons. Ordinary people in this sparsely populated province marked by dry steppes, towering mountain ranges and a shifting sand desert had always depended on trade for many of their household needs. But by 1970 even lorry drivers who had to cross the Gobi desert had to wait for several years before they could buy a thermos flask. At wedding ceremonies simple drinking glasses were in short supply. In Turfan, the centre of a fertile oasis where Red Guards had converted minarets and mosques into factories, a single bar of soap had to be shared by three people each season. In the provincial capital of Urumqi, once a major hub on the silk road, washing powder was restricted to one bag per person every four months. Matches and lighters were luxuries. A ration card was required to buy a flint, necessary for lighting fires.[18]

Xinjiang was at the edge of the empire, but even trading cities along the Pearl Delta near Hong Kong were reeling. Foshan suffered from shortages of matches, soap, toothpaste, batteries and cotton cloth. Further north, in the countryside outside Nanjing, toothbrushes were considered such a luxury that most people started using them only after the death of the Chairman in 1976.[19]

The regime was aware of these problems, and some adjustments were made. Even though the campaign to Learn from Dazhai would not wind down until several years after the Chairman's death, the dogmatic insistence on economic autarky softened. State enterprises, once again, started sending travelling representatives and purchasing agents to renew commercial links across the country after 1971. A good indication of this activity was the Guangzhou Trade Fair, where attendance shot up. In the spring of 1973, the fair attracted up to 127,000 visitors a day, far more than previous years. Every hotel was fully booked. Beds were added to guest rooms, turning them into dormitories, but were still not enough, as hundreds of delegates had to get through the night sitting in hotel lobbies. In Shanghai, too, a resurgence in trade saw a record number of purchasing agents, as some 65,000 visitors crowded every hotel in the early months of 1973. In the Huashan Hotel alone, 400 guests slept in the corridors. In the Xinhua Hotel visitors had to sit in the reception for three nights before they were entitled to a mat in the corridor. Hundreds of people slept on the floors of barber shops.[20]

Trade with the West was encouraged. There was an enthusiastic procession of American businessmen, keen to make the pilgrimage to Beijing. Photos appeared of a genial David Rockefeller in a flowery sports shirt standing among smiling officials from the Bank of China. New equipment and advanced technology was imported, replacing some of the antiquated machinery in a number of state enterprises.[21]

Restrictions imposed on arts and crafts at the height of the Cultural Revolution were relaxed. The Ministry of Light Industry still banned 'reactionary, pornographic and repulsive products', but artefacts hitherto condemned as 'feudal' or 'superstitious' were once again allowed, bringing in several million US dollars from exports alone each year. Ethnic minorities, too, were allowed to resurrect some of the handicrafts banned since 1966, from Korean woks to Tibetan bowls. In general, there was more emphasis on light industrial products than before.[22]

The countryside, too, was allowed to diversify its production and establish small industries, a policy heralded by the premier at a North China Agricultural Conference held in August 1970. The idea was that China should 'walk on two legs', as rural enterprises would support agricultural development, for instance in producing farming tools, chemical fertilisers and cement. But it was hardly a new departure. In Dazhai, the peasants working under Chen Yonggui operated a brick kiln, a noodle factory and a bauxite mine, as agriculture and industry merged to further the collective cause. The whole idea of 'walking on two legs' dated from the Great Leap Forward, when the Chairman thought that his country could overtake its competitors by relocating industry in the countryside, liberating the productive potential of every peasant in giant people's communes. The rural enterprises that the state encouraged remained firmly under collective leadership.[23]

Despite a softening in official rhetoric and some tinkering with government policy, the planned economy remained incapable of improving the livelihood of most ordinary people. As late as 1974, many cities could barely produce half of all commodities required to satisfy the basic needs of the population.[24]

Ziyang county is located in the midst of great natural beauty, as the Han River, a tributary of the Yangtze, flows majestically between several towering mountain chains. Some of the best tea comes from this part of Shaanxi province, as rich soil, a mild climate and plentiful rain produce jade-green leaves rich in selenium. In December 1973, a party official on an inspection tour came across a small shed by the side of the road, cobbled together with bits of thatch and a few planks. It was shared by a family of seven, who slept on the floor, separated from the frozen earth by a thin layer of slate and shredded cotton. They had no clothes and tried to keep warm by wrapping themselves in straw. The stalks barely held together, as the shrivelled breasts of the mother, aged forty, were left exposed. The family boasted no possessions other than a few broken bowls and one corrugated-tin can. An old man sat in a corner quietly sobbing, repeating the same desperate plea over and over again: 'Please allow the government to take care of us!' The inspector wanted to give them his coat, but realised that he still had ten more days on the road, travelling in the middle of the winter with temperatures plunging to minus 10 degrees. 'I felt terrible because I did not take off a single piece of clothing to help them,' he later recalled. When he questioned the head of the local district, he was told that a fifth of the villagers lived in similar circumstances. In a single commune, fifty people had starved to death in the spring, and more would follow that winter.[25]

Little changed in the following two years. In December 1975, some 70 per cent of the population in Ziyang lived on less than 500 grams of grain per day. Poverty was particularly pronounced in the mountainous areas of the county, where up to a third of the villagers could not even afford to buy salt or put oil in their lamps. Many did not have a blanket, a bowl or a tool to work the land.[26]

Across the province as a whole, more than 5 million people went hungry. 'Some villagers only have 125 to 130 kilos of grain for the entire year, and if we take into account the debts they still have to pay, in the months to come they will have less than ten kilos of food per person per month,' one official noted. Many thousands starved to death. Famine oedema and extreme emaciation were common. People who did not die of hunger tried to flee the countryside, begging for a living on the roads. In the south of the province, where Ziyang was located, people ate mud.[27]

Shaanxi was not the only province where millions went hungry. Starvation remained common in large parts of the countryside until 1976. In Hebei, the province that surrounds Beijing and Tianjin, more than 5 million villagers lacked food in 1975. In Qingxian county alone, the average amount of food eaten per day across whole villages was a mere 400 grams.[28]

Across the border from Hebei, to the south-east, the province of Shandong was ravaged by famine in 1973. As a last resort, half of the population in Dongming county consumed the seeds normally set aside for sowing in the following season. They also ate the fodder destined for plough animals, long since gone, and sold the tiles on their roofs, their bedding and sometimes even their own clothes. Thousands took to the road, forming large gangs of beggars that roamed the countryside. The numbers were stark: in the Jining region, 1.6 million people lacked food, while 2.2 million went hungry in Linqin.[29]

Further inland, in Hubei, famine remained common in the years following the Lin Biao affair. In 1972, a third of the population in various counties had to survive on less than 13 kilos of grain a month. In Yichang, the province's second largest city with jurisdiction over large parts of the surrounding countryside, one official report noted that 'as a result of insufficient nutrition, people have started to suffer from oedema, emaciation, a prolapsed uterus, amenorrhoea and other diseases'.[30]

Two years later, in 1974, many of the villagers in Tongshan county had less than 8 kilos of food per month, the rough equivalent of two small sweet potatoes per day. In some villages, an investigator noted, from March to May 'there is only an average of 1.5 kilos per month'. The famine was not confined to Tongshan. In Jianli, on the northern bank of the Yangtze River, tens of thousands of people were reduced to begging for a living. One such was Pi Hanbin, who had no more than 10 kilos of grain a month, to be shared with his wife and their five children. Not all of them were hardy enough to head for the city in the hope of finding some food. Chen Zhengxian, who hailed from a neighbouring village, could no longer bear to listen to the constant cries of hunger from his child and swallowed rat poison. Similar deprivation could be found across the province.[31]

These are but a few examples from the countryside, and no doubt the archives in other provinces contain equally telling examples, yet even in villages just outside once prosperous cities hunger remained a constant worry. In the suburbs of Shanghai, a full third of all people's communes had sunk into poverty by 1973. Outside Wenzhou, a thriving foreign treaty port before the Second World War, in 1976 droves of villagers sold all their belongings and fled mass starvation.[32]

Nobody inside the cities starved to death, since much of the grain procured from the countryside was earmarked for urban residents. But even in the capital the diet was barely sufficient. The canteen at Peking University, according to one of the first foreign students allowed to enrol in the wake of the Sino-American rapprochement, looked like a prisoners' mess straight out of Solzhenitsyn's *One Day in the Life of Ivan Denisovich*, 'a dark sea of plank benches and rough tables'. Staff and students had to queue up with their own enamel bowl at a tiny window for a ladleful of slop. The food would have looked like a feast to starved villagers, but it was always identical: 'tasteless cornmeal mush, with a teaspoonful of inedible salted vegetables. Lunch, the only time my classmates ate meat, was a sliver or two of pork fat mixed with stale cabbage. The rice was dry and tasteless, broken grains, more gray than white, polluted with tiny fragments of gravel and coal. I learned to chew carefully to avoid breaking a tooth.' In the country's premier university, the students were permanently undernourished.[33]

Much as the old guard were unable to tackle the dismal performance of industry, they were unable to change the fundamentals of agricultural production in the people's communes.

Not that the leadership was oblivious to the state of permanent crisis in the countryside. In 1970, China imported a record 6.5 million tonnes of chemical fertiliser and purchased 5.36 million tonnes of grain – the highest amount since the start of the Cultural Revolution. In an effort to improve grain output, the regime introduced a wide range of agricultural innovations from August 1970 onwards. In the same way that advanced technology was bought from abroad to spruce up state enterprises, improved seeds, pesticides, fertilisers and farm machinery were made available in parts of the countryside.[34]

In a shift away from the extreme rhetoric of radical collectivisation, villagers were once again encouraged to cultivate their own private plots in their spare time, provided all collective duties had been completed. Local markets were allowed to operate in the countryside, but within the constraints of the planned economy, meaning that a great variety of products remained off the table, including all foodstuffs over which the state had a monopoly, from cotton, edible oil, meat and grain to tobacco and timber. These measures did not amount to much, and did not go beyond some of the policies introduced in the aftermath of the catastrophe of the Great Leap Forward.

Still, even minor tinkering with a bankrupt economy had an impact, especially after years of military dictatorship. Grain production increased. But it did not raise the income of most villagers. Several economists have used official statistics to calculate that the per capita expenditure for the rural population actually declined in the 1970s. The reason was quite simple: the state took away the surplus. In 1971, the country produced a crop of 240 million tonnes, more than ever before, but as the leaders in Beijing noted, this represented, on paper, a paltry 25 kilos of unprocessed grain per person each month – before the state procured 45 million tonnes.[35]

A similar trend could be seen in other aspects of agricultural production. The leadership did not abolish its narrow focus on the production of grain, but did encourage economic diversification. The people's communes were even allowed to grow a limited quantity of cash crops, to be sold on local markets to achieve the goal of economic self-sufficiency. But here too, the changes were limited. The number of pigs increased in the early 1970s, but as pork remained a state monopoly there were too few incentives to lead to a sizeable improvement in protein for everybody. In 1971, for instance, Gansu province had a million more pigs than the previous year, and close to 2 million more when compared to 1966. But on average one animal weighed a third less when compared to five years earlier. As a result, the provincial capital of Lanzhou consumed 155 tonnes of pork per month in 1971, the equivalent of less than half a kilo per person. In 1965 it had been 240 tonnes, even though fewer people lived in Lanzhou. In grain and in meat, as with basic daily commodities, the regime simply could not keep up with an expanding population base.[36]

When the Chairman died in 1976 at least 20 per cent of the population, equivalent to 200 million people, suffered from chronic malnutrition.[37] A widespread state of semi-starvation was not helped by poor health. In towns and cities across the country, hospitals had been battered by denunciation meetings and factional fighting at the height of the Cultural Revolution. In Wuhan, by the spring of 1967, chaos reigned in most hospitals, as doctors not yet denounced by rebels started fainting with exhaustion, forced to work around the clock for fear of being accused of bourgeois behaviour. A survey of one medical facility showed that nine out of ten staff suffered from liver infections caused by poor hygiene. Wuhan was hardly unique. Reliable statistics are rare, but in the case of Hebei province the number of workers in health care decreased from 88,400 in 1965 to 66,900 five years later. Relative to the overall population, the number was less than it had been in 1952, twenty years earlier.[38]

The decline stabilised somewhat in the years following Lin Biao's death, but many people continued to suffer from a wide variety of chronic diseases, as evidence from the archives shows. In Foshan, some 20 kilometres south of Guangzhou, in 1973 a third of the workforce earned less than 20 yuan a month. Since a family spent an average of 10 to 11 yuan on food alone, even a minor illness could push them into a deficit, adding an extra financial burden of 2 to 3 yuan a month. A more serious condition cost 10 yuan a month. Still, people in Foshan fared better than their counterparts in other cities of Guangdong. In Zhaoqing, a quarter of the workforce was on less than 12 yuan a month in 1974.[39]

In Foshan one in every five workers lived with a chronic disease. It was the same across the province. In some chemical factories more than two-thirds of the workforce were ill. Tuberculosis, liver infections and mental illness were common. Before the Cultural Revolution, a number of medical institutions had specialised in treating these conditions, but they had been absorbed by general hospitals. Thousands of beds had vanished.[40]

Conditions in the countryside were far worse. On 26 June 1965, the Chairman himself had pointed the finger at the Ministry of Health, accusing it of being a Ministry for Urban Lords dedicated only to the needs of the upper crust at the expense of ordinary people, particularly in the countryside. Two years later, as 'Smash Elitist Health Care' became the slogan of the day, Mao offered a magic cure. Education, in his opinion, was overrated, and anybody could become a doctor. Ordinary villagers were put on short courses before being asked to attend to the medical needs of the masses. The Chairman called them 'barefoot doctors'.

In Sichuan, Jung Chang was one of the many students sent to the countryside who was selected to become a doctor. She went to work 'with absolutely no training'. Elsewhere, barely literate farmers were not prepared for even simple courses in medicine, and received training for as little as ten days. One candidate remembers that 'only twenty minutes after the class began some students became sleepy. Their heads dropped bit by bit, like chickens pecking rice. With each passing minute, more and more students were napping. Later, a few even snored loudly in class, with saliva dribbling out of their mouths. They could not be woken up.'[41]

The project was a sham, and one that conveniently moved the burden from the state to the collective. In the spirit of self-reliance, the barefoot doctors received virtually no help from the state, with the exception of preventive vaccines. Many could not even perform simple emergency procedures.[42]

Still, there were large numbers of them, and many were dedicated to their work, if only because the job offered an escape from tilling the fields. Another positive outcome was the reduction in price of the basic medical kit with which barefoot doctors were equipped, for instance stethoscopes, thermometers and blood-pressure monitors. These tools became far more widespread than before.[43]

The price of many medications also dropped. A good example was the reduction in the prevalence of cretinism, a condition of severely stunted physical and mental growth caused by lack of iodine in the diet. Many villagers living in the mountainous areas of Ziyang, for instance, could not afford to buy salt. Thanks to the distribution of cheap tablets containing iodine, in Shaanxi province as a whole the number of cases of cretinism by 1974 was halved from 4 million at the start of the Cultural Revolution.[44]

Yet even something as basic as iodised salt remained in short supply, and in Shaanxi, Hubei and other provinces the state failed to reach many millions of people. And while some easily preventable diseases were on the decline, others increased. The number of cases of malaria, for instance, jumped five-fold in Hubei after 1966, and still blighted the lives of 2.6 million villagers in 1974.[45]

The reality was that the co-operative medicine represented by barefoot doctors thrived only briefly, at the height of the government campaign in 1968. Within a few years it collapsed in large parts of the countryside. In Fuyang county, to take but one example, it had been abandoned by two-thirds of all the people's communes by 1971. Villagers, like many workers in the cities, once again had to pay for medical services, and at 2 to 10 yuan the fees were prohibitive.[46]

As a result, poor health was the norm in large swathes of the countryside. Precise studies are lacking, since the authorities faced many other pressing demands, with one political campaign following on the heels of another throughout much of the Cultural Revolution. Most of all, there were no funds to tackle chronic diseases in the countryside, much less to carry out in-depth medical examinations. But when in 1972 work teams were sent into the villages of dozens of counties in Shandong to check the health of women of reproductive age, they found that between 30 and 38 per cent of the women they examined suffered from a gynaecological disorder. Some had a prolapsed uterus, caused by a combination of work overload and malnutrition. Others suffered from a pelvic inflammatory disease or cervical erosion. Many were so sick that they never got out of bed. In the absence of medical care, infant mortality rates were also high, as villagers fell back on traditional practices, using local midwives who had no medical training. In one village, a traditional midwife delivered thirty babies, of whom ten subsequently died. Puerperal fever as well as maternal deaths were common. In a single commune in Gaotang, thirty-six women died while giving birth in 1971 alone. In most villages, real medical improvements would only come much later, after the people's communes had been abolished in 1982.[47]

The Silent Revolution

Set amid dusty sandstone-coloured hills in northern Shaanxi, Yan'an is one of the most hallowed places in communist propaganda. At the end of the Long March in 1936 it was taken over by the communists, and became their temporary capital during the Second World War. Decades later, Yan'an had become a symbol of the ideal communist man, one who merged with the collective in war and work alike. The 'Yan'an spirit' heralded selfless dedication to the greater good, as people fused into a collective force powerful enough to move mountains.

While Yan'an loomed large in the communist imagination, the place itself was dirt poor and had been largely bypassed by the revolution. But some local people did not wait for an invitation from above to pull themselves out of poverty. When a propaganda team arrived in Yan'an in December 1974, they found a thriving and sophisticated black market. One village had abandoned any attempt to wrench food from the arid and parched soil, specialising in selling pork instead. In order to fulfil their quota of grain deliveries to the state, they used the profit from their meat business to buy back corn from the market. Local cadres supervised the entire operation. No one in the village seemed to have any interest in politics. More than three years after the demise of Lin Biao, posters of the erstwhile heir apparent still fluttered in the wind. Slogans painted on outside walls were fading, and dated mostly from 1969.[1]

Yan'an was not alone in taking to the market. Entire people's communes in Luonan, less than two hours away from Xi'an by bus, had divided up all collective assets and handed responsibility for production back to individual families. Many villagers abandoned two decades of monoculture, imposed by a state keen on grain to feed the cities and barter on the international market, and cultivated crops that performed well on the black market. Some rented out their plots and went to the city instead, working in underground factories and sending back remittances to the village. Other freedoms flourished. The head of one production team, instead of adorning his front door with slogans exalting the Chairman, displayed couplets composed by a Tang dynasty emperor. Traditional geomancy, decried as superstition since liberation, seemed to matter more than the latest party directives, which everybody ignored. Spirit mediums and fortune tellers did the rounds.[2]

In Pucheng, further to the north of Xi'an, some cadres also stood back and allowed the villagers to go about their business. Here, too, propitious couplets in traditional calligraphy largely displaced loud slogans in brash red, and here too, party officials expressed little interest in reading newspapers, let alone keeping up with the party line. 'Not one party meeting has been called, and not one of the prescribed works of Marx, Lenin and Chairman Mao has been studied,' complained one report. In some production brigades, telephone conferences were not a realistic prospect, since the lines had been cut down and were used by the villagers to dry sweet potatoes. Instead of working for the collectives, people with any kind of expertise offered their services to the highest bidder. There were doctors who gave private consultations for a fee. There were self-employed artisans. Chen Hongru, classified as a 'rich peasant' and a 'counter-revolutionary' to boot, worked as a carpenter on the black market, helping out production teams during the busy season for no less than 25 work points a day, more than twice the amount a hard-working male adult could earn in a collective.[3]

This all took place in Shaanxi, where millions went hungry, some of them eating mud or stripping bark from trees. In Ziyang, where one inspector had come across the starving family of seven surviving in a shed in the midst of winter, the local authorities had shrugged their shoulders. But elsewhere in the province, some cadres preferred to hand out the land to the villagers and let them try to survive by their own means rather than watch them die of hunger or steal the grain directly from the fields.

Necessity is the proverbial mother of invention, and the overlap between sheer destitution and the entrepreneurial spirit could be found elsewhere.

The most influential example came from Anhui, one of the first provinces to have sunk into mass starvation in 1959. Anhui had also been one of the first to emerge from Mao's Great Famine by allowing farmers to rent the land in 1961. In the summer of 1962 the Chairman attacked Zeng Xisheng, the provincial leader, as a 'capitalist roader', and the land was recollectivised in the following years.

But as the military dictatorship under Lin Biao collapsed and the soldiers returned to their barracks, villagers in many parts of the countryside tried to regain control over the land and leach power away from the state. In some cases, local cadres took the lead, distributing the land to the farmers. Sometimes a deal was struck between representatives of the state and those who tilled the land, as the fiction of collective ownership was preserved by turning over a percentage of the crop to party officials. Bribery often greased the wheels of free enterprise, as villagers paid cadres to look the other way.

The return to market principles was facilitated by divisions at the top. Throughout the Cultural Revolution, partisan wrangling and factional infighting among the leadership had resulted in constant changes in government policy. On the ground, villagers were often subject to the ebb and flow of radical politics, as the precise contours of the collective economy, from the size of private plots to the number of animals that a family could own, shifted from one campaign to the next. They were also at the mercy of the local cadres, who had some scope to interpret or negotiate the constantly changing rules of the game.

This became particularly prominent after the North China Agricultural Conference in the summer of 1970, as Zhou Enlai tried to move away from the destructive effects of extreme collectivisation. In subsequent months, numerous articles appeared in the press stressing the right of villagers to cultivate their own private plots, the importance of local peasant markets and the contribution of cash crops to the collective economy. These measures did not go beyond what had been introduced after the catastrophe of the Great Leap Forward, but they softened some of the more extreme interpretations of the Learn from Dazhai campaign. On 26 December 1971, precisely seven years after Chen Yonggui had shared a meal with the Chairman to launch the slogan 'In Agriculture, Learn from Dazhai', the People's Daily even cautioned against 'blindly learning from Dazhai'.[4]

A more moderate approach towards agriculture was helped by the purges that followed Lin Biao's death. Half a dozen provincial leaders who had embraced radical collectivisation were replaced. But Chen Yonggui did not simply vanish from the scene after 1971. Throughout the Cultural Revolution the Chairman had pitted one faction against the other. In 1973 Chen Yonggui was elected a member of the powerful Politburo and transferred to Beijing, where two years later he was appointed a vice-premier of the State Council. Throughout he remained influential, and even after the death of the Chairman he continued to denounce private plots as the 'tail of capitalism'. At one point he suggested that the whole of Gansu province should be modelled on Dazhai.

Given these conflicting messages from the top, very different approaches appeared throughout the countryside, as overzealous cadres continued to impose radical collectivisation and ban private plots in some places while elsewhere villagers were allowed more scope for private initiatives. But most of all, as the standing of the party suffered a blow in the aftermath of the Lin Biao affair, some cadres started deliberately twisting and bending various state directives, taking them far beyond what the leadership intended. As one village official put it, the rural cadres, 'after the continuous flip-flop of government policies and after their repeated humiliations in public during struggle sessions', lost interest in politics. They devoted their energy to production instead. Some of them opened up every portion of collective property to negotiation, from control over the pigsty, the fish pond and the forest to the exact dimensions of individual plots. They allowed a black market to thrive, realising that their own livelihoods, including the food they ate, depended on free trade. They encouraged the villagers to leave the collectives and strike out on their own.[5]

A good example comes from Fenghuang, an ancient town in Hunan where giant wooden wheels scooped up water from the river to irrigate the terraced rice fields. As elsewhere, the villagers seized three opportunities to expand their private plots. They did so first during Mao's Great Famine, trying to escape from starvation as best they could. Then they used the initial chaos of the Cultural Revolution to reclaim more land from the state. They were forced to surrender all gains during the campaign to Learn from Dazhai, but in 1972 they expanded their plots by more than 50 per cent.

Private plots were not to constitute more than 5 per cent of the land, and people were allowed to cultivate them only once their daily duties to the collective had been fulfilled. But in Fenghuang, as in many other places, some villagers, with the consent of the cadres, interpreted the loosening of agricultural policy as a licence to withdraw from the people's communes and work all day on their own. Many went private, growing vegetables or fishing for shrimps. Wu Tingzhong, for instance, declined the basic food ration he was entitled to as a member of his production team, and relied instead on his own plot to grow potatoes, vegetables and tobacco in sufficient quantities to feed himself and sell a surplus worth 400 yuan a year. The entire production team soon followed his lead, as they pooled their resources to focus on producing cash crops. It was a socialist world turned upside down, as those who answered the call of the market thrived while members of the collective remained mired in poverty. Wu Qinghua, a loyal follower who obeyed every order from the people's commune, earned barely enough work points to get by. He lived in a converted latrine, dressed in rags and lived in destitution, as he had to borrow money from the collective to help tide him over a bad season. Fenghuang was divided. The cadres leaned towards Wu Tingzhong.[6]

The restrictions on trade remained in place throughout the nation. Even when local officials and team leaders decided to close their eyes or bend the regulations, people like Wu Tingzhong and others still had to evade tax officials and other government agents. In the wake of the North China Agricultural Conference, local peasant markets were once again encouraged, but a ban on trading in commodities over which the state had a monopoly remained in place, from grain, meat, cotton, silk, tea and tobacco to groundnuts. But here too, the grip of the state weakened significantly after the Lin Biao affair.

One example comes from Tang Huangdao, a villager who fried peanuts and cakes at night and sold them by the roadside to travellers. Like many others, he hid most of his wares in the fields, only carrying a small quantity of merchandise with him. When he was caught, everything was confiscated, but there was no other punishment. Outside Tang's village in Henan, a province that had sustained massive devastation during the Great Leap Forward, a blockade was sometimes imposed to prevent the sale of grain, normally requisitioned by the state in a monopoly imposed decades earlier in 1953. In the months before and after the wheat harvest in early summer, checkpoints were set up along the main roads to stop people from carrying away bags filled with corn or wheat on their bicycles. But the villagers knew how to avoid the militia, carrying small amounts under cover of darkness or making multiple trips with hidden containers to avoid detection. In any event, a weakened state was no longer a match for determined individuals who had honed their skills over many years of hardship. Villagers who had survived the horrors of Mao's Great Famine were not about to be intimidated by a tax officer hanging about at a roadblock in a conspicuous uniform.[7]

Much as need ruled large parts of the country, prompting villagers to rely on their own wits to pull themselves out of destitution, opportunity also played an important role. Some villages were better off than others. They capitalised on their advantages to improve their collective lot, whether these were proximity to transportation routes, abundant fish and wildlife, a regular water supply, fertile soil, a level terrain for farming or access to sources of energy such as coal and wood.

Wealthy regions joined those mired in poverty in a silent revolution that subverted the planned economy. In villages along the southern coast, people raised ducks, kept bees, bred fish, baked bricks and cut timber, always in the name of the collective. In the county of Xinchang, Zhejiang, with a population of roughly a quarter of a million people, by late 1971 some two-thirds of all villagers were independent – or 'go-it-aloners' in the parlance of the time. Much of this was done with the tacit consent of the local authorities, who rented the land to individual households in exchange for a portion of the crop. A year before the death of the Chairman, the habit of leaving the collectives to try one's luck on private land or in underground factories was described as 'widespread' throughout the province. Wenzhou took the trend to the extreme, as private capitalism flourished in the city and its isolated delta despite repeated harassment from the government.[8]

Nowhere was this trend more evident than in Guangdong, a subtropical province with plenty of light, heat and water as well as abundant waterways and a long coastline ideal for economic growth. Markets were ubiquitous. In Qingyuan, virtually every commodity normally banned from the market by virtue of a government monopoly was openly on sale, including grain, peanuts, oil and tobacco. Business was swift. It took a team of five youths sent by the village elders no more than half an hour to dispose of 200 kilos of grain.[9]

Further inland, in the county of Puning, some thirty markets covered the needs of more than a million people. They attracted local farmers, artisans and traders, each with their vendible goods on hand, back or cart. Pedlars offered colourful illustrations from traditional operas, books from the imperial and republican eras and collections of traditional poetry that had escaped the clutches of the Red Guards. There were itinerant doctors offering their services. Storytellers used wooden clappers to mark the most dramatic moments of their stories. Blind people sang traditional folk songs for alms. Touts stood outside local restaurants selling ration coupons. Many hundreds came by bicycle from other parts of the province each day. In some markets, organised gangs travelled up and down the coast, going all the way to Shanghai to trade in prohibited goods. A few went as far as Jiangxi to procure tractors, acting on demand from local villages keen to mechanise.[10]

Here, too, the local cadres were reluctant to interfere. Some even encouraged the villagers to abandon grain production, mandated by the state, and pursue more profitable crops instead. Government agents failed to stamp out illegal trading, as 'they are only concerned with collecting fees, and do not care about government policy', the authors of one detailed investigation deplored. Small pedlars could be suppressed, the report continued, but 'the cadres and the villagers will have no vegetables to eat'.[11]

The market exploited the difference between the fixed price set by the command economy for agricultural products and the higher amounts ordinary people were prepared to pay. A difference of 100 per cent was common, but some commodities, for instance soybeans, reached 500 per cent, meaning that the state procured at 0.44 yuan per kilo when the same amount could fetch 2.2 yuan on the market.[12]

The market in Puning, like elsewhere, thrived because the command economy could not deliver sufficient goods to meet the demands of ordinary people. Widespread shortages forced prices up, stimulating private enterprise. Timber was a case in point. By 1973, fir was ten times more expensive than it had been at the beginning of the Cultural Revolution in 1966. Across the county were thousands of unfinished houses that had been abandoned for lack of timber. Some people were willing to pay a premium on the black market. Across the mountains in the north of the province there was random felling of trees. The trade was not limited to a few farmers bringing planks to market on their bicycle carts. There were hundreds of factories in Lechang, Qingyuan and Huaiji trading illegally in timber, up to 70,000 cubic metres in 1973 according to one estimate.[13]

Guangdong had another asset that helped some people sidestep the planned economy. Not far away from the Pearl River Delta, in the midst of a continuous stretch of jade green spread out like a huge carpet, dotted here and there with banana groves, counties like Kaiping and Taishan were traditionally dominated by emigration overseas. Before liberation, whole villages had displayed ostentatious mansions built by returned migrants, including thousands of large, fortified towers influenced by foreign architecture, with features ranging from flushing toilets and marble tiles to Gothic battlements and turrets. Relations between these emigrant communities and the communist party were bad, and in 1952 many bore the brunt of a bloody campaign of land reform. Years later, at the height of the Cultural Revolution, when people lived and died by their class background, many were denounced as 'spies', 'traitors' and 'counter-revolutionaries', further disrupting links with overseas communities. But after 1970 goods and remittances once again started to pour across the border. By 1974 the amount of money reaching the villagers from overseas was twice as high as in 1965. Families with overseas connections had been the first to suffer from the onslaught of the Cultural Revolution, and now they were the first to emerge from uniform poverty. They used foreign remittances to tackle a housing crisis created by years of neglect if not wilful assault on anything bearing the hallmark of imperialism. In Taishan and elsewhere in the region, they bought up steel, timber and concrete. Chen Jijin shared a mud hovel with his family of eight. They were waiting for a remittance of 20,000 yuan to build a new house – a sum representing the annual salary of thirty qualified factory workers.[14]

The number of parcels from abroad went up. In Guangzhou, the provincial capital, more than 200,000 packages had accumulated in 1972, but the backlog was cleared by the end of the year. They contained mainly clothes and edible oil, reflecting local market shortages. Other commodities included beans, bulbs, matches and medicine. Some of them found their way on to the black market.[15]

A measure of decollectivisation could also be seen in other provinces. In Sichuan, the huge inland province that had suffered terribly during Mao's Great Famine before being wrecked by the two Tings who controlled the provincial revolutionary committee, the land was rented to the farmers in the early 1970s. The desire to own land was driven from below and only ratified by local authorities much later.[16]

But returning the land to the cultivators was but one aspect of a silent revolution in the countryside. Some wealthier villages not only planted profitable crops for the market, but also began establishing local factories. This was common in many parts of Guangdong. In Chao'an, just outside Shantou, where entire villages had been reduced to poverty after embroidery was declared 'feudal' at the height of the Cultural Revolution, historic links with the overseas community were revived after the Ministry of Light Industry lifted the trading restrictions in 1972.[17] Two years later up to half the women in some villages once again specialised in drawn work and embroidery. Their output was worth 1.3 million yuan on the foreign market. Others turned to manufacturing hardware and tools. But while some of these village enterprises were collectively owned, many merely used the appearance of a collective to run a business entirely along private lines. A good example was Dongli Village, where all but 40 of the 420 families were members of a nail factory. They worked from home and were paid by the piece. All the profits went straight to the individual workers, who were also responsible for finding the raw material. Some bought it from street pedlars, others obtained recycled iron from the black market, and a few went to Shantou to buy in bulk. A good worker made 5 to 10 yuan a day, the equivalent of what an ordinary farmer made by working in a commune for an entire month.[18]

The village enterprises contributed to the market in more than one way. They not only sold their wares through intermediaries, but also used their earnings to buy grain and fodder for their pigs, as well as imported goods that the planned economy could not provide, from fish oil to aspirin. They sent purchasing agents to compete with the state sector for scarce resources needed to run their businesses, buying up coal, steel and iron.[19]

These examples come from Guangdong, but rural enterprises were not limited to the south. In parts of Jiangsu, contracts were concluded between the production team and individual households as early as 1969, in blatant violation of the radical policies of the time. This process often began in regions where the land was unsuitable for agriculture. Along the coast, for instance, some villagers at first abandoned the sandy soil and switched to raising fish instead. Then they gradually turned their attention to industry. In Chuansha, where villagers were mandated by the state to grow cotton, the industrial portion of total production increased from 54 per cent in 1970 to 74 per cent five years later, a rate of growth far superior to the years of 'economic reform' after 1978. In contrast, in Songjiang county local leaders continued to obey the state's call for grain.[20]

The growth of cottage industries in the Yangtze Delta followed old manufacturing habits and trading routes that predated liberation. They were revived as soon as the hand of the state weakened. Much as Shantou had a long tradition in exporting embroideries to overseas markets, for many centuries the villages around Shanghai had specialised in household goods, ceramics, cloth, silk and other handicrafts. Mechanisation spread from the late nineteenth century onwards, as simple devices for reeling silk, for instance, were incorporated into the village mills, diversifying production even further. Sophisticated guilds, chambers of commerce and banks in Shanghai, often with overseas connections, co-ordinated a flourishing trade. The Shanghai Silk Reeling Industry Trade Association, to name but one, promoted the production and commerce of silk in Shanghai, Jiangsu, Anhui and Zhejiang, before it was disbanded by the communists in 1949.

The extent to which rural industry reconnected with its past in the early 1970s is shown by statistics: in Jiangsu province as a whole, industry represented a mere 13 per cent of total output in the countryside in 1970, but a phenomenal 40 per cent by 1976. These factories were often collective, if in name only. Tangqiao village, with help from the cadres, established a metalworking factory with twenty-five employees in 1970. A year later, it set up a power plant as well as a cardboard-box factory, several other metal shops and an animal-feed processing plant. A brick factory followed in 1972, all of it in blatant disregard of the state's demand that the country-side grow grain and Learn from Dazhai. The village leaders now attracted political attention and started opening new enterprises under the umbrella of a 'comprehensive factory'. The façade of planned unity was abandoned the moment the Chairman died in 1976.[21]

There were also underground factories, dispensing altogether with the pretence of collective ownership. These, too, were run by village leaders. They had appeared during the Great Leap Forward, although many folded during the catastrophe that followed. As the sociologist Fei Xiaotong wrote of these clandestine enterprises, 'peasants did not mind what the nature of ownership was. The only thing they did mind was to keep up their liveli-hood.' Some were run by individuals, who merely used the name, and often the accountant, of the collective. In other words, they attached themselves to production teams and relied for protection on state officials.

Officials in the higher echelons of power could do very little to combat the trend. In Shanghai, Zhang Chunqiao fulminated about the 'sprouts of capitalism in the countryside'. Others railed against the attack on the 'dictatorship of the proletariat'. There were periodic campaigns to 'cut the tail of capitalism', but they were met with widespread sabotage, as villagers slaughtered their animals and diverted collective resources for their own use. Private firms went underground, at least temporarily until the storm blew over. Most of all, outside some of the cities where the radical follow-ers of the Chairman were well entrenched, large parts of the countryside were no longer within their reach.[22]

When the garden economy created by private plots and rented land pro-duced a surplus, villagers sometimes got on their bicycles and went to the city, selling vegetables, fruit, chickens, ducks and fish. A few took their produce from door to door, others gathered outside department stores, by railway stations or near the factory gates, sitting on kerbs and spreading out their wares on the ground or on small card tables. They were regularly chased away by public security services, but they kept on coming back. Sometimes the local authorities turned a blind eye, as people met at an agreed time to trade goods at makeshift bazaars.[23]

But villagers went further in restoring the links that had tied the countryside to the cities. They migrated in large numbers, despite the restrictions imposed by the household registration system. During the Great Leap Forward, millions of villagers had resettled in the cities, working in underground factories or on construction projects. Many were sent home during the famine, but they kept on coming back, carrying out the dirty, dangerous or demeaning jobs that city dwellers were unwilling to do. By the early 1970s, many villages had a well-established tradition of migration, knowing how to evade agents of the state, where to seek employment in the city and how to look after family members left behind. Sometimes the cadres themselves encouraged a form of chain migration by agreeing to take care of children and the elderly, as remittances from workers in the city contributed to the survival of the entire village. The migrants continued to submit their quota of grain, either through relatives or by paying a fee directly to the village leader.

Many millions evaded government control in the wake of the Lin Biao affair, seeping through the holes of the household registration system to settle in the very heart of the city or along its periphery. Circles of relative wealth appeared around the cities, as pedlars and farmers moved to fringe areas where they cultivated vegetables or manufactured small goods sold to urban residents. Some gave up on agriculture to set up food stalls or open small restaurants near the local markets.

Many lived in a twilight zone, constantly evading government control and running the risk of being sent back to their home villages, but large numbers managed to acquire the right to stay in the city. Not all of them were peasants. There were rural cadres keen to acquire urban residency, workers who had been sent to the Third Front and erstwhile city dwellers banned to the countryside after 1968. They pulled strings, offered bribes and pleaded with the authorities. Many of them were recruited by state enterprises, allowing factory leaders to cut labour costs. Those who were formally allowed to stay brought over friends and relatives from the village.

The numbers were staggering, counteracting the efforts the state had made to curb the urban population in 1968–9. In Shaanxi, major cities across the province grew by a quarter of a million people in 1970, and again by a third of a million the following year, reaching a total of 3.6 million. Once natural population growth and changes to the planned economy had been taken into account, it appeared that many were villagers, soldiers and cadres who had managed to bypass the restrictions imposed by the household registration system.[24]

It was the same elsewhere. In Hubei, the urban population grew by a mere third of a million between 1965 and 1970, but by half a million in the following two years. In 1972 alone, more than 300,000 people managed to acquire urban residency. A fifth of these permits were deemed to have been obtained fraudulently. There were also tens of thousands of people without any right of abode, including women married to urban residents and their children. On top of this, in 1971 and 1972 half a million farmers settled in the periphery, on the very edge of urban areas, many of them moving in and out of the city during the day or working on shifts overnight.[25]

Even in Beijing the authorities found it difficult to control the movement of people. By 1973, there were clusters of unemployed people openly wandering about the streets. Some were seeking work, others had secretly returned from exile to the countryside, while whole groups of migrants were in transit, on their way to Heilongjiang. By one estimate some 200,000 to 300,000 people passed through the capital every day. The burden was such that a year later, the Public Security Bureau employed more than 10,000 agents around the clock to try and keep the capital free of undesirable elements.[26]

Not only were more and more people ready to ignore the restrictions imposed on their freedom of movement by the household registration system, but they were also happy to travel for free. In Harbin, the provincial capital of Heilongjiang, the local authorities estimated that 1.3 million people travelled without a ticket in 1973. A more precise example comes from Lanzhou, the capital of Gansu: during a random check carried out on 14 October 1973, two out of every three travellers were unable to produce a ticket on demand. About a third of a million people also scrambled on board freight trains in Lanzhou that same year. The express train from Shanghai to Urumqi, on the other hand, was 'frequently' blocked by whole groups of people who forced it to slow down and then boarded without a ticket. In parts of the country, travelling for free became a habit, as people argued that 'people's trains' were designed for 'the people'. In the station in Zhengzhou, a major railway hub in Henan, over a thousand travellers rushed to get on a train without a ticket each and every day.[27]

The same was true of city transportation, as people boarded buses but refused to buy a ticket. Sometimes the ticket collector and even the driver were beaten up by irate passengers or gangs of thugs. In October 1973 alone, several dozen of them were publicly attacked in Jinan, the capital of Shandong, some of them injured so badly that they were unable to return to work.[28]

There was little that a weakened state could do to curtail the movement of millions of people, but there was a safety valve. In May 1970 the regime formally allowed some migrants to settle in Heilongjiang. With mountains covered in virgin larch, purple linden and Manchurian birch, the region had abundant natural resources that had already attracted people fleeing starvation in the wake of the Great Leap Forward. But for the most part the province remained an uninhabited wilderness. The state hoped that more riches would be tapped through voluntary resettlement – besides massive labour camps. The majority of migrants came from Shandong and Hebei, and many did not wait for the new state policy. In Zhaoyuan county alone, more than 2,000 people pulled up stakes in the single month of July 1969 and left in search of a better life in Heilongjiang. Some villages were almost emptied, as up to a third of the locals voted with their feet, including the accountant and all the party leaders.[29]

Dan Ling, the young man who had listened to a Japanese radio report announcing the death of Lin Biao, tried his luck after being released in January 1973. With other migrants he headed for Heilongjiang, described as a land of plenty for all. He and his fellow travellers slept on benches at a railway station until their situation had been legalised by the local government. After roaming the region for a while, Dan ended up in a Korean settlement where his engineering skills came in handy. All of them were poor, eating nothing but millet, but they were content, at last free members of a community in which 'nobody felt inferior or humiliated for political reasons'. They did not share their tools.[30]

———

Throughout the country people started quietly reconnecting with the past, from local leaders who focused on economic growth to villagers who reconstituted popular markets that had existed long before liberation. Sometimes a farmer merely pushed the boundaries of the planned economy by bringing some corn to market or spending more time on a private plot. In other cases they were bolder, opening underground factories or speculating in commodities normally controlled by the state. But everywhere, in one way or another, people were emboldened by the failure of the Cultural Revolution to take matters into their own hands. As one shrewd observer has noted, 'people decided they did not want to go on living the way they were doing, and they were setting up ways to get themselves out of their predicament'. It was an uneven, patchy revolution from below, and one that remained largely silent, but eventually it would engulf the entire country.[31]

22

The Second Society

If a second economy was quietly finding solutions to the widespread misery created by central planning, a second society was appearing amid people disillusioned with the communist creed. As in Eastern Europe and the Soviet Union, a hidden, underground, largely invisible society lived in the shadow of the formal political system.

The phenomenon was not new. Much as a black market appeared the moment the communist party started to clamp down on basic economic freedoms in 1950, social activities condemned by the new regime continued to survive away from the public eye. When community festivals were stigmatised and cult leaders sent to re-education camps in the early years of liberation, popular religion went underground – quite literally. In north China underground chambers were built with tunnels long enough to connect strategic places throughout entire villages. In Hebei province, some sectarian leaders took refuge for over four years in shelters several metres below the surface. Christianity and Buddhism also had great staying power, as their followers quietly dropped all visible signs of allegiance but clung to their faith. A literary inquisition in the early 1950s consigned entire collections to the pulping press, while even seemingly innocuous titles were taken off the shelves, but for many years people continued to read forbidden books in secret, sometimes with little interference.[1]

The leadership was all too conscious of the extraordinary resilience of the old ideas and institutions it had tried to destroy wholesale after liberation. At the very heart of the Cultural Revolution lay the acknowledgement that despite seventeen years of communist rule, in the hearts and minds of many people the old society continued to exist. Underneath a surface of ideological uniformity lay a world of subcultures, countercultures and alternative cultures that posed a threat to the communist party. In official parlance, once the socialist transformation of the means of production had been completed, a new revolution was required to liquidate once and for all the last remnants of feudal and bourgeois thought, or else the forces of revisionism might very well prevail and undermine the entire communist enterprise.

But despite the house raids, the book burnings, the public humiliations and all the purges, not to mention the ceaseless campaigns of re-education, from study classes in Mao Zedong Thought to May Seventh Cadre Schools, old habits died hard. The Cultural Revolution aimed to transform every aspect of an individual's life, including his innermost thoughts and personal feelings, but in many cases it managed to exact only outward compliance. People fought deception with deception, lies with lies and empty rhetoric with empty slogans. Many were great actors, pretending to conform, knowing precisely what to say when required.

The second society was not so much a separate sphere as a realm of free-dom that continued to exist in some people. Thanks to endless campaigns of thought reform, many individuals learned how to parrot the party line in public but keep their thoughts to themselves. All of them worshipped at the altar of the Chairman, although some quietly maintained faith in their own values, whether political or religious. There must have been many ordinary people who were crushed by the relentless pressure to conform, just as there were true believers or pure opportunists who enthusiastically followed every twist and turn in official ideology. But some people devel-oped two minds or two souls, one for public view, the other strictly private, to be shared with trusted friends and family only. Some were able to move to and fro between these two realms, while others sank into apathy and depression, unable to reconcile the projected values of the world around them with their own beliefs.[2]

––––––––––

Throughout the Cultural Revolution, propaganda trumpeted the impor-tance of socialist education, both for young people who had never experienced the old world and for the older generation tainted by revi-sionist thoughts. But by the 1970s the educational system lay in ruins.

Higher institutes of learning had all but closed down, with some of the best minds in the country confined to May Seventh Cadre Schools. As soon as they finished middle school, students were sent to the country-side for re-education by the peasants. When Jan Wong arrived at Peking University in 1972, one of the two foreign students to be accepted that year, she found a campus that was virtually deserted. The student body amounted to a few hundred, compared to an enrolment that normally ran into the thousands. 'Many buildings were padlocked. Lecture halls were empty. Until we arrived, Building Twenty-Five, a gray brick struc-ture with a curved-tile roof, had been vacant for six years.'[3]

Many primary and middle schools had been invaded by Red Guards at the height of the Cultural Revolution, only to see their premises further encroached by a sprawling bureaucracy in the following years. In Jiangsu province, more than 700,000 square metres of school space had been lost by 1972, equivalent to tens of thousands of classrooms. Factories spilled over into primary schools, while government units converted lecture halls into office space.[4]

Statistics can be misleading, all the more so since most of the avail-able figures were produced by the government for public consumption, but the archives offer some revealing glimpses. In Hebei province close to 8 million students went to school in 1965. Five years later this figure had been slashed to 6 million, or roughly a quarter less. But the biggest drop occurred in institutes of higher education, as the numbers dwindled from 27,000 on the eve of the Cultural Revolution to fewer than 5,000 in 1970.[5]

The education dispensed in schools, not to mention universities, empha-sised ideology. In Shandong, around a third of all language lessons by 1975 were devoted to praising the achievements of the Cultural Revolution, and a further 17 per cent to the latest political campaign. In Jiangsu, half of the excerpts in textbooks adopted for language classes in 1972 were by Marx, Lenin and Mao, and a further one-third came from propaganda outlets like *Red Flag* and the *People's Daily*.[6]

Children may have been able effortlessly to recite passages from the Little Red Book, but otherwise the chaos of the Cultural Revolution did little to enhance their long-term academic development. In Nantong, near the river mouth of the Yangtze, some children could not say when the People's Republic had been established. In Jiangning, also in Jiangsu province, a few were unable to write their own names. This was the case with twenty of the fifty-four children in one class at the Dongtai Sancang Commune. Forty of them could not write arabic numbers.

Basic knowledge of geography was also patchy in middle schools, as some pupils could not even place Beijing on a map. In Funing county a few struggled to find their own country on a globe. In Nantong and Xuzhou many students had not learned how to add or subtract numbers. A test showed that not every middle-school student could tell how many minutes there were in an hour.

Some teachers were also barely literate. A detailed survey of schools in Jiangning county showed that roughly half of the staff could not write the names of many of the country's provincial capitals. In any event, as late as 1974 many of them still lived in fear of being denounced and persecuted, 'so they are very lenient and fail to correct students who make mistakes in writing or using the wrong characters'.[7]

These were not isolated examples. In Shandong, one-third of all young people and 60 per cent of adults were partly or wholly illiterate. In parts of the province, for instance the region of Linqin, half of all young people and two-thirds of all adults could not write their own name or read even a simple article from the *People's Daily*. These figures reflected a nationwide trend. As the State Council admitted, by 1978, as a result of the Cultural Revolution, the rate of illiteracy or semi-literacy reached 30 to 40 per cent among children and youths of all age groups across China. In parts of the country it was more than 50 per cent. Party members were no exception. In Hebei, regimented by 1.45 million cadres, one in three was illiterate. Few had graduated from high school.[8]

But even as general literacy was in decline, the opportunities to read forbidden literature paradoxically increased. Even at the height of the Cultural Revolution, as Red Guards went on a spree, trying to eradicate all signs of a feudal past, some of them quietly pocketed titles that attracted their attention. Many books were pulped or burned, but quite a few found their way on to a thriving black market. In Chengdu, as Jung Chang noted, all sorts of people could be found trading books, including

'Red Guards who wanted to make some cash from the books they had confiscated; frustrated entrepreneurs who smelled money; scholars who did not want their books to be burned but were afraid of keeping them; and book lovers'. Her brother went to the black market every day, trading his way up the ladder by selling books which he had obtained from a paper-recycling shop. He read voraciously, at the rate of one or two volumes a day, but never dared to keep more than a dozen or so at any one time, all of them carefully hidden.[9]

These underground readers were soon joined by others, as people became increasingly disillusioned with politics. After March 1967 some of the students started withdrawing from factional warfare, joining the ranks of those referred to as the 'free and unfettered'. To keep themselves occupied, they turned to reading a whole variety of books that were beyond their reach before the onset of the Cultural Revolution. Underground reading became even more common after the summer of 1968, as millions of young people exiled to the countryside circulated books among themselves to while away the long winter nights. Jung Chang, sent to a small village in Sichuan, had been given a whole stack of reading material by her brother. She was out in the fields every day, but itched to get back to them: 'In the placidity of the village, in the hushed depth of the nights in my damp home, I did a lot of reading and thinking.' Liang Heng, banned from Changsha, was lucky enough to be placed in a middle school, where he discovered a cache of books covered in dust and mildew in a storage room. His heart pounded, as a whole world of the imagination opened up to him: 'My life changed completely.'[10]

As the ideological climate relaxed in the wake of Lin Biao's death, the world of forbidden literature flourished yet further. While the contents of bookshops changed very little, with row after row of works by Mao, Marx, Engels, Lenin and Stalin, the range of books that circulated under the counter expanded enormously. Besides the banned books that had been rescued from private collections and public libraries, the state printed around a thousand translations of modern and contemporary writers for limited circulation, intended for the eyes of party members only. These books, too, found their way to the general public. The daughter of a leading official remembers that her father would lock the restricted books in a drawer, but failed to hide the key very well. She devoured Soviet novels, and was particularly struck by Ivan Shamiakin's *Snowy Winters*, dealing with the wrongful persecution of cadres in the Soviet Union. Jung Chang, on the other hand, relished Nixon's *Six Crises*, even if the translation came expurgated, while the descriptions of the Kennedy administration in David Halberstam's *The Best and the Brightest* made her marvel at the relaxed atmosphere of politics in the United States.[11]

One of the translations that had the biggest impact was William Shirer's *The Rise and Fall of the Third Reich*, as it offered striking parallels with the Cultural Revolution. Harry Truman's *Memoirs*, Milovan Djilas's *The New Class: An Analysis of the Communist System* and Solzhenitsyn's *One Day in the Life of Ivan Denisovich* were also welcome, helping readers to develop critical views of the communist revolution. The work of Trotsky, in a country where people were being shot for being Trotskyists, was also influential, not least his *The Revolution Betrayed: What is the Soviet Union and Where is It Going?* as well as *Stalin: An Appraisal of the Man and his Influence*. There were also notable literary works, including Albert Camus' *The Stranger*, Jack Kerouac's *On the Road*, Samuel Beckett's *Waiting for Godot* and J. D. Salinger's *The Catcher in the Rye*.[12]

Banned books were sometimes copied by hand. There were even reading groups exchanging forbidden material and gathering to discuss common interests. One network of readers based in Beijing, with correspondents in other parts of the country, boldly called themselves the Fourth International Counter-Revolutionary Clique. Despite government suppression, these clubs continued to gain members, as a growing number of readers groped towards a critical perspective on the Cultural Revolution.[13]

Not all the literature that circulated was equally high-minded. On the black market, novels with erotic passages commanded the highest prices, proportionate to the degree of political danger. In this puritanical society, even Stendhal's nineteenth-century classic *Le Rouge et le noir* was considered erotic, and a copy could command the equivalent of two weeks' wages for an ordinary worker. Erotic novels were copied by hand and sometimes even crudely mimeographed with simple stencils or hand-cranked devices. At the height of the Cultural Revolution, many units had begun publishing their own bulletins or newspapers. Some of that equipment had escaped from the hands of the Mao Zedong Thought propaganda teams and was now being put to good use, as erotic novels and lewd songs circulated in factories, schools and even government offices.[14]

One of the most widely read novels was *The Heart of a Maiden*, a story about a college girl and her sexual encounters with her cousin and other young men. The text was short and explicit, which may have accounted for its popularity. No one will ever know just how many copies circulated, but it may well have been one of the most studied texts after the Chairman's Little Red Book.[15]

———

Throughout the Cultural Revolution, people also continued listening secretly to foreign radio broadcasts, despite the risk of being denounced by a neighbour and sentenced for a counter-revolutionary crime. The extent of the practice was revealed during the 'One Strike and Three Antis' campaign in 1970, when millions of ordinary people were persecuted for the merest hint of discontent with the party, whether real or imagined. In one factory in Gansu, deep inside the hinterland, one in every fifty workers listened to radio programmes broadcast from the Soviet Union, the United States, Taiwan, Hong Kong, Japan or India. There was also a Sichuan Underground Station and a Voice of the Liberation Army.[16]

Much as ordinary people had learned how to use printing equipment at the height of the Cultural Revolution, quite a few students had taken classes in radio broadcasting. Gao Yuan, the head of his school's radio club in Zhengding, was able to build everything from the simplest single-diode receiver to seven-transistor radios. The best devices picked up signals from Moscow.[17]

Radio clubs soon became suspect, but there was a thriving black market in radio transistors and semi-conductors. On Fuzhou Street in Shanghai, young people keen to pursue their hobby could meet factory workers who stole the required parts. The authorities repeatedly tried to stamp out the trade, but to no avail.[18]

Their attempt to jam the Voice of America and radio signals from Taiwan was also futile. In the airwave war, no technology existed to prevent strong and stable signals from reaching most listeners. In an odd twist, by reducing the cost of a radio the regime actually made listening to short-wave programmes from abroad easier. In the countryside, just before the onset of the Cultural Revolution, a set could cost the equivalent of a whole pig, a luxury few families could afford. The range varied from 300 to 500 kilometres, meaning that cities like Yining were out of range of the provincial capital Urumchi and did not enjoy daytime reception. In order to spread Mao Zedong Thought, the price was cut by more than a third in following years, and by 1970 four-transistor radios were sold below cost of production in many parts of the country.[19]

Several years later, wired networks reached a majority of the population in entire provinces, supported by broadcasting stations in county towns and amplifying stations in people's communes. Even poor villagers were never far removed from the propaganda. In Hubei, in 1974, there were over 4.8 million loudspeakers, compared to a mere 180,000 prior to the Cultural Revolution. It was equivalent to almost one per household.[20]

Still, the din of the propaganda machine could not drown out a diversity of waves, local and foreign. Even in poor regions like Hainan, the subtropical island off the coast of Guangdong, people occasionally listened to the Voice of the Liberation Army, which was vehemently hostile to Mao Zedong. There was also a Voice of Communist Youth, which broadcast seditious slogans at irregular intervals throughout the day. The station was believed to be run by graduate students of Zhongshan University in Guangzhou. In Guangzhou itself, taxi drivers were openly tuning their radios to Hong Kong programmes. They were not alone. By now, even dedicated party officials were lured by foreign radio, if only because they were keen to discover what was happening in their own country. The same young woman who found Ivan Shamiakin's *Snowy Winters* in a drawer at home one day walked into her parents' room without knocking on the door, only to hear a bright voice calling out: 'This is Radio Moscow!'[21]

Other social activities condemned by the state flourished. There were underground singing clubs, as people gathered under the pretext of singing revolutionary songs, only to enact forbidden plays and sing banned tunes. In the Shanghai Number Two Machine Tool Plant, a group of a hundred young workers played forbidden music every Friday in the winter of 1969–70, attracting a lively audience from other factories.[22]

The old world made a comeback, as people reconnected with pastimes decried as feudal or bourgeois by the Red Guards years earlier. The only widespread children's game by the time of Lin Biao's death was skipping, but soon enough whips and tops, hopscotch and diabolo could be seen in the streets of Beijing. The sale of traditional, painted silk kites was still restricted to foreigners, but some children knew how to fly ingenious contrivances made of strips of wood and bits of the *People's Daily*. Poker appeared in the narrow, winding alleys of the capital. Pigeons could be seen racing across the sky with small bamboo pipes attached to their tail feathers, producing an eerie, harmonious whistle. People started keeping birds in cages again, sometimes heading for the parks in the early morning to air their pets.[23]

Ordinary people became underground artists, seeking refuge from politics in art by painting in a manner deliberately detached from the 'socialist realism' that shaped everything at the time, from the propaganda posters festooned on walls to the 'people's art' officially sponsored by the party. Many were deliberately apolitical, trying to carve out a personal space in which they could reconnect with their inner selves. Their art was clandestine, but like the underground literary salons and singing clubs, informal groups of amateur artists shared their interests, using abandoned factories, deserted parks or private flats in buildings with adequate dark hallways and isolated staircases. Art books and exhibition catalogues were circulated, as people reconnected with everything Western from Michelangelo to Picasso, but also with Chinese traditional paintings.

In Beijing some of these budding artists, all from very diverse backgrounds, came together in a group which received a name only much later: Wuming, or Nameless. 'In an era when free association was a crime, the group had to be nameless, shapeless and spontaneous. There were no regulations, no membership, no unified artistic principles or style.' Many of them came from families defined as 'class enemies' and had endured broken homes, ravaged schools and crumbling communities throughout the Cultural Revolution. They took to the brush, at first honing their skills by following the propaganda campaign and painting portraits of the Chairman. It was a good source of precious oil paint and linen canvas, which they used to begin experimenting in their spare time. Nature was a favourite theme, from peach blossoms and lilacs observed in the Botanical Garden to the sunsets seen from the Ming tombs in the suburbs of Beijing. On one occasion, several members forged a letter of introduction to get past public security and made a trip to the seaside at Beidaihe on National Day. But they also painted from memory, carving a personal realm deep inside themselves. Wang Aihe, herself an accomplished painter and member of Wuming, remembers a fellow factory worker who stared for hours through the window, pondering how to paint a tree he could see in the distance.[24]

Religion also went underground, allowing people to remain secretly connected to their faiths, both organised creeds including Christianity, Buddhism, Taoism and Islam, and folk religions with their local gods and deities.

Throughout the Cultural Revolution, there were even occasional spurts of popular protest. In Hebei, to take but one example, in 1969 Christians openly shouted, 'I don't believe in Mao Zedong, I believe in God!' Elsewhere in the province, slogans appeared on May Day, proclaiming 'Celebrate God the Creator'. But these were isolated incidents, quickly suppressed by the omnipotent military. In most cases, especially in the countryside, ordinary villagers carried on exercising their faiths in a quiet, indirect, non-confrontational way.[25]

In many cases, religious leaders were impotent, but ordinary villagers continued with their beliefs. Ironically, denominations that had borne the brunt of persecution in the 1950s were better prepared for the onslaught of the Cultural Revolution. This was the case for Watchman Nee and the Little Flock, which had been one of the fastest-growing native Protestant movements in China up to 1949, when it boasted as many as 70,000 followers. Within the first five years of liberation, most leaders of the Little Flock were arrested and the congregations systematically crushed. Watchman Nee died in prison in 1972. But ordinary followers viewed the persecution as a test of their faith, organising cell groups and home meetings many years before the Cultural Revolution even began. A pragmatic tradition of clandestine worshipping allowed them to survive.[26]

Other organised religions resorted to similar strategies, adopting a decentralised approach with clusters of worshippers dispersed throughout the countryside. Lamas, imams and priests may well have been in re-education camps, but ordinary followers stepped in to hold their communities together. They also recruited new members among the ever growing number of victims of the Cultural Revolution, offering an explanation for their suffering, a sense of hope and sometimes a promise of salvation or inner peace. Most of all, with government offices in charge of religious affairs in turmoil, besieged by rebels or imploding under the weight of factional infighting, denominations of every hue resurfaced and reorganised themselves, laying a firm foundation for religious revival after the death of Mao Zedong.

Local gods were also stubborn, subverting attempts by the state to replace them with the cult of Mao. In some villages, local festivals and public rituals were discontinued, while temples were closed down, but many villagers continued to worship at a small shrine or altar inside their home. They burned incense, offered vows, invoked the spirits or otherwise communicated with a whole variety of local gods away from the public eye, from ancestral spirits, patron deities and rain gods to fertility goddesses. The ultimate act of subversion was probably to turn the Chairman himself into a local deity. But larger statues also survived, even as temples were often demolished or turned into granaries. In some cases they were moved from one place to another, until by 1972 local communities felt it safe enough to give them a more permanent home. Sometimes a temple was built with collective funds under the pretence of establishing a school, a trend that could be observed throughout Pingliang county in Gansu, and no doubt in other parts of the country.[27]

Folk culture, often intertwined with local religion, also remained resilient, even at the height of the Cultural Revolution. Jiang Qing had made one of her first public appearances at the Peking Opera festival in the summer of 1964, determined to reform traditional opera, one of the most popular art forms in the countryside. Soon enough she banned all opera with the exception of eight revolutionary dramas which glorified the People's Liberation Army and Mao Zedong Thought. The Eight Model Operas appeared on posters, postcards, stamps, plates, teapots, vases and calendars.

They were played by special performing troupes in schools and factories. Zhai Zhenhua, who was sent to Yan'an to till the fields, was lucky enough to be selected by a travelling troupe. They presented their show to factory workers and commune peasants on crude stages in open fields. 'The audience was usually large but applause was sparse. The opera was never really welcomed anywhere except, believe it or not, at Yan'an University.'[28]

But despite all the state propaganda, some communities still went ahead and stuck to their own traditions. In 1968, several villages joined forces in Zhejiang and organised huge gatherings around a performance of traditional opera, with cigarettes and wine laid out on hundreds of tables for honorary guests and local families alike. In Jiangxi, a much poorer province than Zhejiang, there were also occasions on which thousands of people gathered openly to enjoy a traditional play. In parts of the countryside, commune members routinely celebrated traditional festivities and prayed to the local gods and spirits. Some villages had a common fund to allow dragon-boat competitions, which were attended by large crowds, as pigs were slaughtered and food was piled on the tables in a conspicuous display of consumption. By the early 1970s, besides opera performers, a whole range of traditional specialists, including folk musicians, geomancers, spirit mediums and fortune tellers, were making a living in the countryside.[29]

Underground churches are sometimes called house churches, as small groups of believers gathered secretly in private homes to share their faith. While religion could no longer openly function as a social bond holding entire communities together, it survived as a more personal, private experience, retreating from the church, the temple or the mosque into the realm of the home. Paradoxically, as the Cultural Revolution attacked the very notion of privacy as a bourgeois concept, people from all walks of life tried to turn their homes into fragile islands of freedom. This was not easy, especially in the cities where apartments and houses were often shared by several families, while prying eyes and gossiping neighbours were a nuisance everywhere. Still, literary salons, reading clubs and underground artists, like religious believers, sometimes managed to gather clandestinely in a private home, even if they had to change venues regularly to avoid detection.

But it was families rather than religious groups or underground clubs that stubbornly perpetuated their beliefs in the relative privacy of their home. The educational system may have been in disarray, but home schooling allowed some parents to instil the values they cherished into their offspring. Across the country, many millions of children were not allowed to go beyond elementary education because of their bad class background. Not only were they spared much of the state propaganda, but family members sometimes educated them at home. Mothers in particular played an important role, drawing on a rich culture of family education, since their status in the traditional household had often depended on the academic success of their offspring. Liu Wenzhong, who belonged to a family ostracised as 'counter-revolutionaries' in Shanghai, was schooled at home and taught to value human rights and democracy.[30]

Well before liberation, a whole range of traditional skills had also been developed and transmitted through family ties. Sometimes several households or even entire villages specialised in producing paper umbrellas, cloth shoes, silk hats, rattan chairs, wicker creels or twig baskets for the market. Throughout the Cultural Revolution some families continued to maintain their skills, from crafting protective charms and printing popular almanacs to making paper lanterns. Many other skills were family based, for instance martial arts, traditional theatre or opera singing.

The family, of course, endured sustained attack during the Cultural Revolution. Some households were divided right through the middle, as members pledged allegiance to different factions or were caught up in the shifting currents of local politics. Senseless and unpredictable purges were designed to cow the population and rip apart entire communities, producing docile, atomised individuals loyal to no one but the Chairman. Family members were expected to denounce each other at public struggle meetings, and spouses were often enjoined to seek a divorce when their partners were shipped away to the gulag. Most of all, particularly in the cities, many households were ruthlessly broken up, as their members were sent to different parts of the countryside. Children were wrenched away as soon as they graduated from middle school, their parents sometimes split up and confined to different re-education camps. Ordinary workers ended up in improvised factories on the Third Front, while government employees were re-educated by the peasants in Mao Zedong Study Classes or May Seventh Cadre Schools. In Sichuan, Jung Chang's parents were separated and held in two labour camps, controlled directly by the Tings, while her four siblings were tilling the fields in remote villages far away from Chengdu.

But China has one of the world's most complex kinship systems, fine-tuned over many centuries by a sophisticated lexicon with separate designations for almost every family member according to their gender, relative age, lineage and generation. Filial piety was a linchpin of Confucian ethics, while extended families in the form of clans and lineages formed the backbone of a millennial empire that collapsed only in 1911. As a result, families proved to be remarkably resilient. In some cases they actually became closer. Jung Chang and her siblings learned how to look after each other, and became more united by frequently visiting their parents in camp.[31]

The strength of the family bond was clearly demonstrated by the paucity of children who actually denounced their parents. Propaganda was replete with examples of young pioneers who chose loyalty to the state above duty to a parent. In the Soviet Union the case of Pavlik Morozov, a teenage boy killed by relatives in 1932 for having informed on his own father, became a cause célèbre. Though mythical, the story was endlessly exploited by the state. In the cult of Pavlik Morozov, children were encouraged to replace the family bond with one fealty alone, namely to Stalin.[32]

Propaganda in China was equally vociferous. Already during the Socialist Education Campaign, the slogan 'Father is Close, Mother is Close, but Neither is as Close as Chairman Mao' was inculcated into every child. As one student noted, 'We were drilled to think that anyone, including our parents, who was not totally for Mao was the enemy.' Parents themselves encouraged their children to conform to official ideology, recognising that this was the best option to safeguard their future.[33]

Yet in the Soviet Union fanatical denunciations of parents were actually rather unusual. Even fewer cases can be documented for the Cultural Revolution. Those rare children who actually informed on their own relatives were often ostracised. Ma Dingan, who reported his father for dealing in ration coupons on the black market, was expelled from his home, repudiated by the villagers and confined to an abandoned temple, and even local party officials refused to have anything to do with him.[34]

An even more striking case is that of Zhang Hongbing, who as a boy aged fifteen shopped his own mother, demanding that she be shot for her counter-revolutionary crimes. The party granted his wish. The woman, whose only crime was to have thrown portraits of the Chairman into the fire, was executed by firing squad. The son became the object of a cult, briefly celebrated for his revolutionary fervour by the local party commit-tee, before being persecuted himself as the son of a counter-revolutionary element. For decades Zhang was tormented by a guilty conscience, finally coming forward in 2013 to make a public confession in the hope of assuag-ing his pain. By going public he discovered that he was the only case of a son who had actually demanded the death penalty for a close relative. In China as in the Soviet Union, more often than not the norm for young people was to renounce family members rather than denounce them.[35]

Even outside the family, an old code of loyalty occasionally survived, as people stood by their friends or colleagues. Jung Chang was allowed to visit her father on a regular basis thanks to a squad leader in his late twenties who did his best unobtrusively to improve the lot of the people he knew. One translator working in Beijing remembers how she was shunned by her colleagues at work after she became a victim of the campaign to cleanse the ranks in 1969. But their family members, all living in the same compound, carried on as if nothing had happened, helping her with discreet gifts of rationed items. As memoirs and interviews amply testify, there were also random acts of kindness among complete strangers.[36]

In its effort to atomise society, the regime took sword and fire to tradi-tional social bonds, but it failed to destroy the family. Not only did family ties endure, but new bonds were forged. The regime frowned on romantic relationships, and married couples rarely displayed their affection in public during the Cultural Revolution. Love was considered a decadent, bourgeois emotion, and sex was taboo. Many students grew up in sheer ignorance of the most basic physiological facts. Zhuo Fei, for one, was terrified that she might become pregnant after sharing a bicycle with a young man, but she was too afraid to ask anybody, even her own relatives. Rae Yang, the Red Guard from Beijing who had relished the opportunity to go to Manchuria, put it in a nutshell: 'We did not have sex or even think about it. Sex was bourgeois. No doubt about it! In my mind, it was something very dirty and ugly. It was also extremely dangerous. In the books I read and the movies I saw, only the bad guys were interested in sex. Revolutionaries had nothing to do with it. When revolutionaries fell in love, they loved with their hearts. They didn't even touch hands.'[37]

But like so many other students banned to the countryside, Rae learned quickly by watching the farm animals. She was put in charge of breeding boars, having to guide their quivering genitals into a sow's vagina. 'It was like watching pornographic movies day in and day out.' Others found out by reading *The Heart of a Maiden*. Once Lin Biao had vanished, young people began to meet socially and quietly pair up, seeking privacy away from collective dormitories and crowded dining halls. In Manchuria, with temperatures plunging to 30 degrees below zero, young couples on state farms had little choice but to take to the great outdoors. Despite the cold they persisted, rushing back to the dormitories to embrace the heaters after less than twenty minutes.[38]

On the other hand, for students who did not work on agricultural collectives controlled by the army, living among the villagers instead, the opportunities for sexual encounters were much greater. In some cases young people even lived together, a practice unimaginable in the cities. A few had children out of wedlock, refusing to marry for fear of being stuck in the countryside for ever.

But most of all, except for students from the cities, the vast majority of people in the countryside were far less coy about sex. When they first arrived among their peasant hosts, quite a few young students were taken aback by their open displays of affection. One day Wang Yuanyuan, a sixteen-year-old girl sent to Inner Mongolia, saw a couple making love by the side of a ditch and reported the affair to the brigade leader. 'The old peasants, though, didn't treat it as anything and just laughed.' As in so many other aspects of folk culture, the Cultural Revolution ran no more than skin deep.[39]

23

Reversals

The thaw was followed by a freeze. Already in December 1972, the Chairman began worrying that the attack on Lin Biao was undermining the whole Cultural Revolution. At the Tenth Congress, held in Beijing in August 1973, the party constitution was revised to strike out Lin Biao and the principal members of his 'anti-party clique'. The Chairman instead elevated Wang Hongwen, the head of security from the Number Seventeen Cotton Textile Mill who had led the Cultural Revolution in Shanghai. In a great show of political theatre, Wang put the Chairman's vote for the new Central Committee in the ballot box, indicating that he had been personally picked to be Mao's successor. In a delicate balance of power, the old guard, including Deng Xiaoping, Li Jingquan, Ulanfu and Tan Zhenlin, were brought back. But they ranked low in the party hierarchy, overshadowed by members of the old Cultural Revolution Group, including Zhang Chunqiao, Yao Wenyuan and Kang Sheng, all placed in strategic positions designed to contain Zhou Enlai.

The premier himself was increasingly isolated. Mao was wary of his efforts to rehabilitate veteran cadres and restore order to the economy, fearing that the moment he died Zhou would reverse the Cultural Revolution, threatening his political legacy. Zhou had always been loyal, but this was due to pure political calculation, not ideological conviction. As one biographer has put it, 'Always the humble gentleman, practicing tolerance and personal endurance, always considerate and balanced, but profoundly smooth and sophisticated, Zhou, in Mao's view, was really a phony.'[1]

In January 1974, Mao set Jiang Qing and her allies upon the premier, accusing him indirectly of being a modern-day Confucius. The campaign to criticise Lin Biao became a campaign to criticise both Lin Biao and

Confucius. *Red Flag*, the *People's Daily* and the *Liberation Army Daily* published a joint editorial, stating that 'the struggle between the proletariat and the bourgeoisie in political ideology is a long, complicated and sometimes acute struggle . . . The reactionaries both in and out of China and the leaders of various opportunist lines in China's history all worship Confucius.' The propaganda machine never mentioned Zhou Enlai by name, but spewed venom against the ancient sage, denounced for representing an old, aristocratic order and devoting his time to 'reviving the doomed dynasty and recalling those retired from the world'.[2]

Slogans appeared condemning the premier's efforts to open the country. A lightning rod for the campaign against foreign culture was the Italian director Michelangelo Antonioni, who had toured China at the invitation of Zhou Enlai and made a documentary about his trip. In January 1974 Antonioni was denounced as 'anti-Chinese' and 'anti-communist', even though no one in China had heard of him or seen the film. Blind worship of foreign machinery, another dig at the premier, was castigated, in particular in Shanghai. Jiang Qing herself mocked those who 'sniff foreigners' farts and call them sweet'.[3]

Wang Hongwen, closely associated with Jiang Qing and now the latest political star, called the campaign a 'second Cultural Revolution' and even revived the slogan 'To Rebel is Justified'. There were the usual mass meetings, wall posters and newspaper editorials aimed at the forces of revisionism. In Beijing, some schoolchildren once again smashed classroom windows, tables and chairs. In the provinces, some former rebels saw another opportunity to challenge those in authority and 'seize power', reviving the heady days of the Cultural Revolution. In Hangzhou, a mass rally organised by erstwhile rebel leaders attracted thousands of their followers in schools and factories alike. Encouraged by Wang Hongwen, they proclaimed their 'right to rebel against reactionaries' and launched an all-out attack against local officials, crippling the economy and paralysing the party structure. Several charismatic leaders managed to overthrow their enemies in power, becoming de facto leaders of the province. They toured the local army camps, undermining the military leaders they viewed as the main stumbling block in their ascent to power.

In Wuhan, former rebel forces also used widespread popular support to confront the local leadership and gain access to the corridors of power. In Nanjing, on the other hand, it was not so much former rebels as victims of the repression against May Sixteenth Elements who used the campaign to take on military leaders. Tens of thousands of people who had been forcibly relocated to the countryside flocked back to the city, blocking the railway traffic and demonstrating for weeks on end in their demands for redress.[4]

The campaign succeeded in pushing Zhou Enlai to the side and neutralising his growing influence over the party. But Jiang Qing overreached, trying to extend her grip on the party and the army. In July 1974 Mao intervened and blamed his wife for allowing the whole affair to veer out of control.

In order to balance the two factions inside the party further, Mao restored Deng Xiaoping to his office of vice-premier. In a sleight of hand, it was Deng rather than Zhou, the architect of the country's foreign relations and the main diplomat behind the rapprochement with the United States, who was sent to head the Chinese delegation at the United Nations in April 1974. Half a year earlier, on the occasion of another visit by Kissinger, the premier's handling of the United States had come under fire, and Deng Xiaoping had been one those joining Jiang Qing and Yao Wenyuan in criticising the premier. His performance had been sufficiently vicious to lead many cadres in the Ministry of Foreign Affairs to believe that Deng Xiaoping had been brought back by the Chairman specifically to check Zhou Enlai.[5]

Zhou Enlai himself had been diagnosed with bladder cancer in 1972, but his medical team had not told him of his condition and the Chairman denied him adequate treatment. In May 1974 his cancer spread to other parts of his body, but still major surgery was ruled out. He continued to work despite constant loss of blood, remedied by daily transfusions. His first proper operation came in June, but it was too late, and signs of metastasis into other major organs were discovered a few months later. His last public appearance was on 30 September 1974, at a state banquet on the eve of National Day. Frail and thin, he appeared in front of 4,500 people, including more than 2,000 foreign guests. Those present also included several dozen party officials making their first appearance since the Cultural Revolution.[6]

This event seemed a sign that genuine political change was once again in the air. The campaign against Confucius had managed to paralyse several provincial capitals, but by and large it was viewed with apprehension. Few people wanted another Cultural Revolution. In the eyes of many, Zhou Enlai represented a counterbalance to Jiang Qing and her leftist allies. But by now it had become public knowledge that the man who was popularly viewed as the chief obstacle against a return to another Cultural Revolution had been hospitalised. 'People everywhere looked to express the anxiety they felt, while offering Zhou their personal respect and blessings.' That day, the real hero was not the Chairman but the premier, as guests stood up and applauded him when he made his appearance at the state banquet, chanting in unison, 'Premier Zhou! Premier Zhou!'[7]

Mao did not attend the reception under pretext of ill-health, observing Zhou from a distance. The outburst of popular adulation forced him to tone down the attacks on the premier. He reorganised the central leadership instead, making Deng Xiaoping a vice-premier as a counterweight to Zhou Enlai. But Jiang Qing felt that she had not been given her proper reward. She had started to compare herself to the only empress ever to have ruled in Chinese history, namely Wu Zetian. Articles praising the sixth-century empress as a great unifier of the nation appeared in the press, even though she was popularly reviled as a ruthless, wicked ruler who had mercilessly crushed her opponents. Madame Mao had several imperial gowns tailored after those of the empress, although she never wore them in public. She held court, receiving a stream of foreign visitors and signing her photographs in imperial red.

She was also paranoid about a palace coup. Fearing an attack from the sky, she had guns on swivel bases mounted on the roof of the Spring Lotus Chamber, her main residence in the Diaoyutai compound. She relied heavily on a whole range of medications, but became convinced that her medical team was trying to kill her.[8]

Madame Mao resented Deng Xiaoping and tried to sabotage the new power structure. Mao had constantly to intervene as an arbiter, eventually warning his wife not to form a gang with her supporters from Shanghai, namely Wang Hongwen, Zhang Chunqiao and Yao Wenyuan. They would later be called the 'Gang of Four'.

In January 1975, Zhou left the hospital to give one of his final speeches at the National People's Congress. He called on the country to modernise entire fields that were lagging behind the rest of the world, in particular agriculture, industry, national defence and science and technology. With the approval of the Chairman, he called the programme the 'Four Modernisations'.

Deng Xiaoping increasingly took charge, in practice running daily affairs. His work style was the opposite of Zhou Enlai. His experience of the Cultural Revolution seemed to have left him unfazed, despite the rough treatment meted out to him and his family, including a son crippled by Red Guards. He charged ahead, unafraid of alienating his opponents on the way. He was sweeping in his approach, and did not hesitate to stand up to Madame Mao.

Deng wasted no time in getting the transportation system back on track, threatening harsh punishment for railway officials who failed to get the trains moving on schedule. Thousands of people suspected of looting or blocking freight trains were sent to prison in early 1975, while eighty-five offenders were executed. He then turned to industry, warning leading officials in the iron and steel industry that they were 'weak, lazy and lax'. He demanded that they tackle labour disruptions and political infighting and focus on meeting the latest steel quota, imposing strict deadlines and sending high-powered work teams to impose compliance. He pruned the management of the giant Anshan Iron and Steel Corporation in Liaoning province, resulting in a streamlined command structure similar to that in existence before the Cultural Revolution.

Deng also intervened in provinces still reeling from the effects of the second Cultural Revolution. It was he who put heavy pressure on the rebels in Hangzhou, who were still paralysing much of Zhejiang province. In the first quarter of 1975 alone, industrial output had dropped by 20 per cent, with the revenue collected by the province almost halved due to factional fighting. Deng dispatched a team that raided the headquarters of the rebel faction and arrested several of its leaders. A massive campaign to

denounce 'factionalism' took place in the province over the summer. The
fate of the main rebel in Hangzhou was sealed by the Chairman himself,
who described him as an 'evil person'.[9]

Deng also ordered the military to attack Shadian, a Muslim-dominated
county in Yunnan, where ethnic unrest had broken out after the villagers had refused to pay any further grain tax until the freedom of religion
granted in the constitution had been honoured. A large armed force moved
in, razing entire villages to the ground. More than 1,600 people were killed,
including hundreds of children and elderly attempting to flee.[10]

But even as Deng appeared to have the support of the Chairman, quell-
ing popular unrest, arresting major rebels and removing procrastinating
cadres, Jiang Qing launched a new campaign, this time against 'empiricism'. It was a barely veiled attack on Deng Xiaoping, targeting his focus
on economic growth at the expense of communist ideology. Once again
strutting the stage at the Great Hall of the People in front of assembled
workers, Madame Mao identified 'empiricism' as the great enemy, the
accomplice of revisionism that must be struck down. The Gang of Four
controlled the press and most major publications, organising party hacks
to contribute a steady flow of denunciatory articles. Deng had to plead
with the Chairman, who intervened to declare that opposing revisionism
meant opposing both empiricism and dogmatism – the last term being a
coded reference to Madame Mao and her three acolytes from Shanghai,
whom the Chairman was now calling the 'Gang of Four'. Mao was playing
off one faction against the other in the hope that none would be strong
enough to challenge him.[11]

But Mao did have a change of heart. One victim of Deng Xiaoping's
bruising approach was the Chairman's nephew Mao Yuanxin, a young
man who had made a name for himself as party secretary of the provincial
revolutionary committee in Liaoning. He was scathing of Deng Xiaoping's
interference with the Anshan Iron and Steel Corporation, and poured poison in his uncle's ear after becoming one of his private liaison officers in
September 1975. A new wind, he told the Chairman, was blowing, and it
went against the Cultural Revolution. 'I have been paying great attention
to the speeches Comrade Xiaoping makes, and I see a problem in that he
rarely brings up the achievements of the Great Cultural Revolution or

criticises Liu Shaoqi's revisionist line.' The vice-premier, he alleged, was actually doing even more damage than the premier. A whole new bourgeois class was emerging inside the party, he intimated, and Deng Xiaoping had become their spokesman.[12]

Mao was rattled, but decided that Deng could still be saved. The Chairman, by now, suffered from undiagnosed Lou Gehrig's disease, which left his mental faculties intact but caused a gradual deterioration of the nerve cells controlling his muscles, including his throat, pharynx, tongue, diaphragm and rib muscles. He could barely stand unaided, and needed oxygen to breathe. He was fed a liquid diet of chicken broth through a nasal tube. He communicated through the only person who could understand his slurring speech, namely Zhang Yufeng, the train attendant he had seduced more than twenty years earlier.

Sensing that his end was near, Mao wished to cement his legacy, especially where the Cultural Revolution was concerned. His own verdict was that it had been 70 per cent successful and 30 per cent a failure, but he sought a formal resolution to preclude a sweeping reversal after his death. Mao decided to test Deng Xiaoping's loyalty by asking him to chair a gathering of the party elders to consider what the verdict on the Cultural Revolution should be. But at the meeting on 20 November, Deng refused to be drawn, even turning down a request to supervise the drafting of the resolution. It was a direct affront to the Chairman.

On the very same day, hundreds of big-character posters went up at Tsinghua University in a concerted effort to denounce those who dared to 'negate the Cultural Revolution' and 'attack the proletarian revolution in education'. They were the culmination of a year-long campaign to undermine Deng Xiaoping. In Shanghai, tightly controlled by the Gang of Four, newspaper headlines and voices from loudspeakers had been screaming daily, 'Hit back at the rightist wind of reversing the verdict of the Cultural Revolution!' People who incurred the displeasure of the radicals were accused of attempting to 'negate the Cultural Revolution', which became the slogan of the day. Once again, people 'bowed their heads and walked on tiptoe, fearful of treading on dangerous ground or appearing less than totally submissive'. As the tension was cranked up, endless Politburo meetings were organised in Beijing to take Deng Xiaoping to task. He said very little. He offered a limited self-criticism in December, and again in January 1976, but the Chairman deemed it insufficient.[13]

Zhou Enlai passed away on 8 January 1976, thin and shrivelled by three separate cancers but still handsome. Instead of naming Wang Hongwen as acting premier, or appointing a veteran cadre close to Deng Xiaoping, Mao turned to an individual who stood outside the two camps. Hua Guofeng, a tall, amiable lightweight who years earlier had built a sprawling memorial hall in Shaoshan dedicated to the Chairman, stepped into the breach.

The Chairman also did all in his power to prevent Zhou Enlai from stealing his thunder, even in death. A brief radio broadcast announced the premier's passing, but there was no lying in state. Madame Mao and her followers tried to forbid the wearing of black armbands and white chrysanthemums, announcing that there was no need for any memorial service other than the official one. People expressed their anger and indignation as they queued for food or waited for buses. A few brave souls complained loudly and bitterly.[14]

Still, despite all the efforts of the Gang of Four, there was an outpouring of popular emotion. Zhou Enlai had become a symbol of moderation. Many saw him as the only leader who had tried to mitigate the disaster of the Cultural Revolution. He stood for hope. Tens of thousands of people took to the streets, standing in the icy wind to bid farewell to the premier, even though the route to the cemetery had been kept secret. Many had tears in their eyes as the hearse passed by. One foreign student at Peking University was overwhelmed by the reaction to the premier's death: 'I had never seen such universal grief. It seemed everyone was weeping, men and women, old people and children. Some were almost hysterical. Bus drivers, street sweepers and shop clerks all went about their chores with swollen red eyes.' In what would be his last public appearance for a year, Deng Xiaoping delivered a eulogy. He was relieved of his duties as vice-premier a few days later.[15]

Popular resentment mounted against Madame Mao and her cronies, who now enjoyed the upper hand and increased their attacks on Deng Xiaoping. Even the senile, sick Chairman seemed unable to rein in Jiang

Qing. With Zhou Enlai dead and Deng Xiaoping purged once again, people became anxious, fearing for the future.

As the Qingming festival approached, they rebelled. On Tomb Sweeping Day, as the ancient tradition of honouring deceased relatives was also known, families usually gathered to weed graves, clean or touch up headstones and offer flowers to their ancestors. The festival fell on 4 April, but weeks before people had already started displaying wreaths with eulogies for Zhou Enlai. In Nanjing, an elegiac couplet honouring the premier was removed from the Cemetery for Revolutionary Martyrs, prompting students to put up a slogan the following day. They boldly proclaimed their willingness to 'Defend Zhou Enlai with our Lives!'

But what really infuriated ordinary people was an editorial published in Shanghai on 25 March, calling Zhou Enlai a 'capitalist roader inside the party' who had wanted to help Deng Xiaoping the 'unrepentant capitalist roader' regain power. The newspaper was bombarded with letters, telegrams and telephone calls objecting to the article. In Nanjing, students marched on the Cemetery for Revolutionary Martyrs holding a giant portrait of the deceased premier, defying a ban imposed by the local authorities. Soon the entire city was plastered in slogans attacking the Gang of Four. Some people shouted 'Down with Jiang Qing!', and others demanded the overthrow of Zhang Chunqiao. The protesters spread their message to the rest of the country by daubing slogans on the sides of trains and long-distance buses. In Wuxi, an industrial city roughly 200 kilometres to the east of Nanjing, a sea of humanity poured into Red Square, brandishing portraits of the premier and loudly broadcasting a recording of Deng Xiaoping's eulogy.[16]

Trains from Nanjing on their way to the capital were stopped in Tianjin and coated in green paint. But in the capital too, people had started leaving wreaths at the base of the Monument to the People's Heroes, a towering obelisk in Tiananmen Square. They were confiscated by the Public Security Bureau, but still mourners thronged to the square with poems, flowers and wreaths, sometimes tying their tributes with wire to the white, marble railings surrounding the monument to prevent the security forces from removing them. Volunteers stood guard. On 31 March, poems attacking 'Jiang Qing the witch' appeared. Some 4,000 policemen and militia workers were deployed two days later, while the municipal party committee banned government units from sending wreaths, merely encouraging more protesters to join the fight, as poetry and flowers became weapons used against the Gang of Four.[17]

The festival fell on a Sunday. Hundreds of thousands of people streamed into the square, hanging posters on flagpoles and piling wreaths around the monument. Some released bundles of brightly coloured balloons carrying streamers with tributes to Zhou Enlai, hoping that they could be seen from the Chairman's residence in Zhongnanhai. A young man standing on a pedestal, leading several thousand people in singing a slow lament, was deliberately dressed in a traditional gown. On that drizzling day, he held a traditional, oil-paper umbrella, using his archaic appearance to remind the crowd that students had demonstrated against their rulers in the original Tiananmen Square decades earlier, on 4 May 1919. Others were more blunt, holding up a microphone to attack 'the new Empress Dowager'. One student brandished a piece of white brocade on which he had written in blood a pledge to defend the premier. But the atmosphere remained solemn, as people from all walks of life, from high officials in expensive woollen overcoats to ordinary villagers in drab cotton clothing, quietly defied the will of their supreme leader.[18]

The Politburo convened the same day, condemning the incident as counter-revolutionary. Mao Yuanxin reported the decision to his uncle, who approved. In the early hours of 5 April, the police started cleaning the square, loading all the wreaths in a fleet of 200 lorries and using fire hoses to remove the slogans from the walls of the monument. Within hours, enraged demonstrators clashed with the police. Both sides called for reinforcements. Later that day cars were set on fire and a command post was looted.

By the evening more than 10,000 policemen and five battalions of security forces were on standby. Warning messages were broadcast continuously through loudspeakers from 6.30 p.m. onwards, condemning the incident as a 'reactionary plot' and calling on the crowd to disperse. A few hours later, militias armed with clubs and iron bars moved to strategic positions around the square. At 9.30 p.m. the floodlights were suddenly switched on. The square was sealed off, and more than 200 people who remained inside were beaten, dragged away by force and arrested. From the Great

Hall of the People, Jiang Qing observed the events through a pair of binoculars. Later that night she joined her husband for a celebratory meal of peanuts and roast pork. Offering a toast of fiery rice wine, she declared that 'We are victorious.' Just before midnight, a hundred public security officers moved through the square in line abreast, watering and mopping up the blood.[19]

Mao, still clear-headed at this point despite his physical deterioration, was convinced that Deng Xiaoping was behind the incident. Deng was dismissed from all his posts, but retained his party membership. A nationwide crackdown followed, as thousands were arrested for counter-revolutionary crimes. Many more were interrogated. In Shijiazhuang, the capital of Hebei, every person known to have visited the capital was investigated. In schools, factories and offices across Beijing, people were asked about their participation in the Tiananmen incident. More than 100,000 were made to march through the city with red banners condemning Deng Xiaoping. 'We marched with resentment,' remembered one participant.[20]

Across the nation, people who were asked to denounce the erstwhile vice-premier showed resistance, chatting, reading, knitting or even sleeping through the proceedings. Those asked to stand up and speak in public meetings read their prepared scripts in a flat, emotionless voice. Nobody was duped, and the campaign fell flat. People were waiting for the end. In Chengdu, crowds often appeared in the streets, having heard that Mao was about to die.[21]

Aftermath

Natural catastrophes, according to imperial tradition, are harbingers of dynastic change. On the early morning of 28 July 1976, a giant earthquake struck Tangshan, a coal city on the Bohai Sea just over 150 kilometres east of Beijing. The scale of the devastation was enormous. At least half a million people died, although some estimates have placed the death toll at 700,000.[1]

In the summer of 1974, seismographic experts had predicted the likelihood of a very large earthquake in the region within the next two years, but owing to the Cultural Revolution, they were hopelessly short of modern equipment and trained personnel.[2]

Few preparations were made. Tangshan itself was a shoddily built city, with pithead structures, hoist towers and conveyor belts looming over ramshackle, one-storey houses. Below ground there was a vast network of tunnels and deep shafts. In one terrible instant, a 150-kilometre-long fault line ruptured beneath the earth, inflicting more damage than the atomic bombs dropped on either Hiroshima or Nagasaki. Asphalt streets were torn asunder and rails twisted into knots. The earth moved with such lightning speed that the sides of trees in the heart of the earthquake zone were singed. Some houses folded inwards, others were swallowed up. Roughly 95 per cent of the 11 million square metres of living space in the city collapsed.

As soon as the tremor subsided, a freezing rain drenched dazed survivors, blanketing the city in a thick mist mingled with the dust of crumbled buildings. For an hour Tangshan remained shrouded in darkness, lit only by flashes of fire in the rubble of the crushed houses. Some survivors burned to death, but many more were asphyxiated. 'I was breathing in the ashes of the dead,' one victim, then a boy aged twelve, remembered.[3]

Death was everywhere. 'Bodies dangled out of windows, caught as they tried to escape. An old woman lay in the street, her head pulped by flying debris. In the train station, a concrete pillar had impaled a young girl, pinning her to the wall. At the bus depot, a cook had been scalded to death by a cauldron of boiling water.'[4]

The earthquake could not have struck at a worse moment. Beijing was paralysed by the slow death of the Chairman, surrounded by doctors and nurses in Zhongnanhai. Mao felt the quake, which rattled his bed, and must have understood the message. Many buildings in the capital were shaken violently, overturning pots and vases, rattling pictures on the wall, shattering some glass windows. Many residents refused to return to their homes, sleeping on the pavements under makeshift plastic sheets until the aftershocks subsided. Instead of broadcasting the news, some neighbourhood committees turned on the loudspeakers to exhort the population to 'criticise Deng Xiaoping and carry the Cultural Revolution through to the end'. The insensitivity of the authorities to the plight of ordinary people caused widespread anger.[5]

It was weeks before the military authorities, hampered by lack of planning, poor communication and the need to receive approval for every decision from their leaders in Beijing, responded effectively. The rescue was strategic. Tangshan was a mining powerhouse that could not be abandoned, but villagers in the surrounding countryside were left to cope alone. Offers of aid from foreign nations – search teams, helicopters, rescue equipment, blankets and food – were flatly rejected by Hua Guofeng, who used the opportunity to assert his own leadership and suggest national self-confidence. Lacking professional expertise and adequate equipment, the young soldiers relied on muscle power to pull some 16,000 people from the ruins, a fraction of those recovered earlier by the very victims themselves. The People's Liberation Army covered tens of thousands of bodies with bleaching powder and buried them in improvised graveyards outside the city. No national day of mourning was announced. The dead were hardly acknowledged.[6]

A few minutes past midnight on 9 September 1976, the line on the monitor in Beijing went flat. It was one day after the full moon, when families traditionally gathered to count their blessings at the Mid-Autumn Festival.

Jan Wong, the foreign student who had arrived at Peking University in 1972, was cycling to class when she heard the familiar chords of the state funeral dirge on the broadcasting system. The usually strong voice of the Central Broadcasting Station was now full of sorrow, mournfully announcing the death of the Chairman. 'We announce with the deepest grief that Comrade Mao Zedong, our esteemed and beloved great leader, passed away ten minutes after midnight.' Other cyclists looked shocked, but not sad. In the classroom, her fellow students were dry-eyed, busy making white paper chrysanthemums, black armbands and paper wreaths. 'There were no gasps or tears, just a sense of relief.' It was a stark contrast with the outpouring of grief at the premier's death nine months earlier.[7]

In schools, factories and offices, people assembled to listen to the official announcement. Those who felt relief had to hide their feelings. This was the case with Jung Chang, who for a moment was numbed with sheer euphoria. All around her people wept. She had to display the correct emotion or risk being singled out. She buried her head in the shoulder of the woman in front of her, heaving and snivelling.[8]

She was hardly alone in putting on a performance. Traditionally, in China, weeping for dead relatives and even throwing oneself on the ground in front of the coffin was a required demonstration of filial piety. Absence of tears was a disgrace to the family. Sometimes actors were hired to wail loudly at the funeral of important dignitaries, thus encouraging other mourners to join in without feeling embarrassed. And much as people had mastered the art of effortlessly producing proletarian anger at denunciation meetings, some knew how to cry on demand.

People showed less contrition in private. In Kunming, the provincial capital of Yunnan, liquor sold out overnight. One young woman remembers how her father invited his best friend to their home, locked the door and opened the only bottle of wine they had. The next day, they went to a public memorial service where people cried as if they were heartbroken. 'As a little girl, I was confused by the adults' expressions – everybody looked so sad in public, while my father was so happy the night before.'[9]

Still, some people felt genuine grief, in particular those who had benefited from the Cultural Revolution. And plenty of true believers remained,
especially among young people. Ai Xiaoming, a twenty-two-year-old girl
eager to enter the party and contribute to socialism, was so heartbroken
that she wept almost to the point of fainting.[10]

But in the countryside, it seems, few people sobbed. As one poor villager in Anhui recalled, 'not a single person wept at the time'.[11]

Whether or not they shed tears, by the time the state funeral was held
in Tiananmen Square on 18 September, most people had collected their
emotions. The entire leadership was present, with the exception of Deng
Xiaoping, still under house arrest. Luo Ruiqing, one of the first leading
officials to have become a victim of the Cultural Revolution, insisted on
attending the funeral in his wheelchair. He still adored the man who had
persecuted him, and he cried. Hua Guofeng used the occasion to exhort
the masses to continue the campaign against Deng Xiaoping. At precisely
three o'clock, he announced three minutes of silence. Silence fell over the
country, as railway stations came to a standstill, buses pulled over to the
side of the road, workers downed their tools, cyclists dismounted and
pedestrians stopped in their tracks. Then Wang Hongwen called out, 'First
bow! Second bow! Third bow!' A million people in the square bowed three
times before the giant portrait of Mao hanging from the rostrum.[12]

It was the last public display of unity among the leaders before the big
showdown. Even as the Chairman's body was being injected with formaldehyde for preservation in a cold chamber deep beneath the capital, different factions were jockeying for power. The Gang of Four controlled
the propaganda machine, and cranked up the campaign against 'capitalist
roaders'. But they had little clout within the party, and no influence over
the army. Their only source of authority was now dead, and public opinion
was hardly on their side. With the exception of Jiang Qing, their power
base was in Shanghai, a long way from the capital where all the jousting
for control took place.

Most of all, they underestimated Hua Guofeng. A mere two days after
Mao's death, the premier quietly reached out to Marshal Ye Jianying,
by now in charge of the Ministry of Defence. He also contacted Wang
Dongxing, Mao's former bodyguard who commanded the troops in charge

of the leadership's security. On 6 October, less than a month after the
Chairman's death, a Politburo meeting was called to discuss the fifth volume of *Mao's Selected Works*. Members of the Gang of Four were arrested
one by one as they arrived at the meeting hall. Madame Mao, sensing a
trap, stayed away, but was arrested at her residence.

After the official announcement on 14 October, firecrackers exploded
all night. Stores sold out not only of liquor, but of all kinds of items,
including ordinary tinned food, as people splurged to celebrate the downfall of the Gang of Four. 'Everywhere, I saw people wandering around with
broad smiles and big hangovers,' one resident recalled.[13]

There were official celebrations too, 'exactly the same kind of rallies as
during the Cultural Revolution'. In Beijing, columns of hundreds of thousands of people waved huge banners denouncing the 'Gang of Four Anti-
Party Clique'. A mass rally was held on Tiananmen on 24 October, as the
leaders made their first public appearance since the coup. Hua Guofeng,
now anointed as chairman of the party, moved back and forth along the
rostrum, clapping lightly to acknowledge the cheers and smiling beatifi-
cally, very much like his predecessor.[14]

In Shanghai, posters were plastered on buildings along the Bund up to a
height of several storeys. The streets were choked with people exulting over
the fall of the radicals. Nien Cheng was forced to join a parade, carrying
a slogan saying 'Down with Jiang Qing'. She abhorred it, but many demonstrators relished the opportunity, marching four abreast with banners,
drums and gongs.[15]

The political campaigns did not cease. 'Instead of attacking Deng, we
now denounced the Gang of Four.' Madame Mao and her three fanatical
followers became scapegoats, blamed for all the misfortunes of the past
ten years. Some people found it difficult to separate Mao from his wife,
but the strategy had its advantages. As one erstwhile believer put it, 'It is
more comfortable that way, as it is difficult to part with one's beliefs and
illusions.'[16]

———

Deng Xiaoping returned to power in the summer of 1977, much to Hua
Guofeng's disappointment. Chairman Hua's portrait now hung next to that

of Chairman Mao in Tiananmen Square. He slicked his hair to resemble the Great Helmsman, and posed for staged photos, uttering vague aphorisms in the style of his former master. But while the propaganda machine churned out posters exhorting the population to 'Most Closely Follow our Brilliant Leader', the new chairman lacked the institutional clout and political charisma to shore up his power. His clumsy attempt at a cult of personality alienated many party veterans. His reluctance to repudiate the Cultural Revolution was out of tune with a widespread desire for change. Hua was easily outmanoeuvred by Deng, who had the support of many of the older party members humiliated during the Cultural Revolution.

Ordinary people also viewed Deng as a saviour. Many of those wronged in one way or another during the Cultural Revolution pinned their hopes on the man who had survived three purges. Millions of students exiled to the countryside, most of them former Red Guards, were streaming back into the cities, worried about their future. They were joined by tens of thousands of ex-convicts, released from the gulag after suffering wrongful imprisonment during the Cultural Revolution. People from all walks of life petitioned the government for redress, from impoverished villagers who accused local leaders of rape, pillage and murder to the victims of political intrigue in the higher echelons of power. In the capital a shanty town mushroomed, as petitioners camped outside the State Council.[17]

Not far away, a mere kilometre to the west of Tiananmen Square, a long brick wall near an old bus station in Xidan became the focal point for popular discontent with the status quo. In October 1978, a few months before an important party gathering, handwritten posters went up, attracting a huge crowd of onlookers, warmly bundled up against the cold. Some of the demonstrators demanded justice, putting up detailed accounts of their personal grievances. Others clamoured for the full rehabilitation of Deng Xiaoping and other senior officials like Peng Dehuai, purged for having stood up to Mao during the Great Leap Forward. Rumours even circulated that the vice-premier stood behind the people, having told a foreign journalist that 'The Democracy Wall in Xidan is a good thing!' Deng's own slogan, 'Seek Truth from Facts', seemed promising. There were calls for universal suffrage, with one electrician from the Beijing Zoo named Wei

Jingsheng asking for a 'Fifth Modernisation: Democracy', to supplement Zhou Enlai's Four Modernisations.[18]

Deng Xiaoping used the Democracy Wall to shore up his own position at the Third Plenum of the Eleventh Central Committee, held two months later in December 1978. Hua retained many of his titles, but Deng effectively took control of the party. It was Deng who went to the United States in February 1979, thrilling the American public when he donned a cowboy hat at a rodeo in Texas. He circled the arena in a horse-drawn stagecoach, waving to the crowd, and generally charmed business leaders and politicians during his stay.

When Deng returned home, he found growing unrest. The Democracy Wall had been transformed into a hotbed of dissent, as several demonstrators led by a construction worker who had been raped by a party secretary organised a protest march through Tiananmen Square on the anniversary of Zhou Enlai's death. They were arrested, but their daring opposition to the communist party inspired others. In a poster entitled 'Democracy or New Dictatorship', Wei Jingsheng branded Deng Xiaoping a 'fascist dictator'.

There was to be no democracy, and Wei Jingsheng was rounded up together with dozens of other dissidents, some to be imprisoned for twenty years. As one disillusioned observer put it, 'The old guard reverted to the old way of managing the country.' A year later, Peng Zhen, the mayor of Beijing who had been one of the first targets of the Cultural Revolution, moved to eliminate once again four basic rights codified into the constitution after the death of Mao. The rights of citizens to 'speak out freely, air their views fully, engage in great debates and write big-character posters', heralded by the Chairman in 1966, were blamed for having contributed to the chaos of the Cultural Revolution. The right to strike was abolished a year later.[19]

Still, every dictator has to differentiate himself from his predecessor, and Deng was keen to draw a line under the Cultural Revolution. Since roughly half of all members had joined the communist party since 1966, and most of the old guard had at one point or another been tainted by the sordid politics of the Cultural Revolution, a systematic attempt to call perpetrators to account would have led to a gigantic purge. There were many rehabilitations, but very few prosecutions. Liu Shaoqi, together with all his followers, was formally exonerated in February 1980.

The most politically expedient way of assigning blame without implicating either the communist party or the founding father of the regime was to put the Gang of Four on trial. In November 1980, Jiang Qing, Zhang Chunqiao, Wang Hongwen and Yao Wenyuan entered a courtroom at Justice Road near Tiananmen Square, accused of masterminding a decade of murderous chaos. Madame Mao was defiant, hurling abuse at her accusers. At one point she quipped that 'I was Chairman Mao's dog. I bit whomever he asked me to bite.' Behind the scenes, a special team headed by Peng Zhen orchestrated the show trial. Jiang Qing and Zhang Chunqiao were given the death penalty, commuted to life imprisonment. Ten years later, in 1991, Jiang Qing hanged herself inside her cell with a rope made of her own socks and a few handkerchiefs. Wang Hongwen died in prison the following year. But Yao Wenyuan and Zhang Chunqiao were released after serving twenty years, living out their lives under tight police surveillance.

Other prominent members of the Cultural Revolution Group were also condemned, including Chen Boda. The Chairman had already placed him behind bars in 1970, and he would not be released until 1988.

Lacking any independent legal system, party officials at every level decided who would be punished and who would not. 'Some rebels were rightly punished. Some got rough justice. Others were let off lightly.'[20]

In July 1981, to mark its sixtieth birthday, the party issued a formal resolution on its own history. The document barely mentioned Mao's Great Famine and blamed Lin Biao and the Gang of Four for the Cultural Revolution, while largely absolving the Chairman. Mao's own verdict on the Cultural Revolution was used by Deng to evaluate the entire role of the Chairman in the history of the communist party. It was exactly the same assessment that Mao had given of Stalin, namely 70 per cent successful and 30 per cent a failure.

The resolution was designed to terminate all public debate about the party's own past. Academic research on major issues such as the Great Leap Forward and the Cultural Revolution was strongly discouraged, and any interpretation that strayed from the official version was viewed with an unsympathetic eye.[21]

But the document also had other goals, more closely linked to current politics than to past history. Deng Xiaoping used the resolution to criticise Hua Guofeng and establish his own credentials as paramount leader. The reign of Chairman Hua was lumped together with the Cultural Revolution, while the Third Plenum in December 1978 was consecrated as the 'Great Turning Point in History', when under the guidance of Deng Xiaoping the party finally embarked on the 'correct path for socialist modernisation'.

This path involved a programme based on Zhou Enlai's Four Modernisations. Its most remarkable feature was how reluctantly economic reforms were introduced. By 1976, much of the country was reeling from three decades of economic mismanagement and years of political chaos. But change from above was slow in coming. The Third Plenum was not so much a 'Great Turning Point in History' as an attempt to restore the planned economy to its pre-Cultural Revolution days. Deng Xiaoping and his acolytes were looking back, not forward. In agricultural policy, they revived the various measures taken in 1962 to protect the countryside from the radical collectivisation that had run amok during the Great Leap Forward. Small private plots were once again allowed, but the leadership explicitly prohibited dividing the land. In April 1979 it even demanded that villagers who had left the collectives rejoin the people's communes. But it did make one concession: three years after Mao's death, the party finally increased by 20 per cent the price of the grain sold compulsorily to the state. The prices charged for agricultural machinery, fertilisers and pesticides were also reduced by 10 to 15 per cent.[22]

Real change was driven from below. In a silent revolution dating back at least a decade, cadres and villagers had started pulling themselves out of poverty by reconnecting with the past. In parts of the countryside they covertly rented out the land, established black markets and ran underground factories. The extent and depth of these liberal practices are difficult to gauge, as so much was done on the sly, but they thrived even more after the death of Mao. By 1979, many county leaders in Anhui had no choice but to allow families to cultivate the land. As one local leader put it, 'Household contracting was like an irresistible wave, spontaneously topping the limits we had placed, and it could not be suppressed or turned around.' In Sichuan, too, local leaders found it difficult to contain the division of the land. Zhao Ziyang, who had arrived in Sichuan in 1975 to take over as the head of the provincial party committee, decided to go with the flow.[23]

By 1980, tens of thousands of local decisions had placed 40 per cent of Anhui production teams, 50 per cent of Guizhou teams and 60 per cent of Gansu teams under household contracts. Deng Xiaoping had neither the will nor the ability to fight the trend. As Kate Zhou has written, 'When the government lifted restrictions, it did so only in recognition of the fact that the sea of unorganised farmers had already made them irrelevant.'[24]

In the winter of 1982–3, the people's communes were officially dissolved. It was the end of an era. The covert practices that had spread across the countryside in the last years of the Cultural Revolution now flourished, as villagers returned to family farming, cultivated crops that could be sold for a profit on the market, established privately owned shops or went to the cities to work in factories. Rural decollectivisation, in turn, liberated even more labour in the countryside, fuelling a boom in village enterprises. Rural industry provided most of the country's double-digit growth, offsetting the inefficient performance of state-owned enterprises. In this great transformation, the villagers took centre stage. Rapid economic growth did not start in the cities with a trickle-down effect to the countryside, but flowed instead from the rural to the urban sector. The private entrepreneurs who transformed the economy were millions upon millions of ordinary villagers, who effectively out-manoeuvred the state. If there was a great architect of economic reform, it was the people.[25]

Deng Xiaoping used economic growth to consolidate the communist party and maintain its iron grip on power. But it came at a cost. Not only did the vast majority of people in the countryside push for greater economic opportunities, but they also escaped from the ideological shackles imposed by decades of Maoism. The Cultural Revolution in effect destroyed the remnants of Marxism-Leninism and Mao Zedong Thought. Endless campaigns of thought reform produced widespread resistance even among party members themselves. The very ideology of the party was gone, and its legitimacy lay in tatters. The leaders lived in fear of their own people, constantly having to suppress their political aspirations. In June 1989, Deng personally ordered a military crackdown on pro-democracy demonstrators in Beijing, as tanks rolled into Tiananmen Square. The massacre was a display of brutal force and steely resolve, designed to send a signal that still pulsates to this day: do not query the monopoly of the one-party state.

Notes

Preface

1 Sidney Rittenberg, *The Man Who Stayed Behind*, New York: Simon & Schuster, 1993, p. 271.
2 Bo Yibo, *Ruogan zhongda shijian yu juece de huigu* (Recollections of several important decisions and events), Beijing: Zhonggong zongyang dangxiao chubanshe, 1993, vol. 2, p. 1129.
3 Kate Xiao Zhou, *How the Farmers Changed China: Power of the People*, Boulder, CO: Westview Press, 1996, p. 15.
4 Anne F. Thurston, *Enemies of the People*, New York: Knopf, 1987, pp. 208–9.
5 Fifteen years ago, Tony Chang's select bibliography already amounted to more than 200 pages; see Tony H. Chang, *China during the Cultural Revolution, 1966–1976: A Selected Bibliography of English Language Works*, Westport, CT: Greenwood, 1999.

Chapter 1: Two Dictators

1 Alexander V. Pantsov and Steven I. Levine, *Mao: The Real Story*, New York: Simon & Schuster, 2012, p. 366.
2 Li Zhisui, *The Private Life of Chairman Mao: The Memoirs of Mao's Personal Physician*, New York: Random House, 1994, pp. 182–4.
3 Closing Speech at the Second Plenum of the Eighth Central Committee, 15 Nov. 1956, Gansu, 91–18–480, pp. 74–6.
4 Frank Dikötter, *The Tragedy of Liberation: A History of the Chinese Revolution, 1945–1957*, London: Bloomsbury, 2013, pp. 278–80; the figure of over 3 million appears on p. 102.
5 Elizabeth J. Perry, 'Shanghai's Strike Wave of 1957', *China Quarterly*, no. 137 (March 1994), pp. 1–27.
6 *Neibu cankao*, 30 Nov. 1960, p. 17.
7 Hunan, 8 April 1961, 146–1-583, p. 96.
8 The detailed archival evidence on which this estimate is based can be found in Frank Dikötter, *Mao's Great Famine: The History of China's Most Devastating Catastrophe, 1958–1962*, London: Bloomsbury, 2010, ch. 37.

9 Report by Li Xiannian on the issue of grain shortages, 30 July 1961, Zhongyang (61) 540, Gansu, 91–18–211, pp. 136–7.

10 Pitman Potter, *From Leninist Discipline to Socialist Legalism: Peng Zhen on Law and Political Authority in the PRC*, Stanford: Stanford University Press, 2003, pp. 18 and 85–6.

11 Robert Service, *Stalin: A Biography*, Basingstoke: Macmillan, 2004, pp. 312–13; E. A. Rees, *Iron Lazar: A Political Biography of Lazar Kaganovich*, London: Anthem Press, 2012, p. 135.

12 Hao Shengxin, *Nanwang de suiyue* (Unforgettable years), Beijing: Beijing shidai nongchao wenhua fazhan gongsi, 2011, p. 76.

13 Speech by Liu Shaoqi, 27 Jan. 1962, Gansu, 91–18–493, pp. 58–60 and 62.

14 Speech by Lin Biao, 29 Jan. 1962, Gansu, 91–18–493, pp. 163–4.

15 Roderick MacFarquhar, *The Origins of the Cultural Revolution*, vol. 3: *The Coming of the Cataclysm, 1961–1966*, New York: Columbia University Press, 1997, p. 169.

16 Zhang Suhua, *Bianju: Qiqianren dahui shimo* (The whole story of the Seven Thousand Cadres Conference), Beijing: Zhongguo qingnian chubanshe, 2006, p. 71.

17 Li, *The Private Life of Chairman Mao*, p. 386.

18 Speech by Zhou Enlai, 7 Feb. 1962, Gansu, 91–18–493, p. 87.

19 Zhang, *Bianju*, pp. 176–83; MacFarquhar, *The Origins of the Cultural Revolution*, vol. 3, p. 172.

20 Service, *Stalin*, p. 347.

Chapter 2: Never Forget Class Struggle

1 Mao Zedong, *Jianguo yilai Mao Zedong wengao* (Mao Zedong's manuscripts since the founding of the People's Republic), Beijing: Zhongyang wenxian chubanshe, 1996, vol. 9, p. 349.

2 Speech by Mao Zedong, Gansu, 18 Jan. 1961, 91–6-79, p. 4.

3 Josef Stalin, *History of the All-Union Communist Party: A Short Course*, New York: International Publishers, 1939, pp. 324–5.

4 Kees Boterbloem, *The Life and Times of Andrei Zhdanov, 1896–1948*, Montreal: McGill-Queen's Press, 2004, pp. 176–7 and 215.

5 Li Hua-yu, 'Instilling Stalinism in Chinese Party Members: Absorbing Stalin's Short Course in the 1950s', in Thomas P. Bernstein and Li Hua-yu (eds), *China Learns from the Soviet Union, 1949–Present*, Lanham, MD: Lexington Books, 2009, pp. 107–30.

6 Mao Zedong, 'Talk at an Enlarged Working Conference Convened by the Central Committee of the Communist Party of China', 30 Jan. 1962; one manuscript version of this speech is in Gansu, 91–18–493, pp. 3–37; I have used the translation from the *Peking Review*, published on 7 July 1978, in *Selected Works of Mao Zedong*, vol. 8, no pagination, Marxists Internet Archive.

7 Li, *The Private Life of Chairman Mao*, p. 379.

8 Extracts of Minutes of the Xilou Meeting, Oct. 1967, Shanghai, B104-3-41, pp. 7–9 and 13.

9 Extracts of Minutes of the May Meeting and the Beidaihe Meeting, Shanghai, Oct. 1967, B104-3-41, pp. 7-10.

10 Liu Yuan, 'Mao Zedong wei shenma yao dadao Liu Shaoqi', quoted in Gao Wenqian, *Zhou Enlai: The Last Perfect Revolutionary*, New York: PublicAffairs, 2007, pp. 97-8. For a slightly different version from Liu's wife, see Huang Zheng, *Wang Guangmei fangtan lu* (A record of conversations with Wang Guangmei), Beijing: Zhongyang wenxian chubanshe, 2006, p. 288.

11 Jacques Marcuse, *The Peking Papers: Leaves from the Notebook of a China Correspondent*, London: Arthur Barker, 1968, p. 299.

12 Li, *The Private Life of Chairman Mao*, p. 395.

13 Yao Jin, *Yao Yilin baixi tan* (Conversations with Yao Yilin), Beijing: Zhonggong dangshi chubanshe, 2008, p. 229.

14 Mao Zedong, 'Speech at the Tenth Plenum of the Eighth Central Committee', 24 Sept. 1962, *Selected Works of Mao Zedong*, vol. 8, no pagination, Marxists Internet Archive.

15 *Neibu cankao*, 1 March 1963, pp. 7-9; 5 April 1963, pp. 6-9; 9 April 1963, pp. 2-5.

16 *Neibu cankao*, 2 April 1963, pp. 2-3.

17 Zhongfa (63) 368, 26 May 1963, Shandong, A1-2-1157, pp. 11-14.

18 Interview with Zeng Mu, born 1931, Pengzhou, Sichuan, May 2006.

19 Nanjing, 27 May 1959, 4003-1-279, p. 242.

20 Jin Chongji and Huang Zheng (eds), *Liu Shaoqi zhuan* (A biography of Liu Shaoqi), Beijing: Zhongyang wenxian chubanshe, 1998, vol. 2, p. 948.

21 Song Yongyi, 'Bei yancang de lishi: Liu Shao dui "wenge" de dute gongxian' (Hidden history: Liu Shaoqi's special contribution to the Cultural Revolution) in Song Yongyi (ed.), *Wenhua da geming: Lishi zhenxiang he jiti jiyi* (The Cultural Revolution: Historical truth and collective memories), Hong Kong: Tianyuan shuwu, 2007, vol. 2, pp. 45-62; Edward Friedman, Paul G. Pickowicz and Mark Selden, *Revolution, Resistance and Reform in Village China*, New Haven, CT: Yale University Press, 2005, p. 61.

22 Hunan, 6 May 1964, 146-1-743, pp. 103-8; Hunan, 10 Oct. 1964, 146-1-776, p. 163; the slogan is quoted in Xie Chengnian, 'Wo qinli de "siqing" yundong naxie shi' (My personal experience of the 'Four Cleans'), *Wenshi tiandi*, no. 6 (June 2012), pp. 8-9.

23 Hunan, 15 June 1964, 146-1-751, pp. 56-62 and 75-82.

24 Dai Yushan, '"Siqing" dayuanan de zhenxiang: Du Yu Kaiguo "Tongcheng fengyu"' (The truth about the 'Four Cleans'), *Zhengming*, Jan. 2007, pp. 82-3.

25 Pang Xianzhi and Jin Chongji (eds), *Mao Zedong zhuan, 1949-1976* (A biography of Mao Zedong, 1949-1976), Beijing: Zhongyang wenxian chubanshe, 2003, p. 1345; for stylistic reasons I have slightly compressed Liu's words.

26 Several diplomats see this as the main reason for the rift; see Michael Stepanovitch Kapitsa, *Na raznykh parallelakh: Zapiski diplomata*, Moscow: Kniga i Biznes, 1996, pp. 61-3; Arkady N. Shevchenko, *Breaking with Moscow*, New York: Alfred A. Knopf, 1985, p. 122.

27 Sergey Radchenko, *Two Suns in the Heavens: The Sino-Soviet Struggle for Supremacy, 1962-1967*, Stanford: Stanford University Press, 2009, p. 73.

28 Guo Dehong and Lin Xiaobo, *Siqing yundong shilu* (True record of the Four Cleans), Hangzhou: Zhejiang renmin chubanshe, 2005, pp. 130–2; Gao Hua, 'Zai Guizhou "siqing yundong" de beihou' (The background of the 'Four Cleans' campaign in Guizhou), *Ershiyi shiji*, no. 93 (Feb. 2006), p. 83.

29 Li Xin, '"Siqing" ji' (Record of the 'Four Cleans'), in Guo Dehong and Lin Xiaobo (eds), *'Siqing' yundong qinli ji* (Personal accounts of the 'Four Cleans'), Beijing: Renmin chubanshe, 2008, pp. 258–9.

30 The Guizhou case is recounted in Gao, 'Zai Guizhou "siqing yundong" de beihou', pp. 75–89; see also Yan Lebin, *Wo suo jingli de nage shidai* (That era I lived through), Beijing: Shidai wenhua chubanshe, 2012, pp. 90–1.

31 Luo Bing, 'Mao Zedong fadong shejiao yundong dang'an jiemi' (Revelations from the archives on the launching of the Socialist Education Campaign by Mao Zedong), *Zhengming*, Feb. 2006, pp. 10–13.

32 MacFarquhar, *The Origins of the Cultural Revolution*, vol. 3, p. 365.

33 Ibid., p. 417.

34 Bo, *Ruogan zhongda shijian yu juece de huigu*, vol. 2, p. 1131; see also MacFarquhar, *The Origins of the Cultural Revolution*, vol. 3, pp. 421–3.

35 Pang and Jin, *Mao Zedong zhuan, 1949–1976*, p. 1373.

36 Xiao Donglian, *Qiusuo Zhongguo: Wenge qian shinian shi* (Exploring China: A history of the decade before the Cultural Revolution), Beijing: Zhonggong dangshi chubanshe, 2011, vol. 2, pp. 787 and 791.

37 Gao, 'Zai Guizhou "siqing yundong" de beihou', pp. 84–5.

38 MacFarquhar, *The Origins of the Cultural Revolution*, vol. 3, p. 428.

Chapter 3: War on the Cultural Front

1 Stalin, *History of the All-Union Communist Party*, p. 321.

2 Service, *Stalin*, pp. 299–301; see also Sheila Fitzpatrick (ed.), *Cultural Revolution in Russia, 1928–1931*, Bloomington: Indiana University Press, 1978.

3 Dikötter, *The Tragedy of Liberation*, ch. 9.

4 Ibid., pp. 185–6.

5 Mao Zedong, 'Talk at an Enlarged Working Conference Convened by the Central Committee of the Communist Party of China', 30 Jan. 1962, *Selected Works of Mao Zedong*, vol. 8, no pagination, Marxists Internet Archive.

6 John Byron and Robert Pack, *The Claws of the Dragon: Kang Sheng, the Evil Genius behind Mao and his Legacy of Terror in People's China*, New York: Simon & Schuster, 1992, pp. 125–6; Roger Faligot and Rémi Kauffer, *The Chinese Secret Service*, New York: Morrow, 1989, pp. 103–4 and 115–18.

7 David Holm, 'The Strange Case of Liu Zhidan', *Australian Journal of Chinese Affairs*, no. 27 (Jan. 1992), pp. 77–96; MacFarquhar, *The Origins of the Cultural Revolution*, vol. 3, pp. 293–6; Li Kwok-sing, *A Glossary of Political Terms of the People's Republic of China*, Hong Kong: Chinese University of Hong Kong Press, 1995, p. 255.

8 Mao Zedong, 'Speech at the Tenth Plenum of the Eighth Central Committee', 24 Sept. 1962, *Selected Works of Mao Zedong*, vol. 8, no pagination, Marxists Internet Archive.

9 Zhongfa (63) 504, 25 July 1963, and Report from the Shaanxi Office for Propaganda, 16 June 1963, Shandong, A1–2-1153, pp. 74–88.

10 *Neibu cankao*, 16 April 1963, pp. 8–9.

11 *Neibu cankao*, 18 June 1963, p. 5; 12 June 1963, pp. 14–15; 4 June 1963, pp. 7–8.

12 Report from the Office of the Provincial Party Committee, 20 July 1963, Shandong, A1–2-1189, p. 22.

13 Report from the Central Secretariat of the Youth League, 1 and 18 Oct. 1963, Shandong, A1–2-1154, pp. 213–20; Shandong, 26 Sept. 1963, A1–2-1190, pp. 158–9; on the importance of officially sponsored singing, see Dikötter, *The Tragedy of Liberation*, pp. 193–4.

14 Shandong, 23 July 1963, A1–2-1154, pp. 185–8; Dikötter, *Mao's Great Famine*, p. 240.

15 *People's Daily*, 7 Feb. 1963, quoted in Arthur A. Cohen, *The Communism of Mao Tse-tung*, Chicago: University of Chicago Press, 1964, p. 203.

16 David Milton and Nancy D. Milton, *The Wind Will Not Subside: Years in Revolutionary China, 1964–1969*, New York: Pantheon Books, 1976, pp. 63–5; see also Marcuse, *The Peking Papers*, pp. 235–46.

17 Mary Sheridan, 'The Emulation of Heroes', *China Quarterly*, no. 33 (March 1968), pp. 47–72.

18 Zhai Zhenhua, *Red Flower of China*, New York: Soho, 1992, p. 41.

19 Xu Xiaodi, *Diandao suiyue* (Tumultuous years), Beijing: Shenghuo, dushu, xinzhi sanlian shudian, 2012; interview with Xu Xiaodi, Hong Kong, 13 March 2013.

20 Jung Chang, *Wild Swans: Three Daughters of China*, Clearwater, FL: Touchstone, 2003, p. 322.

21 Ibid., p. 325.

22 Nanjing, 24 Oct. 1966, 6001–2-434, pp. 59–61.

23 Chang, *Wild Swans*, p. 325.

24 Li Rui, *Lushan huiyi shilu* (A true record of the Lushan plenum), Zhengzhou: Henan renmin chubanshe, 1999, pp. 204–7.

25 Gao, *Zhou Enlai*, pp. 187–8.

26 Liu Tong, 'Jieshi Zhongnanhai gaoceng zhengzhi de yiba yaoshi: Lin Biao biji de hengli yu yanjiu' (A key to understanding high politics in Zhongnanhai: Sorting out and studying Lin Biao's notes), paper presented at the International Conference on Chinese War and Revolution in the Twentieth Century, Shanghai Communications University, 8–9 Nov. 2008.

27 Lu Hong, *Junbao neibu xiaoxi: 'Wenge' qinli shilu* (An insider's story of the PLA daily), Hong Kong, Shidai guoji chubanshe, 2006, pp. 14–17; Daniel Leese, *Mao Cult: Rhetoric and Ritual in China's Cultural Revolution*, Cambridge: Cambridge University Press, 2011, pp. 111–13.

28 Li, *The Private Life of Chairman Mao*, p. 412.

29 Lynn T. White, *Policies of Chaos: The Organizational Causes of Violence in China's Cultural Revolution*, Princeton: Princeton University Press, 1989, pp. 194–5, 206, 214–16.

30 PRO, Letter by D. K. Timms, 6 Oct. 1964, FO 371–175973; see also Laszlo Ladany, *The Communist Party of China and Marxism, 1921–1985: A Self-Portrait*, London: Hurst, 1988, p. 273.

31 Mao Zedong, 'Remarks at the Spring Festival', 13 Feb. 1964, in *Selected Works of Mao Zedong*, vol. 9, no pagination, Marxists Internet Archive.

32 Susan L. Shirk, *The Political Logic of Economic Reform in China*, Berkeley: University of California Press, 1993, ch. 3.

33 Hua Linshan, *Les Années rouges*, Paris: Seuil, 1987, p. 46; Gong Xiaoxia, 'Repressive Movements and the Politics of Victimization', doctoral dissertation, Harvard University, 1995, p. 69.

34 Mao, *Jianguo yilai Mao Zedong wengao*, vol. 10, 12 Dec. 1963, p. 436; vol. 11, 27 June 1964, p. 91.

35 Ross Terrill, *Madame Mao: The White-Boned Demon*, Stanford: Stanford University Press, 1990, pp. 107–35.

36 Li, *The Private Life of Chairman Mao*, pp. ix and 255–6.

37 Ibid., pp. 407–8; 'China: The Women', *Time*, 19 Oct. 1962, p. 29.

38 Li, *The Private Life of Chairman Mao*, p. 401.

39 Ibid., pp. 402–3.

40 MacFarquhar, *The Origins of the Cultural Revolution*, vol. 3, p. 389.

41 Xiao, *Qiusuo Zhongguo*, vol. 2, p. 773; see also Guo and Lin, *Siqing yundong shilu*, p. 132.

42 Hu Jinzhao, *Wenren luonan ji* (Record of intellectuals in distress), self-published, 2011, pp. 18–20.

43 MacFarquhar, *The Origins of the Cultural Revolution*, vol. 3, pp. 392–8.

Chapter 4: Clique of Four

1 Edgar Snow, 'Interview with Mao', *New Republic*, 27 Feb. 1965, pp. 17–23; Mao Zedong, 'South of the Mountains to North of the Seas', *Selected Works of Mao Zedong*, vol. 9, no pagination, Marxists Internet Archive; Milton and Milton, *The Wind Will Not Subside*, p. 82.

2 David Halberstam, *The Coldest Winter: America and the Korean War*, London: Macmillan, 2008, p. 372.

3 Radchenko, *Two Suns in the Heavens*, pp. 143–6.

4 Luo Ruiqing, *Commemorate the Victory over German Fascism! Carry the Struggle against U.S. Imperialism through to the End!*, Beijing: Foreign Languages Press, 1965, pp. 28–9.

5 Lin Biao, 3 Sept. 1965, *Long Live the Victory of People's War!*, Beijing: Foreign Languages Press, 1965.

6 Milton and Milton, *The Wind Will Not Subside*, pp. 94–5; some of the first scholars to point at the different strategies adopted by Luo Ruiqing and Lin Biao include Donald Zagoria, *Vietnam Triangle: Moscow, Peking, Hanoi*, New York: Pegasus, 1967, pp. 70–83, and Byungjoon Ahn, *Chinese Politics and the Cultural Revolution: Dynamics of Policy Processes*, Seattle: University of Washington Press, 1976, pp. 186–90 and 203–4.

7 MacFarquhar, *The Origins of the Cultural Revolution*, vol. 3, pp. 448–50; Roderick MacFarquhar and Michael Schoenhals, *Mao's Last Revolution*, Cambridge, MA: Harvard University Press, 2006, p. 26, with minor stylistic changes.

8 Victor Usov, 'The Secrets of Zhongnanhai: Who Wiretapped Mao Zedong, and How?', *Far Eastern Affairs*, no. 5 (May 2012), pp. 129–39.

9 Roderick MacFarquhar, *The Origins of the Cultural Revolution*, vol. 1: *Contradictions among the People, 1956–1957*, London: Oxford University Press, 1974, especially pp. 193–4 and 202–7.

10 Li, *The Private Life of Chairman Mao*, p. 451.

11 Shen Yuan, 'Deng Xiaoping Peng Zhen de fanyou jiaose' (The roles of Deng Xiaoping and Peng Zhen in the anti-rightist campaign), *Kaifang*, no. 4 (April 2007), pp. 67–9; Yin Yi, *Huishou canyang yi hanshan* (The Setting of the Sun over the Mountain), Beijing: Shiyue wenyi chubanshe, 2003), pp. 25–6, quoted in Wang Ning, 'The Great Northern Wilderness: Political Exiles in the People's Republic of China', doctoral dissertation, University of British Columbia, 2005.

12 Hao Ping, 'Reassessing the Starting Point of the Cultural Revolution', *China Review International*, 3, no. 1 (Spring 1996), pp. 66–86.

13 Li, *The Private Life of Chairman Mao*, pp. 295–7.

14 Milton and Milton, *The Wind Will Not Subside*, p. 110.

15 Li, *The Private Life of Chairman Mao*, p. 391.

16 Ibid., pp. 440–1; MacFarquhar and Schoenhals, *Mao's Last Revolution*, p. 17.

17 MacFarquhar and Schoenhals, *Mao's Last Revolution*, pp. 32–3.

18 Pang and Jin, *Mao Zedong zhuan, 1949–1976*, p. 1373.

19 Li, *The Private Life of Chairman Mao*, p. 452.

20 'Lin Biao zai Zhongyang zhengzhiju kuodahui de jianghua quanwen he Qiu Shike de pizhu' (Lin Biao's speech at the enlarged Politburo meeting and Qiu Shike's annotations), 18 May 1966; see also Qinghai bayiba geming zaofan-pai lianhe weiyuanhui (ed.), *Ziliao xuanbian: Zhongyang shouzhang jianghua zhuanji* (Selected materials: Compendium of talks by central party leaders), 5 Dec. 1967, quoted in Song Yongyi, 'Wenge Zhou Enlai: Yige bei yangaile de xingxiang' (A contradictory image from diverse sources: The role of Zhou Enlai in the Cultural Revolution), unpublished paper, March 1999.

Chapter 5: Poster Wars

1 Nanjing, 30 May 1966, 5003-3-1154, p. 40.

2 Yan Jiaqi and Gao Gao, *Turbulent Decade: A History of the Cultural Revolution*, Honolulu: University of Hawai'i Press, 1996, p. 37.

3 Gao Yuan, *Born Red: A Chronicle of the Cultural Revolution*, Stanford: Stanford University Press, 1987, p. 34.

4 Ibid., p. 40.

5 Shandong, 17 May 1966, A1–2-1356, pp. 185–6 and 191–2.

6 'Circular of the Central Committee of the Communist Party of China on the Great Proletarian Cultural Revolution', 16 May 1966.

7 Pang and Jin, *Mao Zedong zhuan, 1949–1976*, p. 1413.

8 Jack Chen, *Inside the Cultural Revolution*, London: Sheldon, 1976, p. 200.

9 Li, *The Private Life of Chairman Mao*, p. 390; Pamela Tan, *The Chinese Factor: An Australian Chinese Woman's Life in China from 1950 to 1979*, Dural, New South Wales: Roseberg, 2008, p. 130.

10 Wang Guangyu, *Qingshi nanyin: Zuihou yici jiaodai* (Ineluctable history: My last confession), self-published, 2011, pp. 34–5.

11 'Sweep Away All Monsters', *People's Daily*, 1 June 1966, translation from the *Peking Review*, 9, no. 23, 3 June 1966, pp. 4–5.

12 MacFarquhar and Schoenhals, *Mao's Last Revolution*, pp. 57–8.

13 PRO, 'Telegram no. 422', 4 June 1966, FO 371–186980; Douwe W. Fokkema, *Report from Peking: Observations of a Western Diplomat on the Cultural Revolution*, London: Hurst, 1971, pp. 8–9.

14 Fokkema, *Report from Peking*, pp. 9–10.

15 PRO, Donald C. Hopson, 'Some Impressions of Shantung', 7 June 1966, FO 371–186986.

16 PRO, Alan E. Donald, 'A Journey in the Yellow River Valley', 21 June 1966, FO 371–186986.

17 Ibid.

18 Mao Zedong, 'Notes on the Report of Further Improving the Army's Agricultural Work by the Rear Service Department of the Military Commission', 7 May 1966, *Selected Works of Mao Zedong*, vol. 9, no pagination, Marxists Internet Archive.

19 Chen, *Inside the Cultural Revolution*, p. xvii.

20 Li, *The Private Life of Chairman Mao*, p. 459.

21 Rae Yang, *Spider Eaters: A Memoir*, Berkeley: University of California Press, 1997, p. 117.

22 Chang, *Wild Swans*, p. 196.

23 Ken Ling, *The Revenge of Heaven*, New York: Ballantine, 1972, pp. 9–10.

24 Gao, *Born Red*, p. 53.

25 Ling, *The Revenge of Heaven*, pp. 9–10.

26 Ibid.; Ye Qing, '"Wenge" shiqi Fujian qunzhong zuzhi yanjiu' (A study of mass organisations in Fujian during the 'Cultural Revolution'), Fujian Normal University, doctoral dissertation, 2002, vol. 1, p. 39.

27 Gao, *Born Red*, p. 56.

28 Zhai, *Red Flower of China*, pp. 63–4.

29 Yan and Gao, *Turbulent Decade*, pp. 47–8.

30 MacFarquhar and Schoenhals, *Mao's Last Revolution*, pp. 72–3; Gong, 'Repressive Movements and the Politics of Victimization', p. 74; the quota and the number of 300,000 is from Song, 'Bei yancang de lishi'.

31 Hao, *Nanwang de suiyue*, pp. 96–8.

32 Jiang Hongsheng, 'The Paris Commune in Shanghai: The Masses, the State, and Dynamics of "Continuous Revolution"', doctoral dissertation, Duke University, 2010, pp. 217 and 230–1.

33 Chen, *Inside the Cultural Revolution*, pp. 217–18.

Chapter 6: Red August

1 PRO, L.V. Appleyard, Letter, 30 July 1966, FO 371–186987.

2 Fokkema, *Report from Peking*, p. 14; PRO, Douglas Brookfield, 'Visit to Shanghai', FO 371–186986; Wang Duanyang, *Yige hongweibing de riji* (Diary of a Red Guard), self-published, 2007, p. 44; Gao, *Born Red*, p. 62; Nanjing, 26 July and 3 Aug. 1966, 5003–3-1155, pp. 23 and 34–5.

3 Ye Yonglie, *Chen Boda zhuan* (Biography of Chen Boda), Beijing: Zuojia chu-banshe, 1993, p. 305; other historians date this encounter to 24 July; it is not included in the official biography of Mao Zedong, Pang and Jin, *Mao Zedong zhuan, 1949–1976*.

4 Jiang Qing Meets Cadres from the Secretariat of the Municipal Party Committee, 19 July 1966, Nanjing, 4003-1-293, pp. 77–84.

5 Ye, *Chen Boda zhuan*, pp. 306–9.

6 Pang and Jin, *Mao Zedong zhuan, 1949–1976*, pp. 1422–3.

7 Zhai, *Red Flower of China*, p. 68; Gao Shuhua and Cheng Tiejun, *Nei Meng wenge fenglei: Yiwei zaofanpai lingxiu de koushu shi* (The Cultural Revolution in Inner Mongolia: The oral history of a rebel leader), Carle Place, NY: Mingjing chubanshe, 2007, p. 189.

8 Song Bolin, *Hongweibing xingshuailu: Qinghua fuzhong lao hongweibing shouji* (The rise and fall of Red Guards: Diary of an old Red Guard from the Middle School attached to Tsinghua University), Hong Kong: Desai chuban youxian gongsi, 2006, p. 105; Li, *The Private Life of Chairman Mao*, p. 470.

9 Pang and Jin, *Mao Zedong zhuan, 1949–1976*, pp. 1427–30.

10 Chen, *Inside the Cultural Revolution*, pp. 221–3.

11 MacFarquhar and Schoenhals, *Mao's Last Revolution*, p. 90.

12 Liang Heng and Judith Shapiro, *Son of the Revolution*, New York: Alfred A. Knopf, 1983, pp. 46–7.

13 Elizabeth J. Perry, *Challenging the Mandate of Heaven: Social Protest and State Power in China*, Armonk, NY: M. E. Sharpe, 2002, p. 244.

14 Chen, *Inside the Cultural Revolution*, pp. 231–4.

15 Li, *The Private Life of Chairman Mao*, p. 469.

16 Verity Wilson, 'Dress and the Cultural Revolution', in Valerie Steele and John S. Major (eds), *China Chic: East Meets West*, New Haven, CT: Yale University Press, 1999, pp. 167–86; Antonia Finnane, *Changing Clothes in China: Fashion, History, Nation*, New York: Columbia University Press, 2008, pp. 227–56; Chang, *Wild Swans*, p. 390.

17 The quotation comes from Yiching Wu, *The Cultural Revolution at the Margins: Chinese Socialism in Crisis*, Cambridge, MA: Harvard University Press, 2014, pp. 60–1; the percentage is based on Wang Youqin, 'Student Attacks against Teachers: The Revolution of 1966', *Issues and Studies*, 37, no. 2 (March 2001), pp. 29–79.

18 This paragraph and the following also rely on Wang, 'Student Attacks against Teachers'.

19 Wang Nianyi, *Da dongluan de niandai* (The years of great turmoil), Zhengzhou: Henan renmin chubanshe, 1988, p. 74.

20 Ma Bo, *Xue yu tie* (Blood and iron), Beijing: Zhongguo shehui kexue chu-banshe, 1998, p. 304; Bu Weihua, 'Beijing hongweibing yundong dashi ji' (Chronology of the Red Guard movement in Beijing), *Beijing dangshi yanjiu*, no. 84 (1994), p. 57.

21 Among some of the witness accounts of this mass rally are Yang, *Spider Eaters*, pp. 122–3; Zhai, *Red Flower of China*, pp. 84–8; Song, *Hongweibing xing-shuailu*, pp. 117–19.

22 Wang, 'Student Attacks against Teachers'.

23 Song Yongyi, 'The Enduring Legacy of Blood Lineage Theory', *China Rights Forum*, no. 4 (2004), pp. 13–23.

24 Wang, 'Student Attacks against Teachers'.

25 The events surrounding his death remain in doubt, as is so often the case with victims of the Cultural Revolution; see Fu Guangming and Zheng Shi, *Taiping hu de jiyi: Lao She zhi si koushu shilu* (Memories of Taiping Lake: Record of oral testimonies about Lao She's death), Shenzhen: Haitian chubanshe, 2001.

26 Wang Youqin, 'Da "xiao liumang" he Nan Baoshan fuzi zhi si' (Beating 'hooligans' and the death of Nan Baoshan and his son), Chinese Holocaust Memorial.

27 PRO, Letter from John D. I. Boyd to David Wilson, 31 Aug. 1966, FO 371–186982.

28 Zhai, *Red Flower of China*, pp. 96–7; Wen Dayong, *Hongweibing chanhui lu* (A Red Guard repents), Hong Kong: Mingbao chubanshe youxian gongsi, 2000, pp. 74–5; Ma, *Xue yu tie*, pp. 12–13 and 129.

29 PRO, Letter from John D. I. Boyd to David Wilson, 31 Aug. 1966, FO 371–186982; MacFarquhar and Schoenhals, *Mao's Last Revolution*, p. 122.

30 Yu Luowen, 'Beijing Daxing xian can'an diaocha' (Investigation into the killings in Daxing county during the Cultural Revolution) in Song Yongyi, *Wenge datusha* (Mass killings during the Cultural Revolution), Hong Kong: Kaifang zazhi she, 2003, translated as 'Enquête sur la tragédie de Daxing' in Song Yongyi, *Les Massacres de la Révolution Culturelle*, Paris: Gallimard, 2009, pp. 43–66.

31 Wang, *Qingshi nanyin*, p. 6.

32 MacFarquhar and Schoenhals, *Mao's Last Revolution*, p. 120; Zhai, *Red Flower of China*, p. 92.

33 Wang, 'Student Attacks against Teachers'.

Chapter 7: Destroying the Old World

1 Wang, 'Student Attacks against Teachers'.

2 Ibid.; Chen Yinan, *Qingchun wuhen: Yige zaofanpai gongren de shinian wenge* (Scarless youth: A rebel worker's experience of the Cultural Revolution), Hong Kong: Chinese University of Hong Kong Press, 2006, ch. 2; Dong Shengli, 'Guanyu Xi'an hongse kongbudui de koushu huiyi' (Oral reminiscences about the Red Terror teams in Xi'an), *Jiyi*, no. 10 (Dec. 2008), pp. 47–9.

3 Rittenberg, *The Man Who Stayed Behind*, p. 348.

4 PRO, Theo Peters, 'The Cultural Revolution Stage III', 19 Sept. 1966, FO 371–186982; Huang Yanmin, 'Posijiu yundong de fazhan mailuo' (The development of the campaign to destroy the 'four olds'), *Ershiyi shiji*, no. 137 (June 2013), pp. 71–82.

5 Gao, *Born Red*, p. 92.

6 Ling, *The Revenge of Heaven*, pp. 36–8.

7 PRO, K. Godwin, Letter from Shanghai, 29 Aug. 1966, FO 371–186982; Nien Cheng, *Life and Death in Shanghai*, New York: Penguin Books, 2008, pp. 62–3.

8 Lu, *Junbao neibu xiaoxi*, pp. 109–10.

9 Ling, *The Revenge of Heaven*, pp. 46–7.

10 Shanghai, 28 Aug. 1966, B3–2-198, pp. 41–4; Wen Guanzhong, interview, 22 Aug. 2012.

11 Shanghai, 28 Aug. 1966, B3–2-198, pp. 41–4; Shanghai, 29 May and 13 Oct. 1967, B172–3-5, pp. 20–1 and 31–6.

12 Weili Fan, '"Land Mines" and Other Evils', *China Outlook*, 4 Dec. 2013.

13 Ying Shanhong (ed.), *Yanzheng jinghan: Hunan Hengyang 'wenge' shishi* (Historical facts about Hunan's Hengyang), self-published, 2002, pp. 155–7.

14 Zhou Zehao, 'The Anti-Confucian Campaign during the Cultural Revolution, August 1966–January 1967', doctoral dissertation, University of Maryland, 2011, pp. 148 and 178.

15 Shanghai, 24 Dec. 1966, B257–1-4714, pp. 46–9; Shanghai, 20 Oct. 1966, B168–2-89, pp. 27–32.

16 Shanghai, 24 Dec. 1966, B257–1-4714, pp. 46–9; Shanghai, 20 Sept. 1966, B109–2-1158, p. 119; Shanghai, 3 Oct. 1966, B109–2-1159, pp. 132–3; Jiangsu, 4 Sept. 1966, 4007–3-1308; the ultimatum was issued in Beijing, but similar bans were passed in many other cities; see PRO, John D. I. Boyd to David Wilson, 31 Aug. 1966, FO 371–186982. Some of the lists of banned objects and activities published by the Red Guards ran into dozens of pages.

17 Report from the Ministry of Foreign Affairs, 16 Nov. 1974, Shandong, A47–2-247, pp. 144–6.

18 MacFarquhar and Schoenhals, *Mao's Last Revolution*, p. 120.

19 Shanghai, 13 and 17 Oct. 1966, B326–5-531, pp. 1–3 and 18–23.

20 Dikötter, *The Tragedy of Liberation*, p. 151.

21 Rae, *Spider Eaters*, p. 127; PRO, John D. I. Boyd to David Wilson, 31 Aug. 1966, FO 371–186982.

22 Shanghai, 30 Nov. 1966, B326–5-531, pp. 24–6; Shanghai, 26 March 1968, B248–2-41, pp. 12–13; Shanghai, 21 and 26 June 1968, B248–2-54, pp. 1–22.

23 Wen Guanzhong, interview, 22 Aug. 2012.

24 Cheng, *Life and Death in Shanghai*, pp. 70–82 and 105–7.

25 Rae, *Spider Eaters*, p. 126; Kang Zhengguo, *Confessions: An Innocent Life in Communist China*, New York: Norton, 2007, p. 105.

26 Liang and Shapiro, *Son of the Revolution*, p. 72.

27 Chang, *Wild Swans*, p. 394.

28 Examples for Beijing are in Chen, *Inside the Cultural Revolution*, pp. 227–8; Fokkema, *Report from Peking*, p. 20; for Shanghai, see Cheng, *Life and Death in Shanghai*, p. 125.

29 David Tsui, interview, 26 July 2012.

30 Hubei, 27 Feb. 1968, SZ139–6-49, pp. 54–5.

31 Shanghai, 27 March 1980, B1–9-228, pp. 73–6.

32 Ling, *The Revenge of Heaven*, pp. 46–7.

33 Ibid., pp. 52–3; Dong, 'Guanyu Xi'an hongse kongbudui de koushu huiyi', p. 48.

34 Party Disciplinary Committee, Report on Art Stolen by Kang Sheng, 23 July 1979, Shandong, A145–38–93; Zhonggong zhongyang wenxian yanjiushi

(ed.), *Sanzhong quanhui yilai zhongyao wenxian xuanbian* (Selection of important documents from the Third Plenum onwards), Beijing: Renmin chubanshe, 1982, vol. 2.

35 Shanghai, 26 Jan. 1969, B105–4-325, p. 3; Shanghai, 5 Sept. 1972, B105–4-953, pp. 107–8; Shanghai, 29 May 1967, B172–3-5, pp. 20–1.

36 Shanghai, 17 Feb. 1967, B172–3-5.

37 Shanghai, 29 May and 13 Oct. 1967, B172–3-5, pp. 20–1 and 31–6.

38 Hubei, SZ139–6-49, 27 Feb. 1968, pp. 54–5.

39 Cheng, *Life and Death in Shanghai*, pp. 86–7 and 111–27.

40 Yang, *Spider Eaters*, pp. 210–11.

41 Yue Daiyun, *To the Storm: The Odyssey of a Revolutionary Chinese Woman*, Berkeley: University of California Press, 1985, p. 176.

42 Shanghai, 7 Sept. 1969, B246–1-269, pp. 142–7.

43 PRO, 'Report from Shanghai', 29 Aug. 1966, FO 371–186982; MacFarquhar and Schoenhals, *Mao's Last Revolution*, p. 122.

Chapter 8: Mao Cult

1 Jiangsu, 25 Nov. 1966, 4007–3-1287, pp. 1–11.

2 Guangdong, 6 June 1967, 286–1-93, pp. 119–22.

3 Shanghai, 29 Dec. 1966, B123–6-1362, pp. 187–90; Shanghai, 2 Nov. 1966, B134–6-1406, p. 4.

4 Shanghai, 22 Nov. 1968, B123–8-117, pp. 57–8.

5 Shanghai, 9 April 1968, B123–8-117, pp. 51–5.

6 Shanghai, 7 Nov. 1966, B163–2-2192, p. 22.

7 Jiangsu, 26 Aug., 8 and 15 Dec. 1966, 4016–3-119, pp. 1–19; Shanghai, 24 March 1967, B123–8-24, p. 24; Shanghai, 15 May 1967, B168–3-132, pp. 49–50.

8 Shanghai, Report from the Office for Finance and Trade, 21 Sept. 1966, B6–1-130, pp. 195–6; PRO, Goodwin to Wilson, 19 Sept. 1966, FO 371–186982.

9 PRO, Leonard Appleyard to John Benson, 'Manifestations of the Mao Cult', 28 Sept. 1966, FO 371–186983.

10 Louis Barcata, *China in the Throes of the Cultural Revolution: An Eye Witness Report*, New York: Hart Publishing, 1968, p. 48.

11 Shandong, 27 Aug. 1966, A1–1-1010, pp. 183–4.

12 Ministry of Culture, 11 July 1966, Shandong, A1–1-1010, pp. 67–9; Instructions from the Centre, 5 April and 12 July 1967, Nanjing, 5038–2-107, pp. 2 and 58–9.

13 Shanghai, 11 Dec. 1967, B167–3-21, pp. 70–3; Instructions from the Centre, 5 April and 12 July 1967, Nanjing, 5038–2-107, pp. 2 and 58–9.

14 Directive from the Ministry of Trade, 30 Aug. 1966, Hebei, 999–4-761, p. 149.

15 *Chinese Propaganda Posters: From the Collection of Michael Wolf*, Cologne: Taschen, 2003, p. 5.

16 Shanghai, 12 May 1967, B244–2-116, pp. 52–4; Shanghai, 13 April 1968, B244–3-66, pp. 42–5.

17 Shanghai, 3 Aug. 1967, B167–3-17, p. 31.

18 Shanghai, 2 May 1967, B182–2-8, pp. 5–8; Nanjing, 4 Feb. 1967, 5020–2-42, pp. 1–13; Hebei, Directive from Centre, 7 Feb. 1968, 999–4-765, pp. 40–1.

19 Shanghai, 2 May 1967, B182–2-8, pp. 5–8.

20 Shanghai, 7 May and 16 July 1967, B182–2-8, pp. 2–4 and 9–11, see also Shanghai, 10 July 1968, B182–3-66, pp. 30–3.

21 Helen Wang, *Chairman Mao Badges: Symbols and Slogans of the Cultural Revolution*, London: British Museum, 2008; see also Melissa Schrift, *Biography of a Chairman Mao Badge: The Creation and Mass Consumption of a Personality Cult*, New Brunswick, NJ: Rutgers University Press, 2001.

22 Interview with Xu Xiaodi, Hong Kong, 13 March 2013; Wang, *Chairman Mao Badges*, p. 19.

23 Wang, *Chairman Mao Badges*, p. 21.

Chapter 9: Linking Up

1 PRO, K. Godwin, 'Letter from Shanghai', 29 Aug. 1966, FO 371–186982.

2 PRO, Theo Peters, 'Red Guard Activity', 9 Sept. 1966, FO 371–186982.

3 *Renmin ribao*, 1 Sept. 1966; Wang, *Da dongluan de niandai*, p. 77.

4 Zhai, *Red Flower of China*, p. 110; Wang, *Da dongluan de niandai*, p. 77.

5 Ling, *The Revenge of Heaven*, pp. 86–7; Ye, '"Wenge" shiqi Fujian qunzhong zuzhi yanjiu', vol. 1, pp. 56–63.

6 PRO, K. Godwin, 'Letter from Shanghai', 29 Aug. 1966, FO 371–186982; Wang, *Yige hongweibing de riji*, p. 63.

7 PRO, Boyd to Wilson, 'Invasion of Peking', 28 Sept. 1966, FO 371–186982.

8 Wen Guanzhong, interview, 22 Aug. 2012.

9 Gao, *Born Red*, p. 146; Ling, *The Revenge of Heaven*, pp. 111–15.

10 Gao, *Born Red*, p. 116.

11 Ling, *The Revenge of Heaven*, pp. 159–60; Chang, *Wild Swans*, p. 403.

12 Shen Fuxiang, *Zhengrong suiyue: Shoudu gongren zaofanpai huiyilu* (The years of glory: Memories of a rebel worker), Hong Kong: Shidai guoji chuban youxian gongsi, 2010, p. 325; MacFarquhar and Schoenhals, *Mao's Last Revolution*, p. 109.

13 Reports from the People's Congress, 1 and 9 Nov. 1966, Shanghai, B172–5-1085, pp. 15 and 20.

14 Liu Zuneng, *Wo de gushi* (My story), Beijing: Beijing shidai nongchao wenhua fazhan gongsi, 2011, p. 328; Zhou Chenghao, *Wangshi huiyi* (Memories of things past), Beijing: Beijing shidai nongchao wenhua fazhan gongsi, 2011, pp. 154–5; Ling, *The Revenge of Heaven*, p. 163.

15 PRO, Theo Peters, 'Red Guard Activity', 9 Sept. 1966, FO 371–186982; Gao, *Born Red*, p. 119; Ling, *The Revenge of Heaven*, p. 165.

16 Liu, *Wo de gushi*, pp. 329–30; Ling, *The Revenge of Heaven*, pp. 176–7.

17 Liang Xiaosheng, *Yige hongweibing de zibai* (Confessions from a Red Guard), Hong Kong: Tiandi tushu youxian gongsi, 1996, pp. 265–7; David Tsui, interview, 26 July 2012.

18 Chang, *Wild Swans*, p. 413.

19 Howard W. French, 'Hearts Still Scarred 40 Years after China's Upheaval', *New York Times*, 10 June 2006; also Yu Xiguang, *Weibei weigan wang youguo:*

'*Wenhua da geming' shangshu ji* (Humble people do not forget their country: A collection of petitions from the Cultural Revolution), Changsha: Hunan renmin chubanshe, 1989, p. 52.

20 Liu Wenzhong, *Fengyu rensheng lu: Yige canji kuqiu xinsheng ji* (A record of my stormy life), Macau: Aomen chongshi wenhua, 2004, pp. 40 and 65.

21 Ling, *The Revenge of Heaven*, pp. 178–9.

22 Zhou, *Wangshi huiyi*, p. 156; Liang, *Yige hongweibing de zibai*, pp. 272–3.

23 Ling, *The Revenge of Heaven*, pp. 179–80.

24 Guo Faliang, *Guxiang, guren, gushi* (Home town, home people, home stories), Beijing: Beijing shidai nongchao wenhua fazhan gongsi, 2011, p. 348; Liang, *Yige hongweibing de zibai*, pp. 271–2; Li Shihua, *Gongyong de mubei: Yige Zhongguoren de jiating jishi* (A common tombstone: The story of one Chinese family), Carle Place, NY: Mingjing chubanshe, 2008, p. 243.

25 Li, *Gongyong de mubei*, pp. 243–5.

26 Zhai, *Red Flower of China*, pp. 113–14.

27 Wen Guanzhong, interview, 22 Aug. 2012.

28 Report from the Jiangxi Provincial Party Committee, 6 Jan. 1967, Shanghai, B243-2-754, p. 2; an eyewitness account is in Liang and Shapiro, *Son of the Revolution*, pp. 109–10.

29 Liang and Shapiro, *Son of the Revolution*, p. 104; Wong Siu Kuan, 'Why the Cultural Revolution?', *Eastern Horizon*, 6, no. 2 (Feb. 1967), p. 15.

30 Interview with Li Zhengan, born 1922, Chengdu, Sichuan, April 2006; Liu, *Wo de gushi*, p. 330.

31 This section is based on Fan Ka Wai, 'Epidemic Cerebrospinal Meningitis during the Cultural Revolution', *Extrême-Orient, Extrême-Occident*, 37 (Sept. 2014), pp. 197–232.

Chapter 10: Rebels and Royalists

1 PRO, Boyd to Wilson, 'Invasion of Peking', 28 Sept. 1966, FO 371–186982; Wang, *Yige hongweibing de riji*, p. 62; Wang, 'Student Attacks against Teachers'.

2 Song, 'The Enduring Legacy of Blood Lineage Theory', p. 15; see also Andrew G. Walder, 'Tan Lifu: A "Reactionary" Red Guard in Historical Perspective', *China Quarterly*, no. 180 (Dec. 2004), pp. 965–88.

3 Ling, *The Revenge of Heaven*, p. 15.

4 'Zai Mao Zedong sixiang de dalushang qianjin' (Forward on the road on Mao Zedong Thought), *Hongqi*, no. 13, 1 Oct. 1966, pp. 4–6; Ye, '"Wenge" shiqi Fujian qunzhong zuzhi yanjiu', vol. 1, pp. 63–4.

5 Chen Boda, 'Chen Boda zai Zhongyang gongzuo huiyishang de jianghua' (Talk by Chen Boda at a party centre work conference), 16 Oct. 1966, Cultural Revolution Database; Song, 'The Enduring Legacy of Blood Lineage Theory', pp. 17–18.

6 Song, 'The Enduring Legacy of Blood Lineage Theory', pp. 13–23; one should also read Wu, *The Cultural Revolution at the Margins*, ch. 3.

7 Shui Luzhou, *Wenge jianlun* (Short history of the Cultural Revolution), web-based version, ch. 46; Ling, *The Revenge of Heaven*, p. 135; Wang Shengze,

"'Wenge" fengbao zhong de Ye Fei shangjiang' (General Ye Fei during the Cultural Revolution), *Dangshi bolan*, no. 12 (Dec. 2008), pp. 41–6.

8 'Yi Mao zhuxi daibiao de wuchanjieji geming luxian de shengli' (Victory for the Proletarian Revolutionary Line Represented by Chairman Mao), *Hongqi*, no. 14, 1 Nov. 1966, pp. 1–3.

9 Kang, *Confessions*, p. 108.

10 White, *Policies of Chaos*, pp. 180–1.

11 Tiejun Cheng and Mark Selden, 'The Construction of Spatial Hierarchies: China's *hukou* and *danwei* Systems', in Timothy Cheek and Tony Saich (eds), *New Perspectives on State Socialism in China*, Armonk, NY: M. E. Sharpe, 1997, pp. 23–50.

12 Dikötter, *Mao's Great Famine*, pp. 238–9.

13 White, *Policies of Chaos*, p. 180; Christopher Howe, 'Labour Organisation and Incentives in Industry before and after the Cultural Revolution', in Stuart Schram (ed.), *Authority, Participation and Cultural Change in China*, London: Contemporary China Institute, 1973, p. 235.

14 White, *Policies of Chaos*, p. 185; descriptions of daily life among temporary workers appear in Ying Hong, *Daughter of the River: An Autobiography*, New York: Grove Press, 1998.

15 Shanghai, 2, 14 and 17 July 1966, A36-2-757, pp. 7–9, 13–14 and 33; Elizabeth J. Perry and Li Xun, *Proletarian Power: Shanghai in the Cultural Revolution*, Boulder, CO: Westview Press, 2000, p. 31.

16 Shanghai, August 1966, A36-2-757, pp. 103–12.

17 'Yi Mao zhuxi daibiao de wuchanjieji geming luxian de shengli' (Victory for the Proletarian Revolutionary Line Represented by Chairman Mao), *Hongqi*, no. 14, 1 Nov. 1966, pp. 1–3; also Zhou Enlai, 'Zhou Enlai zai buzhang huiyi de baogao zhong guanyu dang'an wenti de jianghua' (Comments by Zhou Enlai on personal dossiers during a ministerial meeting), 19 Nov. 1966, Cultural Revolution Database.

18 Liu Guokai, *A Brief Analysis of the Cultural Revolution*, Armonk, NY: M. E. Sharpe, 1987, pp. 35–6; Chen Yinan, *Qingchun wuhen*, pp. 42–6.

19 Shanghai, 7 Aug. 1975, B127-4-77, pp. 1–5.

20 Liu, *A Brief Analysis of the Cultural Revolution*, pp. 74–6.

21 Report from the Nanjing Municipal Revolutionary Committee, Dec. 1966, Nanjing, 5020-2-8, pp. 111–22.

22 Tan, *The Chinese Factor*, p. 131; 'Jiang Qing Chen Boda yu quanguo hongse laodongzhe zaofan zongtuan daibiao de tanhua' (Jiang Qing and Chen Boda speak to representatives of the All-China Red Worker Rebels General Corps), 26 Dec. 1966, Cultural Revolution Database; Milton and Milton, *The Wind Will Not Subside*, pp. 186–8; Shen, *Zhengrong suiyue*, pp. 330–1.

23 'Jiang Qing Chen Boda yu quanguo hongse laodongzhe zaofan zongtuan daibiao de tanhua' (Jiang Qing and Chen Boda speak to representatives of the All-China Red Worker Rebels General Corps), 26 Dec. 1966, Cultural Revolution Database; 'Yingjie gongkuang qiye wenhua da geming de gao-chao' (Welcoming the upsurge in the Great Cultural Revolution in factories and mines), *Renmin ribao*, 26 Dec. 1966, Cultural Revolution Database;

Wang, *Da dongluan de niandai*, p. 164; on the toast, see also MacFarquhar and Schoenhals, *Mao's Last Revolution*, p. 155.

24 Li Xun, *Da bengkui: Shanghai gongren zaofanpai xingwang shi* (The rise and fall of Shanghai's worker rebels), Taipei: Shibao chubanshe, 1996, and Perry and Li, *Proletarian Power*, pp. 32–4.

25 Jiang, 'The Paris Commune in Shanghai', pp. 255–7; PRO, Letter from Ray W. Whitney, 23 Nov. 1966, FO 371–186984; Wang Rui, '"Anting shijian" de zai renshi he zai yanjiu' (Revisiting the Anting incident), *Ershiyi shiji*, no. 55, 31 Oct. 2006.

26 Jiang, 'The Paris Commune in Shanghai', p. 281, as well as Wu, *The Cultural Revolution at the Margins*, p. 110; see also Gerald Tannebaum, 'How the Workers Took over their Wharves', *Eastern Horizon*, 6, no. 6 (July 1967), pp. 6–17; Raymond F. Wylie, 'Shanghai Dockers in the Cultural Revolution: The Interplay of Political and Economic Issues', in Christopher Howe (ed.), *Shanghai: Revolution and Development in an Asian Metropolis*, Cambridge: Cambridge University Press, 1981, pp. 91–124.

27 Shanghai, Jan. 1966, B250-1-1, pp. 33–8; Report by the People's Congress, 4 Jan. 1967, Shanghai, B248-2-4, pp. 1–3.

28 Nanchu, *Red Sorrow: A Memoir*, New York: Arcade, 2001, p. 29.

Chapter 11: Enter the Army

1 Wang Chenglin, *Chongqing 'zalan gong, jian, fa' qinli ji* (Personal account of the 'smashing of the legal apparatus' in Chongqing), self-published, 2003, pp. 20–40; Fokkema, *Report from Peking*, p. 62.

2 Report from the Centre, 11 Jan. 1967, Hebei, 921–5-3, p. 41; Pang and Jin, *Mao Zedong zhuan, 1949–1976*, p. 1473.

3 Zhang Guanghua, *Zhenshi de huiyi* (Real memories), Beijing shidai nongchao wenhua fazhan gongsi, 2010, p. 232; Liu, *Wo de gushi*, pp. 351–3; see also MacFarquhar and Schoenhals, *Mao's Last Revolution*, pp. 170–1.

4 Pang and Jin, *Mao Zedong zhuan, 1949–1976*, p. 1474; Zhang, *Zhenshi de huiyi*, p. 232.

5 Tan, *The Chinese Factor*, p. 132.

6 Gao, *Zhou Enlai*, pp. 145–7.

7 Pang and Jin, *Mao Zedong zhuan, 1949–1976*, pp. 1474–5; Liu, *A Brief Analysis of the Cultural Revolution*, pp. 59–60.

8 PRO, P. M. Hewitt, 'Letter from Shanghai', 31 Jan. 1967, FCO 21–8.

9 Neale Hunter, *Shanghai Journal: An Eyewitness Account of the Cultural Revolution*, New York: Praeger, 1969, pp. 232–43.

10 PRO, P. M. Hewitt, 'Letter from Shanghai', 14 Feb. 1967, FCO 21–8.

11 Wu, *The Cultural Revolution at the Margins*, p. 129.

12 Ibid., pp. 129–30.

13 PRO, P. J. Weston, 'Letter from Shanghai', 1 March 1967, FCO 21–21.

14 Song Yongyi, 'Chronology of Mass Killings during the Chinese Cultural Revolution (1966–1976)', Online Encyclopedia of Mass Violence, published on 25 August 2011, accessed 23 March 2015.

15 Wu, *The Cultural Revolution at the Margins*, pp. 151–2; see also Wang, *Qingshi nanyin*, p. 142; Chen, *Qingchun wuhen*, pp. 97–108; Yu Xiguang, 'Hunan', *Wenge zaofan duoquan dadian* (Great encyclopedia on rebels and power seizures during the Cultural Revolution), web-based text.

16 Ling, *The Revenge of Heaven*, pp. 254–98; Shui, *Wenge jianlun*, ch. 46.

17 Ding Shu, 'L'Événement du 23 février au Qinghai', in Song, *Les Massacres de la Révolution Culturelle*, pp. 67–88; Liu, *A Brief Analysis of the Cultural Revolution*, p. 61.

18 Pang and Jin, *Mao Zedong zhuan, 1949–1976*, pp. 1480–1; Bu Weihua, *Zalan jiu shijie: Wenhua da geming de dongluan yu haojie* (Smashing the old world: The chaos and catastrophe of the Great Cultural Revolution), Hong Kong: Chinese University of Hong Kong Press, 2008, pp. 447–8.

19 Wang, *Qingshi nanyin*, p. 121.

20 Gao, *Zhou Enlai*, p. 159.

21 Pang and Jin, *Mao Zedong zhuan, 1949–1976*, pp. 1482–3; Bu, *Zalan jiu shijie*, pp. 452–3; Gao, *Zhou Enlai*, p. 160.

22 Gao, *Zhou Enlai*, p. 164.

23 Ding, 'L'Événement du 23 février au Qinghai', pp. 86–7; Xue Tingchen, *Wuhui rensheng* (A life without regrets), Beijing: Beijing shidai nongchao wenhua fazhan gongsi, 2011, pp. 180–93.

24 The policy, in the unwieldy vocabulary of the time, was referred to as the 'three supports and two militaries'; the quotation from Kang Sheng can be found in MacFarquhar and Schoenhals, *Mao's Last Revolution*, p. 160.

25 Zhai, *Red Flower of China*, p. 119.

26 Gao, *Born Red*, pp. 200–2.

27 Fokkema, *Report from Peking*, pp. 79–80.

28 Shanghai, 4, 16 and 21 March 1967, B105-4-58, pp. 1–3, 36–7 and 74–6.

29 MacFarquhar and Schoenhals, *Mao's Last Revolution*, pp. 177–8.

30 'Zhengque de duidai geming xiaojiang', *Renmin ribao*, 2 April 1967; 'Zhongyang junwei shitiao mingling' (Ten-point command from the Military Commission), 6 April 1967, Cultural Revolution Database; one of the earliest and most lucid analyses of the reversal in favour of the rebels is a CIA Intelligence Report, RSS 0028/68, 'Mao's "Cultural Revolution" in 1967: The Struggle to "Seize Power"', 24 May 1968; see also MacFarquhar and Schoenhals, *Mao's Last Revolution*, pp. 181–2.

31 Liu, *A Brief Analysis of the Cultural Revolution*, pp. 68–9; Ling, *The Revenge of Heaven*, p. 307.

32 Wang, *Qingshi nanyin*, pp. 144–7; Zhai, *Red Flower of China*, p. 126; Ling, *The Revenge of Heaven*, pp. 214–15.

33 Gao, *Born Red*, p. 203.

34 Guo, *Guxiang, guren, gushi*, pp. 352–3.

35 Gao, *Zhou Enlai*, p. 166.

36 Ling, *The Revenge of Heaven*, pp. 324–39.

37 Gao, *Born Red*, p. 251.

38 Dikötter, *Mao's Great Famine*, pp. 52 and 299.

39 Chang, *Wild Swans*, p. 435.

40 Interview with Li Zhengan, born 1922, Chengdu, Sichuan, April 2006.

41 Andrew G. Walder, *Fractured Rebellion: The Beijing Red Guard Movement*, Cambridge, MA: Harvard University Press, 2009, p. 252.

Chapter 12: The Arms Race

1 Report by the State Council, June 1967, Guangdong, 235-2-261, pp. 39–41; also Guangdong, 29 May 1967, 235-2-261, pp. 24–8.
2 Shanghai, 20 May 1967, B105-4-57, pp. 25–6; see also Shanghai, 29 May 1967, B246-2-170, p. 14.
3 Shanghai, 18 May 1967, B246-2-177, pp. 37–8.
4 Shanghai, 19 June 1967, B168-3-136, pp. 29–32.
5 Milton and Milton, *The Wind Will Not Subside*, pp. 253–8; Thomas W. Robinson, 'The Wuhan Incident: Local Strife and Provincial Rebellion during the Cultural Revolution', *China Quarterly*, no. 47 (July 1971), pp. 413–38; Zhang, *Zhenshi de huiyi*, pp. 66–9; MacFarquhar and Schoenhals, *Mao's Last Revolution*, pp. 210–13.
6 'Wuchan jieji bixu laolao zhangwo qianggunzi' (The Proletariat Must Take Firm Hold of the Gun), *Hongqi*, 1 Aug. 1967, pp. 43–7; Milton and Milton, *The Wind Will Not Subside*, p. 257; for a different interpretation, see Michael Schoenhals, '"Why Don't We Arm the Left?": Mao's Culpability for the Cultural Revolution's "Great Chaos" of 1967', *China Quarterly*, no. 182 (June 2005), pp. 277–300.
7 Fokkema, *Report from Peking*, pp. 122–3.
8 Lin Biao's Important Speech on 9 August, 9 Aug. 1967, Hubei, SZ1–3–567, pp. 2–8.
9 MacFarquhar and Schoenhals, *Mao's Last Revolution*, pp. 210–13.
10 Perry and Li, *Proletarian Power*, pp. 139–41; Yan and Gao, *Turbulent Decade*, p. 390; Wu, *The Cultural Revolution at the Margins*, p. 139.
11 Shanghai Municipal Revolutionary Committee, Report on the Militia, Sept. 1971, Hebei, 919–3-100, pp. 2–7.
12 Several Decisions by the Centre on the Hunan Issue, 10 Aug. 1967, Hunan, 182-2-52, pp. 1–3.
13 Liang and Shapiro, *Son of the Revolution*, pp. 128–37.
14 Hunan, 9 Sept. and 26 Oct. 1967, 194–1-939, pp. 62–5 and 79–82; Hunan, 4 Oct. 1967, 182–2-52, p. 135.
15 Hunan, 27 June 1967, 194–1-939, pp. 1–3; Hunan, 26 Oct. 1967, 194–1-939, pp. 62–5.
16 Report on Chief Crimes of Wang Feng and Pei Mengfei, 16 Feb. 1969, Gansu, 129–6-33, n.p.; see also Li, *The Private Life of Chairman Mao*, p. 396.
17 Instructions from the Centre, 12 May 1967, Gansu, 129–2-1, pp. 9–12; Note from Zhou Enlai to Lin Biao, 14 May 1967, Gansu, 129–1-1, pp. 13–16.
18 Gansu, 1 Sept. 1967, 129–6-4, pp. 133–4; Gansu, 2 and 8 Sept. 1967, 129–6-4, pp. 136–7 and 148–9.
19 Report on the Cultural Revolution, 2 and 3 Aug. 1967, Gansu, 129–6-1, pp. 80–5; Gansu, 30 Aug. 1967, 129–6-1, p. 2; George Watt, *China 'Spy'*, London: Johnson, 1972, pp. 115–20.

20 Barbara Barnouin and Yu Changgen, *Ten Years of Turbulence: The Chinese Cultural Revolution*, London: Kegan Paul International, 1993, pp. 185–6.

21 Minutes of Kang Sheng and Guan Feng meeting with Hongsansi Delegation, 18 Aug. 1967, Gansu, 129–2-1, pp. 51–66; Rehabilitation of Zhang Tao [alias Sha Tao], 1974, Gansu, 191–12–73, pp. 1–4; see also Wei Xiaolan, '"Wo xin tianzonghui liang": Kang Sheng mishu tan "Sha Tao shijian"' ('I believe the sky will always be clear': Kang Sheng's secretary on the 'Sha Tao case'), *Bainianchao*, no. 9 (Sept. 2007), pp. 52–6.

22 Philip Pan, *Out of Mao's Shadow: The Struggle for the Soul of a New China*, Basingstoke: Picador, 2009, p. 97.

23 *Nanning shi 'wenge' da shijian* (Major events in Nanning during the Cultural Revolution), Nanning: Zhonggong Nanning shiwei zhengdang lingdao xiaozu bangongshi, Aug. 1987, p. 11.

24 'Communists: Closer to a Final Split', *Time*, 17 Feb. 1967, p. 34.

25 Fokkema, *Report from Peking*, pp. 136 and 167.

26 'Hong Kong: Mao-Think v. the Stiff Upper Lip', *Time*, 26 May 1967, p. 36; 'Hong Kong: As Usual', *Time*, 18 Aug. 1967, p. 90; John Cooper, *Colony in Conflict: The Hong Kong Disturbances, May 1967–January 1968*, Hong Kong: Swindon, 1970; Christine Loh, *Underground Front: The Chinese Communist Party in Hong Kong*, Hong Kong: Hong Kong University Press, 2010, pp. 113–14; on the riots, one should also read Gary Cheung, *Hong Kong's Watershed: The 1967 Riots*, Hong Kong: Hong Kong University Press, 2009, and Robert Bickers and Ray Yep (eds), *May Days in Hong Kong: Riot and Emergency in 1967*, Hong Kong: Hong Kong University Press, 2009.

27 Frank Welsh, *A History of Hong Kong*, London: HarperCollins, 1993, pp. 469–70.

28 Gao, *Zhou Enlai*, pp. 169–70; Jin Chongji (ed.), *Zhou Enlai zhuan, 1898–1949* (A biography of Zhou Enlai, 1898–1949), Beijing: Zhongyang wenxian chubanshe, 1989, pp. 1732–4; Barnouin and Yu, *Zhou Enlai*, pp. 236–7.

29 Wang Li, 'Wang Li dui Waijiaobu geming zaofan lianluozhan daibiao Yao Dengshan deng tongzhi de tanhua' (Wang Li speaks to rebel representatives Yao Dengshan and others at the Ministry of Foreign Affairs Liaison Station), 7 Aug. 1967, Cultural Revolution Database; Milton and Milton, *The Wind Will Not Subside*, pp. 267–8; Fokkema, *Report from Peking*, pp. 136–7.

30 Milton and Milton, *The Wind Will Not Subside*, p. 271.

31 The most frequently quoted account comes from Donald C. Hopson, and can be found in PRO, 'The Burning of the British Office in Peking', 8 Sept. 1967, FCO 21–34; Hopson's version was made public in 1991 (see, for instance, Gary Finn, 'Diplomatic "Carry On" in Mob Siege: Public Records 1968', *Independent*, 1 Jan. 1999); this file also contains accounts by other members of the mission; see also Percy Cradock, *Experiences of China*, London: John Murray, 1994, pp. 59–71, and James Hoare, *Embassies in the East: The Story of the British Embassies in Japan, China and Korea from 1859 to the Present*, Richmond: Curzon Press, 1999, pp. 82–6; some of the detail here comes from Tony Blishen, interview, 24 July 2012.

32 Pang and Jin, *Mao Zedong zhuan, 1949–1976*, p. 1503.

Chapter 13: Quenching the Fires

1 MacFarquhar and Schoenhals, *Mao's Last Revolution*, p. 230.
2 Kang Sheng and Jiang Qing, 'Zhongyang shouzhang disanci jiejian Anhui shuangfang daibiaotuan de zhishi' (Talk with Delegates from Both Factions from Anhui), 5 Sept. 1967, Cultural Revolution Database; 'Zhonggong zhongyang guowuyuan zhongyang junwei zhongyang wenge xiaozu guanyu buzhun qiangduo renmin jiefangjun wuqi zhuangbei he gezhong junyong wuzi de mingling' (Order Forbidding the Seizure of Weapons from the People's Liberation Army), 5 Sept. 1967, Cultural Revolution Database; Milton and Milton, *The Wind Will Not Subside*, pp. 285–8.
3 Milton and Milton, *The Wind Will Not Subside*, pp. 292–3.
4 PRO, Donald C. Hopson, 'Letter from Beijing', 7 Oct. 1967, FCO 21–41; Yue, *To the Storm*, p. 225.
5 PRO, Donald C. Hopson, 'Letter from Beijing', 7 Oct. 1967, FCO 21–41; Milton and Milton, *The Wind Will Not Subside*, pp. 295–9.
6 Milton and Milton, *The Wind Will Not Subside*, p. 305.
7 Ling, *The Revenge of Heaven*, pp. 383–4.
8 Chang, *Wild Swans*, p. 469.
9 Kang, *Confessions*, p. 123.
10 Zhai, *Red Flower of China*, pp. 229–30.
11 Song Yongyi, interview, 8 and 13 January 2013.
12 Fang Zifen, interview, 5 Nov. 2013.
13 Liang and Shapiro, *Son of the Revolution*, pp. 153–4.
14 Ibid., pp. 138–43.
15 Tan, *The Chinese Factor*, p. 131.
16 Gao, *Born Red*, pp. 317–18.
17 PRO, Percy Cradock, 'Letter from Peking', 3 June 1968, FCO 21–19.
18 Chang, *Wild Swans*, pp. 520–1.
19 Shanghai, B103-4-1, 11 July 1967, pp. 1–3; Shanghai, 9 Dec. 1969, B98-5-100, pp. 10–11; Shanghai, 1 Aug. 1968, B109-4-80, p. 31; on statues in Shanghai, one should read Jin Dalu, *Feichang yu zhengchang: Shanghai 'wenge' shiqi de shehui bianqian* (The extraordinary and the ordinary: Social change in Shanghai during the Cultural Revolution), Shanghai: Shanghai cishu chubanshe, 2011, vol. 2, pp. 198–228.
20 Shanghai, 13 June 1968, B244-2-110, pp. 71–2.
21 Pang Laikwan, 'The Dialectics of Mao's Images: Monumentalism, Circulation and Power Effects', in Christian Henriot and Yeh Wen-hsin (eds), *Visualising China, 1845–1965: Moving and Still Images in Historical Narratives*, Leiden: Brill, 2013, pp. 419–20.
22 Fang Zifen, interview, 5 Nov. 2013.
23 Xiao Mu, *Fengyu rensheng* (A stormy life), New York: Cozy House Publisher, 2003, pp. 178–83.
24 Guo Jian, Yongyi Song and Yuan Zhou (eds), *The A to Z of the Chinese Cultural Revolution*, Lanham, MD: Scarecrow Press, 2009, p. 334.
25 Guo Xuezhi, *China's Security State: Philosophy, Evolution, and Politics*, Cambridge: Cambridge University Press, 2012, pp. 286–7.

26 Milton and Milton, *The Wind Will Not Subside*, pp. 309–11; Yang Chengwu, 'Dashu teshu weida tongshuai Mao zhuxi de jueda quanwei' (Establish the absolute authority of Mao Zedong Thought in a big way and a special way), *Renmin ribao*, 3 Nov. 1967; Mao Zedong, 'Dui dashu teshu jueda quanwei de tifa deng de piyu' (Comments on establishing the absolute authority of Mao Zedong Thought in a big way and a special way), 17 Dec. 1967, Cultural Revolution Database; Zhou Enlai, Kang Sheng and Jiang Qing, 'Zhongyang shouzhang jiejian Sichuan sheng gechou xiaozu lingdao chengyuan de zhishi' (Speech to delegates from Sichuan), 15 March 1968, and 'Zhongyang shouzhang jiejian Zhejiang sheng fujing daibiaotuan shi de zhongyao jianghua' (Speech to delegates from Zhejiang), 18 March 1968, both in the Cultural Revolution Database.

27 Lin Biao, 'Zai jundui ganbu dahuishang de jianghua' (Speech at a meeting of military cadres), 24 March 1968; Zhou Enlai, Jiang Qing and Chen Boda, 'Zhongyang shouzhang zai jiejian jundui ganbu huishang de jianghua' (Speeches by central leaders at a meeting of military cadres), 24 March 1968, Cultural Revolution Database; CIA Intelligence Report, 'Mao's "Cultural Revolution" III: The Purge of the P.L.A. and the Stardom of Madame Mao', June 1968, pp. 42–4.

28 Gao, *Born Red*, p. 334.

29 Patrick Fuliang Shan, 'Becoming Loyal: General Xu Shiyou and Maoist Regimentation', *American Journal of Chinese Studies*, 18, no. 2 (Fall 2011), pp. 133–50; Dong Guoqiang and Andrew G. Walder, 'From Truce to Dictatorship: Creating a Revolutionary Committee in Jiangsu', *China Journal*, no. 68 (July 2012), pp. 4–5.

30 Shen Xiaoyun, 'The Revolutionary Committee Grows out of the Barrel of a Gun during the Great Proletarian Cultural Revolution: The Unknown Truth of "Armed Conflict" in Guangxi', *Modern China Studies*, 20, no. 1 (2013), pp. 141–82.

31 Ibid.

32 *Nanning shi 'wenge' da shijian* (Major events in Nanning during the Cultural Revolution), Nanning: Zhonggong Nanning shiwei zhengdang lingdao xiaozu bangongshi, 1987, pp. 30–2.

33 Kuo Yao-hua, *Free China Review*, 18, no. 8 (1 Aug. 1968), p. 275.

34 Xu Yong, 'Wei Guoqing extermine la faction du "22 Avril"', in Song Yongyi, *Les Massacres de la Révolution Culturelle*, Paris: Gallimard, 2009, pp. 255–6; Zheng Yi, *Scarlet Memorial: Tales of Cannibalism in Modern China*, Boulder, CO: Westview Press, 1996.

35 Zheng, *Scarlet Memorial*, pp. 73–5, 84–6; see also *Wuxuan shi 'wenge' da shijian* (Major events in Wuxuan during the Cultural Revolution), 1987, Nanning: Zhonggong Wuxuan shiwei zhengdang lingdao xiaozu bangongshi, p. 316.

36 *Qinghua daxue zhi* (Annals of Tsinghua University), Beijing: Qinghua daxue chubanshe, 2001, pp. 758–9; Milton and Milton, *The Wind Will Not Subside*, p. 319.

37 Zhou Enlai, Chen Boda and Kang Sheng, 'Zhongyang shouzhang jiejian Guangxi laijing xuexi de liangpai qunzhong zuzhi bufen tongzhi he jundui

bufen ganbu shi de zhishi' (Meeting with representatives of both factions from Guangxi), 25 July 1968, Cultural Revolution Database.

38 Mao Zedong, 'Zhaojian shoudou hongdaihui "wuda lingxiu" shi de tanhua' (Talk with Red Guard representatives), 28 July 1968, Cultural Revolution Database.

39 Cheng, *Life and Death in Shanghai*, p. 206.

40 Milton and Milton, *The Wind Will Not Subside*, pp. 319 and 330.

41 George Y. Tang, *Liangdairen de xuanze* (The choices of two generations), Beijing: Beijing shidai nongchao wenhua fazhan gongsi, 2011, p. 126; on mango mania, see Michael Dutton, 'Mango Mao: Infections of the Sacred', *Public Culture*, 16, no. 2 (spring 2004), pp. 161–87; Alice de Jong, 'The Strange Story of Chairman Mao's Wonderful Gift', *Reminiscences and Ruminations: China Information Anniversary Supplement*, 9, no. 1 (Summer 1994), pp. 48–54; Alfreda Murck, 'Golden Mangoes: The Life Cycle of a Cultural Revolution Symbol', *Archives of Asian Art*, 57 (2007), pp. 1–21; Alfreda Murck (ed.), *Mao's Golden Mangoes and the Cultural Revolution*, Zurich: Scheidegger & Spiess, 2013.

42 Zhou Enlai, 'Zhou Enlai zai qingzhu quanguo shengshi zizhiqu chengli geming weiyuanhui shang de jianghua' (Congratulatory speech on the establishment of revolutionary committees), 7 Sept. 1968, Cultural Revolution Database; 'Zhongyang zhuan'an shencha xiaozu "guanyu pantu, neijian, gongzei Liu Shaoqi zuixing de shencha baogao" ji "pantu, neijian, gongzei Liu Shaoqi zuizheng"' (Report on Liu Shaoqi by the Central Case Examination Group), 18 Oct. 1968, Cultural Revolution Database; with a few minor changes, I have used the translation in Milton and Milton, *The Wind Will Not Subside*, pp. 335–9.

Chapter 14: Cleansing the Ranks

1 Gansu, 2 March 1968, 129-1-40, pp. 10–13; 'Zhonggong zhongyang, guowuyuan, zhongyang junwei, zhongyang "wenge" zhuanfa Heilongjiang sheng geming weiyuanhui "guanyu shenwa pantu gongzuo qingkuang de baogao" de pishi ji fujian' (Report on digging out renegades from Heilongjiang province), 5 Feb. 1968, Cultural Revolution Database.

2 Milton and Milton, *The Wind Will Not Subside*, p. 315; the original is in Zhou Enlai, Kang Sheng and Jiang Qing, 'Zhongyang shouzhang jiejian Zhejiang sheng fujing daibiaotuan shi de zhongyao jianghua' (Speech to Delegates from Zhejiang), 18 March 1968, Cultural Revolution Database.

3 Mao Zedong, 'Guanyu "Beijing Xinhua yinshuachang junguanhui fadong qunzhong kaizhan duidi douzheng de jingyan" de pishi' (Comments on report on the uncovering of renegades in the Beijing New China Printing Plant), 25 May 1968, Cultural Revolution Database.

4 Bu, *Zalan jiu shijie*, p. 677.

5 Frank Dikötter, *China before Mao: The Age of Openness*, Berkeley: University of California Press, 2008, pp. 78–80; Wang Youqin, 'The Second Wave of Violent Persecution of Teachers: The Revolution of 1968', Presented at the

35th International Congress of Asian and North African Studies, Budapest, 7–12 July 1997.

6 Cheng, *Life and Death in Shanghai*, pp. 251, 254 and 259.

7 Bu, *Zalan jiu shijie*, p. 677.

8 Yue, *To the Storm*, pp. 240–1.

9 Ibid., pp. 161–2; Wang, 'The Second Wave of Violent Persecution of Teachers'.

10 Bu, *Zalan jiu shijie*, pp. 677–8.

11 Hebei, 7 April 1969, 919–1-288, pp. 142–3; Report to Xie Fuzhi, 1969, Hebei, 919–1-274.

12 Hebei, 7 Jan. 1969, 919–1-288, pp. 30–1; Hebei, 27 Jan. 1969, 919–1-288, pp. 46–7; Report on Policy Implementation at the Baigezhuang Farming Area, 10 July 1974, Hebei, 925–1-51, pp. 27–31.

13 Hebei, 28 May 1969, 919–1-290, pp. 42–3; Hebei, 27 Dec. 1969, 919–1-295, p. 57.

14 Ding Shu, 'Wenge zhong de "qingli jieji duiwu" yundong' (The campaign to cleanse the class ranks during the Cultural Revolution), *Huaxia wenzhai zeng-kan*, no. 244, 14 Dec. 2004; Jonathan Unger, 'The Cultural Revolution at the Grass Roots', *China Journal*, no. 57 (Jan. 2007), p. 113.

15 'Kang Sheng Xie Fuzhi jiejian Kunming junqu he Yunnan qunzhong daibiao shi de jianghua' (Talks by Kang Sheng and Xie Fuzhi at a meeting with the Kunming Military Region and representatives of the masses from Yunnan), 21 Jan. 1968, Cultural Revolution Database; *Dangdai Yunnan dashi jiyao* (Chronology of major events in contemporary Yunnan), Kunming: Dangdai Zhongguo chubanshe, 2007, pp. 285–9.

16 Documents on the North China Conference, sessions of 12, 17, 18 June and 24 July 1966, Inner Mongolia, 11–2-555, 23 Jan. 1967; Qi Zhi (ed.), *Nei Menggu wenge shiji* (True record of the Cultural Revolution in Inner Mongolia), Hong Kong: Tianxingjian chubanshe, 2010, p. 70.

17 Tumen and Zhu Dongli, *Kang Sheng yu 'Neirendang' yuan'an* (Kang Sheng and the unjust case of the 'Inner Party'), Beijing: Zhonggong zhongyang dangxiao chubanshe, 1995, pp. 202–3.

18 Ba Yantai, *Nei Menggu wasu zainan shilu* (True record of the cleansing of the class ranks in Inner Mongolia), Hohhot: Nei Menggu renquan xinxi zhongxin, 1999, self-published; the term 'genocide' is used by Yang Haiying, 'Yi "routi de xiaomie" shixian "minzu de xiaowang"' (Realising ethnic cleansing by physical extermination), *Minzu xuebao*, no. 29 (Dec. 2009), pp. 1–23; see also Gao and Cheng, *Nei Meng wenge fenglei*; the dismemberment of the province was reversed in 1979.

Chapter 15: Up the Mountains, Down to the Villages

1 Zhou Enlai, 'Zhou Enlai zai qingzhu quanguo shengshi zizhiqu chengli geming weiyuanhui de dahuishang de jianghua' (Congratulatory speech on the establishment of revolutionary committees), 7 Sept. 1968, Cultural Revolution Database.

2   *Renmin ribao*, 22 Dec. 1968; on the exile of young students, often referred to as 'sent-down youth' or even 'rusticated youth' in the somewhat esoteric language of sinology, one should read Michel Bonnin, *The Lost Generation: The Rustication of China's Educated Youth (1968–1980)*, Hong Kong: Chinese University of Hong Kong Press, 2013; Pan Yihong, *Tempered in the Revolutionary Furnace: China's Youth in the Rustication Movement*, Lanham, MD: Lexington Books, 2009; Ding Yizhuang, *Zhongguo zhiqing shi: Chulan, 1953–1968* (A history of China's sent-down youth: The first waves, 1953–1968), Beijing: Dangdai Zhongguo chubanshe, 2009; Liu Xiaomeng, *Zhongguo zhiqing shi: Dachao, 1966–1980* (A history of China's sent-down youth: The big wave, 1966–1980), Beijing: Zhongguo shehui kexue chubanshe, 1998; a detailed case-study can be found in Zhu Zhenghui and Jin Guangyao (eds), *Zhiqing buluo: Huangshang jiaoxia de 10,000 ge Shanghai ren* (The tribe of educated youth: The lives of 10,000 students from Shanghai in Huangshan), Shanghai: Shanghai guji chubanshe, 2004.

3   Roger Garside, interview, 19 July 2012; Zhai, *Red Flower of China*, p. 156.

4   Gao, *Born Red*, p. 353.

5   Yang, *Spider Eaters*, p. 159.

6   Xu Xiaodi, interview, 13 March 2013.

7   Hunan, 25 and 30 June 1968; 5 and 9 July 1968, 182-2-44, pp. 2–3, 6, 9 and 41–5.

8   Yang, *Spider Eaters*, pp. 174–9.

9   Hubei, 30 May 1973, SZ139-6-510, pp. 187–92; Hunan, 7 Sept. 1972, 182-2-52, pp. 52–5.

10 Dikötter, *Mao's Great Famine*, pp. 174–5; Liang and Shapiro, *Son of the Revolution*, p. 162; Hubei, 19 Aug. 1973, SZ139-6-510, pp. 199–201.

11 Liang and Shapiro, *Son of the Revolution*, p. 23; Xiao, *Fengyu rensheng*, pp. 275–6.

12 To be precise, the amount of coal sold to the local population went down to 5.5 million tonnes in 1968 from 8 million tonnes in 1966; Shandong, 19 March 1969, A47-2-87, p. 157.

13 Report on Market Conditions, Nanjing, 18 March 1966, 5003-3-1139, pp. 78–86.

14 Ling, *The Revenge of Heaven*, pp. 149–50; Shandong, 17 April 1966, A1-2-1356, pp. 107–9; Report from the Bureau for Grain, 11 March 1967, Shandong, A131-2-853, p. 16.

15 Wen Guanzhong, interview, 22 Aug. 2012.

16 Hunan, 12 March 1971, 182-2-50, pp. 14–19.

17 Zhai, *Red Flower of China*, p. 173.

18 Nanchu, *Red Sorrow*, p. 91; Shanghai, March 1973, B228-2-335, pp. 65–70.

19 Shanghai, March 1973, B228-2-335, pp. 65–70; Shanghai, 5 July 1969, B228-2-224, p. 77, and Shanghai, 1 July 1969, B228-2-223, p. 160.

20 Hunan, 8 Sept. 1972, 182-2-52, p. 154; Liu, *Zhongguo zhiqing shi*, pp. 320–1.

21 Hunan, 23 Oct. 1970, 182-2-50, pp. 116–17; Hunan, 24 Feb. 1971, 182-2-50, pp. 95–7.

22 Yang, *Spider Eaters*, p. 181; Hunan, 23 Oct. 1970, 182-2-50, pp. 116–17; Hou Yonglu, *Nongmin riji: Yige nongmin de shengcun shilu* (Diary of a farmer), Beijing: Zhongguo qingnian chubanshe, 2006, p. 164.

23 Hubei, 30 May 1973, SZ139–6-510, pp. 187–92; see also Hubei, 15 Dec. 1969 and 7 April 1970, SZ139–2-94, n.p.

24 Hubei, 27 May 1970, SZ139–2-303, n.p.; Hubei, 19 Aug. 1973, SZ139–6-510, pp. 199–201.

25 Hunan, Dec. 1971, 182–2-50, p. 148.

26 Li Qinglin is the subject of a wonderful article by Elya J. Zhang, 'To Be Somebody: Li Qinglin, Run-of-the-Mill Cultural Revolution Showstopper', in Joseph W. Esherick, Paul G. Pickowicz and Andrew Walder (eds), *The Chinese Cultural Revolution as History*, Stanford: Stanford University Press, 2006, pp. 211–39.

27 Hubei, 19 Aug. 1973, SZ139–6-510, pp. 199–201.

28 Hubei, Minutes of Meeting on 26 June 1973, SZ139–6-510, pp. 142–9; Fujian Provincial Archives, 1973, C157–1-10, quoted in Zhang, 'To Be Somebody', p. 219; Hubei, 9 March 1974, SZ139–6-589, pp. 62–75.

29 See Dikötter, *Mao's Great Famine*, chapter entitled 'Exodus'.

30 Zhou Enlai, 'Zhou Enlai zai qingzhu quanguo shengshi zizhiqu chengli geming weiyuanhui shang de jianghua' (Congratulatory speech on the establishment of revolutionary committees), 7 Sept. 1968, Cultural Revolution Database.

31 Shanghai, 7 Aug. 1975, B127–4-77, p. 1; Hunan, 12 March 1971, 182–2-50, pp. 14–19; on kilos of grain as a measure of calories, see Jean C. Oi, *State and Peasant in Contemporary China: The Political Economy of Village Government*, Berkeley: University of California Press, 1989, pp. 48–9.

32 Hunan, 27 Aug. 1971, 182–2-50, pp. 35–41.

33 Hebei, 19 Nov. 1969, 919–1-294, pp. 11–12.

34 Shanghai, 23 Jan. 1970, B228–2-240, pp. 124–6; Shanghai, 1 April 1968, B227–2-39, pp. 1–5.

35 Mao Zedong, 'Dui Liuhe "wuqi" ganxiao wei jiguan geminghua zouchu tiao xinlu" yiwen de piyu' (Comment on the Liuhe May Seventh School for Cadres), 30 Sept. 1968, Cultural Revolution Database; 'Liuhe "wuqi" ganxiao wei jiguan geminghua tigongle xin de jingyan', *Renmin ribao*, 5 Oct. 1968.

36 Yue, *To the Storm*, pp. 259–60.

37 Gansu, March 1970, 129–4-202, p. 73; Gansu, 3 March 1972, 129–6-83, pp. 11–12; Gansu, 1969, 129–4-33, pp. 38–40; Hebei, 25 Oct. 1967, 919–1-147, pp. 1–3.

Chapter 16: Preparing for War

1 See the memoirs of Vitaly Bubenin, *Krovavyĭ Sneg Damanskogo: Sobytiia 1966–1969 gg.*, Moscow: Granitsa, 2004.

2 Yang Kuisong, 'The Sino-Soviet Border Clash of 1969: From Zhenbao Island to Sino-American Rapprochement', *Cold War History*, 1, no. 1 (Aug. 2000), pp. 21–52; see also Lyle J. Goldstein, 'Return to Zhenbao Island: Who Started Shooting and Why It Matters', *China Quarterly*, no. 168 (Dec. 2001), pp. 985–97.

3 'Mao Zedong's Speech at the First Plenary Session of the CCP's Ninth Central Committee', 28 April 1969, History and Public Policy Program Digital Archive, Wilson Center, Washington DC.

4 A detailed analysis of the Ninth Party Congress can be found in MacFarquhar and Schoenhals, *Mao's Last Revolution*, pp. 285–301.

5 MacFarquhar and Schoenhals, *Mao's Last Revolution*, p. 301.

6 Christian F. Ostermann, 'East German Documents on the Border Conflict, 1969', *Cold War International History Project Bulletin*, nos 6–7 (Winter 1995), p. 187; Harvey W. Nelsen, *Power and Insecurity: Beijing, Moscow and Washington, 1949–1988*, Boulder, CO: Lynne Rienner, 1989, pp. 72–3; Yang, 'The Sino-Soviet Border Clash of 1969', pp. 32–3; see also Lorenz Lüthi, 'The Vietnam War and China's Third-Line Defense Planning before the Cultural Revolution, 1964–1966', *Journal of Cold War Studies*, 10, no. 1 (Winter 2008), pp. 26–51.

7 Dikötter, *Mao's Great Famine*, p. 239.

8 'The CCP Central Committee's Order for General Mobilization in Border Provinces and Regions', 28 Aug. 1969, *Cold War International History Project Bulletin*, no. 11 (Winter 1998), pp. 168–9.

9 PRO, Roger Garside, 'War Preparations: Peking', 30 Dec. 1969, FCO 21–483; 'China: War Scare', 28 Nov. 1969.

10 PRO, Roger Garside, 'War Preparations: Shanghai', 2 Dec. 1969, FCO 21–483; George Walden, 'Preparations against War', 27 Jan. 1970, FCO 21–683.

11 PRO, Roger Garside, 'War Preparations: Shanghai', 2 Dec. 1969, FCO 21–483.

12 Hebei, 6, 26 and 30 Dec. 1969, 919–1–295, pp. 27–8, 72, 114–15; Hebei, 26 Dec. 1969, 919–1–294, p. 124.

13 Zhai, *Red Flower of China*, p. 199.

14 PRO, 'Shanghai', 4 Nov. 1969, FCO 21–513; Roger Garside, 'War Preparations: Peking', 30 Dec. 1969, FCO 21–483; George Walden, 'Preparations against War', 27 Jan. 1970, FCO 21–683.

15 Shanghai, List of Quotations by Mao Zedong on Air Raids Dating from 1964 to 1974, B105–9-638, pp. 15–16.

16 PRO, J. N. Allan, 'Air Raid Shelters, Tunnels', November 1970, FCO 21–683.

17 Craig S. Smith, 'Mao's Buried Past: A Strange, Subterranean City', *New York Times*, 26 Nov. 2001.

18 For examples, see Shanghai, 25 Jan. and 14 Sept. 1971, B120–3-23, pp. 32 and 43.

19 Shanghai, 28 May 1971, B120–3-23, pp. 1–2; Shanghai, 30 May 1970, B120–3-15, pp. 3–4; on the building of shelters in Shanghai, one should read Jin, *Feichang yu zhengchang*, vol. 2, pp. 357–99.

20 PRO, 'Underground construction in Peking', 25 Aug. 1970, FCO 21–683; Shanghai, 29 August 1970, B120–2-7, pp. 1–11; 3 March 1973, B120–2-26, pp. 45–6.

21 Shanghai, 14 Sept. 1971, B120–3-23, p. 32; 5 Dec. 1975, B120–3-63, pp. 3–4.

22 Smith, 'Mao's Buried Past'; on Shanghai, see 3 March 1973, B120-2-26, pp. 45–6; Hebei, 19 Nov. 1969, 919–1-294, pp. 11–12.

23 Shandong, 25 Nov. 1971, A1–8-15, pp. 47–8; Zhang Zhong, Talk on Anti Air Raid Shelters, 20 Sept. 1970, Gansu, 91–7-50, p. 3; Zhai, *Red Flower of China*, pp. 198–200.

24 PRO, J. N. Allan, 'Air Raid Shelters, Tunnels', November 1970, FCO 21–683.

25 Walter S. Dunn, *The Soviet Economy and the Red Army, 1930–1945*, Westport, CT: Greenwood, 1995, pp. 30–7.

26 Yang, 'The Sino-Soviet Border Clash of 1969', p. 24.

27 The best account of the Third Front appears in Chen Donglin, *Sanxian jianshe: Beizhan shiqi de xibu kaifa* (Building the Third Front: Opening up the West during the era of war preparation), Beijing: Zhonggong zhongyang dangxiao chubanshe, 2003.

28 Bryan Tilt, *The Struggle for Sustainability in Rural China: Environmental Values and Civil Society*, New York: Columbia University Press, 2009, pp. 23–4, first quotation with a minor stylistic change.

29 Judith Shapiro, *Mao's War against Nature: Politics and the Environment in Revolutionary China*, New York: Cambridge University Press, 2001, p. 152; Barry Naughton, 'The Third Front: Defence Industrialization in the Chinese Interior', *China Quarterly*, no. 115 (Sept. 1988), pp. 351–86.

30 Naughton, 'The Third Front', pp. 359–60.

31 Hubei, SZ81–4-12, 25 April and 9 June 1970, pp. 1–3 and 19–24.

32 Ibid.

33 Hebei, 19 Sept. 1972, 999–7-41, pp. 76–82.

34 Naughton, 'The Third Front', pp. 378–82; White, *Policies of Chaos*, p. 184.

Chapter 17: Learning from Dazhai

1 Directive about Learning from Dazhai, 13 Jan. 1968, Zhejiang, J116–25–60, pp. 20–9.

2 Nanjing shi dang'anguan (eds), *Nanjing wenhua da geming da shiji chugao* (Draft chronology of major events during the Cultural Revolution in Nanjing), Nanjing: Nanjing shi dang'anguan, 1985, date of 18 Aug. 1966; see also the attack on households with private cows six weeks earlier, in Nanjing, 27 June 1966, 5003–3-1139, pp. 21–4.

3 Gao, *Born Red*, pp. 126–7.

4 Order from the Centre, 14 Sept. 1966, Nanjing, 4003–1-298, p. 124; Zhou Enlai and Wang Renzhong, 'Zhou Enlai Wang Renzhong dui Beijing shi hongweibing daibiao de jianghua' (Meeting with a delegation of Red Guards from Beijing), 1 Sept. 1966, Cultural Revolution Database.

5 Liang and Shapiro, *Son of the Revolution*, pp. 98–9.

6 On the Daoxian massacre, one should read Su Yang, *Collective Killings in Rural China during the Cultural Revolution*, Cambridge: Cambridge University Press, 2011, as well as Tan Hecheng, *Xue de shenhua: Gongyuan 1967 nian Hunan Daoxian wenge da tusha jishi* (A bloody tale: A historical account of

the Cultural Revolution massacre of 1967 in Daoxian, Hunan), Hong Kong: Tianxingjian chubanshe, 2010.

7   Shaanxi, 215-1-1363, 8 April and 21 Aug. 1967, pp. 67–8 and 81–3.

8   Shaanxi, 215-1-1363, 13 Jan. 1968, p. 190.

9   Shaanxi, 215-1-1363, 3 Dec. 1967 and 13 Jan. 1968, pp. 190 and 236–40.

10 Report by the Guangzhou Military Committee, 20 Dec. 1967, Shaanxi, 215-1-1363, pp. 146–52.

11 Shaanxi, 21 May 1967, 194-1-1274, pp. 1–22; Shaanxi, 25 April 1967, 194-1-1283, p. 86.

12 Report from the Bureau for Forestry, 6 April 1967, Gansu, 129-4-62, pp. 112–17; Jiangsu, 21 Aug. 1967, 4028-3-1611, pp. 28–9; Shanxi Revolutionary Committee, 'Disanhao tonggao' (Number three circular), 7 Feb. 1967, Cultural Revolution Database; *Renmin ribao*, 11 Feb. 1967, also in Hebei, 11 Feb. 1967, 921-5-3, pp. 42–3; Shaanxi, 31 March and 15 April 1967, 194-1-1283, pp. 33 and 70.

13 Dikötter, *Mao's Great Famine*, p. 88.

14 Zhou Enlai Meets Delegates of Fourteen Provinces and Cities at the Conference on Grain and Oil Procurements, 3 May 1967, Shandong, A131-2-851, pp. 6–10; see also Directives on the Economy from the Centre, 1 and 13 July 1967, Shandong, A131-2-853, pp. 62–3 and 66–7; Zhou Enlai Talks at the National Conference on Grain, 28 Oct. 1967, Shandong, A131-2-851, pp. 51–4.

15 On Zhejiang, see Keith Forster, *Rebellion and Factionalism in a Chinese Province: Zhejiang, 1966–1976*, Armonk, NY: M. E. Sharpe, 1990.

16 Directive from the Military, 13 Jan. 1968, Zhejiang, J116-25-60, pp. 20–9.

17 Zhejiang, 8 Sept. 1971, J116-25-159, pp. 160–2; Zhejiang, 17 March 1972, J116-25-250, pp. 73–6.

18 Gansu, 1 Sept. 1969, 129-4-179, pp. 95–104.

19 Ibid.; Liang and Shapiro, *Son of the Revolution*, p. 182.

20 Hebei, 5 Sept. 1974, 925-1-51, pp. 69–72; Hebei, 10 Feb., 5 and 11 March 1972, 925-1-19, pp. 44, 83–4 and 93–6; Hebei, 6 April 1971, 999-7-20, pp. 83–5.

21 Shapiro, *Mao's War against Nature*, p. 101; on Dazhai, see also Song Liansheng, *Nongye xue Dazhai shimo* (The history of the Learn from Dazhai campaign), Wuhan: Hubei renmin chubanshe, 2005.

22 Shapiro, *Mao's War against Nature*, p. 101.

23 Zhai, *Red Flower of China*, p. 190; Shapiro, *Mao's War against Nature*, p. 108.

24 Zhang Xianliang, *Half of Man is Woman*, quoted in Shapiro, *Mao's War against Nature*, p. 108.

25 Hebei, 18 Aug. 1970, 940-10-1, pp. 54–8; Shapiro, *Mao's War against Nature*, p. 113.

26 Shapiro, *Mao's War against Nature*, pp. 116–36.

27 Nanchu, *Red Sorrow*, pp. 97–100.

28 Sun Qinghe, *Shengsi yitiao lu* (The road between life and death), Beijing: Beijing shidai nongchao wenhua fazhan gongsi, 2012, p. 42.

29 Shapiro, *Mao's War against Nature*, p. 137.

Chapter 18: More Purges

1 Milton and Milton, *The Wind Will Not Subside*, p. 256.
2 MacFarquhar and Schoenhals, *Mao's Last Revolution*, p. 233.
3 'Zhou Enlai jianghua' (Speech by Zhou Enlai), 24 Jan. 1970, Cultural Revolution Database; 'Zhonggong zhongyang guanyu qingcha "wuyao-liu" fangeming yinmou jituan de tongzhi' (Notice on the May Sixteenth Conspiracy), 27 March 1970, Cultural Revolution Database; Barnouin and Yu, *Ten Years of Turbulence*, p. 198; Ding Qun, 'Yuanyu biandi de Jiangsu qingcha "Wu Yao Liu" yundong' (The campaign against the May Sixteenth Elements in Jiangsu), *Wenshi jinghua*, no. 1 (2009), pp. 24–31.
4 Shan, 'Becoming Loyal', pp. 142–3, gives 270,000 victims, a number repeated in other books on the Cultural Revolution, but a more reliable source is Ding Qun, who quotes over 26,100 victims; see Ding, 'Yuanyu biandi de Jiangsu qingcha "Wu Yao Liu" yundong', p. 30.
5 Thurston, *Enemies of the People*, pp. 202–3.
6 Ding, 'Yuanyu biandi de Jiangsu qingcha "Wu Yao Liu" yundong', p. 29; Thurston, *Enemies of the People*, p. 144.
7 Guo, Song and Zhou (eds), *The A to Z of the Chinese Cultural Revolution*, p. xxxi.
8 Yan, *Turbulent Decade*, pp. 159–63.
9 Huang Zheng, *Liu Shaoqi de zuihou suiyue 1966–1969* (Liu Shaoqi's last years, 1966–1969), Beijing: Jiuzhou chubanshe, 2012; see also Ding Shu, 'Fengyu rupan de suiyue: 1970 nian yida sanfan yundong jishi' (Turbulent years: The One Strike and Three Antis campaign of 1970), *Huanghuagang zazhi*, no. 5 (March 2003), pp. 69–80.
10 Hubei, 25 Nov. 1970, SZ139-2-290, n.p. (to be precise, 173,000 people were implicated in the One Strike campaign, and 87,000 of these were prosecuted; 434,000 people were implicated in the Three Antis campaign, and 207,000 of these were prosecuted); Hubei, 17 Sept. 1971, SZ139-2-114, n.p. (the 107,000 include 2,000 May Sixteenth Elements and 15,000 followers of the *Yangtze Tribune*); a different set of numbers appears in Hubei, SZ139-2-290, p. 98, giving more than 99,000 confirmed cases of counter-revolutionary activity falling under the One Strike campaign and over 330,000 confirmed cases of corruption between February 1970 and April 1971.
11 Wang Shaoguang, *Failure of Charisma: The Cultural Revolution in Wuhan*, Oxford: Oxford University Press, 1995, pp. 219–20; the figure of 15,000 is in Hubei, 17 Sept. 1971, SZ139-2-114, n.p.
12 Hubei, 16 Feb. and 11 April 1970, SZ139-2-303, n.p.; Hubei, 17 Sept. 1971, SZ139-2-114, n.p.
13 Hubei, 25 Sept. 1971, SZ139-2-316, n.p.
14 Hubei, 13 March 1970, SZ139-2-303, n.p.
15 Gansu, 6 May 1970, 129-6-45, pp. 46–7; Gansu, 17 Oct. 1970, 129-6-48, pp. 105–20; Gansu, 3 March 1970, 129-6-39, p. 21.
16 Gansu, 17 Oct. 1970, 129-6-48, pp. 105–20; Gansu, 18 May 1970, 129-6-46, p. 1.

17 Gansu, 6 May 1970, 129–6-45, pp. 46–7; Gansu, 24 March 1970, 129–6-41, pp. 44–5; Gansu, 4 March 1970, 129–6-39, pp. 47–50.

18 Gansu, 11 May 1970, 129–6-45, pp. 119–22; Gansu, 4 March 1970, 129–6-39, pp. 47–50; Gansu, 30 Sept. 1970, 129–6-48, pp. 70–2.

19 Gansu, 6 May 1970, 129–6-45, pp. 46–7; Gansu, 28 Feb. 1970, 129–6-39, pp. 10–14.

20 Gansu, 28 Feb. 1970, 129–6-39, pp. 10–14; Gansu, March 1970, 129–4-202, p. 73; Lanzhou broadcast, 15 Oct. 1969, *BBC Summary of World Broadcasts* FE/3212, with a few stylistic changes, quoted in Dennis Woodward, 'Rural Campaigns: Continuity and Change in the Chinese Countryside – The Early Post-Cultural Revolution Experience (1969–1972)', *Australian Journal of Chinese Affairs*, no. 6 (July 1981), p. 101.

21 Woodward, 'Rural Campaigns', p. 107.

22 Gansu, 16 Nov. 1971, 129–6-62, pp. 1–3; Hebei, 1 Dec. 1971, 999–7-20, p. 37.

23 Gansu, 6 May 1970, 129–6-45, pp. 46–7; see also Gansu, 17 Oct. 1970, 129–6-48, pp. 105–20.

Chapter 19: Fall of an Heir

1 Yan and Gao, *Turbulent Decade*, p. 163.

2 Li, *The Private Life of Chairman Mao*, p. 121.

3 Ibid., p. 518.

4 The following paragraphs are based on a much more detailed account in MacFarquhar and Schoenhals, *Mao's Last Revolution*, pp. 325–33, and Gao, *Zhou Enlai*, pp. 201–6.

5 MacFarquhar and Schoenhals, *Mao's Last Revolution*, p. 300.

6 Xia Yafeng, 'China's Elite Politics and Sino-American Rapprochement, January 1969–February 1972', *Journal of Cold War Studies*, 8, no. 4 (Fall 2006), pp. 3–28.

7 Jonathan Fenby, *Modern China: The Fall and Rise of a Great Power, 1850 to the Present*, New York: Ecco, 2008, p. 497.

8 Jean Lacouture, 'From the Vietnam War to an Indochina War', *Foreign Affairs*, July 1970, pp. 617–28; see also Chen Jian, 'China, the Vietnam War and the Sino-American Rapprochement, 1968–1973', in Odd Arne Westad and Sophie Quinn-Judge (eds), *The Third Indochina War: Conflict between China, Vietnam and Cambodia, 1972–79*, London: Routledge, 2006, pp. 49–50.

9 Yan and Gao, *Turbulent Decade*, pp. 261–2 and 433; see also Nicholas Griffin, *Ping-Pong Diplomacy: The Secret History behind the Game that Changed the World*, New York: Scribner, 2014.

10 PRO, 'Visit to the Forbidden City', 4 May 1971, 'Diplomatic Tour', 4 May 1971, FCO 21–858.

11 PRO, 'The Canton Fair Trade', 1 June 1971, FCO 21–842.

12 Cheng, *Life and Death in Shanghai*, p. 307.

13 Margaret MacMillan, *Nixon and Mao: The Week that Changed the World*, New York: Random House, 2007; William Burr (ed.), *The Kissinger Transcripts: The Top-Secret Talks with Beijing and Moscow*, New York: The New Press, 1999.

14 Jung Chang and Jon Halliday, *Mao: The Unknown Story*, London: Jonathan Cape, 2005, p. 605.

15 Barnouin and Yu, *Ten Years of Turbulence*, p. 229.

16 Peter Hannam and Susan V. Lawrence, 'Solving a Chinese Puzzle: Lin Biao's Final Days and Death, after Two Decades of Intrigue', *US News and World Report*, 23 Jan. 1994.

17 Qiu Jin, *The Culture of Power: The Lin Biao Incident in the Cultural Revolution*, Stanford: Stanford University Press, 1999, p. 161, with a few minor stylistic changes.

18 According to Lin Doudou's confession after the incident; see ibid., pp. 173–4.

19 Ibid., p. 173.

20 Hannam and Lawrence, 'Solving a Chinese Puzzle'.

21 Yan and Gao, *Turbulent Decade*, p. 334.

22 MacFarquhar and Schoenhals, *Mao's Last Revolution*, p. 353.

23 Cheng, *Life and Death in Shanghai*, p. 335.

24 Sun Youli and Dan Ling, *Engineering Communist China: One Man's Story*, New York: Algora Publishing, 2003, pp. 175–6.

25 Nanchu, *Red Sorrow*, p. 152.

26 Li Jianglin, interview, 26 June 2014.

27 Li, *The Private Life of Chairman Mao*, p. 538.

28 Hannam and Lawrence, 'Solving a Chinese Puzzle'.

Chapter 20: Recovery

1 Li, *The Private Life of Chairman Mao*, pp. 544–6; Milton and Milton, *The Wind Will Not Subside*, p. 348.

2 PRO, Michael J. Richardson, 'Local Colour', 10 Feb. 1972, FCO 21–969; Michael J. Richardson, 'Naming of Streets', 26 Jan. 1972, FCO 21–962.

3 Report on Shanghai, 7 March 1973, Guangdong, 296-A2.1–25, pp. 189–98; PRO, Michael J. Richardson, 'Naming of Streets', 26 Jan. 1972, FCO 21–962.

4 Shanghai, 9 Dec. 1969, B98-5-100, pp. 10–11; Shanghai, 17 Feb. 1971 and 12 Feb. 1972, B50–4-52, pp. 44 and 67.

5 Shanghai, 18 Dec. 1972, B123-8-677, p. 1.

6 Shanghai, 28 Dec. 1978, B1-8-11, pp. 17–19; Shanghai, 11 Jan. 1972, B246-2-730, pp. 54–5; Shanghai, 10 Dec. 1971, B326-1-49, p. 30.

7 Li, *The Private Life of Chairman Mao*, p. 564.

8 Talk on Government Administration, October 1972, Hubei, SZ91-3-143, pp. 44–61.

9 William Bundy, *A Tangled Web: The Making of Foreign Policy in the Nixon Presidency*, New York: Hill & Wang, 1998.

10 Milton and Milton, *The Wind Will Not Subside*, p. 348; MacFarquhar and Schoenhals, *Mao's Last Revolution*, p. 339.

11 On renewed steel targets, see Yu Qiuli, Telephone Conference, 8 Sept. 1972, Hubei, SZ91-3-143, pp. 1–16; on blackouts, Hubei, 1 Feb. 1973, SZ21-4-107, pp. 221–3.

12 Xie Shengxian, *Hei yu bai de jiyi: Cong wenxue qingnian dao 'wenge fan'* (Black and white memories: From literary youth to criminal of the Cultural Revolution), Hong Kong: Sanlian shudian, 2012, pp. 202–5.

13 Guangdong, 29 Sept. 1975, 253–2-183, pp. 114–19; Report from the Bureau for Finance, 7 May 1975, 129–2-84, pp. 43–4; Shaanxi, 1975, 123–71–217, p. 23; Jan Wong, *Red China Blues: My Long March from Mao to Now*, New York: Doubleday, 1996, p. 42.

14 Letter from Transportation Supervisor to the Ministry of Transportation, Shaanxi, 26 Sept. 1975, 144–1-1225, pp. 234–5.

15 Gansu, 16 June 1972, 129–4-360, p. 2; Report from the Bureau for Finance, 7 May 1975, Gansu, 129–2-84, pp. 43–4.

16 Shaanxi, 1975, 123–71–217, p. 23.

17 Report on Trade by an Investigation Team from Shanghai, Shanghai, Oct. 1970, B123–8-344, pp. 17–19.

18 Ibid.

19 Guangdong, 5 Aug. 1968, 229–4-2, pp. 68–9; Zhang Man, interview with Zhang Shiming, Shuyang County, Jiangsu, 22 Nov. 2013.

20 Guangdong, 2 and 4 May 1973, 296–A2.1–25, pp. 151–8 and 166–9; Hebei, 13 April 1973, 919–3-100, pp. 44–5.

21 Milton and Milton, *The Wind Will Not Subside*, p. 366.

22 Report by the Ministry of Light Industry, 13 Dec. 1972, Hebei, 919–3-100, pp. 17–21; Report by the Ministry of Trade, 25 Aug. 1972, Hebei, 919–3-100, pp. 29–32.

23 See PRO, 'Economic Situation in China', 1971, FCO 21–841; see also Y. Y. Kueh, 'Mao and Agriculture in China's Industrialization: Three Antitheses in a 50-Year Perspective', *China Quarterly*, no. 187 (Sept. 2006), pp. 700–23.

24 Guangdong, 229–6-202, 26 June 1974, pp. 24–9; Kueh, 'Mao and Agriculture in China's Industrialization', notes that the policies in support of rural industries were widely hailed by foreign observers as the 'Chinese road to industrialisation', although they all evolved from the catastrophic campaign for 'backyard furnaces' at the height of the Great Leap Forward in 1958.

25 Shaanxi, Dec. 1973, 123–71–55, p. 39.

26 Shaanxi, 3 and 24 Dec. 1975, 123–71–209, pp. 16–19 and 34; Shaanxi, 28 April 1975, 123–71–204, pp. 104–5.

27 Report by Investigation Team of the Provincial Revolutionary Committee, 10 April 1976, Shaanxi, 123–71–294, pp. 13–14; Shaanxi, 10 Dec. 1976, 123–71–304, pp. 1–22; see also Report by Bureau for Grain, 10 Jan. 1977, 123–71–294, pp. 9–11.

28 Report from the Bureau for Grain, 1 March 1975, Hebei, 997–7-44, pp. 5–8.

29 Shandong, 19 and 23 April 1973, A131–4-35, pp. 1–3 and 10; Shandong, 16 Jan. and 3 March 1973, A131–4-37, pp. 12 and 17.

30 Hubei, 8 and 18 Jan., 28 March 1972, SZ75–6-77, pp. 47, 56 and 73.

31 Hubei, 15 March 1974, SZ75–6-194, pp. 5–7 and 20–1.

32 Shanghai, 10 Feb. 1973, B250–1-376, pp. 2–5; Zhejiang, 21 May 1976, J002–998–197606, p. 2.

33 Wong, *Red China Blues*, p. 49.

34 Chad J. Mitcham, *China's Economic Relations with the West and Japan, 1949–79: Grain, Trade and Diplomacy*, New York: Routledge, 2005, p. 207.

35 Nicholas R. Lardy, *Agriculture in China's Modern Economic Development*, Cambridge: Cambridge University Press, 1983; Carl Riskin, *China's Political Economy: The Quest for Development since 1949*, Oxford: Oxford University Press, 1987; Report on Grain Conference in Beijing, 10 Nov. 1971, Shaanxi, 123–71–35, pp. 11–12.

36 Gansu, 29 March 1972, 129–4-356, pp. 20–1.

37 Lardy, *Agriculture in China's Modern Economic Development*, p. 166.

38 Hubei, 3 May 1967, SZ115–2-826, p. 47; Hebei, 1973, 942–8-55, pp. 63–4.

39 Guangdong, 24 Nov. 1973, 231-A1.3–8, pp. 122–9; Guangdong, 1 March 1974, 231-A1.3–8, p. 66.

40 Guangdong, 25 March 1974, 231-A1.3–8, pp. 64–8.

41 Chang, *Wild Swans*, p. 558; Liu Zhongyi, *Cong chijiao yisheng dao Meiguo dafu* (From barefoot doctor to American doctor), Shanghai: Shanghai renmin chubanshe, 1994, p. 25, quoted in Fang Xiaoping, 'Barefoot Doctors in Chinese Villages: Medical Contestation, Structural Evolution, and Professional Formation, 1968–1983', doctoral dissertation, National University of Singapore, 2008, p. 117, with minor stylistic changes.

42 Zhou, *How the Farmers Changed China*, p. 39.

43 Fang, 'Barefoot Doctors in Chinese Villages', pp. 146–58.

44 Shaanxi, 15 March 1975, 123–71–204, pp. 3–9.

45 Hubei, 20 Feb. 1974, SZ115–5-32 (this survey of more than thirty counties showed that 2 million out of 15 million people, or more than one in seven, suffered from goitre); Hubei, SZ115–5-32, 19 July 1974, p. 94.

46 Fang, 'Barefoot Doctors in Chinese Villages', pp. 205–13.

47 Reports from the Bureau for Health, 31 March and 20 June 1972, Shandong, A188–1-3, pp. 108 and 149–52.

Chapter 21: The Silent Revolution

1 Shaanxi, 24 Jan. 1975, 123–71–209, pp. 1–7.

2 Shaanxi, 6 Jan. 1975, 123–71–209, pp. 8–15.

3 Shaanxi, 6 Feb. 1975, 123–71–209, pp. 34–48.

4 David Zweig, *Agrarian Radicalism in China, 1968–1981*, Cambridge, MA: Harvard University Press, 1989, pp. 61–2; in communist parlance these measures were referred to as the Sixty Articles.

5 Huang Shu-min, *The Spiral Road: Change in a Chinese Village through the Eyes of a Communist Party Leader*, Boulder, CO: Westview Press, 1989, pp. 109–10; there are clear parallels with Zhou, *How the Farmers Changed China*, p. 55; see also Ralph Thaxton, *Catastrophe and Contention in Rural China: Mao's Great Leap Famine and the Origins of Righteous Resistance in Da Fo Village*, Cambridge: Cambridge University Press, 2008, p. 278; see also Daniel Kelliher, *Peasant Power in China: The Era of Rural Reform, 1979–1989*, New Haven, CT: Yale University Press, 1992.

6 Hunan, 7 July 1976, 146–2-61, pp. 81–4.

7 Thaxton, *Catastrophe and Contention in Rural China*, pp. 278–84.

8 The expression was *jietian daohu*, to 'lend the land to individual households': Zhejiang, 8 Sept. 1971, J116–25–159, p. 155; Lynn T. White, *Unstately Power: Local Causes of China's Economic Reforms*, Armonk, NY: M. E. Sharpe, 1998, pp. 120–1.

9 Guangdong, 1 Nov. 1975, 294-A2.14–6, p. 52.

10 Guangdong, 20 Dec. 1973, 296-A2.1–51, pp. 44–53; Guangdong, 20 March 1974, 294-A2.13–8, pp. 1–28.

11 Guangdong, 20 Dec. 1973, 296-A2.1–51, pp. 44–53.

12 Ibid.

13 Report from Guangdong Provincial Revolutionary Committee, 26 Nov. 1973, Shandong, A47-2-247, pp. 37–9; Guangdong, 20 Dec. 1973, 296-A2.1–51, pp. 44–53.

14 Guangdong, 26 Sept. 1975, 253-2-183, pp. 95–9.

15 Report from the Ministry of Trade, 13 Dec. 1972, Hebei, 919–3-100, p. 37; on the contents of overseas parcels, see Guangdong, 26 Sept. 1975, 253-2-183, pp. 95–9.

16 Chris Bramall, 'Origins of the Agricultural "Miracle": Some Evidence from Sichuan', *China Quarterly*, no. 143 (Sept. 1995), pp. 731–55.

17 Report by the Ministry of Light Industry, 13 Dec. 1972, Hebei, 919–3-100, pp. 17–21.

18 Guangdong, 20 March 1974, 294-A2.13–8, pp. 1–28.

19 Ibid.

20 White, *Unstately Power*, pp. 94 and 101.

21 Ibid., pp. 112–15.

22 Ibid., pp. 119–21.

23 For a good example, see Thaxton, *Catastrophe and Contention in Rural China*, pp. 286–91.

24 Shaanxi, 20 Aug. 1973, 123–71–70, pp. 1–6.

25 Hubei, 20 Oct. 1972, SZ75–6-77, p. 12; Hubei, 26 Nov. 1973, SZ75–6-107, pp. 58–9; see also Bonnin, *The Lost Generation*.

26 PRO, 'Letter from Embassy', 23 May 1973, FCO 21–1089, p. 2; Report from the Ministry of Public Security, 30 Aug. 1974, Shandong, A47-2-247, pp. 103–6.

27 Report from the State Council, 3 March 1974, Shandong, A47-2-247, pp. 26–9.

28 Report from the Public Security Bureau, 20 Nov. 1973, Shandong, A1–8-24, pp. 45–6.

29 The directive was repeated in the following years; see Order from State Council, 5 June 1973, Hebei, 919–3-100, pp. 14–15; Report from the State Planning Committee, 25 July 1974, Shandong, A47-2-247, pp. 85–7; Shandong, 19 Aug. 1969, A47–21–100, pp. 38–9.

30 Sun and Ling, *Engineering Communist China*, pp. 191–4.

31 O. Arne Westad, 'The Great Transformation', in Niall Ferguson, Charles S. Maier, Erez Manela and Daniel J. Sargent (eds), *The Shock of the Global: The 1970s in Perspective*, Cambridge, MA: Harvard University Press, 2010, p. 79.

Chapter 22: The Second Society

1 Dikötter, *The Tragedy of Liberation*, pp. 190, 199–203.
2 The idea of the second society comes from Elemér Hankiss, and I have paraphrased several of his statements from his 'The "Second Society": Is There an Alternative Social Model Emerging in Contemporary Hungary?', *Social Research*, 55, nos 1–2 (Spring 1988), pp. 13–42. I much prefer the unedited version of this article, which can be found on the website of the Wilson Center, Washington DC.
3 Wong, *Red China Blues*, p. 46.
4 Jiangsu, 17 April and 13 Oct. 1972, 4013–20–122, pp. 51, 163–4 and 181.
5 Hebei, 1973, 942–8-55, pp. 60–1.
6 Bureau for Education, 9 Oct. 1975, Shandong, A29-4-47, p. 61; Jiangsu, 3 June 1972, 4013–20–108, pp. 113–14.
7 Jiangsu, 25 Jan. 1975, 4013–20–106, pp. 1–3 and 38.
8 Bureau for Education, 15 May and 3 June 1975, Shandong, A29-4-47, pp. 75, 87 and 99; Report from the State Council, 6 Nov. 1978, Shanghai, B1-8-11, pp. 14–16; Hebei, 11 Dec. 1968, 919–1-148, n.p.
9 Chang, *Wild Swans*, pp. 476–7.
10 Ibid., p. 552; Liang and Shapiro, *Son of the Revolution*, pp. 201–2.
11 Li Jianglin, interview, 7 Sept. 2014; Chang, *Wild Swans*, pp. 593–4.
12 On these translations, see Guo, Song and Zhou (eds), *The A to Z of the Chinese Cultural Revolution*, p. 107; Mark Gamsa, *The Chinese Translation of Russian Literature: Three Studies*, Leiden: Brill, 2008, p. 24; Yang Jian, *Zhongguo zhiqing wenxue shi* (A literary history of educated youth), Beijing: Zhongguo gongren chubanshe, 2002, chs 4 to 6.
13 Guo, Song and Zhou (eds), *The A to Z of the Chinese Cultural Revolution*, pp. 98–9.
14 See, for instance, Shandong, 30 May 1975, A1-8-59, p. 3.
15 *The Heart of a Maiden* (*Shaonü zhi xin*), also called *Memoirs of Manna* (*Manna huiyilu*); see Yang Dongxiao, 'Wenge jinshu: "Shaonü zhi xin". Nage niandai de xingyuzui' (A book banned during the Cultural Revolution: 'The Heart of a Maiden'. The first pornographic novel hand-copied during the Cultural Revolution), *Renwu huabao*, no. 23 (2010), pp. 68–71.
16 Gansu, 26 May 1970, 129–6-48, p. 100.
17 Gao, *Born Red*, p. 29.
18 Shanghai, 6 May 1974, B123-8-1044, pp. 4–9.
19 Ministry of Trade, 18 May 1966, Hebei, 999–4-761, pp. 116–24; Shaanxi, 27 Oct. and 20 Nov. 1970, 215–1-1844, pp. 50 and 53–9.
20 PRO, 'China News Summary', 25 Sept. 1974, FCO 21–1223.
21 PRO, 'Overt Intelligence Reports, January to April 1972', 1 June 1973, FCO 21–1089; PRO, 'Letter from Embassy', 10 May 1973, FCO 21–1089; Li Jianglin, interview 7 Sept. 2014.
22 Shanghai, 12 Jan. 1970, B246-2-554, p. 1.
23 PRO, Richard C. Samuel, 'Play Games Not War', 17 April 1972, FCO 21–969; M. J. Richardson, 'Local Colour', 3 Oct. and 6 Dec. 1972, FCO 21–969.

24 Wang Aihe, '*Wuming*: Art and Solidarity in a Peculiar Historical Context', in *Wuming (No Name) Painting Catalogue*, Hong Kong: Hong Kong University Press, 2010, pp. 7–9; see also Wang Aihe, 'Wuming: An Underground Art Group during the Cultural Revolution', *Journal of Modern Chinese History*, 3, no. 2 (Dec. 2009), pp. 183–99; Julia F. Andrews, *Painters and Politics in the People's Republic of China, 1949–1979*, Berkeley: University of California Press, 1994; and Ellen Johnston Laing, *The Winking Owl: Art in the People's Republic of China*, Berkeley: University of California Press, 1988.

25 Hebei, 31 May 1969, 919-1-290, pp. 54–5.

26 Joseph Tse-Hei Lee, 'Watchman Nee and the Little Flock Movement in Maoist China', *Church History*, 74, no. 1 (March 2005), pp. 68–96; see also Chen-yang Kao, 'The Cultural Revolution and the Emergence of Pentecostal-style Protestantism in China', *Journal of Contemporary Religion*, 24, no. 2 (May 2009), pp. 171–88.

27 Gansu, 26 May 1974, 91-7-283, pp. 1–7.

28 Zhai, *Red Flower of China*, pp. 226–7; see also Barbara Mittler, '"Eight Stage Works for 800 Million People": The Great Proletarian Cultural Revolution in Music – A View from Revolutionary Opera', *Opera Quarterly*, 26, nos 2–3 (Spring 2010), pp. 377–401.

29 Report from the Ministry of Grain, 23 Jan. 1968, Hebei, 919-1-185, pp. 24–5; Report from the Public Security Bureau, 20 Nov. 1973, Shandong, A1-8-24, p. 46; Shaanxi, 25 April 1968, 194-1-1317, p. 59.

30 Liu, *Fengyu rensheng lu*, p. 40.

31 Chang, *Wild Swans*, p. 576; on the family during the Cultural Revolution, see also Zang Xiaowei, *Children of the Cultural Revolution: Family Life and Political Behavior in Mao's China*, Boulder, CO: Westview Press, 2000.

32 Orlando Figes, *The Whisperers: Private Life in Stalin's Russia*, New York: Picador, 2007, p. 300.

33 Chang, *Wild Swans*, p. 330.

34 Gansu, July 1975, 91-7-351, n.p.

35 The most extensive interview and research on Zhang Hongbing appears in Philippe Grangereau, 'Une Mère sur la conscience', *Libération*, 28 April 2013, pp. 5–7.

36 Chang, *Wild Swans*, p. 574; Tan, *The Chinese Factor*, p. 157.

37 Zhuo Fei, *Yingzujie mingliu zai wenge de gushi* (Celebrities from the British concession in Shanghai during the Cultural Revolution), Hong Kong: Mingbao chubanshe youxian gongsi, 2005, p. 249.

38 Yang, *Spider Eaters*, pp. 197 and 248–9.

39 Emily Honig, 'Socialist Sex: The Cultural Revolution Revisited', *Modern China*, 29, no. 2 (April 2003), pp. 143–75.

Chapter 23: Reversals

1 Gao, *Zhou Enlai*, p. 252.

2 Guo, Song and Zhou, *The A to Z of the Chinese Cultural Revolution*, p. 61; Yan and Gao, *Turbulent Decade*, p. 430.

3 PRO, 'Shanghai Attacks Blind Worship of Foreign Things', 2 Oct. 1974, FCO 21–1224.

4 Dong Guoqiang and Andrew G. Walder, 'Nanjing's "Second Cultural Revolution" of 1974', *China Quarterly*, no. 212 (Dec. 2012), pp. 893–918.

5 MacFarquhar and Schoenhals, *Mao's Last Revolution*, p. 366.

6 Gao, *Zhou Enlai*, pp. 259–63; PRO, R. F. Wye, 'Appearances at the National Day Reception', 4 Oct. 1974, FCO 21–1224.

7 Gao, *Zhou Enlai*, p. 264.

8 Li, *The Private Life of Chairman Mao*, p. 586; Terrill, *Madame Mao*, p. 279.

9 Zhejiang, 13 May 1975, J002–998–197509–2, pp. 1–6; Forster, *Rebellion and Factionalism in a Chinese Province*.

10 MacFarquhar and Schoenhals, *Mao's Last Revolution*, pp. 384–8; Dru Gladney, *Muslim Chinese: Ethnic Nationalism in the People's Republic*, Cambridge, MA: Harvard University Press, 1996, pp. 137–40.

11 MacFarquhar and Schoenhals, *Mao's Last Revolution*, pp. 393–7.

12 Li, *The Private Life of Chairman Mao*, p. 601; MacFarquhar and Schoenhals, *Mao's Last Revolution*, pp. 404–5.

13 Cheng, *Life and Death in Shanghai*, p. 459; MacFarquhar and Schoenhals, *Mao's Last Revolution*, pp. 409–11.

14 Cheng, *Life and Death in Shanghai*, p. 466; Tan, *The Chinese Factor*, p. 221.

15 MacFarquhar and Schoenhals, *Mao's Last Revolution*, p. 416; Wong, *Red China Blues*, p. 165.

16 Yan and Gao, *Turbulent Decade*, pp. 489–92.

17 Ibid., pp. 492–5.

18 Roger Garside, *Coming Alive: China after Mao*, London: Deutsch, 1981, pp. 115–28.

19 Li, *The Private Life of Chairman Mao*, p. 612; Yan and Gao, *Turbulent Decade*, pp. 497–9.

20 Tan, *The Chinese Factor*, p. 228; MacFarquhar and Schoenhals, *Mao's Last Revolution*, pp. 431–2.

21 Chang, *Wild Swans*, p. 647.

Chapter 24: Aftermath

1 James Palmer, *The Death of Mao: The Tangshan Earthquake and the Birth of the New China*, London: Faber & Faber, 2012, p. 236.

2 Report from the Chinese Academy of Science, 29 June 1974, Shandong, A47–2-247, pp. 76–9.

3 Palmer, *The Death of Mao*, p. 131.

4 Ibid., p. 132.

5 Tan, *The Chinese Factor*, p. 241.

6 Palmer, *The Death of Mao*, pp. 167–71.

7 Wong, *Red China Blues*, pp. 173–4.

8 Chang, *Wild Swans*, p. 651.

9 Jean Hong, interview, 7 Nov. 2012, Hong Kong; Rowena Xiaoqing He, 'Reading Havel in Beijing', *Wall Street Journal*, 29 Dec. 2011.

10 Ai Xiaoming interviewed by Zhang Tiezhi, 22 Dec. 2010, Guangzhou.

11 Wu Guoping interviewed by Dong Guoqiang, 1 Dec. 2013, Zongyang county, Anhui.
12 Shan, 'Becoming Loyal', p. 145; Wong, *Red China Blues*, p. 175; Tan, *The Chinese Factor*, p. 245.
13 Wong, *Red China Blues*, p. 177.
14 PRO, 'Confidential Wire', 25 Oct. 1976, FCO 21–1493.
15 Cheng, *Life and Death in Shanghai*, pp. 483–4; Garside, *Coming Alive*, p. 164.
16 Wong, *Red China Blues*, p. 181; Tan, *The Chinese Factor*, p. 251.
17 Wong, *Red China Blues*, pp. 188–9.
18 George Black and Robin Munro, *Black Hands of Beijing: Lives of Defiance in China's Democracy Movement*, London: Wiley, 1993, p. 50.
19 Tan, *The Chinese Factor*, p. 257; Potter, *From Leninist Discipline to Socialist Legalism*, p. 113.
20 Chang, *Wild Swans*, p. 656.
21 MacFarquhar and Schoenhals, *Mao's Last Revolution*, p. 457.
22 Yang Dali, *Calamity and Reform in China: State, Rural Society, and Institutional Change since the Great Leap Famine*, Stanford: Stanford University Press, 1996, pp. 147–9.
23 Ibid., p. 157.
24 White, *Unstately Power*, p. 96; Zhou, *How the Farmers Changed China*, p. 8.
25 Zhou, *How the Farmers Changed China*, pp. 231–4.

Select Bibliography

Archives

Non-Chinese Archives

PRO, Hong Kong – Public Record Office, Hong Kong
PRO – The National Archives, London

Provincial Archives

Gansu – Gansu sheng dang'anguan, Lanzhou
91   Zhonggong Gansu shengwei (Gansu Provincial Party Committee)
93   Zhonggong Gansu shengwei xuanchuanbu (Gansu Provincial Party Committee's Department for Propaganda)
96   Zhonggong Gansu shengwei nongcun gongzuobu (Gansu Provincial Party Committee Department for Rural Work)
129   Gansu sheng geming weiyuanhui (Gansu Province Revolutionary Committee)
144   Gansu sheng jihua weiyuanhui (Gansu Province Planning Committee)
180   Gansu sheng liangshiting (Gansu Province Bureau for Grain)
192   Gansu sheng shangyeting (Gansu Province Bureau for Commerce)

Guangdong – Guangdong sheng dang'anguan, Guangzhou
217   Guangdong sheng nongcunbu (Guangdong Provincial Bureau for Rural Affairs)
231   Guangdong sheng zonggonghui (Guangdong Province Federation of Trade Unions)
235   Guangdong sheng renmin weiyuanhui (Guangdong Provincial People's Congress)
253   Guangdong sheng jihua weiyuanhui (Guangdong Province Planning Committee)
314   Guangdong sheng jiaoyuting (Guangdong Province Bureau for Education)

Hebei – Hebei sheng dang'anguan, Shijiazhuang
879   Zhonggong Hebei shengwei nongcun gongzuobu (Hebei Provincial Party Committee Department for Rural Work)

919   Hebei sheng geming weiyuanhui (Hebei Province Revolutionary Committee)

921   Hebei shenggewei shengchanbu yuanhui (Hebei Province Revolutionary Committee's Bureau for Production)

925   Hebei sheng nongye shengchan weiyuanhui (Hebei Province Committee on Agricultural Production)

926   Hebei sheng caizheng maoyi weiyuanhui (Hebei Province Committee on Finances and Trade)

940   Hebei sheng jihua weiyuanhui (Hebei Province Planning Committee)

942   Hebei sheng tongjiju (Hebei Province Office for Statistics)

979   Hebei sheng nongyeting (Hebei Province Agricultural Bureau)

997   Hebei sheng liangshiting (Hebei Province Bureau for Grain)

999   Hebei sheng shangyeting (Hebei Province Bureau for Trade)

Hubei – Hubei sheng dang'anguan, Wuhan

SZ1   Zhonggong Hubei sheng weiyuanhui (Hubei Provincial Party Committee)

SZ29   Hubei sheng zonggonghui (Hubei Province Federation of Trade Unions)

SZ34   Hubei sheng renmin weiyuanhui (Hubei Provincial People's Congress)

SZ75   Hubei sheng liangshiting (Hubei Province Bureau for Grain)

SZ81   Hubei sheng shangyeting (Hubei Province Bureau for Trade)

SZ90   Hubei sheng gongyeting (Hubei Province Bureau for Industry)

SZ107   Hubei sheng nongyeting (Hubei Province Agricultural Bureau)

SZ115   Hubei sheng weishengting (Hubei Province Bureau for Health)

SZ139   Hubei sheng geming weiyuanhui (Hubei Province Revolutionary Committee)

Hunan – Hunan sheng dang'anguan, Changsha

146   Zhonggong Hunan shengwei nongcun gongzuobu (Hunan Provincial Party Committee Department for Rural Work)

163   Hunan sheng renmin weiyuanhui (Hunan Provincial People's Congress)

182   Hunan sheng laodongju (Hunan Province Office for Labour)

194   Hunan sheng liangshiju (Hunan Province Office for Grain)

Jiangsu – Jiangsu sheng dang'anguan, Nanjing

4007   Jiangsu sheng minzhengting (Jiangsu Province Bureau for Civil Affairs)

4013   Jiangsu sheng jiaoyuting (Jiangsu Province Bureau for Education)

4016   Jiangsu sheng wenhuating (Jiangsu Province Bureau for Culture)

4018   Jiangsu sheng weishengting (Jiangsu Province Bureau for Health and Hygiene)

4028   Jiangsu sheng jiansheting (Jiangsu Province Bureau for Construction)

4060   Jiangsu sheng liangshiting (Jiangsu Province Bureau for Grain)

Shaanxi – Shaanxi sheng dang'anguan, Xi'an

123   Zhonggong Shaanxi shengwei (Shaanxi Provincial Party Committee)

144   Shaanxi sheng jiaotongting (Shaanxi Province Transportation Bureau)

194   Shaanxi sheng nongyeting (Shaanxi Province Agricultural Bureau)

215   Shaanxi sheng shangyeting (Shaanxi Province Bureau for Trade)

Shandong – Shandong sheng dang'anguan, Jinan
A1   Zhonggong Shandong shengwei (Shandong Provincial Party Committee)
A27   Shangdong sheng wenhuaju (Shandong Province Office for Culture)
A29   Shangdong sheng jiaoyuting (Shandong Province Education Bureau)
A47   Shandong sheng geming weiyuanhui (Shandong Province Revolutionary
        Committee)
A103 Shandong sheng tongjiju (Shandong Province Office for Statistics)
A108 Shandong sheng jingji weiyuanhui (Shandong Province Economic
        Commission)
A131 Shandong sheng liangshiting (Shandong Province Bureau for Grain)
A147 Shandong sheng xinfangju (Shandong Province Office for Visits)

Sichuan – Sichuan sheng dang'anguan, Chengdu
JC1   Zhonggong Sichuan shengwei (Sichuan Provincial Party Committee)

Zhejiang – Zhejiang sheng dang'anguan, Hangzhou
J116 Zhejiang sheng nongyeting (Zhejiang Province Bureau for Agriculture)

Municipal Archives

Nanjing – Nanjing shi dang'anguan, Nanjing, Jiangsu
4003 Nanjing shiwei (Nanjing Municipal Party Committee)
5003 Nanjing shi renmin zhengfu (Nanjing Municipal People's Government)
5013 Nanjing shi laodongju (Nanjing Municipal Office for Labour)
5020 Nanjing shi jingji weiyuanhui (Nanjing City Economic Commission)
5023 Nanjing shi tongjiju (Nanjing Municipal Bureau for Statistics)
5038 Nanjing shi qinggongyeju (Nanjing Municipal Bureau for Light Industry)
6001 Nanjing shi zonggonghui (Nanjing Municipal Federation of Trade Unions)

Shanghai – Shanghai shi dang'anguan, Shanghai
A36   Shanghai shiwei gongye zhengzhibu (Shanghai Municipal Party Committee's
        Bureau for Industry and Politics)
A38   Shanghai shiwei gongye shengchan weiyuanhui (Committee for Industrial
        Production of the Shanghai Municipal Party Committee)
B1   Shanghai shi renmin zhengfu (Shanghai Municipal People's Government)
B3   Shanghai shi renmin weiyuanhui wenjiao bangongshi (Bureau for Culture
        and Education of the Shanghai Municipal People's Congress)
B6   Shanghai shi renmin weiyuanhui cailiangmao bangongshi (Bureau for
        Finances, Grain and Trade of the Shanghai Municipal People's Congress)
B45   Shanghai shi nongyeting (Shanghai Municipality's Bureau for Agriculture)
B50   Shanghai shi renwei jiguan shiwu guanliju (Bureau for Office Work of the
        Shanghai Municipal People's Congress)
B74   Shanghai shi minbing zhihuibu (Shanghai City's Militia Command Post)
B92   Shangha shi renmin guangbo diantai (Shanghai City Radio)
B98   Shanghai shi di'er shangyeju (Shanghai City's Number Two Bureau for Trade)
B104   Shanghai shi caizhengju (Shanghai Municipal Bureau for Finance)

B105   Shanghai shi jiaoyuju (Shanghai Municipal Bureau for Education)

B109   Shanghai shi wuzi (Shanghai Municipal Bureau for Goods and Materials)

B120   Shanghai Shi renmin fangkong bangongshi (Shanghai Municipal Office for Air Defence)

B123   Shanghai shi diyi shangyeju (Shanghai City's Number One Bureau for Trade)

B127   Shanghai shi laodongju (Shanghai Municipal Bureau for Labour)

B134   Shanghai shi fangzhi gongyeju (Shanghai Municipal Bureau for Textile Industry)

B163   Shanghai shi qinggongyeju (Shanghai Municipal Bureau for Light Industry)

B167   Shanghai shi chubanju (Shanghai Municipal Bureau for Publishing)

B168   Shanghai shi minzhengju (Shanghai Municipal Bureau for Civil Administration)

B172   Shanghai shi wenhuaju (Shanghai Municipal Bureau for Culture)

B173   Shanghai shi jidian gongye guanliju (Shanghai Municipal Bureau for Machinery and Electronics)

B182   Shanghai shi gongshanghang guanliju (Shanghai Municipal Bureau for Supervision of Business)

B227   Shanghai shi geming weiyuanhui laodong gongzizu (Shanghai Municipal Revolutionary Committee's Team on Wages)

B228   Shanghai shi renmin zhengfu zhishi qingnian shangshan xiaxiang ban-gongshi (Bureau for Sending Educated Youth to the Countryside of the Shanghai Municipal People's Government)

B244   Shanghai shi jiaoyu weisheng bangongshi (Shanghai Municipal Bureau for Education and Health)

B246   Shanghai shi renmin zhengfu jingji weiyuanhui (Committee on the Economy of the Shanghai Municipal People's Government)

B248   Shanghai shi renmin zhengfu caizheng maoyi bangongshi (Office for Finance and Trade of the Shanghai Municipal People's Government)

B250   Shanghai shi nongye weiyuanhui (Shanghai Municipal Committee on Agriculture)

Published Works

Ahn, Byungjoon, *Chinese Politics and the Cultural Revolution: Dynamics of Policy Processes*, Seattle: University of Washington Press, 1976.

Andrews, Julia F., *Painters and Politics in the People's Republic of China, 1949–1979*, Berkeley: University of California Press, 1994.

Andrieu, Jacques, 'Les gardes rouges: Des rebelles sous influence', *Cultures et Conflits*, no. 18 (Summer 1995), pp. 2–25.

Andrieu, Jacques, 'Mais que se sont donc dit Mao et Malraux? Aux sources du maoïsme occidental', *Perspectives chinoises*, no. 37 (Sept. 1996), pp. 50–63.

Ba Yantai, *Nei Menggu wasu zainan shilu* (True record of the cleansing of the class ranks in Inner Mongolia), Hohhot: Nei Menggu renquan xinxi zhongxin, 1999, self-published.

Baehr, Peter, 'China the Anomaly: Hannah Arendt, Totalitarianism, and the Maoist Regime', *European Journal of Political Theory*, 9, no. 3 (July 2010), pp. 267–86.

Barcata, Louis, *China in the Throes of the Cultural Revolution: An Eye Witness Report*, New York: Hart Publishing, 1968.

Barnouin, Barbara and Yu Changgen, *Ten Years of Turbulence: The Chinese Cultural Revolution*, London: Kegan Paul International, 1993.

Barnouin, Barbara and Yu Changgen, *Zhou Enlai: A Political Life*, Hong Kong: Chinese University of Hong Kong Press, 2009.

Bickers, Robert and Ray Yep (eds), *May Days in Hong Kong: Riot and Emergency in 1967*, Hong Kong: Hong Kong University Press, 2009.

Black, George and Robin Munro, *Black Hands of Beijing: Lives of Defiance in China's Democracy Movement*, London: Wiley, 1993.

Bo Yibo, *Ruogan zhongda shijian yu juece de huigu* (Recollections of several important decisions and events), Beijing: Zhonggong zongyang dangxiao chubanshe, 1993.

Bonnin, Michel, *The Lost Generation: The Rustication of China's Educated Youth (1968–1980)*, Hong Kong: Chinese University of Hong Kong Press, 2013.

Boterbloem, Kees, *The Life and Times of Andrei Zhdanov, 1896–1948*, Montreal: McGill-Queen's Press, 2004.

Bramall, Chris, 'Origins of the Agricultural "Miracle": Some Evidence from Sichuan', *China Quarterly*, no. 143 (Sept. 1995), pp. 731–55.

Brown, Jeremy, 'Burning the Grassroots: Chen Boda and the Four Cleanups in Suburban Tianjin', *Copenhagen Journal of Asian Studies*, 26, no. 1 (2008), pp. 50–69.

Bu Weihua, 'Beijing hongweibing yundong dashi ji' (Chronology of the Red Guard movement in Beijing), *Beijing dangshi yanjiu*, no. 84 (1994), pp. 56–61.

Bu Weihua, *Zalan jiu shijie: Wenhua da geming de dongluan yu haojie* (Smashing the old world: The chaos and catastrophe of the Great Cultural Revolution), Hong Kong: Chinese University of Hong Kong Press, 2008.

Bubenin, Vitaly, *Krovavyi Sneg Damanskogo: Sobytiia 1966–1969 gg.*, Moscow: Granitsa, 2004.

Bundy, William, *A Tangled Web: The Making of Foreign Policy in the Nixon Presidency*, New York: Hill & Wang, 1998.

Burr, William (ed.), *The Kissinger Transcripts: The Top-Secret Talks with Beijing and Moscow*, New York: The New Press, 1999.

Byron, John and Robert Pack, *The Claws of the Dragon: Kang Sheng, the Evil Genius behind Mao and his Legacy of Terror in People's China*, New York: Simon & Schuster, 1992.

Chan, Anita, 'Dispelling Misconceptions about the Red Guard Movement: The Necessity to Re-Examine Cultural Revolution Factionalism and Periodization', *Journal of Contemporary China*, 1, no. 1 (Sept. 1992), pp. 61–85.

Chan, Anita, 'Self-Deception as a Survival Technique: The Case of Yue Daiyun, *To the Storm – The Odyssey of a Revolutionary Chinese Woman*', *Australian Journal of Chinese Affairs*, nos 19–20 (Jan.–July 1988), pp. 345–58.

Chan, Anita, Stanley Rosen and Jonathan Unger, 'Students and Class Warfare: The Social Roots of the Red Guard Conflict in Guangzhou (Canton)', *China Quarterly*, no. 83 (Sept. 1980), pp. 397–446.

Chang Jung, *Wild Swans: Three Daughters of China*, Clearwater, FL: Touchstone, 2003.

Chang Jung and Jon Halliday, *Mao: The Unknown Story*, London: Jonathan Cape, 2005.

Chang, Tony H., *China during the Cultural Revolution, 1966–1976: A Selected Bibliography of English Language Works*, Westport, CT: Greenwood, 1999.

Cheek, Timothy, *Propaganda and Culture in Mao's China: Deng Tuo and the Intelligentsia*, Oxford: Oxford University Press, 1997.

Chen Donglin, *Sanxian jianshe: Beizhan shiqi de xibu kaifa* (Building the Third Front: Opening up the West during the era of war preparation), Beijing: Zhonggong zhongyang dangxiao chubanshe, 2003.

Chen, Jack, *Inside the Cultural Revolution*, London: Sheldon, 1976.

Chen Jian, *Mao's China and the Cold War*, Chapel Hill: University of North Carolina Press, 2001.

Chen Jian, 'China, the Vietnam War and the Sino-American Rapprochement, 1968–1973', in Odd Arne Westad and Sophie Quinn-Judge (eds), *The Third Indochina War: Conflict between China, Vietnam and Cambodia, 1972–79*, London: Routledge, 2006, pp. 33–64.

Chen Ruoxi, *The Execution of Mayor Yin and Other Stories from the Great Proletarian Cultural Revolution*, revised edn, Bloomington: Indiana University Press, 2004.

Chen Yinan, *Qingchun wuhen: Yige zaofanpai gongren de shinian wenge* (Scarless youth: A rebel worker's experience of the Cultural Revolution), Hong Kong: Chinese University of Hong Kong Press, 2006.

Cheng, Nien, *Life and Death in Shanghai*, New York: Penguin Books, 2008.

Cheng, Tiejun and Mark Selden, 'The Construction of Spatial Hierarchies: China's *hukou* and *danwei* Systems', in Timothy Cheek and Tony Saich (eds), *New Perspectives on State Socialism in China*, Armonk, NY: M. E. Sharpe, 1997, pp. 23–50.

Cheng Yinghong, *Creating the 'New Man': From Enlightenment Ideals to Socialist Realities*, Honolulu: University of Hawai'i Press, 2009.

Cheung, Gary, *Hong Kong's Watershed: The 1967 Riots*, Hong Kong: Hong Kong University Press, 2009.

Chinese Propaganda Posters: From the Collection of Michael Wolf, Cologne: Taschen, 2003.

Clark, Paul, *The Chinese Cultural Revolution: A History*, Cambridge: Cambridge University Press, 2008.

Cohen, Arthur A., *The Communism of Mao Tse-tung*, Chicago: University of Chicago Press, 1964.

Cook, Alexander C. (ed.), *The Little Red Book: A Global History*, Cambridge: Cambridge University Press, 2014.

Cooper, John, *Colony in Conflict: The Hong Kong Disturbances, May 1967–January 1968*, Hong Kong: Swindon, 1970.

Cradock, Percy, *Experiences of China*, London: John Murray, 1994.

Dai Yushan, '"Siqing" dayuanan de zhenxiang: Du Yu Kaiguo "Tongcheng fengyu"' (The truth about the 'Four Cleans'), *Zhengming*, Jan. 2007, pp. 82–3.

Dangdai Yunnan dashi jiyao (Chronology of major events in contemporary Yunnan), Kunming: Dangdai Zhongguo chubanshe, 2007.

Diamant, Neil J., *Embattled Glory: Veterans, Military Families, and the Politics of Patriotism in China, 1949–2007*, Lanham, MD: Rowman & Littlefield, 2009.

Dikötter, Frank, *China before Mao: The Age of Openness*, Berkeley: University of California Press, 2008.

Dikötter, Frank, *Exotic Commodities: Modern Objects and Everyday Life in China*, New York: Columbia University Press, 2006.

Dikötter, Frank, *Mao's Great Famine: The History of China's Most Devastating Catastrophe, 1958–1962*, London: Bloomsbury, 2010.

Dikötter, Frank, *The Tragedy of Liberation: A History of the Chinese Revolution, 1945–1957*, London: Bloomsbury, 2013.

Ding Qun, 'Yuanyu biandi de Jiangsu qingcha "Wu Yao Liu" yundong' (The campaign against the May Sixteenth Elements in Jiangsu), *Wenshi jinghua*, no. 1 (2009).

Ding Shu, 'Fengyu rupan de suiyue: 1970 nian yida sanfan yundong jishi' (Turbulent years: The One Strike and Three Antis campaign of 1970), *Huanghuagang zazhi*, no. 5 (March 2003), pp. 69–80.

Ding Shu, 'Wenge zhong de "qingli jieji duiwu" yundong' (The campaign to cleanse the class ranks during the Cultural Revolution), *Huaxia wenzhai zengkan*, no. 244, 14 Dec. 2004.

Ding Yizhuang, *Zhongguo zhiqing shi: Chulan, 1953–1968* (A history of China's sent-down youth: The first waves, 1953–1968), Beijing: Dangdai Zhongguo chubanshe, 2009.

Domenach, Jean-Luc, *L'Archipel oublié*, Paris: Fayard, 1992.

Dong Guoqiang and Andrew G. Walder, 'Factions in a Bureaucratic Setting: The Origins of Cultural Revolution Conflict in Nanjing', *China Journal*, no. 65 (Jan. 2011), pp. 1–25.

Dong Guoqiang and Andrew G. Walder, 'From Truce to Dictatorship: Creating a Revolutionary Committee in Jiangsu', *China Journal*, no. 68 (July 2012), pp. 1–31.

Dong Guoqiang and Andrew G. Walder, 'Local Politics in the Chinese Cultural Revolution: Nanjing under Military Control', *Journal of Asian Studies*, 70, no. 2 (May 2011), pp. 425–47.

Dong Guoqiang and Andrew G. Walder, 'Nanjing's "Second Cultural Revolution" of 1974', *China Quarterly*, no. 212 (Dec. 2012), pp. 893–918.

Dong Shengli, 'Guanyu Xi'an hongse kongbudui de koushu huiyi' (Oral reminiscences about the red terror teams in Xi'an), *Jiyi*, no. 10 (Dec. 2008), pp. 47–9.

Dunn, Walter S., *The Soviet Economy and the Red Army, 1930–1945*, Westport, CT: Greenwood, 1995.

Dutton, Michael, 'Mango Mao: Infections of the Sacred', *Public Culture*, 16, no. 2 (Spring 2004), pp. 161–87.

Esherick, Joseph W., Paul G. Pickowicz and Andrew G. Walder, *China's Cultural Revolution as History*, Stanford: Stanford University Press, 2006.

Faligot, Roger and Rémi Kauffer, *The Chinese Secret Service*, New York: Morrow, 1989.

Fan Ka Wai, 'Epidemic Cerebrospinal Meningitis during the Cultural Revolution', *Extrême-Orient, Extrême-Occident*, 37 (Sept. 2014), pp. 197–232.

Fang Xiaoping, *Barefoot Doctors and Western Medicine in China*, New York: University of Rochester Press, 2012.

Fenby, Jonathan, *Modern China: The Fall and Rise of a Great Power, 1850 to the Present*, New York: Ecco, 2008.

Feng Jicai, *Ten Years of Madness: Oral Histories of China's Cultural Revolution*, San Francisco: China Books, 1996.

Figes, Orlando, *The Whisperers: Private Life in Stalin's Russia*, New York: Picador, 2007.

Finnane, Antonia, *Changing Clothes in China: Fashion, History, Nation*, New York: Columbia University Press, 2008.

Fitzpatrick, Sheila (ed.), *Cultural Revolution in Russia, 1928–1931*, Bloomington: Indiana University Press, 1978.

Fokkema, Douwe W., *Report from Peking: Observations of a Western Diplomat on the Cultural Revolution*, London: Hurst, 1972.

Forster, Keith, *Rebellion and Factionalism in a Chinese Province: Zhejiang, 1966–1976*, Armonk, NY: M. E. Sharpe, 1990.

Friedman, Edward, Paul G. Pickowicz and Mark Selden, *Revolution, Resistance and Reform in Village China*, New Haven, CT: Yale University Press, 2005.

Fu Guangming and Zheng Shi, *Taiping hu de jiyi: Lao She zhi si koushu shilu* (Memories of Taiping Lake: Record of oral testimonies about Lao She's death), Shenzhen: Haitian chubanshe, 2001.

Gamsa, Mark, *The Chinese Translation of Russian Literature: Three Studies*, Leiden: Brill, 2008.

Gao Hua, 'Zai Guizhou "siqing yundong" de beihou' (The background of the 'Four Cleans' campaign in Guizhou), *Ershiyi shiji*, no. 93 (Feb. 2006), pp. 75–89.

Gao Shuhua and Cheng Tiejun, *Nei Meng wenge fenglei: Yiwei zaofanpai lingxiu de koushu shi* (The Cultural Revolution in Inner Mongolia: The oral history of a rebel leader), Carle Place, NY: Mingjing chubanshe, 2007.

Gao Wenqian, *Zhou Enlai: The Last Perfect Revolutionary*, New York: PublicAffairs, 2007.

Gao Yuan, *Born Red: A Chronicle of the Cultural Revolution*, Stanford: Stanford University Press, 1987.

Garside, Roger, *Coming Alive: China after Mao*, London: Deutsch, 1981.

Gladney, Dru, *Muslim Chinese: Ethnic Nationalism in the People's Republic*, Cambridge, MA: Harvard University Press, 1996.

Goldstein, Lyle J., 'Return to Zhenbao Island: Who Started Shooting and Why It Matters', *China Quarterly*, no. 168 (Dec. 2001), pp. 985–97.

Gong Xiaoxia, 'Repressive Movements and the Politics of Victimization', doctoral dissertation, Harvard University, 1995.

Griffin, Nicholas, *Ping-Pong Diplomacy: The Secret History behind the Game that Changed the World*, New York: Scribner, 2014.

Guo Dehong and Lin Xiaobo (eds), *'Siqing' yundong qinli ji* (Personal accounts of the 'Four Cleanups'), Beijing: Renmin chubanshe, 2008.

Guo Dehong and Lin Xiaobo, *Siqing yundong shilu* (True record of the Four Cleanups), Hangzhou: Zhejiang renmin chubanshe, 2005.

Guo Faliang, *Guxiang, guren, gushi* (Home town, home people, home stories), Beijing: Beijing shidai nongchao wenhua fazhan gongsi, 2011.

Guo Jian, Yongyi Song and Yuan Zhou (eds), *The A to Z of the Chinese Cultural Revolution*, Lanham, MD: Scarecrow Press, 2009.

Guo Xuezhi, *China's Security State: Philosophy, Evolution, and Politics*, Cambridge: Cambridge University Press, 2012.

Grey, Anthony, *Hostage in Peking*, London: Weidenfeld & Nicholson, 1988.

Halberstam, David, *The Coldest Winter: America and the Korean War*, London: Macmillan, 2008.

Hankiss, Elemér, 'The "Second Society": Is There an Alternative Social Model Emerging in Contemporary Hungary?', *Social Research*, 55, nos 1–2 (Spring 1988), pp. 13–42.

Hao Ping, 'Reassessing the Starting Point of the Cultural Revolution', *China Review International*, 3, no. 1 (Spring 1996), pp. 66–86.

Hao Shengxin, *Nanwang de suiyue* (Unforgettable years), Beijing: Beijing shidai nongchao wenhua fazhan gongsi, 2011.

Hoare, James, *Embassies in the East: The Story of the British Embassies in Japan, China and Korea from 1859 to the Present*, Richmond: Curzon Press, 1999.

Holm, David, 'The Strange Case Of Liu Zhidan', *Australian Journal of Chinese Affairs*, no. 27 (Jan. 1992), pp. 77–96.

Honig, Emily, 'Socialist Sex: The Cultural Revolution Revisited', *Modern China*, 29, no. 2 (April 2003), pp. 143–75.

Hou Yonglu, *Nongmin riji: Yige nongmin de shengcun shilu* (Diary of a farmer), Beijing: Zhongguo qingnian chubanshe, 2006.

Howe, Christopher, 'Labour Organisation and Incentives in Industry before and after the Cultural Revolution', in Stuart Schram (ed.), *Authority, Participation and Cultural Change in China*, London: Contemporary China Institute, 1973, pp. 233–56.

Hu Jinzhao, *Wenren luonan ji* (Record of intellectuals in distress), self-published, 2011.

Hua Linshan, *Les Années rouges*, Paris: Seuil, 1987.

Huang Shu-min, *The Spiral Road: Change in a Chinese Village through the Eyes of a Communist Party Leader*, Boulder, CO: Westview Press, 1989.

Huang Yanmin, 'Posijiu yundong de fazhan mailuo' (The development of the campaign to destroy the 'four olds'), *Ershiyi shiji*, no. 137 (June 2013), pp. 71–82.

Huang Zheng, *Liu Shaoqi de zuihou suiyue 1966–1969* (Liu Shaoqi's last years, 1966–1969), Beijing: Jiuzhou chubanshe, 2012.

Huang Zheng, *Liu Shaoqi yisheng* (Liu Shaoqi: A life), Beijing: Zhongyang wenxian chubanshe, 2003.

Huang Zheng, *Wang Guangmei fangtan lu* (A record of conversations with Wang Guangmei), Beijing: Zhongyang wenxian chubanshe, 2006.

Hunter, Neale, *Shanghai Journal: An Eyewitness Account of the Cultural Revolution*, New York: Praeger, 1969.

Ji Fengyuan, *Linguistic Engineering: Language and Politics in Mao's China*, Honolulu: University of Hawai'i Press, 2004.

Jiang Hongsheng, 'The Paris Commune in Shanghai: The Masses, the State, and Dynamics of "Continuous Revolution"', doctoral dissertation, Duke University, 2010.

Jiang Weiqing, *Qishi nian zhengcheng: Jiang Weiqing huiyilu* (A seventy-year journey: The memoirs of Jiang Weiqing), Nanjing: Jiangsu renmin chubanshe, 1996.

Jin Chongji (ed.), *Zhou Enlai zhuan, 1898–1949* (A biography of Zhou Enlai, 1898–1949), Beijing: Zhongyang wenxian chubanshe, 1989.

Jin Chongji and Huang Zheng (eds), *Liu Shaoqi zhuan* (A biography of Liu Shaoqi), Beijing: Zhongyang wenxian chubanshe, 1998.

Jin Dalu, *Feichang yu zhengchang: Shanghai 'wenge' shiqi de shehui bianqian* (The extraordinary and the ordinary: Social change in Shanghai during the Cultural Revolution), Shanghai: Shanghai cishu chubanshe, 2011.

Jin, Qiu, *The Culture of Power: The Lin Biao Incident in the Cultural Revolution*, Stanford: Stanford University Press, 1999.

Jong, Alice de, 'The Strange Story of Chairman Mao's Wonderful Gift', *China Information*, 9, no. 1 (Summer 1994), pp. 48–54.

Kang Zhengguo, *Confessions: An Innocent Life in Communist China*, New York: Norton, 2007.

Kao, Chen-yang, 'The Cultural Revolution and the Emergence of Pentecostal-style Protestantism in China', *Journal of Contemporary Religion*, 24, no. 2 (May 2009), pp. 171–88.

Kapitsa, Michael Stepanovitch, *Na raznykh parallelakh: Zapiski diplomata*, Moscow: Kniga i Biznes, 1996.

Kelliher, Daniel, *Peasant Power in China: The Era of Rural Reform, 1979–1989*, New Haven, CT: Yale University Press, 1992.

King, Richard (ed.), *Art in Turmoil: The Chinese Cultural Revolution, 1966–76*, Vancouver: University of British Columbia Press, 2010.

Kueh, Y. Y., 'Mao and Agriculture in China's Industrialization: Three Antitheses in a 50-Year Perspective', *China Quarterly*, no. 187 (Sept. 2006), pp. 700–23.

Lacouture, Jean, 'From the Vietnam War to an Indochina War', *Foreign Affairs*, July 1970, pp. 617–28.

Ladany, Laszlo, *The Communist Party of China and Marxism, 1921–1985: A Self-Portrait*, London: Hurst, 1988.

Laing, Ellen Johnston, *The Winking Owl: Art in the People's Republic of China*, Berkeley: University of California Press, 1988.

Lardy, Nicholas R., *Agriculture in China's Modern Economic Development*, Cambridge: Cambridge University Press, 1983.

Law Kam-yee (ed.), *The Cultural Revolution Reconsidered: Beyond a Purge and a Holocaust*, London: Macmillan, 2002.

Lee, Hong Yung, 'The Radical Students in Kwangtung during the Cultural Revolution', *China Quarterly*, no. 64 (Dec. 1975), pp. 645–83.

Lee, Joseph Tse-Hei, 'Watchman Nee and the Little Flock Movement in Maoist China', *Church History*, 74, no. 1 (March 2005), pp. 68–96.

Leese, Daniel, *Mao Cult: Rhetoric and Ritual in China's Cultural Revolution*, Cambridge: Cambridge University Press, 2011.

Leys, Simon, *Broken Images: Essays on Chinese Culture and Politics*, New York: St Martin's Press, 1980.

Leys, Simon, *The Chairman's New Clothes: Mao and the Cultural Revolution*, New York: St Martin's Press, 1977.

Li Hua-yu, 'Instilling Stalinism in Chinese Party Members: Absorbing Stalin's Short Course in the 1950s', in Thomas P. Bernstein and Li Hua-yu (eds), *China*

Learns from the Soviet Union, 1949–Present, Lanham, MD: Lexington Books, 2009, pp. 107–30.

Li Jie, 'Virtual Museums of Forbidden Memories: Hu Jie's Documentary Films on the Cultural Revolution', *Public Culture*, 21, no. 3 (Fall 2009), pp. 539–49.

Li Kwok-sing, *A Glossary of Political Terms of the People's Republic of China*, Hong Kong: Chinese University of Hong Kong Press, 1995.

Li Rui, *Lushan huiyi shilu* (A true record of the Lushan plenum), Zhengzhou: Henan renmin chubanshe, 1999.

Li Shihua, *Gongyong de mubei: Yige Zhongguoren de jiating jishi* (A common tombstone: The story of one Chinese family), Carle Place, NY: Mingjing chubanshe, 2008.

Li Xun, *Da bengkui: Shanghai gongren zaofanpai xingwang shi* (The rise and fall of Shanghai's worker rebels), Taipei: Shibao chubanshe, 1996.

Li Zhisui, *The Private Life of Chairman Mao: The Memoirs of Mao's Personal Physician*, New York: Random House, 1994.

Liang Heng and Judith Shapiro, *Son of the Revolution*, New York: Alfred A. Knopf, 1983.

Liang Xiaosheng, *Yige hongweibing de zibai* (Confessions from a Red Guard), Hong Kong: Tiandi tushu youxian gongsi, 1996.

Liao Yiwu, *God is Red: The Secret Story of How Christianity Survived and Flourished in Communist China*, New York: HarperCollins, 2011.

Ling, Ken, *The Revenge of Heaven*, New York: Ballantine, 1972.

Liu Guokai, *A Brief Analysis of the Cultural Revolution*, Armonk, NY: M. E. Sharpe, 1987.

Liu Tong, 'Jieshi Zhongnanhai gaoceng zhengzhi de yiba yaoshi: Lin Biao biji de hengli yu yanjiu' (A key to understanding high politics in Zhongnanhai: Sorting out and studying Lin Biao's notes), paper presented at the International Conference on Chinese War and Revolution in the Twentieth Century, Shanghai Communications University, 8–9 Nov. 2008.

Liu Wenzhong, *Fengyu rensheng lu: Yige canji kuqiu xinsheng ji* (A record of my stormy life), Macau: Aomen chongshi wenhua, 2004.

Liu Xiaomeng, *Zhongguo zhiqing shi: Dachao, 1966–1980* (A history of China's sent-down youth: The big wave, 1966–1980), Beijing: Zhongguo shehui kexue chubanshe, 1998.

Liu Zuneng, *Wo de gushi* (My story), Beijing: Beijing shidai nongchao wenhua fazhan gongsi, 2011.

Loh, Christine, *Underground Front: The Chinese Communist Party in Hong Kong*, Hong Kong: Hong Kong University Press, 2010.

Lu Hong, *Junbao neibu xiaoxi: 'Wenge' qinli shilu* (An insider's story of the PLA daily), Hong Kong, Shidai guoji chubanshe, 2006.

Lü Xiuyuan, 'A Step toward Understanding Popular Violence in China's Cultural Revolution', *Pacific Affairs*, 67, no. 4 (Winter 1994–5), pp. 533–63.

Luo Bing, 'Mao Zedong fadong shejiao yundong dang'an jiemi' (Revelations from the archives on the launching of the Socialist Education Campaign by Mao Zedong), *Zhengming*, Feb. 2006, pp. 10–13.

Luo Ruiqing, *Commemorate the Victory over German Fascism! Carry the Struggle against U.S. Imperialism through to the End!*, Beijing: Foreign Languages Press, 1965.

Lüthi, Lorenz, 'The Vietnam War and China's Third-Line Defense Planning before the Cultural Revolution, 1964–1966', *Journal of Cold War Studies*, 10, no. 1 (Winter 2008), pp. 26–51.

Ma Bo, *Xue yu tie* (Blood and iron), Beijing: Zhongguo shehui kexue chubanshe, 1998.

MacFarquhar, Roderick, *The Origins of the Cultural Revolution*, vol. 1: *Contradictions among the People, 1956–1957*, London: Oxford University Press, 1974.

MacFarquhar, Roderick, *The Origins of the Cultural Revolution*, vol. 3, *The Coming of the Cataclysm, 1961–1966*, New York: Columbia University Press, 1997.

MacFarquhar, Roderick and Michael Schoenhals, *Mao's Last Revolution*, Cambridge, MA: Harvard University Press, 2006.

MacMillan, Margaret, *Nixon and Mao: The Week that Changed the World*, New York: Random House, 2007.

Mao Zedong, *Jianguo yilai Mao Zedong wengao* (Mao Zedong's manuscripts since the founding of the People's Republic), Beijing: Zhongyang wenxian chubanshe, 1987–96.

Mao Zedong, *Mao Zedong waijiao wenxuan* (Selection of writings on foreign affairs by Mao Zedong), Beijing: Zhongyang wenxian chubanshe, 1994.

Marcuse, Jacques, *The Peking Papers: Leaves from the Notebook of a China Correspondent*, London: Arthur Barker, 1968.

Milton, David and Nancy D. Milton, *The Wind Will Not Subside: Years in Revolutionary China, 1964–1969*, New York: Pantheon Books, 1976.

Mitcham, Chad J., *China's Economic Relations with the West and Japan, 1949–79: Grain, Trade and Diplomacy*, New York: Routledge, 2005.

Mittler, Barbara, '"Eight Stage Works for 800 Million People": The Great Proletarian Cultural Revolution in Music – A View from Revolutionary Opera', *Opera Quarterly*, 26, nos 2–3 (Spring 2010), pp. 377–401.

Murck, Alfreda, 'Golden Mangoes: The Life Cycle of a Cultural Revolution Symbol', *Archives of Asian Art*, 57 (2007), pp. 1–21.

Murck, Alfreda (ed.), *Mao's Golden Mangoes and the Cultural Revolution*, Zurich: Scheidegger & Spiess, 2013.

Nanchu, *Red Sorrow: A Memoir*, New York: Arcade, 2001.

Nanjing shi dang'anguan (eds), *Nanjing wenhua da geming da shiji chugao* (Draft chronology of major events during the Cultural Revolution in Nanjing), Nanjing: Nanjing shi dang'anguan, 1985.

Naughton, Barry, 'The Third Front: Defence Industrialization in the Chinese Interior', *China Quarterly*, no. 115 (Sept. 1988), pp. 351–86.

Nelsen, Harvey W., *Power and Insecurity: Beijing, Moscow and Washington, 1949–1988*, Boulder, CO: Lynne Rienner, 1989.

Oi, Jean C., *State and Peasant in Contemporary China: The Political Economy of Village Government*, Berkeley: University of California Press, 1989.

Ostermann, Christian F., 'East German Documents on the Border Conflict, 1969', *Cold War International History Project Bulletin*, nos 6–7 (Winter 1995), pp. 186–91.

Palmer, James, *The Death of Mao: The Tangshan Earthquake and the Birth of the New China*, London: Faber & Faber, 2012.

Pan, Philip, *Out of Mao's Shadow: The Struggle for the Soul of a New China*, Basingstoke: Picador, 2009.

Pan Yihong, *Tempered in the Revolutionary Furnace: China's Youth in the Rustication Movement*, Lanham, MD: Lexington Books, 2009.

Pang Laikwan, 'The Dialectics of Mao's Images: Monumentalism, Circulation and Power Effects', in Christian Henriot and Yeh Wen-hsin (eds), *Visualising China, 1845–1965: Moving and Still Images in Historical Narratives*, Leiden: Brill, 2013, pp. 407–38.

Pang Xianzhi, Guo Chaoren and Jin Chongji (eds), *Liu Shaoqi*, Beijing: Xinhua chubanshe, 1998.

Pang Xianzhi and Jin Chongji (eds), *Mao Zedong zhuan, 1949–1976* (A biography of Mao Zedong, 1949–1976), Beijing: Zhongyang wenxian chubanshe, 2003.

Pantsov, Alexander V. and Steven I. Levine, *Mao: The Real Story*, New York: Simon & Schuster, 2012.

Pasqualini, Jean, *Prisoner of Mao*, Harmondsworth: Penguin, 1973.

Perry, Elizabeth J., *Challenging the Mandate of Heaven: Social Protest and State Power in China*, Armonk, NY: M. E. Sharpe, 2002.

Perry, Elizabeth J., 'Shanghai's Strike Wave of 1957', *China Quarterly*, no. 137 (March 1994), pp. 1–27.

Perry, Elizabeth J. and Li Xun, *Proletarian Power: Shanghai in the Cultural Revolution*, Boulder, CO: Westview Press, 2000.

Potter, Pitman, *From Leninist Discipline to Socialist Legalism: Peng Zhen on Law and Political Authority in the PRC*, Stanford: Stanford University Press, 2003.

Qinghua daxue zhi (Annals of Tsinghua University), Beijing: Qinghua daxue chubanshe, 2001.

Radchenko, Sergey, *Two Suns in the Heavens: The Sino-Soviet Struggle for Supremacy, 1962–1967*, Stanford: Stanford University Press, 2009.

Rees, E. A., *Iron Lazar: A Political Biography of Lazar Kaganovich*, London: Anthem Press, 2012.

Riskin, Carl, *China's Political Economy: The Quest for Development since 1949*, Oxford: Oxford University Press, 1987.

Rittenberg, Sidney, *The Man Who Stayed Behind*, New York: Simon & Schuster, 1993.

Robinson, Thomas W., 'The Wuhan Incident: Local Strife and Provincial Rebellion during the Cultural Revolution', *China Quarterly*, no. 47 (July 1971), pp. 413–38.

Rosen, Stanley, *Red Guard Factionalism and the Cultural Revolution in Guangzhou*, Boulder, CO: Westview Press, 1982.

Salisbury, Harrison E., *The New Emperors: China in the Era of Mao and Deng*, Boston: Little, Brown, 1992.

Schoenhals, Michael, *China's Cultural Revolution, 1966–1969: Not a Dinner Party*, Armonk, NY: M. E. Sharpe, 1996.

Schoenhals, Michael, '"Why Don't We Arm the Left?" Mao's Culpability for the Cultural Revolution's "Great Chaos" of 1967', *China Quarterly*, no. 182 (June 2005), pp. 277–300.

Schrift, Melissa, *Biography of a Chairman Mao Badge: The Creation and Mass Consumption of a Personality Cult*, New Brunswick, NJ: Rutgers University Press, 2001.

Service, Robert, *Stalin: A Biography*, Basingstoke: Macmillan, 2004.

Shakya, Tsering, *The Dragon in the Land of Snows*, New York: Columbia University Press, 1999.

Shan, Patrick Fuliang, 'Becoming Loyal: General Xu Shiyou and Maoist Regimentation', *American Journal of Chinese Studies*, 18, no. 2 (Fall 2011), pp. 133–50.

Shapiro, Judith, *Mao's War against Nature: Politics and the Environment in Revolutionary China*, New York: Cambridge University Press, 2001.

Shen Fuxiang, *Zhengrong suiyue: Shoudu gongren zaofanpai huiyilu* (The years of glory: Memories of a rebel worker), Hong Kong: Shidai guoji chuban youxian gongsi, 2010.

Shen Xiaoyun, 'The Revolutionary Committee Grows out of the Barrel of a Gun during the Great Proletarian Cultural Revolution: The Unknown Truth of "Armed Conflict" in Guangxi', *Modern China Studies*, 20, no. 1 (2013), pp. 141–82.

Sheng, Michael M., *Battling Western Imperialism: Mao, Stalin, and the United States*, Princeton: Princeton University Press, 1997.

Sheridan, Mary, 'The Emulation of Heroes', *China Quarterly*, no. 33 (March 1968), pp. 47–72.

Shevchenko, Arkady N., *Breaking with Moscow*, New York: Alfred A. Knopf, 1985.

Shirk, Susan L., *The Political Logic of Economic Reform in China*, Berkeley: University of California Press, 1993.

Smith, Craig S., 'Mao's Buried Past: A Strange, Subterranean City', *New York Times*, 26 Nov. 2001.

Song Bolin, *Hongweibing xingshuailu: Qinghua fuzhong lao hongweibing shouji* (The rise and fall of Red Guards: Diary of an old Red Guard from the Middle School attached to Tsinghua University), Hong Kong: Desai chuban youxian gongsi, 2006.

Song Liansheng, *Nongye xue Dazhai shimo* (The history of the Learn from Dazhai campaign), Wuhan: Hubei renmin chubanshe, 2005.

Song Yongyi, 'The Enduring Legacy of Blood Lineage Theory', *China Rights Forum*, no. 4 (2004), pp. 13–23.

Song Yongyi, *Les Massacres de la Révolution Culturelle*, Paris: Gallimard, 2009.

Song Yongyi, 'Bei yancang de lishi: Liu Shao dui "wenge" de dute gongxian' (Hidden history: Liu Shaoqi's special contribution to the Cultural Revolution), in Song Yongyi (ed.), *Wenhua da geming: Lishi zhenxiang he jiti jiyi* (The Cultural Revolution: Historical truth and collective memories), Hong Kong: Tianyuan shuwu, 2007, vol. 2, pp. 45–62.

Stalin, Josef, *History of the All-Union Communist Party: A Short Course*, New York: International Publishers, 1939.

Su Yang, *Collective Killings in Rural China during the Cultural Revolution*, Cambridge: Cambridge University Press, 2011.

Sun Qinghe, *Shengsi yitiao lu* (The road between life and death), Beijing: Beijing shidai nongchao wenhua fazhan gongsi, 2012.

Sun Youli and Dan Ling, *Engineering Communist China: One Man's Story*, New York: Algora Publishing, 2003.

Tan Hecheng, *Xue de shenhua: Gongyuan 1967 nian Hunan Daoxian wenge da tusha jishi* (A bloody tale: A historical account of the Cultural Revolution massacre of 1967 in Daoxian, Hunan), Hong Kong: Tianxingjian chubanshe, 2010.

Tan, Pamela, *The Chinese Factor: An Australian Chinese Woman's Life in China from 1950 to 1979*, Dural, New South Wales: Roseberg, 2008.

Tang, George Y., *Liangdairen de xuanze* (The choices of two generations), Beijing: Beijing shidai nongchao wenhua fazhan gongsi, 2011.

Tannebaum, Gerald, 'How the Workers Took over their Wharves', *Eastern Horizon*, 6, no. 6 (July 1967), pp. 6–17.

Taubman, William, *Khrushchev: The Man and his Era*, London, Free Press, 2003.

Terrill, Ross, *Madame Mao: The White-Boned Demon*, Stanford: Stanford University Press, 1990.

Thaxton, Ralph, *Catastrophe and Contention in Rural China: Mao's Great Leap Famine and the Origins of Righteous Resistance in Da Fo Village*, Cambridge: Cambridge University Press, 2008.

Thurston, Anne F., *Enemies of the People*, New York: Knopf, 1987.

Tilt, Bryan, *The Struggle for Sustainability in Rural China: Environmental Values and Civil Society*, New York: Columbia University Press, 2009.

Tumen and Zhu Dongli, *Kang Sheng yu 'Neirendang' yuan'an* (Kang Sheng and the unjust case of the 'Inner Party'), Beijing: Zhonggong zhongyang dangxiao chubanshe, 1995.

Tyler, Christian, *Wild West China: The Taming of Xinjiang*, London: John Murray, 2003.

Unger, Jonathan, 'The Cultural Revolution at the Grass Roots', *China Journal*, no. 57 (Jan. 2007), pp. 109–37.

Unger, Jonathan, 'Cultural Revolution Conflict in the Villages', *China Quarterly*, no. 153 (March 1998), pp. 82–106.

Usov, Victor, 'The Secrets of Zhongnanhai: Who Wiretapped Mao Zedong, and How?', *Far Eastern Affairs*, no. 5 (May 2012), pp. 129–39.

van der Heijden, Marien, Stefan R. Landsberger, Kuiyi Shen, *Chinese Posters: The IISH-Landsberger Collections*, München: Prestel, 2009.

Walder, Andrew G., *Fractured Rebellion: The Beijing Red Guard Movement*, Cambridge, MA: Harvard University Press, 2009.

Walder, Andrew G., 'Tan Lifu: A "Reactionary" Red Guard in Historical Perspective', *China Quarterly*, no. 180 (Dec. 2004), pp. 965–88.

Walder, Andrew G. and Yang Su, 'The Cultural Revolution in the Countryside: Scope, Timing and Human Impact', *China Quarterly*, no. 173 (March 2003), pp. 74–99.

Wang Aihe, *Wuming (No Name) Painting Catalogue*, Hong Kong: Hong Kong University Press, 2010.

Wang Aihe, 'Wuming: An Underground Art Group during the Cultural Revolution', *Journal of Modern Chinese History*, 3, no. 2 (Dec. 2009), pp. 183–99.

Wang Chenglin, *Chongqing 'zalan gong, jian, fa' qinli ji* (Personal account of the 'smashing of the legal apparatus' in Chongqing), self-published, 2003.

Wang Duanyang, *Yige hongweibing de riji* (Diary of a Red Guard), self-published, 2007.

Wang Guangyu, *Qingshi nanyin: Zuihou yici jiaodai* (Ineluctable history: My last confession), self-published, 2011.

Wang, Helen, *Chairman Mao Badges: Symbols and Slogans of the Cultural Revolution*, London: British Museum, 2008.

Wang Nianyi, *Da dongluan de niandai* (The years of great turmoil), Zhengzhou: Henan renmin chubanshe, 1988.

Wang Rui, '"Anting shijian" de zai renshi he zai yanjiu' (Revisiting the Anting incident), *Ershiyi shiji*, no. 55, 31 Oct. 2006.

Wang Shaoguang, *Failure of Charisma: The Cultural Revolution in Wuhan*, Oxford: Oxford University Press, 1995.

Wang Shengze, '"Wenge" fengbao zhong de Ye Fei shangjiang' (General Ye Fei during the Cultural Revolution), *Dangshi bolan*, no. 12 (Dec. 2008), pp. 41–6.

Wang Youqin, 'Finding a Place for the Victims: The Problem in Writing the History of the Cultural Revolution', *China Perspectives*, no. 4, 2007, pp. 65–74.

Wang Youqin, 'The Second Wave of Violent Persecution of Teachers: The Revolution of 1968', Presented at the 35th International Congress of Asian and North African Studies, Budapest, 7–12 July 1997.

Wang Youqin, 'Student Attacks against Teachers: The Revolution of 1966', *Issues and Studies*, 37, no. 2 (March 2001), pp. 29–79.

Watt, George, *China 'Spy'*, London: Johnson, 1972.

Wei Guoqing, 'Kazhan "siqing" yundong' (Launching the "Four Cleans" Campaign), in Guo Dehong and Lin Xiaobo (eds), *'Siqing' yundong qinli ji* (Personal reminiscences on the 'Four Cleans' campaign), Beijing: Renmin chubanshe, 2008, pp. 36–65.

Wei Xiaolan, '"Wo xin tianzonghui liang": Kang Sheng mishu tan "Sha Tao shijian"' ('I believe the sky will always be clear': Kang Sheng's secretary on the 'Sha Tao case'), *Bainianchao*, no. 9 (Sept. 2007), pp. 52–6.

Welch, Holmes, *Buddhism under Mao*, Cambridge, MA: Harvard University Press, 1972.

Welsh, Frank, *A History of Hong Kong*, London: HarperCollins, 1993.

Wen Dayong, *Hongweibing chanhui lu* (A Red Guard repents), Hong Kong: Mingbao chubanshe youxian gongsi, 2000.

Westad, O. Arne, 'The Great Transformation', in Niall Ferguson, Charles S. Maier, Erez Manela and Daniel J. Sargent (eds), *The Shock of the Global: The 1970s in Perspective*, Cambridge, MA: Harvard University Press, 2010, pp. 65–79.

Westad, O. Arne and Sophie Quinn-Judge (eds), *The Third Indochina War: Conflict between China, Vietnam and Cambodia, 1972–79*, London: Routledge, 2006.

White, Lynn T., *Policies of Chaos: The Organizational Causes of Violence in China's Cultural Revolution*, Princeton: Princeton University Press, 1989.

White, Lynn T., *Unstately Power: Local Causes of China's Economic Reforms*, Armonk, NY: M. E. Sharpe, 1998.

Williams, Philip F. and Yenna Wu, *The Great Wall of Confinement: The Chinese Prison Camp through Contemporary Fiction and Reportage*, Berkeley: University of California Press, 2004.

Wilson, Verity, 'Dress and the Cultural Revolution', in Valerie Steele and John S. Major (eds), *China Chic: East Meets West*, New Haven, CT: Yale University Press, 1999, pp. 167–86.

Wolin, Richard, *The Wind from the East: French Intellectuals, the Cultural Revolution, and the Legacy of the 1960s*, Princeton: Princeton University Press, 2010.

Wong, Frances, *China Bound and Unbound: History in the Making: An Early Returnee's Account*, Hong Kong: Hong Kong University Press, 2009.

Wong, Jan, *Red China Blues: My Long March from Mao to Now*, New York: Doubleday, 1996.

Woodward, Dennis, 'Rural Campaigns: Continuity and Change in the Chinese Countryside – The Early Post-Cultural Revolution Experience (1969–1972)', *Australian Journal of Chinese Affairs*, no. 6 (July 1981), pp. 97–124.

Wu, Harry, *Bitter Winds: A Memoir of my Years in China's Gulag*, New York: Wiley, 1993.

Wu, Harry Hongda, *Laogai: The Chinese Gulag*, Boulder, CO: Westview Press, 1992.

Wu Ningkun and Li Yikai, *A Single Tear: A Family's Persecution, Love, and Endurance in Communist China*, London: Hodder & Stoughton, 1993.

Wu, Tommy Jieqin, *A Sparrow's Voice: Living through China's Turmoil in the 20th Century*, Shawnee Mission, KS: M.I.R. House International, 1999.

Wu, Yiching, *The Cultural Revolution at the Margins: Chinese Socialism in Crisis*, Cambridge, MA: Harvard University Press, 2014.

Wylie, Raymond F., 'Shanghai Dockers in the Cultural Revolution: The Interplay of Political and Economic Issues', in Christopher Howe (ed.), *Shanghai: Revolution and Development in an Asian Metropolis*, Cambridge: Cambridge University Press, 1981, pp. 91–124.

Xia Yafeng, 'China's Elite Politics and Sino-American Rapprochement, January 1969–February 1972', *Journal of Cold War Studies*, 8, no. 4 (Fall 2006), pp. 3–28.

Xiao Donglian, *Qiusuo Zhongguo: Wenge qian shinian shi* (Exploring China: A history of the decade before the Cultural Revolution), Beijing: Zhonggong dangshi chubanshe, 2011.

Xiao Mu, *Fengyu rensheng* (A stormy life), New York: Cozy House Publisher, 2003.

Xie Chengnian, 'Wo qinli de "siqing" yundong naxie shi' (My personal experience of the 'Four Cleans'), *Wenshi tiandi*, no. 6 (June 2012), pp. 8–12.

Xie Shengxian, *Hei yu bai de jiyi: Cong wenxue qingnian dao 'wenge fan'* (Black and white memories: From literary youth to criminal of the Cultural Revolution), Hong Kong: Sanlian shudian, 2012.

Xu Xiaodi, *Diandao suiyue* (Tumultuous years), Beijing: Shenghuo, dushu, xinzhi sanlian shudian, 2012.

Xu Yong, 'Wei Guoqing extermine la faction du "22 Avril"', in Song Yongyi, *Les Massacres de la Révolution Culturelle*, Paris: Gallimard, 2009, pp. 249–78.

Xue Tingchen, *Wuhui rensheng* (A life without regrets), Beijing: Beijing shidai nongchao wenhua fazhan gongsi, 2011.

Yan Jiaqi and Gao Gao, *Turbulent Decade: A History of the Cultural Revolution*, Honolulu: University of Hawai'i Press, 1996.

Yan Lebin, *Wo suo jingli de nage shidai* (That era I lived through), Beijing: Shidai wenhua chubanshe, 2012.

Yang Dongxiao, 'Wenge jinshu: "Shaonü zhi xin". Nage niandai de xingyuzui' (A book banned during the Cultural Revolution: 'The Heart of a Maiden'. The first pornographic novel hand-copied during the Cultural Revolution), *Renwu huabao*, no. 23 (2010), pp. 68–71.

Yang Jian, *Zhongguo zhiqing wenxue shi* (A literary history of educated youth), Beijing: Zhongguo gongren chubanshe, 2002.

Yang Kuisong, 'The Sino-Soviet border clash of 1969: From Zhenbao Island to Sino-American *Rapprochement*', *Cold War History*, 1, no. 1 (Aug. 2000), pp. 21–52.

Yang Lan, 'Memory and Revisionism: The Cultural Revolution on the Internet', in Ingo Cornils and Sarah Waters (eds), *Memories of 1968: International Perspectives*, Oxford: Peter Lang, 2010, pp. 249–79.

Yang, Rae, *Spider Eaters: A Memoir*, Berkeley: University of California Press, 1997.

Yang Xiaokai, *Captive Spirits: Prisoners of the Cultural Revolution*, New York: Oxford University Press, 1997.

Yao Jin, *Yao Yilin baixi tan* (Conversations with Yao Yilin), Beijing: Zhonggong dangshi chubanshe, 2008.

Ye Qing, '"Wenge" shiqi Fujian qunzhong zuzhi yanjiu' (A study of mass organisations in Fujian during the 'Cultural Revolution'), Fujian Normal University, doctoral dissertation, 2002.

Ye Tingxing, *My Name is Number 4: A True Story from the Cultural Revolution*, Basingstoke, NH: St. Martin's Griffin, 2008.

Ye Yonglie, *Chen Boda zhuan* (Biography of Chen Boda), Beijing: Zuojia chubanshe, 1993.

Ying Shanhong (ed.), *Yanzheng jinghan: Hunan Hengyang 'wenge' shishi* (Historical facts about Hunan's Hengyang), self-published, 2002.

Yu Xiguang, *Weibei weigan wang youguo: 'Wenhua da geming' shangshu ji* (Humble people do not forget their country: A collection of petitions from the Cultural Revolution), Changsha: Hunan renmin chubanshe, 1989.

Yue Daiyun, *To the Storm: The Odyssey of a Revolutionary Chinese Woman*, Berkeley: University of California Press, 1985.

Zagoria, Donald, *Vietnam Triangle: Moscow, Peking, Hanoi*, New York: Pegasus, 1967.

Zang Xiaowei, *Children of the Cultural Revolution: Family Life and Political Behavior in Mao's China*, Boulder, CO: Westview Press, 2000.

Zhai Zhenhua, *Red Flower of China*, New York: Soho, 1992.

Zhang, Elya J., 'To be Somebody: Li Qinglin, Run-of-the-Mill Cultural Revolution Showstopper', in Joseph W. Esherick, Paul G. Pickowicz and Andrew Walder (eds), *The Chinese Cultural Revolution as History*, Stanford: Stanford University Press, 2006, pp. 211–39.

Zhang Guanghua, *Zhenshi de huiyi* (Real memories), Beijing: Beijing shidai nongchao wenhua fazhan gongsi, 2010.

Zhang Suhua, *Bianju: Qiqianren dahui shimo* (The whole story of the Seven Thousand Cadres Conference), Beijing: Zhongguo qingnian chubanshe, 2006.

Zheng Yi, *Scarlet Memorial: Tales of Cannibalism in Modern China*, Boulder, CO: Westview Press, 1996.

Zhou Chenghao, *Wangshi huiyi* (Memories of things past), Beijing: Beijing shidai nongchao wenhua fazhan gongsi, 2011.

Zhou, Kate Xiao, *How the Farmers Changed China: Power of the People*, Boulder, CO: Westview Press, 1996.

Zhou Zehao, 'The Anti-Confucian Campaign during the Cultural Revolution, August 1966–January 1967', doctoral dissertation, University of Maryland, 2011.

Zhu Zhenghui and Jin Guangyao (eds), *Zhiqing buluo: Huangshang jiaoxia de 10,000 ge Shanghai ren* (The tribe of educated youth: The lives of 10,000 students from Shanghai in Huangshan), Shanghai: Shanghai guji chubanshe, 2004.

Zhuo Fei, *Yingzujie mingliu zai wenge de gushi* (Celebrities from the British concession in Shanghai during the Cultural Revolution), Hong Kong: Mingbao chubanshe youxian gongsi, 2005.

Zweig, David, *Agrarian Radicalism in China, 1968–1981*, Cambridge, MA: Harvard University Press, 1989.

Acknowledgements

I acknowledge with gratitude a joint research grant A-HKU701/12 from the Research Grants Council, Hong Kong, and the Agence Nationale de la Recherche, Paris, which allowed me to carry out the research for this book. The joint grant is designed to encourage collaboration between specialists of the Cultural Revolution at the University of Hong Kong and the French Centre for Research on Contemporary China, and I should like to express my gratitude to Jean-Philippe Béja, Michel Bonnin, Sebastian Veg and Wang Aihe. Nelson Chiu, Carol Nga Yee Lau and Zardas Lee helped as research assistants by sifting through printed sources and checking endnotes for the final text. A number of people have read and commented on draft versions, especially Gail Burrowes, Christopher Hutton, Françoise Koolen, Robert Peckham, Priscilla Roberts, Patricia Thornton, Andrew Walder and Lynn White. Jean Hung, at the Universities Service Centre for China Studies at the Chinese University of Hong Kong, was exceptionally helpful, especially in bringing memoirs of ordinary people to my attention. Tony and Elizabeth Blishen, David Cheng Chang, Thomas DuBois, Nancy Hearst, Karl Gerth, Guo Jian, Guo Zijian, Kenneth Kuo (Ken Ling), Li Xiaolin, Roderick MacFarquhar, Lynn Pan, Jennifer Ruth, Eve Song, Song Yongyi, Helen Sun, Yao Shuping, David Tsui, Wang Youqin, Matthew Wills, Wu Yiching, Jennifer Zhu Scott, Zhou Zehao and Zhu Jiaming were all very generous in sharing stories, suggestions and sources. Like other students of the Cultural Revolution, I owe a special debt to Roderick MacFarquhar, without whose erudite and elegantly written volumes about elite politics under Mao, in particular his *Mao's Last Revolution*, co-authored with Michael Schoenhals, this book would have been impossible.

I also received help from friends and colleagues in mainland China, but I prefer not to single them out. This may seem overly prudent, but developments in the People's Republic over the last few years show, once again, that it may be wise to err on the side of caution. The endnotes, on the other hand, demonstrate how the best and most courageous research on the Mao era often comes from the People's Republic, even if their authors have to publish abroad.

I would also like to extend my thanks to several people who have dedicated extraordinary time and effort to assembling and maintaining digital databases of source material on the Cultural Revolution. Song Yongyi and his team have painstakingly collected a whole array of documents that can be found in their Cultural Revolution Database. Wu Yiching's website project (difangwenge.org) has also become one of the most invaluable open research libraries on the Cultural Revolution.

I wish to give special thanks to those who kindly shared their memories of the Cultural Revolution with me. Even if I have not been able to quote from every interview, the memories of people from all walks of life, including many outcasts (*heiwulei*) who have so often been marginalised in accounts that focus on Red Guards, have been at the forefront of my mind when writing this narrative history.

I am indebted to my publishers, namely Michael Fishwick in London and George Gibson in New York, and my copy-editor Peter James, as well as Anna Simpson, Marigold Atkey, Laura Brook and all the team at Bloomsbury. I would like to convey my gratitude to my literary agent Andrew Wylie in New York and Sarah Chalfant and James Pullen in London. I thank my wife Gail Burrowes, with love.

Hong Kong, December 2015

Index

Aeronautics Institute, 117
agricultural production, 228–9, 265–6,
    320–1
    see also collectivisation and
    decollectivisation
Ai Xiaoming, 315
Albania, 23
All-China Federation of Literature and
    Art, 38
All-China Federation of Trade
    Unions, 107, 124
aluminium, 99–100
Amur River, 208
An Ziwen, 183
Anhui province
    beggars and vagabonds, 196
    collectivisation, 16, 18–19
    decollectivisation, 320–1
    and Mao's death, 315
    rebels attempt to seize power, 129
    silk production, 279
    starvation continues, 272
    students exiled to countryside, 196, 198
Ankang, 225
Anshan Iron and Steel
    Corporation, 305–6
antibiotics, shortages of, 114
Antonioni, Michelangelo, 301
army
    and course of Cultural
        Revolution, 129–32, 136–8
    and Cultural Revolution Group, 135–8,

163–4, 171–2
    and Dazhai campaign, 230–1
    and death of Lin Biao, 255, 258
    factionalism in, 142–5
    fortieth anniversary celebrations, 151
    imposes military control, 138–9
    loses privileges, 44
    moves towards military
        dictatorship, 185
    promotes Little Red Book, 97
    promotes Mao Zedong
        Thought, xiv–xv, 35–7, 167, 171,
        243
    restored to power, 163–4
    restrictions on, 140–2
    summer camps, 36–7, 72–3
artists, 169–71
    underground, 293–4

badges, Mao, 99–100, 108, 166, 247
Baiyin, 22, 46
Bank of China, 158, 261
barefoot doctors, 267–9
Beckett, Samuel, 290
Beidaihe, 17, 21, 250, 294
Beijing
    banners denounce Gang of Four, 316
    building of metro, 212
    children's games, 293
    clean-up of posters, 164
    demonstrations, 8
    dismissal of Peng Zhen, 45–9

exodus of students, 32–3, 192–3
Nixon's visit, 256
preparations for war, 211–14
Red Guards converge on, 104–11, 113, 115
soldiers swim across lake, 66
students seek redress, 101–2
underground literature, 290
victims of cleansing campaign, 187
violence in, 74–80, 93
see also British mission, burning of;
Forbidden City; Tiananmen Square
Beijing Military Region, 244, 250
Beijing Municipal Party Committee, 47, 49, 53, 55, 57, 75
Beijing Normal University, 64, 73, 75
Beijing Railway Station, 212
Beijing Teachers' College, 75
Beijing Zoo, 11, 317
Bian Zhongyun, death of, 73, 75
big-character poster campaign, 53–4, 57, 60–1, 63, 65, 69–71, 81, 108, 121, 123, 129, 148, 178, 187, 307
black markets, 225, 239, 270–1, 278, 285, 290, 298
blood donations, appeals for, 211
Bo Yibo, 64
book burnings, 83–4, 87–8, 285–6
Boxers, 161
Brezhnev, Leonid, xiii, 25, 43, 210
British mission, burning of, 157–8, 160–1, 163, 171, 233
Buddhism, 285, 294
Buddhist shrines and temples, 31–2
burial sites, 223–4
burials, ban on, 85

cadre schools, 202–5, 210, 258, 286–7, 298
Cambodia, 214, 246, 258
Camp David, 23
Camus, Albert, 290
cannibalism, 17, 176–7

canteens, collective, 237
Cao Diqiu, 104, 120, 125
Capital West Hotel, 138, 150, 189, 207
'Case of the Sixty-One Traitors', 156, 183
cats, massacre of, 86
cemeteries, 84–5
see also burial sites
Cemetery for Revolutionary Martyrs, 309
Central People's Radio, 57, 81
Chang, Jung, xvii, 35, 61, 72, 89, 107, 109, 117, 145, 268
and her family, 298–9
and forbidden literature, 288–90
and Mao's death, 314
Changsha, 70, 80, 133, 167, 195, 289
clashes between Red Guards, 102–3
factionalism in, 153–4
Chen Boda, 56–7, 67, 85, 91, 102, 116–18, 125, 172, 178
and army, 133–8, 143, 145, 153
fall of, 244–5, 248–9
protects Zhou Enlai, 160
Chen Yi, Marshal, 136–8, 160, 164, 245, 251
death and funeral, 255, 257
Chen Yonggui, 219–21, 227, 229, 262, 272–3
Chen Youxin, 185
Chen Yun, 17
Chen Zaidao, 149–51, 163, 255
Chengdu, 61, 89, 113, 140, 145, 169, 216, 288, 311
Chiang Kai-shek, 31, 36, 39, 62, 87, 184, 223, 246
China Youth Daily, 81
Chinese Communist Party
absorbs Mongolian People's Party, 190
creates post of honorary chairman, 6–7
dependence on Soviet Union, 4
elects new Central Committee, 208, 219
see also Lushan plenum; Seven Thousand Cadres Conference

Chinese Communist Party Congresses
  Eighth, 6, 30, 207
  Ninth, 207, 219, 235, 240, 243–5
  Tenth, 301
Chongqing, 147–8, 157, 229
Christianity, 32, 285, 294
class struggle, 16–18, 21–2, 28, 30–1, 43,
    54, 62, 73
  and Inner Mongolia, 190
  'Never Forget Class Struggle'
    slogan, 17–18, 35, 39–40, 58, 190
coffins, 85, 195, 224
collectivisation and decollectivisation
  collectivisation, 6, 8, 15–20, 144, 190,
    209
  and Dazhai campaign, 220–1, 227–8
  decollectivisation, 224–6, 265–6,
    270–80, 320–1
Confucianism, 31, 298
Confucius, campaign against, 301–2, 304
Congress of Victors (Soviet), 11, 14, 27
corruption, xiv, 20–1, 33, 236, 240
countryside
  Cultural Revolution and, 221–4
  and Dazhai model, 226–31, 239
  exiled populations, 192–202
  and movement of people, 200, 280–4
  and preparations for war, 210
  and sex, 300
  students in, 192–200, 232
  see also collectivisation, and
    decollectivisation
crime, 20, 147–8
criminal gangs, 167
Cuban Missile Crisis, 23, 43
Cultural Revolution
  army challenges, 136–8
  army joins, 129–32
  beginning of, 48
  beginning of end, 252
  claims first victims, 53
  disaffection with, 165–7
  draws in workers, 120–7

ends under Deng Xiaoping, xv, 318–19
public inauguration of, 57
reaches turning point, 116–17
sanctioned by leadership, 69
suspension of, 179
and 'Yan'an spirit', 202, 212
Cultural Revolution Group
  backing for Zhang Chunqiao, 131
  and cleansing campaign, 184
  and countryside, 221–4
  decline of, 165–7, 208, 216
  and fall of Lin Biao, 243–4
  formation of, 56–7, 67, 69
  limited influence in provinces, 145
  and looting, 90–1
  promotes factionalism, 153–7
  and Red Guards, 75, 78, 80, 104, 108,
    112, 114, 177–8
  relations with army, 135–8, 163–4,
    171–2
  targets Zhou Enlai, 159–62, 232–3
  and Third Front, 216, 218
  and workers' unrest, 124–5
  and Wuhan incident, 149–52
Curie, Marie, 166

Dalian, 147
Damansky Island, 206, 208, 216
dance, loyalty, 169
Daoist monks, 230
Daoxian county, 21, 222
Daxing county, 78, 179, 193
Dazhai campaign, 219–20, 226–7, 230–1,
    239, 260–2, 272–3, 280
deforestation, 195
'Democracy Wall', 8, 317–18
Democratic Party, 238
Deng Tuo, 11, 46, 53–4, 57, 61, 76,
    91–2, 98
Deng Xiaoping, 6, 8, 11, 16, 18, 25–6,
    28, 136–7, 173
  ends Cultural Revolution, xv,
    318–19

fall of, 155, 183–4, 308–9, 311, 313, 315
and fall of Peng Zhen, 47, 49
and fall of Ulanfu, 190
and Luo Ruiqing, 44–5
restored as vice-premier, 303–8
returns to power, 316–22
and rise of Wei Guoqing, 174
targeted in Cultural Revolution, xii, 116–17, 122
and work teams, 60, 68
Deng Zihui, 18
Dianchi Lake, 230–1
Diaoyutai State Guesthouse, 56, 58, 67, 135, 160, 171, 304
Djilas, Milovan, 290
dogs, 86
Donald, Alan, 58
dunce's caps, 62, 73, 80

education system, 286–7
and home schooling, 297
Mao criticises, 37–8, 75
see also students
Eight Model Operas, 295
employment, conditions of, 120–4
Engels, Friedrich, 289
ethnic minorities, 189–90, 209, 262, 306

factories, unrest in, 65, 70, 121–3
family and kinship, 296–300
famine oedema, 196, 263–4
Fang Zifen, 166, 170
Fei Xiaotong, 280
films, foreign, 28
folk culture, 295–6
folk songs and ballads, 31, 166, 276
'Foolish Old Wan Who Moved the Mountain, The', 59
Forbidden City, 3, 56, 71, 108
foreigners visit, 246–7
Foshan, 261, 267
'Four Modernisations' programme, 305,

318, 320
Fourth Field Army, 152–3, 173–4
Fu Chongbi, 171–2
Fudan University, 131
Fujian province
preparations for war, 210
rebels attempt to seize power, 134
teachers commit suicide, 63
Fuzhou, 103–4, 115–18
Fuzhou Millitary Region, 142–3

Gang of Four, 48, 65, 305–6, 308–10, 315–16, 319
Gansu province
agricultural production, 266
cadre schools, 204–5
and Dazhai campaign, 227–8, 273
decollectivisation, 225, 321
factionalism, 154–5
industrial production, 260
preparations for war, 214, 218
and 'Three Antis' campaign, 238–41
Gao Yuan, 54, 63, 66, 82, 106, 139, 141, 168, 172, 188, 228
exiled to countryside, 193, 221
and fighting between factions, 143–4
and radio broadcasts, 291
geomancy, 271, 296
Golden Lotus, The, 166
Göring, Hermann, 90
grain production, 228–9, 265–6
state monopoly of, 274–5
Great Famine
and end of collective canteens, 237
and ethnic minorities, 190, 209
impact in countryside, 224–5, 272–3, 275, 278
and Seven Thousand Cadres Conference, 11–13, 15–16
starvation continues, 196, 263–4, 266
Great Leap Forward
brutalisation under, 9–10
compared with Third Front, 218

and counter-revolutionary
    ideology, 32–3
criticism of, 9–13, 17, 29, 36, 53, 319
and Dazhai campaign, 219–21, 227–8,
    231, 272
and deforestation, 195
and *The Dismissal of Hai Rui*, 47–8
and economic losses, 120–1
impact in countryside, 223
and movement of people, 200, 281,
    283
and rise of entrepreneurialism, 19–20
and steel output, 3–4, 9, 149, 195, 213
Ulanfu condemns, 190
and underground factories, 280
and 'walking on two legs', 262
    Yangtze Tribune Group and, 236
Great Northern Wilderness, *see* Manchuria
Great Wall of China, 246
Group of Five, 40, 46, 49, 56
Guangdong province
    army intervention, 135
    and cleansing campaign, 189
    decollectivisation, 7, 19, 275–9
    factionalism, 173–4, 223
    healthcare, 267
    industrial production, 259
    preparations for war, 210
    unemployment, 94–5
Guangxi province
    factionalism, 173–8, 223
    and May Sixteenth campaign, 235
    raids on freight trains, 157
Guangzhou, 80, 89, 147, 158, 225, 246,
    278
    factional fighting, 174–5
    and Hong Kong radio broadcasts,
    292
Guangzhou Trade Fair, 247, 261
Guilin, 38
Guiyang, 24
Guizhou province
    collectivisation, 19

decollectivisation, 321
and Great Famine, 13–14
preparations for war, 215
purge of leadership, 24, 26, 144

Hai Rui, 47–9, 85
Hainan Island, 85, 292
Han Xianchu, 118, 134
Hangzhou, 60, 165, 302, 305–6
Hankou, 259
Hanoi, 43
Harbin, 282
He Long, Marshal, 25, 130, 183–4
healthcare, 267–9
Heart of a Maiden, The, 291, 300
Hebei province
    Christians in, 294
    and cleansing campaign, 187–8
    collectivisation, 18–19
    and counter-revolutionary ideology,
    31
    and Dazhai campaign, 228
    deportations to countryside, 202
    education system, 287
    and Great Famine, 12–13
    healthcare, 267
    inflated agricultural production
        figures, 13
    and movement of people, 283
    popular religion, 285
    preparations for war, 214, 218
    starvation continues, 263–4
    and 'Three Antis' campaign, 240
Heilongjiang province
    cadre schools, 202–3, 205
    and cleansing campaign, 183
    population growth, 282–3
    preparations for war, 215
Henan province, 274
heroes, emulation of, 33–6
Hitler, Adolf, 109
Ho Chi Minh, 43
Hohhot, 191

Hong Kong, 7, 32–3, 175, 237, 246–7, 261
  and burning of British mission, 158–60
  radio broadcasts, 291–2
Hongwu emperor, 53
Hopson, Donald, 158, 161
household registration system, 120, 154, 200, 224, 281–2
Hu Feng, 28, 31
Hua Guofeng, 153, 308, 313, 315–17, 320
Hua Linshan, 38
Huang Yongsheng, 152, 172, 174, 251
Hubei province
  army intervention, 135
  and Dazhai campaign, 230
  deforestation, 195
  and Great Famine, 13
  healthcare, 268
  looting, 89–90
  power shortages, 259
  preparations for war, 215, 217
  starvation continues, 264
  students exiled to countryside, 195, 198–200
  and 'Three Antis' campaign, 236–40
Hunan province
  corruption, 21
  and Dazhai campaign, 228, 230
  deforestation, 195–6
  deportations to countryside, 201
  factionalism, 155, 163, 173, 223
  and Great Famine, 11
  influx of Red Guards, 113
  students exiled to countryside, 194–9
Hundred Flowers campaign, 6–7, 28, 46, 53, 55, 60, 64, 170, 234
Hungarian revolt, 7

Indonesian embassy, siege of, 157
industrial production, 148–9, 259–62, 305
  impact of Cultural Revolution, 95
  see also steel production

industrialisation, China seeks Soviet assistance, 5
infant mortality rates, 269
Inner Mongolia, 135, 189–91, 193, 215, 229, 258, 300
  extremes of torture in, 190–1
Institute for Foreign Languages, 160
intellectuals
  and cadre schools, 204
  and cleansing campaign, 186–7
  purging of, 8, 27–30, 37, 40–1, 46
  and Red Guard violence, 76–7
Islam, 294

Japan
  radio broadcasts, 291
  and US–China rapprochement, 257–8
Jesuits, 84
'jet-plane' torture, 21, 63, 129–30
Jiang Qing (Madame Mao)
  and army, 135–8, 143, 145, 151, 163–4, 172, 303
  arrest and imprisonment, 316, 319
  and cleansing campaign, 184
  elected to Central Committee, 208
  emerges as radical ideologist, 172–3
  and fall of Deng Xiaoping, 184
  and fall of Lin Biao, 244
  and fall of Liu Shaoqi, 141
  and fall of Peng Dehuai, 130
  and fall of Wang Feng, 154–6
  and Gang of Four, 301–6, 308–11, 315–16
  paranoia, 304
  personal vendettas, 13–7
  popular resentment of, 308–9
  rise to power, 38–41
  secret mission to Shanghai, 41, 47–9
  and rise of Cultural Revolution Group, 56
  and rise of Red Guards, 75, 178
  supports rebel students, 67
  targets Zhou Enlai, 159–60, 233

and workers' unrest, 124
and Wuhan incident, 150–2
Jiang Weiqing, 23
Jiangning county, 288
Jiangsu province
    decollectivisation, 279
    education system, 287–8
    and Great Famine, 12
    and May Sixteenth campaign, 234–5
Jiangxi province
    cadre schools, 203
    decollectivisation, 225
    influx of Red Guards, 112–13
    students exiled to countryside, 197
Jinan, 55, 58, 214
Johnson, Lyndon B., 42
Jurmed, Tuvany, 249

Kang Sheng, 29–30, 41, 46–7, 49–50,
    56–7, 172, 174, 301
    and army, 135, 138–9
    and 'Case of the Sixty-One
        Traitors', 156, 183
    and cleansing campaign, 183–4, 189–90
    engineers Shanxi coup, 129, 142
    and fall of Lin Biao, 243–4
    and fall of Wang Feng, 156
    and Inner Mongolia terror, 190
    meeting with Tsinghua students, 177–8
    personal vendettas, 156–7
    wife elected to Central Committee, 208
Kang Zhengguo, 88, 118, 166–7
Kazakhs, 209
Ke Qingshi, 48, 104, 120
Kerouac, Jack, 290
Khmer Rouge, 258
Khrushchev, Nikita, x–xii, 8, 16, 32, 43,
    55, 57, 116
    byword for revisionism, 22–3
    denunciation of Stalin, x, xii, 5–6, 16,
        45, 207, 215
    fall of, 25, 45, 215
    'mini-Khrushchevs' uncovered, 41

kilns, makeshift, 213
Kim Il-sung, 257
Kissinger, Henry, 247–8, 303
Korean War, xi, 4, 42–3
Kosygin, Alexei, 43, 209
Kuai Dafu, 64, 67–8, 136, 141, 177–8
Kunming, 216, 314

labour camps, 45–6, 122, 188, 198, 298
Lam Bun, 159
land reform, 5, 29, 211
Lanzhou, 65, 101, 163, 266
    factionalism, 155–7
    and 'Three Antis' campaign, 239–40
Lanzhou Military Region, 155–6, 163
Lao She, 76
Laos, 246
Lei Feng, 33–6, 54, 63, 98, 211
Lenin, Vladimir, x–xi, 10, 16, 271, 287,
    289
Lenin in October, 28
Li Jingquan, 144–5, 258, 301
Li Qinglin, 199
Li Xiannian, 10, 199–200
Li Zuopeng, 150–2, 243, 251
Liang Shuming, 29
Liaoning province, 173, 199
Liberation Army Daily, 36, 83, 257, 302
libraries, destruction of, 83–4
Lin Biao
    and army, xiv, 130, 135, 137–8, 140,
        142, 163, 171–3
    and civil war, 12
    death, 100, 236
    denounced by Chen Yi, 136–8, 255
    fall of, 242–4, 248–52
    and fall of Lu Dingyi, 49–50
    and fall of Wang Feng, 154–6
    foreword to Little Red Book, 243, 251
    and Fourth Field Army, 152–3, 173–4
    and 'guardian warriors', 152, 172, 251
    Mao's heir apparent, 17, 25, 69, 137,
        207–8, 242–4

and personality cult, 167–8
and 'Politics in Command' slogan, 37,
    44
and preparations for war, 208–9
and rebellion in Shanxi, 129
replaces Liu Shaoqi, 69
and Red Guards, 71, 74, 81, 83, 96,
    178, 221
and self-reliance, 44
struggle with Luo Ruiqing, 44–5
Tiananmen Square speech, 74, 109,
    221
wife elected to Central Committee, 208
and Wuhan incident, 150–2
and 'Yan'an spirit', 59, 202
Lin Doudou, 249–50
Lin Liguo, 249–50
Ling, Dan, 251, 283
Ling, Ken, 62, 82–3, 115, 118, 134, 165,
    196
    and factional fighting, 142–3
    with Red Guards in Beijing, 103–4,
        105–8, 110
literacy, decline in, 288
literature and drama, 28, 30–1, 38, 40–1,
    166
    erotic, 290–1
    forbidden, 288–91
    see also book burnings
Little Red Book, see Quotations from
    Chairman Mao Zedong
Liu Geping, 129, 142
Liu Jieting, 144
Liu Lantao, 156, 227
Liu Shaoqi, xii, 6, 11–12, 16–18, 39–40,
    135–7, 145, 307, 319
    and 'Case of the Sixty-One
        Traitors', 156–7
    death in prison, 235, 242
    fall of, 69, 95–6, 141, 180, 183–4
    and fall of Peng Zhen, 46
    and fall of Ulanfu, 190
    How to be a Good Communist essay, 17

and Luo Ruiqing, 44–5
and Socialist Education
    Campaign, 21–6, 144, 190
targeted in Cultural
    Revolution, 116–17, 122–4
and work teams, 60, 64–5, 67–8, 101
Liu Zihou, 13
Long March, 19, 112, 123, 144, 173, 270
Long March teams, 112–13
Lop Nur nuclear test site, 209
loudspeakers, 97, 158, 192, 206, 221,
    292, 307, 313
Lu Dingyi, 49–50, 95, 183–4
Luo Ruiqing, 43–5, 50, 255
    attends Mao's funeral, 315
    fall of, 128–30, 151, 171, 183–4
Lushan plenum, 9, 12, 18, 29–30, 35, 44,
    47, 69, 130, 137

Macau, 175, 237
malaria, 268
Manchuria (Great Northern
    Wilderness), 8, 46, 147, 217
    and border dispute, 206, 208
    and Dazhai campaign, 229, 231
    students exiled to countryside, 193–4,
        196–8, 251–2
mangoes, sacred, 178–9
Mao, Madame, see Jiang Qing
Mao Yuanxin, 306–7, 310
Mao Zedong
    capacity for malice, xi
    death, 266, 280, 295, 313–15
    distrust of Lin Biao, 242–4, 248–52
    ill health, 248, 252, 255, 257, 307, 311
    influence of Stalin, 4–6, 14–16, 214–15
    marriage and infidelities, 39–40
    personality cult, xii, 36, 96–100,
        167–71
    statues and portraits, 169–71, 179, 186,
        247, 256, 299
    swims in Yangtze, 66, 111
    and threat of deStalinisation, x, 6

Mao Zedong Thought
    army promotes, 35–7, 167, 171, 243
    and university propaganda
        campaign, 177–9, 192, 203
    written out of constitution, xii, 6, 8,
        30, 207
markets, unregulated, 224–5
Marx, Karl, 131, 271, 287, 289
May Fourth Movement, 8
May Sixteenth campaign, 232–6, 240
meningitis, 114
mental illness, 267
Military Affairs Commission, 138, 140
Million Heroes, 149–51
Ministry of Foreign Affairs, 161, 233
Ministry of Health, 114, 267
Ministry of Labour, 124
Ministry of Light Industry, 262, 278
Mongolia, 190–1, 209
    Lin Biao killed in air crash, 249–52
    see also Inner Mongolia
Mongolian embassy, siege of, 157
Mongolian People's Party, 190
Monument to the People's Heroes, 309
Morozov, Pavlik, 298
mosquitoes, 194
music, see songs and music

Nan Baoshan, 77
Nanjing
    cultural life, 166–7
    demonstrations, 7
    destruction by Red Guards, 85
    drownings, 67
    industrial production, 148
    and May Sixteenth campaign, 233–4,
        303
    and mourning for Zhou Enlai, 309
    and rise of Xu Shiyou, 173–4
    shadow economy, 20
    and socialist education, 35
Nanjing Military Region, 173
Nanjing University, 234

Nanning, 174–5, 177
National Day, 37, 101, 164, 173, 213,
    245, 251, 294
Nee, Watchman, and the Little Flock,
    294
New China News Agency, 81
Nie Rongzhen, Marshal, 245
Nie Yuanzi, 46, 57, 60, 68, 148, 178, 187,
    204
Nien Cheng, xvii, 87–8, 90–2, 101,
    178–9, 186, 247, 251, 316
Ningxia province, desertification,
    229–30
Nixon, Richard M., 245–6, 248, 255–8
    Six Crises, 290
North China Agricultural
    Conference, 262, 272, 274
North Korea, 257
North Vietnam, 246
nuclear weapons, 23, 42

October Revolution, xi, 8
'One Strike and Three Antis'
    campaign, 236–41, 291
opera, 30, 38, 295–6
opium, 19
Ouyang Hai, 34

Panzhihua steel plant, 216, 218, 231
Paris Commune, 131
parks and gardens, 257
Pearl River, 175, 261, 277
Peking Opera Festival, 38, 41, 295
Peking University, 29, 46, 64, 68, 75, 92,
    117
    and big-character poster campaign, 57,
        60, 148
    and cadre schools, 203
    and cleansing campaign, 187
    exodus of students, 32–3
    foreign students at, 287, 314
    Madame Mao visits, 67
    suicides at, 187

Peng Dehuai, Marshal, xii, xiv, 9, 12, 18,
     29–30, 35–6
  compared with Hai Rui, 48–9
  fall of, 130, 151, 183–4
  rehabilitation of, 317
Peng Peiyun, 204
Peng Zhen (mayor of Beijing), ix, xiii, 11,
     14, 21, 37–8, 40, 92, 136, 187, 232
  fall of, 45–50, 53–7, 68, 95, 102, 155,
     183–4
  and trial of Gang of Four, 319
People's Daily
  and anti-Confucius campaign, 302
  and beginnings of Cultural
     Revolution, 53–4, 56–7, 61
  extols Dazhai campaign, 220, 272
  and 'January Storm', 126–7
  and literacy, 287–8
  warns against decollectivisation, 225–6
pigeons, 86–7, 293
'ping-pong diplomacy', 246
porcelain, 88–91, 95, 100, 259
ports, backlogs of freight, 147
posters
  anticipate fall of Zhou Enlai, 232–3
  attacking Xu Shiyou, 234
  and fall of Liu Shaoqi, 141
  of Mao, 98, 169–70
  removed from Beijing, 164
  see also big-character poster campaign
Pravda, 208, 237
privacy, and the home, 296–7

Qi Benyu, 171
Qingdao, 32, 58, 84
Qinghai province
  desertification, 230
  military intervention, 134–5, 138, 140
Qingming festival, 309–10
Qiu Huizuo, 150–2, 251
Qufu, 84–5, 153
Quotations from Chairman Mao Zedong
     (Little Red Book), 36, 44, 59, 94,
     100, 102, 105, 109

  army promotes, 97, 131
  Lin Biao's foreword to, 243, 251
  misreading of, 186–7
  printing of, 98
  quotation contests, 168–9
  royalties from, 216
  and song lyrics, 192

radio broadcasts, 291–2
Rae Yang, 61, 86, 88, 92
  exiled to countryside, 193–5, 198
railway system, paralysis in, 147
Red Flag, 116, 118, 122, 125, 141, 151,
     155, 163, 171, 287
  and anti-Confucius campaign, 302
  falls silent, 165
Red Guards
  clashes among, 102–4, 107–8
  converge on Beijing, 104–11
  and cycle of violence, 74–80, 146,
     221–2
  destruction and looting, 80–93, 222
  divisions among, 115–17
  end of, 177–9
  expropriations, 91–3
  and forbidden literature, 288–9
  'free and unfettered', 165–7
  and free travel, 101–2, 113–14, 147,
     166
  house searches, 87–9
  impact in countryside, 221–2
  and Mao badges, 99–100, 108, 166
  rise of, 71–80
religion, 27–8, 31–2, 285, 294–5
revisionism, 22–3, 25–6, 38, 41, 55, 140,
     167, 232, 306
Ricci, Matteo, 84
Rittenberg, Sidney, 81
Rockefeller, David, 261

Salinger, J. D., 290
Scarlet Guards, 104, 126
School of Oriental and African Studies, 76
security apparatus, distrust of, 128–9

'self-reliance', 219–20, 226
Service, Robert, 14
Seven Thousand Cadres
    Conference, 10–14, 16, 18, 22–3,
    29, 48, 190
sex, 299–300
Sha Tao, 157
Sha Tau Kok, 158
Shaanxi province
    industrial production, 259–60
    poverty and starvation, 262–3, 271
    preparations for war, 215
    unregulated markets operate, 224–6
Shamiakin, Ivan, 290, 292
Shandong province
    deforestation, 196
    education system, 287–8
    factionalism, 173
    healthcare, 269
    preparations for war, 214
    starvation, 196, 264
Shanghai
    and cleansing campaign, 185–6
    and countryside trade, 279–80
    and deportations to countryside,
        201–2
    expropriations, 92–3
    factional fighting, 152–3
    Gang of Four and, 307, 315–16
    'January Storm', 126–8, 133
    Jiang Qing's secret mission, 41, 47–9
    Mao statues and portraits, 169–70
    and May Sixteenth campaign, 235
    Nixon visits, 256–8
    preparations for war, 210–11, 213–14,
        217
    production Mao-branded goods, 98–9
    suicides, 185–6
Shanghai Diesel Engine Factory, 152–3
Shanghai International Settlement, 213
Shanghai Municipal Revolutionary
    Committee, 132
Shanghai Number Seventeen Cotton
    Textile Mill, 65, 70, 125, 301

Shanghai Number Two Machine Tool
    Plant, 292
Shanghai People's Commune, 131–2, 135
Shantou, 95, 278
Shanxi province
    decollectivisation, 225
    factionalism, 173
    rebel coup, 129, 142
    Red Guards descend on Beijing, 105
Shaoshan (Mao's birthplace), 112, 153,
    308
Shenyang, 19
Shijiazhuang, 188, 311
Shirer, William, 87, 290
Siberia, 4, 179, 215
Sichuan province
    army intervention, 135, 140
    barefoot doctors in, 268
    decollectivisation, 278, 321
    factionalism, 173
    preparations for war, 215–16
Sichuan Cotton Mill, 145
Sichuan Revolutionary Committee, 145
Sihanouk, Prince, 214, 246
singing clubs, 293
'Sixteen Articles', 69, 83
Snow, Edgar, 42, 214, 245–7
Socialist Education Campaign, 46, 54, 63,
    66, 72, 110, 120, 122, 144
    and the family, 298
    launch of, 18, 20–6, 29–31, 33, 35–6
    Mongolian opposition to, 190
Socialist High Tide, 5–6, 9, 207
Solzhenitsyn, Alexander, 265, 290
Song Yaowu, 75, 111
Song Yongyi, 166
songs and music, 28, 32, 97, 167, 169,
    192, 221, 238
    see also folk songs and ballads
Soviet advisers, withdrawal of, 23, 44
Soviet embassy, blockade of, 157
Soviet Union
    alleged spies from, 186, 193
    anti-Soviet propaganda, 210

border clashes and threat of
    war, 206–18, 242–3, 245
collectivisation, 4–5, 11, 15
economic aims, 8–9
evacuation plan, 215
Great Terror, 14, 26
internal passport system, 120
retrieves Lin Biao's body, 252
and US–China rapprochement, 247–8,
    257
and Vietnam War, 43, 246
withdraws advisers, 23, 44
spirit mediums, 271, 296
Spring Festival report, 37–8
Stalin, Joseph, 9, 11, 22, 26, 30, 289, 298,
    319
    Khrushchev denounces, x, xii, 5–6, 16,
        45, 207, 215
    influence on Mao, 4–6, 14–16, 214–15
    and Korean War, 43
    and purge of intellectuals, 27, 29
Stalingrad, battle of, 212
statues, of Mao, 169–71
steel production, 3–4, 9, 149, 195, 213,
    216, 218, 259
students
    exiled to countryside, 192–200, 232
    exodus from Beijing, 32–3, 192–3
    immunity under Cultural
        Revolution, 133
    return to classes, 139–40, 167
    seek redress, 101–2
    and work teams, 61–5, 67–8
    see also Red Guards
Sukarno, President, 39, 141
Sun Yat-sen, 36
Suzhou, 209, 242
swimming, 66–7

Taiwan, 31, 62, 116, 188, 246–7, 291
Tan Lifu, 115–16, 118
Tan Zhenlin, 136, 138, 184, 301
Tanaka, Kakuei, 257

Tangshan, 188, 202
    earthquake, 312–13
Tao Zhu, 16, 183
Taoism, 294
Tcherepnin, Alexander, 185
teachers, violence against, 61–4, 73–5,
    80, 140
Teng Haiqing, General, 191
Third Front, 215–18, 259, 281, 297
'Three Loyalties and Four Boundless Loves'
    campaign, 168–71
Thurston, Anne, xvi
Tian Han, 40–1, 76
Tiananmen Square
    demonstrations, 309–11
    Lin Biao speech, 74, 109, 221
    Mao appears at mass rallies, 108–11
    and Mao's funeral, 315
    massacre under Deng Xiaoping, 322
    student rallies, 74–5, 80, 82, 96, 102
Tianjin, 102, 217–18, 309
Tibet, Chinese invasion of, 144
trade, with West, 261–2
Trotsky, Leon, 290
Truman, Harry, 290
Tsinghua University, 60, 64, 67–8, 71–2,
    107–8, 117, 136, 141, 307
    and propaganda campaign, 177–9
tuberculosis, 267
Twentieth Army, 226–7
'two Tings', the, 144–5, 258, 278, 298

Uighurs, 209
Ukraine, 5
Ulanfu, 190, 258, 301
unemployment, 94–5
United Nations, 247
United States
    and Chinese–Soviet tensions, 208–11
    Deng Xiaoping visits, 318
    offers medical assistance, 114
    politics, 290
    rapprochement with China, 245–8,

255–9, 303
see also Korean War Vietnam War
Urumqi, 261, 283
Ussuri River, 206–8

Vietnam War, 42–3, 174, 215, 245–6,
    258

Wang Aihe, 294
Wang Dongxing, 15, 45
Wang Feng, 154–6, 227
Wang Guangmei, 21, 39–40, 60, 63–4,
    67, 141, 184
Wang Hongwen, 65, 70, 125–7, 129, 152
    death in prison, 319
    and Gang of Four, 301–2, 308
    and Mao's funeral, 315
Wang Li, 149–51, 160–3, 233
Wang Renzhong, 13, 23, 74
Wang Rongfen, 109
Wang Yugeng, 103, 115–16
war, preparations for, 206–18
Wei Guoqing, 174–5, 177, 235
Wei Jingsheng, 318
Wen Guanzhong, 84, 87, 105, 112,
    196
Wenzhou, 104, 265
women, sold into wedlock, 32
women's health, 197, 264, 269
Wong, Jan, 287, 314
Wong Yee-man, 159–60
work teams, 60–5, 67, 70, 72, 101–2,
    121–2, 139
Wu Faxian, 150–2, 172, 227, 243, 249,
    251
Wu Han, 47–8, 53–5, 57, 61, 68, 76, 98
Wuhan, 19, 31, 89, 91, 99, 199, 303
    industrial production, 148–9
    power shortages, 259
    Red Guards visit, 111–12
    'Wuhan incident', 148–52, 159–60,
        163, 174, 243
    and *Yangtze Tribune* group, 236–7

Wuhan Military Region, 163
Wuxi, 234

Xi Zhongxun, 30, 41
Xi'an, 19, 65, 80, 88, 90, 102, 118, 166,
    270–1
Xiamen, 61–3, 82–3, 90, 103, 115, 165
    factional fighting, 142–3
Xiamen People's Commune, 134
Xie Fuzhi, 78, 149–51, 178, 189–90
Xinjiang province
    army intervention, 133
    ethnic minorities, 209
    preparations for war, 208–9, 215, 245
    and purge of students and
        intellectuals, 8
    students exiled to countryside, 193
Xu Shiyou, 173–4, 233–4, 250
Xu Xiangqian, Marshal, 130, 135–6, 138,
    150, 164, 173, 245
Xu Xiaodi, 35, 100, 193

Yan'an
    cradle of revolution, 38, 59, 72, 136
    and Dazhai campaign, 229
    decollectivisation, 270–1
    purge of intellectuals, 27–30
    Red Guards visit, 112
    students exiled to countryside, 193, 197
'Yan'an spirit', 202, 212, 270
Yang Chengwu, Marshal, 151, 162, 255
    fall of, 171–3
Yang Shangkun, 45, 48, 50, 183
Yangtze River, 19, 31, 58, 111, 144, 173,
    196, 262, 264, 279, 288
    Mao swims in, 66, 111
Yangtze Tribune group, 236–7
Yao Dengshan, 233
Yao Wenyuan, 48, 53–6, 124, 132, 179,
    207
    and Gang of Four, 301, 303, 305
    trial and imprisonment, 319
Ye Fei, 103–4, 111, 115, 118, 134

Ye Jianying, Marshal, 130, 135–6, 138, 164, 245, 315
Ye Qun, 44, 91, 100, 137, 151, 172, 178, 250, 252
Yezhov, Nikolai, 30
Yue Daiyun, 204
Yunnan province
  and cleansing campaign, 189
  and Dazhai campaign, 230–1
  ethnic minorities, 189, 306
  students exiled to countryside, 197
  and 'Three Antis' campaign, 240

Zeng Xisheng, 16, 18–19, 272
Zhai Zhenhua, 34, 63, 67, 77, 111–12, 139, 166, 229
  exiled to countryside, 192–3, 197–8
  and opera, 296
  and preparations for war, 211, 214
Zhang Chunqiao, 48, 56, 125, 131–2, 135–6, 139, 152, 166, 207, 235, 280
  and fall of Lin Biao, 243–4
  and Gang of Four, 301, 305, 309
  trial and imprisonment, 319
Zhang Guotao, 173
Zhang Hongbing, 299
Zhang Tixue, 111
Zhang Xiting, 144
Zhang Yufeng, 39, 45, 307
Zhang Zhongliang, 22
Zhao Ziyang, 321
Zhejiang province
  imposition of military rule, 226–7

rebellion suppressed, 305–6
Zhengding, 54–5, 62–3, 66, 82–3, 139, 141, 143, 168, 172, 188, 221, 228, 291
Zhengzhou, 283
Zhou Enlai
  devotion to Mao, 68
  and fall of conspirators, 49–50
  and fall of Lin Biao, 250–2
  and fall of Liu Shaoqi, 141, 235
  and fall of Wang Li, 163
  and 'Four Modernisations', 305, 318, 320
  and household registration system, 120
  humiliated by Mao, 9, 13
  ill health and death, 303–5, 308–10
  Moscow mission, 25
  and Peking Opera Festival, 38
  and preparations for war, 207, 209
  and rapprochement with US, 246
  and Red Guards, 74, 147, 178–80, 222, 232–3
  relations with army, 136–8, 155, 171–2
  and release of Hua Guofeng, 153
  and students exiled to countryside, 192–3, 199–200
  and 'Three Antis' campaign, 236
  wife elected to Central Committee, 208
  and Wuhan incident, 149–51
  and Xi'an students, 65, 102
Zhou, Kate, 321
Zhou Lin, 13, 19, 24, 26

A Note on the Author

Frank Dikötter is Chair Professor of Humanities at the University of Hong Kong. He has pioneered the use of archival sources and published ten books that have changed the way historians view and understand China, including the classic *The Discourse of Race in Modern China* (1992), the Samuel Johnson Prize-winning *Mao's Great Famine* (2010) and his most recent, *The Tragedy of Liberation* (2013). Frank Dikötter is married and lives in Hong Kong.

A Note on the Type

The text of this book is set Adobe Garamond. It is one of several versions of Garamond based on the designs of Claude Garamond. It is thought that Garamond based his font on Bembo, cut in 1495 by Francesco Griffo in collaboration with the Italian printer Aldus Manutius. Garamond types were first used in books printed in Paris around 1532. Many of the present-day versions of this type are based on the *Typi Academiae* of Jean Jannon cut in Sedan in 1615.

Claude Garamond was born in Paris in 1480. He learned how to cut type from his father and by the age of fifteen he was able to fashion steel punches the size of a pica with great precision. At the age of sixty he was commissioned by King Francis I to design a Greek alphabet, and for this he was given the honourable title of royal type founder. He died in 1561.